DEATHS IN CENTRAL TEXAS

1935-1944

Compiled by
Monyene Stearns

HERITAGE BOOKS
2019

HERITAGE BOOKS
AN IMPRINT OF HERITAGE BOOKS, INC.

Books, CDs, and more—Worldwide

For our listing of thousands of titles see our website
at
www.HeritageBooks.com

Published 2019 by
HERITAGE BOOKS, INC.
Publishing Division
5810 Ruatan Street
Berwyn Heights, Md. 20740

Copyright © 2003 Monyene Stearns

Heritage Books by the author:
Deaths in Central Texas, 1925–1934
Deaths In Central Texas, 1935–1944
Deaths in Central Texas, 1945–1954

All rights reserved. No part of this book may be reproduced or transmitted in any form or by any means, electronic or mechanical, including photocopying, recording or by any information storage and retrieval system without written permission from the author, except for the inclusion of brief quotations in a review.

International Standard Book Numbers
Paperbound: 978-0-7884-2354-3

INTRODUCTION

Because of the lack of information published about people who died in western McLennan County and eastern Coryell County, Texas, the material in this volume has been gathered from local records, newspaper obituaries, cemetery records, funeral home records, and tombstone inscriptions and has been combined into the entries on the following pages.

Each entry is followed by a notation of the source of that material. Newspaper excerpts are followed by the name of the newspaper, the date of publication, and the page and column where each appears. If only funeral home records were found, the name of the funeral home will appear after the entry.

Since all of the records (except those found in newspapers) were transcribed from handwritten pages, it would be wise to check the index for all possible spellings of a name.

DEATHS IN CENTRAL TEXAS

CHAPTER 1

JIM "JACK" KEMP died in Dallas, January 6, 1935, at age 38. He was born in Texas, March 18, 1897, the son of Washington Kemp and Lucy Hood of Texas. His wife was Mildred Kemp. Burial was in McGregor Cemetery by Amsler Funeral Home. Informant was Lucy Kemp Hood Willis of McGregor and Sam Kroft of Dallas. Amsler Funeral Home Records, Book 1, 1935.

DR. DOWELL M. JORDAN, a prominent Oglesby physician, died Wednesday, January 2, at his home. He was born in Alabama, April 26, 1857, the son of Wiley Jordan and Melinda Nickerson but lived in Oglesby for 50 years. Burial was in Moody by Lee Undertakers. Survivors include his wife; two daughters, Mrs. Segale DeJarnett of Dallas and Mrs. Monette Draper of Oglesby; and two sons, Windell of Commerce and Dr. D. W. Jordan of Bardy. McGregor Mirror: Jan 4 (1-3), 1935. If Dr. Jordan had lived until April 26th, he would have been 78 years old. Survivors include two sons; and two daughters, Mrs. C. R. DeJournett and Mrs. Guy Draper. McGregor Mirror: Jan 11 (6-3), 1935.

MRS. C. G. HARTT died Sunday night, December 23, 1934, at her home in Edcouch, Texas. Burial was in Weslaco Cemetery. She and her husband lived in McGregor ten years ago when he was employed as telegraph operator with the railroads. Survivors include her husband; two daughters, Mrs. Dale S. Washburn of Donna and Miss Rosemary Hartt of Edcouch; four sisters; and four brothers including John D. Anderson of McGregor. McGregor Mirror: Jan 4 (1-3), 1935.

A. G. BUSTER died recently in Pidcoke. Mr. W. L. Warnick of Oglesby attended the funeral of his old friend. McGregor Mirror: Jan 4 (2-4), 1935.

CHESTER WILHITE. Funeral services were held December 23, 1934, for 80 year old, Chester Wilhite. He was born in Tennessee, September 1, 1854. Mr. Wilhite lived in the Comanche Spring community for 40 years after moving here from Tennessee. The only surviving member of his immediate family is his brother, who lives in Sparkman, Tennessee. Burial was in Harris Creek Cemetery beside his wife, Alice J. Wilhite, and a daughter, who preceded him in death several years ago. Lee Undertakers was in charge of the funeral. McGregor Mirror: Jan 4 (4-6), 1935.

THOMAS ODIS "TOL" LUNA, age 50, of South Bosque died Sunday in a Waco hospital. He was born in Middle, Tennessee, in 1884 and came to Texas when young. He had resided in McLennan County for over 40 years. Burial was in Harris Creek Cemetery by Lee Undertakers. Survivors include his wife; eight children, Mrs. Eva Mae Fambrough and Coy D. Luna of California, T. O. Luna, Jr., Dorothy Blanche Luna, Altha May

Luna, Edison Luna, Alka Fay Luna and Joe Duncan Luna of South Bosque. McGregor Mirror: Jan 11 (1-4), 1935.

JOHN LANDFRIED, age 72, died at his home west of Crawford, December 30, 1934. Burial was in the German Baptist Cemetery near Coryell City by Amsler Funeral Home. The pallbearers were all sons-in-laws. Mr. Landfried was born in Galicia, Hungary. He came to America in 1894 and settled in the Prairie Chapel community, where he has resided since. His wife, Elizabeth Massier Landfried, preceded him in death less than a year ago. Survivors include two sons, John and Will; eight daughters, Mrs. Martin Freyer, Mrs. Jacob Freyer, Mrs. Adolph Falkenberg, Mrs. Henry Gauer, Mrs. Henry Groff, Mrs. Adolph Mack, Mrs. H. T. Englebrecht and Miss Martha Landfried. All these children live near Crawford and Coryell City, except Mrs. Groff, who resides at Henrietta. McGregor Mirror: Jan 11 (1-5), 1935.

MR. STORY, brother of Rev. T. G. Story of Weatherford, died in Nolanville this week. Rev. Story stopped in McGregor to visit friends at the Methodist Church where he was the former pastor before attending his brother's funeral Sunday. McGregor Mirror: Jan 11 (4-4), 1935.

MRS. CHARLIE JONES of Moody died Monday, January 7, 1935. She was the daughter of Mr. and Mrs. W. W. Nelson of the Jones Hill community. Survivors include her husband and seven children. One sister, Mrs. George White, was too sick to attend the funeral. (Place of burial not mentioned). McGregor Mirror: Jan 11 (8-3), 1935.

BILL ROBERTS died Sunday in Mound at the home of his daughter, Mrs. Charlie Parrish. If he had lived until April, he would have been 86 years of age. Mr. Roberts had lived in Oglesby for about 30 years. Burial was in Davidson Cemetery beside his wife and two daughters who preceded him in death several years ago. Survivors include several children and grandchildren. McGregor Mirror: Jan 25 (7-1), 1935.

CARL WHITE INFANT. The little babe of Mr. and Mrs. Carl White died recently in a Waco hospital. Burial was in Post Oak Cemetery near Oglesby. This was their first born child. McGregor Mirror: Jan 25 (7-3), 1935.

CHRISTINA HOPPE, age 58, died Friday, January 25, in the family home near McGregor. She was born July 18, 1876, in Germany, coming to America at age one. Her parents were Mr. Kneschk and Miss Wolschk of Germany. In November of 1894 she married Oscar Hoppe near Taylor. They moved to the Osage community in 1903 but have lived in McGregor for 23 years. Burial was in the McGregor Cemetery by Amsler Funeral Home. Survivors include her husband and the following children: Mrs. Arthur Schroeder and Oscar Hoppe, Jr. of Saegerton, Mrs. Newt Edmonds and Mark Hoppe of Oglesby, Carl Hoppe of Turnersville, and Mrs. W. J. Siler, Mrs. George B. Raschke, Walter Hoppe, Miss Irma Lee Hoppe, Mrs. Luther Doty and Mrs. Terry Wells, all of McGregor; brothers and sisters, Mrs. August Marasko of Paige, Miss Emma Kneschk of Austin, Miss Agnes Kneschk of Taylor, Mr. Gus Wolschk of Granger and Mr. Adolph Kneschk of Turnersville. McGregor Mirror: Feb 1 (1-5), 1935.

MRS. M. L. JACKSON (Mary Louise Jackson) died at her home in McGregor Wednesday, February 6. She was born in 1863. In 1881 she married Mr. J. F. Jackson. Mrs. Jackson was the daughter of Mr. and Mrs. Richard Grantham, well known pioneer residents of McGregor, and had lived in McGregor since 1895. Burial was in Harris Creek Cemetery by Amsler Funeral Home beside her husband. Survivors include seven children: S. D. Jackson, E. A. Jackson, C. S. Jackson and F. M. Jackson, all of California, W. W. Jackson of Center, Texas, J. R. Jackson of Tyler, and Richard of Waco; three daughters, Mrs. Ray Swanson of Malakoff, Mrs. Roger Elkins of Hammon, Oklahoma, and Mrs. Jess Ross of Whitney. Six brothers and one sister also survive: W. B. Grantham of Corsicana, J. D. Grantham, J. R. Grantham and N. J. Grantham of McGregor, H. T. Grantham of Clifton, Luther Grantham of Arkansas, and Mrs. E. C. Huckabee of Corsicana. Three of her children preceded her in death. Informant was Mrs. W. C. Huckabee of Corsicana. McGregor Mirror: Feb 8 (1-1), 1935.

MRS. F. W. BISCHOFF, age 72, died in a Waco hospital Tuesday, February 5. Burial was in the German Methodist Cemetery at Buckhorn by Amsler Funeral Home. She was born in Oppendorf, Germany, February 1, 1863, and came to America in 1882. On January 28, 1886, she married F. W. Bischoff. Five of their ten children preceded her in death. Survivors include her husband; one daughter, Mrs. Ben Wiese; four sons, Herman, Louis, Fred, and Edwin Bishoff, all of McGregor; two brothers and one sister. McGregor Mirror: Feb 8 (1-6), 1935.
    Mrs. E. Nitsche and Mr. and Mrs. V. B. Rankin of Dallas were among those out-of-town who were in McGregor for the funeral of Mrs. William Bischoff Wednesday. McGregor Mirror: Feb 8 (4-2), 1935.

J. BAKER HALL, age 45, died in McGregor February 8, 1935. He was the son of C. B. Hall and Jennie Davis. Mr. Hall was a jeweler. Burial was in McGregor Cemetery by Lee Undertakers. Lee Undertaker Records, 1935.

SOPHIA FREDERIKA ANNA FEHLER, age 54, died in Austin February 9, 1935. She was born in Germany, March 21, 1880. At the time of her death she was a resident of the Austin State Hospital. Burial was in McGregor Cemetery by Amsler Funeral Home. Informants were H. Fehler and J. F. Fehler of McGregor. Pallbearers were C. W. Fehler, Ben Fehler, Herbert Fehler, Robert Sanders of McGregor, Fritz Fehler of Clifton and Charles Fehler of Clifton. Amsler Funeral Home Records, Book 1, 1935.

MRS. C. N. CHAPIN (Liby Florence Chapin) died February 19, at her home seven miles southwest of McGregor, in the Whitson Community, where she had lived for 45 years. She was born in 1871 in Indiana, the daughter of D. B. Hinman and Emma Hinman. Mrs. Chapin died as a result of a stroke of paralysis suffered a few days before her death. Burial was in Eagle Springs Cemetery by Lee Undertakers. Seven sons acted as pallbearers. Survivors include her husband, Charlie Chapin (12 Mar 1863 -12 Mar 1946) and nine children: Mrs. H. Simms of Moody, Ernest Chapin and Joe Chapin of Waco, Hugh and Brady Chapin of McGregor, Ross Chapin of Longview, Cecil Chapin of Moody and Elbert Chapin of Prairie Hill. McGregor Mirror: Feb 22 (1-2), 1935.

WILLIS INFANT. The infant daughter of Mr. and Mrs. John B. Willis died at the family home in Waco Friday, February 16. Burial was in McGregor Cemetery. Survivors include her parents; two sisters, Jimmie Louise and Martha Jane Willis; and her grandparents, Mr. and Mrs. Jim Cass. McGregor Mirror: Feb 22 (1-5), 1935.

PEGGY NELL ATKINS, three year old daughter of W. Tharpe Atkins and Mattie Lee Atkins, died Friday, February 15, of pneumonia. She was born September 9, 1931. Burial was in McGregor Cemetery by Lee Undertakers. Survivors include her parents; two brothers, Jerry and Billie Atkins; and two sisters, Owana and Bonnie June Atkins. McGregor Mirror: Feb 22 (4-3), 1935.

MRS. R. MONROE CASEY (Frances Elizabeth Casey), 69, died in Oglesby Thursday, February 14. She was born December 20, 1865, in Mississippi, the daughter of John T. Hollbrook and Emby Mae Wade. Funeral services were at the Old Salem Primitive Church near Oglesby. Burial was in Post Oak Cemetery by Lee Undertakers. Survivors include four children, John Casey of Oglesby, Mrs. Charlie Sharp of Waco, Mrs. Charles Patterson of Oglesby, and Mrs. Ernest Pollard of Oglesby. Her husband died about 5 years ago. McGregor Mirror: Feb 22 (7-3), 1935.

THOMAS HAROLD MUIR, the infant baby of Bill Muir and Della Tolbert of Lorena, Texas, died in a Waco hospital Wednesday, February 20, at age 2 days. Burial was in the McGregor Cemetery by Amsler Funeral Home. McGregor Mirror: Feb 22 (8-6), 1935.

ELIZABETH VIRGINIA ACREE, age 77, died February 25, 1935. She was born February 26, 1857, in Texas, the daughter of Frederic Miller Grimes and Elmira Susan Grimes. Burial was in McGregor Cemetery. Fred Acree, her son, lives in Waco. Lee Undertakers Records, Book 1, 1935.

WILLIAM R. LIPPE, JR., died at Hearst Springs, Texas, February 25, 1935, at age 8 days. He was born in Hearst Springs, the son of W. R. Lippe of McGregor and Lena Steinkamp Lippe. Burial was in McGregor Cemtery by Amsler Funeral Home. Informant was H. W. Lippe of McGregor. Amsler Funeral Home Records, 1935.

IVIN ENGLAND, age 47, died February 23, 1935, in McGregor. He was born October 13, 1887, in Kentucky, the son of Jerry England and Lou Amanda England. Burial was in McGregor Cemetery by Lee Undertakers. Mr.

England was a taylor by trade. Lee Undertakers Records, 1935.

JAMES D. JOHNSON, age 83, died February 24. He was born in Tennessee, November 15, 1851, the son of William Johnson and Thersa Jane White. (Place of burial not mentioned) Lee Undertakers Records.

L. E. BLACK, 47, died by his own hand Thursday in Athens, Texas. He was the son of Dr. and Mr. W. T. Black who lived in McGregor some 20 years ago. Mr. Black was a salesman but because of bad health was unable to work. Despondency over his condition was credited for his actions. Survivors include his wife; two daughters; his mother, Mrs. W. T. Black; one sister, Mrs. C. M. Weekly of Athens; two brothers, Tom Black of Gilmer and Bob Black of Tennessee. (Place of burial not mentioned.) McGregor Mirror: Mar 8 (1-1), 1935.

MRS. R. M. PEACE (EMMA PEACE), a resident of Plainview since 1908, died Friday. Burial was in the Plainview Cemetery by Wood Funeral Home. Emma, daughter of Mr. and Mrs. J. T. Riley, was born November 30, 1866, in McLennan County, Texas. She married R. M. Peace December 2, 1885, and they lived in McGregor until moving to Plainview in 1908. Mrs. Peace's mother, Mrs. J. T. Riley, was a cousin of Cynthia Ann Parker, mother of the Indian Chief, Quanah Parker. And, Mrs. Peace's grandfather, J. T. Riley, was a Captain in the Confederate Army. Survivors include her husband; four children, Mrs. Frank Armstrong of Plainview, Mrs. Ross Rogers (the wife of Amarillo's mayor), and Joe Pratt Peace of Wichita, Kansas; two brothers, Bud Riley of Plainview and Zack Riley of Lockney, Texas. McGregor Mirror: Mar 8 (1-3), 1935.

JAMES. E. JOHNSON, age 57, died in his home in Crawford, Saturday, March 3. Burial was in the Moody Cemetery by Amsler Funeral Home. Survivors include his wife; four daughters, Mrs. Rachel England of Lindale, Mrs. Lula Short of Waco, Miss Florine Johnson and Miss Helen Johnson of Crawford. ; seven sons, Harry of Levelland, James, Jr., John Varney, William, Samuel, Loy and Floy Johnson all of Crawford, and two brothers. McGregor Mirror: Mar 8 (1-5), 1935.

WILLIAM HENRY JONES, a blacksmith in Patton, Texas, died February 25, 1935. He was born in Alabama, July 1, 1877, the son of James Jones and Harriett Bramlett. Burial was in Valley Mills Cemetery. Lee Undertakers Records, 1935.

MR. SAM WEAVER, husband of the former Allie D. Wood of McGregor, died in Memphis, Texas. Mr. and Mrs. E. J. Thomason attended the funeral Monday. McGregor Mirror: Mar 8 (5-5), 1935.

DR. J. B. YOUNG of Moody died Sunday at his home. Burial was Monday, March 4, 1935. Dr. Young was a brother-in-law to Mrs. M. L. Jordan of Oglesby. Mrs. Jordan and daughter, Mrs. Draper, attended the funeral. McGregor Mirror: Mar 8 (7-3), 1935

WATSON (WALTON) W. STONE, 84, resident of Oglesby for the past 43 years, died Wednesday, March 13, at the home of his daughter, Mrs. Tom Rucker. Burial was in the Howard Cemetery in Hamilton by Lee Undertakers. Mr. Stone was born in Mississippi (Alabama) February 18, 1851, the son of Thomas Stone, but came to McLennan County many years ago. Survivors include his children: Mrs. Charlie Crouch of Grapevine, Mrs. Jesse Pruitt of Hamilton, Mrs. Jack Mayer of Beeville, Miss Eva Stone of Oglesby, Mrs. Tom Rucker of Oglesby, Mrs. Charlie Coleman of Oglesby, J. L. Stone and Earl Stone of Weslaco. McGregor Mirror: Mar 15 (1-1), /Lee Undertaker Records, 1935.

MRS. E. S. WARNICK, sister of Mrs. J. R. McEntire, died in Ballinger Tuesday. Survivors include several daughters. Mrs. McEntire of McGregor attended the funeral in Ballinger accompanied by Mr. and Mr. Dan Harris and Ralph McEntire. McGregor Mirror: Mar 15 (5-6), 1935.

MARY ANN LOWRIMORE, the infant daughter of Mr. and Mrs. Olin Lowrimore, died March 12, after living only three hours. Burial was in Post Oak Cemetery. They christened the baby and gave her the name, Mary Ann. McGregor Mirror: Mar 22 (7-2), 1935.

MRS. CLAIRBORNE, mother of Mr. I. P. Clairborne of Oglesby, died last Sunday in her home in Dyersburg, Tennessee. She was 82. Burial was in Tennessee. McGregor Mirror: Mar 22 (7-3), 1935.

ADOLPH G. LOWE died at his home in the Irene Community last Saturday. Funleral services were held at St. Peter's Lutheran Church in Walling Sunday with durial in the Walling Cemetery. Mr. Lowe was the father of Miss Minnie Lowe of McGregor. McGregor Mirror: Mar 22 (1-3), 1935.

NICK EDWARD ANDERSON, 8 year old son of Mr. and Mrs. Leonard Anderson, died Friday, March 15, in a Waco hospital from pneumonia. He was born in McGregor, the son of Leonard Anderson and _____ Lynch. Burial was in the Moody Cemetery by Lee Undertakers. Survivors include his parents; his grandparents, Mr. and Mrs. E. Anderson and Mrs. T. N. Lynch. Pallbearers were Truman Anderson, Garland Anderson, Travis Anderson, Francis Lynch, Morris Lynch and Nick Lynch. McGregor Mirror: Mar 22 (5-5), 1935.

REV. C. G. HOWARD, former pastor of the First Baptist Church of McGregor, died in a Dallas hospital Saturday. Burial was in Oakwood Cemetery in Waco. Rev. Howard was pastor at Handley at the time of his death. McGregor Mirror: Mar 29 (1-4), 1935.

TOM McEVER (Thomas J.), age 57, died Saturday, March 23, at his home in the Horne Community. He was born April 24, 1877 in Georgia, the son of Ed McEver and Maggie Connally. Funeral services were held at the Goshen Church near Moody with burial in Old Perry Cemetery by Lee Undertakers. Survivors include his wife; three sons, Tommie J. McEver, Earl Lawson McEver and Bobbie Joe McEver; daughter, Mrs. R. C. Hodges;

two brothers, Brice McEver of Hillsboro and Dick McEver of Lampasas; and a sister, Mrs. W. A. Turner. Mr. McEver was the son-in-law of J. T. Lawson. McGregor Mirror: Mar 29 (1-5)/Lee Undertakers Records, 1935.

DAN LESLIE MOORE. The five month old son of C. O. Moore and Willie May Lee died Saturday, March 23. He was born October 11, 1934. Burial was in Post Oak Cemetery near Oglesby. McGregor Mirror: Mar 29 (7-1), 1935/Lee Undertakers Records, 1935.

CECIL COOK, age 20, was killed in a plane crash at Brownwood Sunday. The youth, whose home was in DeLeon, was the son of Tom Cook of DeLeon and a nephew of A. F. Cook of McGregor. McGregor Mirror: Apr 5 (1-3), 1935.

J. C. DEFORD, father of Dick DeFord of McGregor, died in Hillsboro Wednesday at the home of his daughter, Mrs. L. E. Tinsley. Burial was in Bold Spring Cemetery. Mr. DeFord was born in Georgia 80 years ago, but had lived in Texas since 1898. During most of those years he had resided in West. Survivors include his wife; three sons; and two daughters. McGregor Mirror: Apr 5 (1-3), 1935.

MRS. LAURA CASEY, age 86, died Thursday, April 4th, at the home of her daughter, Mrs. J. C. Mize. She suffered a broken hip in a fall the Sunday before her death. Mrs. Casey, a sister of the late Newt and Bob Cox, moved from McGregor to Coleman County, Texas, in 1904. She was born January 1, 1849 in Mississippi, the daughter of Caleb and Elizabeth Cox. Burial was in the Novice Cemetery in Coleman County. Survivors include her daughters, Mrs. J. C. Mize of McGregor and Mrs. Ella Reeves of Novice; three sons, R. E. Casey of Clyde, J. C. Casey of Novice, and J. T. Casey of Winters; two sisters, Mrs. Tom Casey of Lockney and Mrs. Frances Newman of Frisco. Her husband preceded her in death some 53 years ago. McGregor Mirror: Apr 12 (1-3), 1935.

MRS. S. V. CHRISTIE, age 85, died Thursday, April 11, at her home just west of McGregor. Mrs. Christie, the daughter of Mr. and Mrs. Miller, was born in Cave Springs, Virginia, January 17, 1850. She was first married on August 6, 1866, to Mr. C. H. Chapman, a Confederate soldier from Virginia, and they came to Texas in 1871, settling near the present town of McGregor. Seven children were born to this union, five daughters and two sons. All of these children are still living except one son who died at the age of 11 years. Mr. Chapman, who was born in 1836, died April 17, 1884 and on September 20, 1888, she married Mr. W. F. Christie. One daughter was born to this marriage. Mr. Christie died on February 6, 1894. Mrs. Christie was buried in the McGregor Cemetery by Amsler Funeral Home. Survivors include the following children: Mrs. Mollie Owens of Kansas City, Mrs. A. M. Handley of Beeville, Mrs. N. D. Lewellen of Santa Cruz, California, Mrs. J. L. Maclin of Waco, Mrs. Jessie Earp, Mrs. Frankie McBride and H. C. Chapman, all of McGregor. McGregor Mirror: Apr 12 (1-4),

1935/Amsler Funeral Home Records, Book 1, 1935.

MINNIE LOU ANNIE VASSELL, age 55, died in Crawford, April 13. She was born in Georgia, January 10, 1880, the daughter of C. D. Daniel and Mary Griffin, both of Georgia. Burial was in Prairie Chapel. Informant was J. R. Vassell of Waco. Amsler Funeral Home Records, Book 1, 1935.

MRS. JOSIE SALES, step-mother of Mrs. L. Pettway and Mr. R. W. Sales, died Monday in a Waco hospital. Burial was in Oakwood Cemetery in Waco by Compton's Chapel. Survivors include her children: R. W. Sales of McGregor, T. S. Sales of Littlefield, Gordon Sales of Waco and Mrs. J. C. McDaniel and Mrs. L. Pettway, both of Waco. McGregor Mirror: Apr 19 (1-5), 1935.

MRS. WALTER MITCHELL (Lula Mae), age 24, died in Temple Saturday, April 19. She was born April 13, 1911, in Oglesby, the daughter of Roy Dawson and Odessa Moats. Burial was Easter Sunday in McGregor Cemetery by Lee Undertakers. Mrs. Mitchell was buried beside the infant babe who preceded her in death only a few hours. Survivors include her parents, Mr. and Mrs. Roy Dawson; her husband; and a 2 year old daughter. McGregor Mirror: Apr 26 (1-2), 1935.

WALDENE MITCHELL, infant daughter of Walter and Lula Mae Mitchell, died April 19, 1935. She lived only a few hours. Burial was in McGregor Cemetery beside her mother who died the same day. Lee Undertakers Records, 1935.

WILLIAM W. WHITLOCK, 60, died in a Temple hospital last Saturday. Mr. Whitlock was born in 1875. He lived in the Osage community 40 years, but for the past three years had been a resident of Kopperl. In 1807 he married Jessie M. Edwards and to this union nine children were born. Survivors include his wife; four daughters; and three sons. Two daughters preded him in death: Alpha Whitlock (April 21, 1899 - April 21, 1899) and Robbie Lora Whitlock (Jan 23, 1907- Feb 3, 1909). McGregor Mirror: Apr 26 (1-5), 1935/Osage Cemetery Records, 1935.

MR. W. D. LEE died in Gatesville last week. Mr. and Mrs. W. L. Warnick of Oglesby and son, Willie of Waco, were called to Gatesville Wednesday of last week for the funeral of her father, Mr. W. D. Lee. Mr. Lee was an old pioneer of this country and would have been 88 if he had lived until July. (Place of burial not mentioned.) McGregor Mirror: Apr 26 (7-3), 1935.

CHARLES JACKSON SHOUMAN, age 73, died in Crawford, April 24, 1935. He was born in Tennessee August 5, 1861, the son of J. K. Shouman and Eliza Kelly, both of Tennessee. Burial was in Crawford by Amsler Funeral Home. Informant was W. J. Shouman of Merkel, Texas. Amsler Funeral Home Records, Book 1, 1935.

MARTHA JANE PATTON, age 71, died in Crawford May 5, 1935. She was born in Tennessee, the daughter of Robert Hatton and Mary Hearne, both of Tennessee. Burial was in Osage Cemetery by Amsler Funeral Home. Informant was W. E. Patton of Crawford. Amsler Funeral Home Records, Book 1, 1935.

GEORGE PERRY HOLBROOK, age 62, died Monday, May 6, of pneumonia. Burial was in Post Oak Cemetery by Lee Undertakers. He was born May 10, 1872 in Georgia, the son of George and Shirley Holbrook. Mr. Holbrook joined the Baptist church at age 21 in Rome, Georgia. He and his family had lived in and around McGregor for the past 23 years. Survivors include his wife, Lillie; daughters, Mrs. Ted Killough, Mrs. Olan Rozelle, Miss Jessie Holbrook and Miss Mary Holbrook; five sons, George, Carlton, J. W, Walter, and Marburt Holbrook. McGregor Mirror: May 10 (1-4), 1935.

SELMA BOHNE died Friday, April 26. She was the youngest daughter of Mr. and Mrs. Henry Bohne, who live near Coryell City. Miss Bohne was born in Coryell City June 3, 1919 and in 1933 she joined the Lutheran Church. Amsler Funeral Home was in charge of services and burial was in St. John Cemetery. Survivors include her parents, three brothers and five sisters: John Bohne of Coryell City, Bill Bohne of McGregor, Rueben Bohne of Coryell City, Mrs. Herman Bolte of Coryell City, Mrs. Louie Haynes and Mrs. Albert Haynes of McGregor, Mrs. Alfred Westerfield and Elda Bohne of Coryell City. McGregor Mirror: May 10 (5-1), 1935.

MRS. MAE NOLAN, sister-in-law of Mrs. M. V. Dalton of Oglesby died in Floydada this week. Mr. and Mrs. M. V. Dalton and Alton Dalton and wife left for Floydada last Sunday for the funeral. McGregor Mirror: May 17 (6-1), 1935.

VACIE VERNE STONE, age 21, daughter of Mr. and Mrs. William J. Stone, died in McGregor Sunday, May 19, 1935. She was born September 13, 1913, the daughter of William Stone of Arkansas and Sarah (Sallie) Berry of Georgia. She had been an invalid for over 14 years. Burial was in the McGregor Cemetery by Amsler Funeral Home. Survivors include her parents, two sisters and six brothers. McGregor Mirror: May 24 (1-4), 1935/Amsler Funeral Home Records, Book 1, 1935.

GOODE INFANT. We sympathize with Mr. and Mrs. Vernon Goode in the death of their little infant babe, who was born last Friday and buried Saturday. Mr. Goode was from the Jones Hill community. McGregor Mirror: May 24 (5-2), 1935.

ALBERT OMER JORDAN, a citizen of Crawford, died May 16, 1935. He was born in Alabama March 19, 1869, the son of Jim Jordan of Alabama and _____ Gober of Alabama. Mr. Jordan became a citizen of Crawford some 40 years ago, moving there from Alabama. Burial was in the Crawford Cemetery by Amsler Funeral Home. Survivors include seven daughters and one son, his wife, Florie Jordan, having preceded him in death some six years ago. Informant was O. K. Jordan of Crawford. McGregor Mirror: May 24 (5-4), 1935/Amsler Funeral Home Records, Book 1, 1935.

MR. R. N. PEACE, age 71, died in Plainview. News of his death reached McGregor last Saturday. Mr. Peace, with his family, left McGregor 26 years ago for Plainview. His wife preceded him in death March 1, 1935. Survivors include two daughters, Mrs. Ross Rogers of Amarillo and Mrs. Franklin Armstrong of Plainview; two sons, Joe C. Peace of Wichita, Kansas, and R. R. Peace of Amarillo. McGregor Mirror: May 31 (1-2), 1935.

MAGGIE SHEPARD, age 59, died in McGregor May 24, 1935. She was born in Seguin, Texas, July 11, 1874, the daughter of Dike Allen. Her husband was Will Shepard. Burial was in McGregor Cemetery by Amsler Funeral Home. Informant was Willie Kirksey of McGregor. Amsler Funeral Home Records, Book 1, 1935.

MRS. MEEKS, died Monday, May 27, 1935, in Hamilton. Mr. and Mrs. Oma Pennington and children went to Moffatt last Tuesday to attend the funeral of her grandmother, Mrs. Meeks. McGregor Mirror: May 31 (5-2), 1935.

MARTHA CAMILLE JONES, age 11, died late Tuesday of injuries received in a cave-in at the gravel pit. She accompanied her father who was hauling gravel. A bank caved in, covering her to a depth of several feet. She was dug out but died an hour later in the hospital in Hamilton. Mr. and Mrs. M. B. Martin and family, Mr. and Mrs. G. W. Lee and family attended the funeral there Thursday. The mother, Mrs. A. T. Jones, is a sister to Mr. Martin and Mrs. Lee. McGregor Mirror: May 31 (8-1)/Jun 7 (6-2), 1935.

MRS. MARVIN STOVER, aunt of Mrs. Lee George, died in Childress Monday. Mrs. George and her husband attended the funeral in Childress and Mrs. George's sister returned home with them for a few days. McGregor Mirror: Jun 7 (4-1), 1935.

EDGAN SIMS, brother of Henry and Clyde Sims of Oglesby, died Thursday in Turnersville. McGregor Mirror: Jun 7 (3-3), 1935.

MRS. ANNA MANSKE, age 59, died in Waco Tuesday, June 18. Anna was born August 2, 1876. She had lived in Osage, nine miles northwest of McGregor, with her son, Walter Manske, since the death of her husband, Paul K. Manske. Burial was in McGregor Cemetery by Wilkerson-Hatch Funeral Home of Waco. Survivors include four sons: Walter Manske of Osage, Herbert Manske of Osage, Otto Manske of Brownsville and Dr. Gayart Manske of Wichita Falls. McGregor Mirror: Jun 21 (1-3), 1935.

PRISCILLA (DRUCILLA) ANN JOHNSON, age 71, died at the home of her granddaughter, Mrs. Otha Spradley, Monday, June 17. She was born in

Texas, March 5, 1864, the daughter of Isaac and Alcindy Hodges. Burial was in McGregor Cemetery beside her husband, J. Sheldon Johnson who died in 1926. Lee Undertakers were in charge of services. Survivors include five children: Alf Johnson and Kee Johnson of Waco, Ernest Johnson of California, and Howard Johnson of Aransas Pass; and one daughter, Mrs. P. P. Morrison of McGregor. McGregor Mirror: Jun 21 (1-5), 1935.

CARL JALONICK, age 84, died at the home of Gus Mertins, 5 miles southwest of Mcgregor Saturday. Carl was born in Germany, August 7, 1850, and came to America in 1886, settling in St. Paul, Minnesota. In 1889, he moved to Texas and settled at William Penn, where he resided until the death of his wife, Minnie, on January 18, 1928. After her death he moved to McGregor to spend the remainder of his life with the Mertins family. Burial was in Brenham by Amsler Funeral Home. Survivors include two granddaughters. Informant was Gus Mertins. McGregor Mirror: Jun 21 (5-4), 1935/Amsler Funeral Home Records, Book 1, 1935.

AGNES LORENZ died in McGregor June 9, 1935, at birth. She was the daughter of Fred Lorenz and _____ Lippe of McGregor. Burial was in McGregor Cemetery by Amsler Funeral Home. Informant was Fred Lippe. Amsler Funeral Home Records, Book 1, 1935.

ROBERT THOMAS BLAIR, age 76, of Holland, died at his home Sunday. Burial was in the Holland Cemetery. Mr. Blair was one of the early settlers in Bell County. He was born in Aniston, Alabama in 1858 and came to Texas at age 14. In 1881 he married Miss Sallie Whatley. Survivors include his wife and several children: W. O. Blair of Belton, E. E. and Herbert Blair, Mrs. Will Swan and Mrs. R. G. Sutton of Holland; Mrs. C. C. Curry of McGregor and T. E. Blair of Houston. McGregor Mirror: Jun 21 (5-6), 1935.

MRS. T. O. HUMPHRIES (Ida Maud Humphries), age 53, died June 21, 1935, at her home. She was born in Flakner, Mississippi, October 3, 1881, the daughter of C. T. Nance and Mary Leona Jamison. Survivors include her husband, Thomas O. Humphries; four daughters: Mrs. J. F. Jones of Gatesville, Miss Thelma, Miss Freda and Miss Juanita Humphries of Oglesby; one son, Curtis Humphries of Flat, Texas; six brothers: Tom Nance of Waco, Wesley, Joel, Morris, Lonnie and Charlie Nance of western Texas; two sisters, Mrs. Noland of Arkansas and Mrs. Noland in the western part of the state. Burial was in Post Oak Cemetery near Oglesby by Lee Undertakers. McGregor Mirror: Jun 28 (6-1), 1935/Lee Undertakers Records, 1935.

IRVIN PALMER CLAIBORNE, Cotton Belt Agent in Oglesby, died in a Waco hospital Thursday from injuries suffered in a head-on auto accident earlier in the day. Mr. Clairborn was in a new 1935 Chevrolet with L. S. Walker, R. D. Wright and Joe Sawyers when the accident occurred. The car Mr. Claiborne was riding in was headed toward Waco when it struck a car headed toward McGregor. Both cars attempted to pass a wagon loaded with hay which obscured the view of the road ahead. Wesley Daniels and J. H. Cousins were riding in the other car. Mr. Claiborne's body was brought back to McGregor by Lee Undertakers and burial was in a Oak Lawn Cemetery in Waco after funeral services in Oglesby where he had lived for 22 years. He was born in Dyersburg, Tennessee, February 12, 1888, the son of Chas Clairborne and Susan Light. At the time of his death, June 27, 1935, he was 47 years old. Survivors include his wife; two sons, Rae Smith and Delmar Clairborne; and relatives in Tennessee. McGregor Mirror: Jul 5 (1-1)/(8-5), 1935.

SARAH ELIZA WITT died in a Temple hospital Saturday, June 29, 1935. She was born in Fannin County, Georgia in 1856 but moved to Texas with her parents during childhood. In 1876, she married Mr. W. P. Witt and she and her husband were one of the first of the pioneer families to establish their home in the Comanche Springs neighborhood. When Mr. Witt died in 1913, Mrs. Witt and her daughter moved to McGregor. Survivors include three children: Miss Pearl Witt of McGregor, Albert Witt of Perryton and Raymond Witt of Wesleco; five grandchildren; and several brothers and sisters: John M. Patterson of Hillsboro, L. S. Patterson of Mexia, Walter Patterson of McKinney, Mrs. G. S. West of Lubbock and Mrs. Helen Edney of Washington. Burial was in McGregor Cemetery by Amsler Funeral Home. McGregor Mirror: Jul 5 (1-2), 1935/Amsler Funeral Home Records, Book 2, 1935.

AUGUSTUS LAFAYETTE (GUS) BLANTON, age 70, died at his home in McGregor last Friday, June 28, 1935. For the past 10 years he had been a mail messanger in McGregor. Mr. Blanton was born in Dalton, Georgia, December 4, 1864, the son of James Blanton and Edith Smith, but at the age of 7 moved to Texas. When the original town lots of McGregor were sold in 1882, he was present. Survivors include his wife; one son, Billie Blanton; one daughter, Anna of McGregor. Burial was in McGregor Cemetery by Amsler Funeral Home. McGregor Mirror: Jul 5 (1-4), 1935/Amsler Funeral Home Records, Book 1, 1935.

MISS ADA LEE BANDO, age 39, died at her home in Newcastle on Saturday, June 28, 1935. She was born in McGregor, September 15, 1895, but had moved to Newcastle several years ago. She was preceded in death by her father and her mother, Charles and Ada Bando, only ten months ago. Survivors include one brother, M. L. Bando of Waco; and two sisters, Mrs. S. W. Taylor of Milano and Mrs. Stine of Vernon. Burial was beside her mother in McGregor Cemetery by Amsler Funeral Home. McGregor Mirror: Jul 5 (5-1), 1935/Amsler Funeral Home Records, Book 1, 1935.

VIRGIL CHANEY, an enrollee at the CCC camp located near Mother Neff Park, was struck and killed by lightning Thursday, July 18, 1935. He was working at the camp when a thunderstorm came up. Lighning struck the shovel he was carrying over his shoulder, killing him instantly. Mr. Chaney was from Morgan Mill near Stephenville, Texas. He was born in Carlton, Texas, May 2, 1914, the son of Nute Chaney and Neoma Harris. Burial was in Bluff Dale Cemetery, Bluff Dale, Texas, by Lee Undertakers. McGregor Mirror: Jul 19 (1-1), 1935/Lee Undertakers Records, 1935.

J. B. PACK, age 24, of Crawford, died in a Waco hospital last Friday, July 12, 1935. Mr. Pack was born in Moody, September 28, 1910, the son of W. H. Pack and Amanda Derting, but for the past 15 years had lived near Crawford. In 1932, he married Eula Boren. Survivors include his wife; his father; and a half-sister. Amsler Funeral Home was in charge of burial arrangements at Crawford Cemetery. Mr. Pack's mother was born in Burksville, Kentucky. McGregor Mirror: Jul 19 (8-3), 1935/ Amsler Funeral Home Records, Book 2, 1935.

WILLIAM OWENS, age 62, one of McGregor's best known colored citizens, died July 11, 1935. He was born in Texas, the son of Harry Owens. Burial was Friday, July 12, in the McGregor Cemetery by Amsler Funeral Home. Informant was his son, Charles Owens. McGregor Mirrro: Jul 19 (8-3), 1935/Amsler Funeral Home Records, Book 2, 1935.

ROY HARRIS, son of Mr. and Mrs. Obe Harris of Jones Hill community, was killed in Moody last Friday when he was struck by the car driven by Eldon Caruthers. Rain caused the accident. McGregor Mirror: Jul 19 (8-5), 1935.

J. H. WOMACK, SR., uncle of Mrs. Sam Powell of Oglesby, died at his home in Riviera, Texas, July 24. Mr. Woamck lived near McGregor for a number of years. Survivors include his wife; five children: Ramsey, Ted, Presley, J. B. Jr., and Nina Lea Womack; one grandson, Jack; three sisters, Mrs. Thomas Darey, Miss Adeline Womack of Waco and Miss Corda Womack of Houston; two brothers, Waymon and Lawson Womack of Waco. McGregor Mirror: Aug 2 (7-2), 1935.

W. R. GRICE, brother-in-law of Mrs. H. T. Hall of McGregor, died in Fort Worth last Thursday. Mr. Grice had lived in McGregor many years ago. Mrs. Hall attended the funeral in Fort Worth. McGregor Mirror: Aug 9 (4-4), 1935.

JOHN F. HAMILTON, age 63, died at his home in McGregor Monday, August 5. Burial was in McGregor Cemetery by Amsler Funeral Home. He was born September 20, 1869, in Franklin, Texas, the son of J. T. Hamilton and Mattie Knight, both of Tennessee. Mr. Hamilton has lived in this area for 57 years, farming until 15 years ago when he and his family moved to town. Survivors include his wife, Anna Oliver Hamilton; two daughters, Mrs. Albert Terry and Mrs. A. E. Reynolds; sons, Oliver Hamilton of McGregor and Roy Hamilton of Hewitt; a sister, Mrs. Jess S. Jones of Ballinger; and a brother, W. A. Hamilton of McGregor. McGregor Mirror: Aug 9 (4-6), 1935/Amsler Funeral Home Records, Book 2, 1935.

F. B. GAGE, brother of Mrs. H. T. Hall of McGregor, died Monday in Houston. He was reared in Crawford, having learned the printing trade in McGregor. Mrs. Hall attended the funeral in Houston. McGregor Mirror: Aug 9 (5-5), 1935.

GILFORD J. MORRIS died at his home in Gatesville Thursday, August 8. Mr. and Mrs. A. E. Morris, Mrs. Paul Morris, Mr. and Mrs. Park Donaldson and children were among those who attended the funeral in Oglesby. Gilford J. Morris, age 63, was the oldest son of the late Mr. and Mrs. J. H. Morris. He was born July 29, 1872. At the time of his death, Gilford was working at the State Training School. Burial was in Post Oak Cemetery. Survivors include his wife; three daughters, Miss Mary Lou, Miss Lilla Mae and Miss Charlie Bob Morris; four brothers: F. A. Morris of Oglesby, A. E. Morris of McGregor, Ernest Morris of Waxahachie and Willard Morris of Hamilton; three sisters, Mrs. J. L.
Allison of McGregor, Mrs. W. B. Alexander of Temple and Mrs. Julia Burleson of Los Angeles, California. McGregor Mirror: Aug 16 (4-4)/(7-1), 1935.

MRS. TOM DARSEY of Merkel died Tuesday. Mrs. J. F. Fields and Miss Willie Darsey, her sisters-in-law, attended the funeral in Merkel. McGregor Mirror: Aug 16 (4-4), 1935.

MRS. B. HICKERSON, age 62, died Tuesday, August 13, 1935, in a Waco hospital. She was born January 27, 1873, the daughter of H. G. Bennett. When she was about 4 years of age, she came to Texas from Tennessee. Mrs. Hickerson lived near Crawford most of her life. Burial was in Crawford Cemetery by Amsler Funeral Home. Survivors include her husband, Buck Hickerson; four daughters: Mrs. Odie McCollum of Lorena, Mrs. R. D. Wiley of Wellington, Mrs. Harvey Hawkins of Waco and Mrs. W. R. Hicks of Baytown; one son, Marcus Hickerson of Lorena; one sister, Mrs. John Cooper of Lockney; one brother, John Bennett of McGregor. Other relatives include Miss Emma and Miss Mattie Hickerson of McGregor. McGregor Mirror: Aug 16 (4-6), 1935/Amsler Funeral Home Records, Book 2, 1935.

HENRY RABBE, age 72, of Coryell City, died in a Waco hospital Saturday, August 10, 1935. He was born in Germany, October 5, 1863, but came to America as a youth, settling first in Washington County, Texas, but soon moved to McGregor, where he lived for many years. After his marriage to Malinda Englebrecht, they moved to Coryell City. Burial was in Prairie Chapel German Baptist Cemetery by Amsler Funeral Home. Survivors include his wife; three sons: Henry, W. L. and Wallace Rabbe; five daughters: Mrs. Charles Westerfield, Mrs. Ernest Westerfield, Mrs. Herbert Gohlke, Mrs. John Bohne and Mrs. William Rabbe. McGregor Mirror: Aug 16 (5-2), 1935/Amsler Funeral Home Records, Book 2, 1935.

DEATHS IN CENTRAL TEXAS, VOL. II

MRS. TOM CONNALLY, wife of Senator Connally of Texas, died of a heart attack in the office of her husand Monday in Washington. Her body will be brought back to Texas on the train. Services were in Marlin Thursday. Ben Connally of Houston joined his father at St. Louis, as did Mr. and Mrs. F. M. Burkhead and Walton Taylor. Mrs. Burkhead is a sister of Mrs. Connally. McGregor Mirror: Aug 30 (1-5), 1935.

RUSSELL INFANT. Little Joe Bob Russell, infant son of Mr. and Mrs. Glenn Russell, died in a Waco hospital last Thursday. Burial was in Crawford Cemetery. CARD OF THANKS. We wish to thank our many friends for their kindnesses during the illness and death of our darling baby. Mr. and Mrs. Glenn Russell. McGregor Mirror: Aug 30 (5-1)/(5-5), 1935.

FERRELL INFANT. Twin boys were born to Mr. and Mrs. Charlie Farrell in a Waco Hospital last week. One of the babies only lived a short while. Burial will be in Post Oak Cemetery. McGregor Mirror: Aug 30 (7-4), 1935.

WILL BANKHEAD, age 63, died at his home in Coryell City Monday. Burial was in Post Oak Cemetery. Survivors include his wife, Ida Bankhead; several brothers and sisters. McGregor Mirror: Sep 6 (7-1), 1935.

CLARENCE BUTLER. The Jones Hill and Horne communities sympathize with Mr. and Mrs. Miles Butler when the sad news came from Colorado that Clarence Butler was killed in a train wreck. McGregor Mirror: Sep 6 (7-4), 1935.

L. PETTWAY died Tuesday in Sanatorium, Texas. He had lived in McGregor with his wife and daughter for many years. The family moved to Waco 2 years ago after the marriage of their daughter, Mildred Nell, where they reside at the present time. Burial was in Oakwood Cemetery by Compton's Funeral Home of Waco. Mr. Pettway is survived by his wife and daughter. McGregor Mirror: Sep 20 (1-1), 1935.

J. T. PARKEE, nephew of Dr. F. R. Wingrove, was killed in Breckenridge Tuesday. McGregor Mirror: Sep 20 (5-5), 1935.

CHARLES WHITE, age 78, died in Temple last Thursday. He was the uncle of Mrs. W. R. Cavitt, Mrs. Carl White, and Mrs. Smith White. Funeral services were in Temple. McGregor Mirror: Sep 20 (7-2), 1935.

JOHN A. WOOD of Memphis, Texas, died Monday in a Dallas hospital. Mr. Wood was at one time one of McGregor's leading citizens. He was an uncle of Mrs. E. J. Thomason, Miss Willie Mae Hall and Charles B. Hall of McGregor. McGregor Mirror: Sep 27 (1-5), 1935.

AMANDA KIRBY died Tuesday. Burial was in Osage by Lee Undertakers. Survivors include her husband, Jess Kirby; several daughters and several sons. McGregor Mirror: Sep 27 (3-1), 1935.

MRS. O. S. POTTER died at her home in Dallas Tuesday. Funeral services were held in Dallas then the body was carried to Waco for graveside services in Oakwood Cemetery. Survivors include her husband; two children, Mrs. Oliver Winchell and Gerald Potter of Waco; three sisters, Mrs. R. F. Senterfit of Lampasas, Mrs. R. R. Bowie of El Paso, and Mrs. E. L. Gibson of Big Springs. McGregor Mirror: Oct 4 (1-4), 1935.

W. R. MEADOWS, son-in-law of Mrs. M. F. Smith, died in Fort Worth. Mrs. Smith, of Raymondville, was in McGregor this week visiting her brother, Jake H. Smith. She had been in Fort Worth where she attended the funeral of her son-in-law. McGregor Mirror: Oct 4 (4-2), 1935.

BILLY GENE SHELTON, age 10 months, died in a Temple hospital October 5, 1935. He was the son of Mr. and Mr. Pete Shelton who live near Stampede. Burial was in Old Perry Cemetery near Moody. McGregor Mirror: Oct 11 (5-4), 1935.

CALVIN J. EDWARDS, age 73, of Osage was buried Monday. His body was shipped to Amsler Funeral Home from Washington, D. C.. W. A. Hamilton, Clay Chapman, R. H. Alexander, A. J. Mann, D. B. Scott, F. M. Lyon and J. F. Ellis attended the funeral in Osage. McGregor Mirror: Oct 18 (4-2), 1935/Amsler Funeral Home Records, Book 2, 1935.

C. O. JONES of Moody was buried Monday. Survivors include his wife; two daughters, Mrs. Tump Grady of Oglesby and Mrs. Howell Hundley of Moody; a son, H. H. Jones of Moody; two grandsons; his mother, Mrs. Frank Jones of Moody; three brothers and two sisters. McGregor Mirror: Oct 18 (7-1), 1935.

MRS. W. H. OWEN (Willie Mae Owens), age 19, died in a Waco hospital Thursday. She was born in Osage, July 13, 1916, the daughter of J. B. Swift and Jennie Clearman. Survivors include her husband; two little children; her parents, Mr. and Mrs. Joe Swift; four sisters; six brothers. Funeral services were at the Bluff Creek Baptist Church near Oglesby by Lee Undertakers. McGregor Mirror: Oct 18 (7-2), 1935/Lee Undertakers Records, 1935.

ELLIE WILLIAMS, age 50, died Friday, October 25, in a Waco hospital. She was the daughter of Thomas Walters and Mahaley Short. The remains were brought to the home of Mrs. Sam Williams and burial was at Flint Creek Cemetery Saturday. (Jones Hill Community news.) Mr. Williams, age 50, was from Flat, Texas. Survivors include his wife; five children; five brothers, John Williams of Moody, Tom of Waco, Rev. Ollie and Gip Williams of Flat, and Jim Williams of McGregor. McGregor Mirror: Oct 25 (4-5)/Nov 1 (5-2), 1935.

MRS. OLIVIA BIRD MORRISON, age 81, died Saturday, October 25, in Waco. She was born in Bowling Green, Kentucky. Burial was in McGregor

Cemetery by Lee Undertakers. Survivors include four sons, P. P. Morrison of McGregor, Johnnie Morrison of Itasca, Lucian Morrison of Troy, Oscar Morrison of Sulphur, Oklahoma; three daughters, Mrs. Christine Harris of Houston, Mrs. Florence Marrs and Mrs. John Absker of Rotan, Texas. McGregor Mirror: Nov 1 (5-1), 1935.

ALVIN GREEN died of pneumonia last Friday, October 25, at his home in Borger. He was the son of Park Green, who formerly lived in McGregor. Mrs. Minnie Kerley and Jim Green were his aunt and uncle. McGregor Mirror: Nov 1 (5-3), 1935.

MRS. PAULINE RAPP, formerly Miss Mogle, died October 24, at Indian Gap. She was born in Plueniger, Germany, August 21, 1869. At age 17 she came to America to make her home with her uncle, Mr. John Wilderer, who lives at Jonesboro in Coryell County. A year later she married Pius Rapp. Several years later they moved to Indian Gap in Mills County. They had nine children, the youngest one died 12 years ago. Mr. Rapp died 4 years later. Mrs. Rapp lived alone until sickness forced her to move into the home of her daughter, Mrs. August Serger. She died October 22, 1935, at age 66. Survivors include her children: Mrs. August Serger, Mrs. Ida Spiker, Mrs. Tina Spiker, all of Priddy, Mrs. Helene Eilers of Hamilton County, Mrs. Clara Kopp of Shine, George Rapp of Schertz, Henry and Carl Rapp of Indian Gap; one brother, Carl Mogle of McGregor; a half-brother and a half-sister in Plueniger, Germany. Burial was in St. John's Cemetery near Priddy by Amsler Funeral Home of McGregor. McGregor Mirror: Nov 1 (5-5), 1935.

EMMA MORRIS, age 48, died at her home in Sanatorium, Texas, October 26. She was born January 26, 1887, the daughter of John Mattiza and Mary Kutacek, both born in Germany. Survivors include her husband, Mr. R. E. Morris of Pittsburg, Texas and one step-son of Pittsburg, Texas; one brother, Mr. Henry Mattiza; two sisters, Mrs. Henry Mattlage and Mrs. Annie Roloff, all of Crawford. Burial was in Coryell Lutheran Church cemetery by Amsler Funeral Home. McGregor Mirror: Nov 1 (5-6), 1935/Amsler Funeral Home Records, Book 2.
Friends of Mrs. W. W. Webb of Comanche Springs community sympathized with her in the loss of one of her brothers recently. He and his wife both died in less than a month. McGregor Mirror: Nov 1 (8-4), 1935.

EDWARD M. MOONEY died Wednesday in Shreveport, Louisiana. His body was shipped to McGregor by train. Funeral services were held at the home of his parents, Mr. and Mrs. T. L. Allison with burial in McGregor Cemetery by Lee Undertakers. Mr. Mooney had made his home in Mooringsport, Louisiana, for the past 17 years. He was married to Georgia Allison on August 6, 1915. He was born in Hollow Springs, Mississippi, December 6, 1889, but at the age of 3 moved to Texas, settling near Oglesby. Survivors include his wife; one son, Thomas Edward Mooney of Mooringsport, Louisiana; his mother, Mrs. N. B. Mooney of Oglesby; four brothers, Will, Carl, O. L. of Floydada and Jim Mooney of Oglesby; one sister Mrs. Luther Sullins of Oglesby.

Pallbearers were his four sons, his brother-in-law, L. Sullins of Oglesby, and his employer, W. F. Harding of Mooringsport, Louisiana. McGregor Mirror: Nov 8 (1-3)/ Nov 15 (7-2), 1935.

MRS. FRITZ WEBER of Marlin died last Sunday, November 3. Burial was in Marlin in the Calvary Cemetery by Adams Funeral Home of Marlin. Survivors include her husband; two sons and a daughter, Willie Rathjen, Arnold Weber and Mary Frances Weber, all of Marlin; a daughter and a son, Mrs. Rudolph Krollage and Herbert Rathjen of Waco; and a daughter, Mrs. John Wallace of McGregor. Mrs. Weber made her home in McGregor for a number of years before moving to Marlin. McGregor Mirror: Nov 8 (4-4), 1935.

B. W. HORN, age 64, died in a Gatesville hotel Saturday. Burial was in Oakwood Cemetery. Mr. Horn was well known in McGregor, being an employee of the Cotton Belt Railroad as a pumper for more than 30 years. Survivors include one son, Leon Horn of Wichita Falls; four daughters, Mrs. Edward Hoehn and Miss Frances Horn of Waco, Miss Curtis Horn of DeLand, Florida, and Mrs. J. E. Parnum of Philadelphia. McGregor Mirror: Nov 8 (5-2), 1935.

MILLIE BARRON (Mrs. Sam Barron), sister of Mrs. Keltner of Jone Hill community, died Sunday at her home near Neff Park. She was born in Kentucky, September 25, 1899, the daughter of Frank and Mary Shirley. Burial was in Post Oak Cemetery by Lee Undertakers. Mrs. Barron, age 36, died at her home near Whitson. Survivors include her husband; two sons; one daughter. McGregor Mirror: Nov 8 (5-3)/ (7-1), 1935/Lee Undertakers Records, 1935.

MR. DAN JONES died Monday. He was a resident of the Jones Hill community. McGregor Mirror: Nov 15 (5-1), 1935.

MYRTLE GREEN JACKSON died in a Temple hospital November 7, 1935. Burial was in Post Oak Cemetery. She was the daughter of Curtis and Ellen Ross Green and was born near Leon Junction December 22, 1889. On November 9, 1913 she married Frank J. Jackson. Survivors include her husband, J. F. Jackson; one son; two sisters, Mrs. Lizzie Walter and Mrs. Lillie Casey; five brothers, Dr. F. C. Green, C. E., George I., Grundy and Newton Green. Pallbearers were six nephews: Otis, Curtis and Benton Walter, John D. Wright, Frederick and Price Green. McGregor Mirror: Nov 15 (7-2), 1935.

ADOLF WEISS, a resident of Coryell City community for 20 years, died Tuesday, November 12. He was born in Brenham 69 years ago, the son of Fritz Weiss and Charlotte Hamberg Weiss, both born in Germany. In 1888 he married Anna Loesch of Brenham. Burial was in Coryell City Lutheran Cemetery by Amsler Funeral Home. Survivors include eight sons and three daughters, Ed and Ernest of McGregor, Walter of Waco, Emanuel of Houston, Albert of Coryell City, Ben of Gatesville, Adolf of Sherman, Lonnie of Palestine and Mrs. Ernest Niemier of Osage, Mrs. Emil

Poetzch and Mrs. W. W. Cooper of Dallas. One brother, Fritz Weiss of Brenham also survives him. Justice of the Peace, Martin Dalton and Peace Officer, John Crouch, were called to the home of Mr. Weiss because he died alone at his home. An inquest was held with Dr. Wheeler and it was ruled that Mr. Weiss died of apoplexy, a heart trouble. McGregor Mirror: Nov 15 (8-4)/Nov 22 (3-4), 1935.

DAN JONES, uncle of Wendell Jordan of Commerce, was buried here a few days ago in Moody. Mrs. I. T. Jones of Florida was also here to attend the funeral with Wendell. McGregor Mirror: Nov 22 (3-4), 1935.

LENA WYNN, Mrs. Joe Wynn, died this last week in Houston. She will be remembered as Miss Lena Kirk Ingram of Shreveport, Louisiana, who visited here often in the home of her aunt, Mrs. W. H. Kirk. McGregor Mirror: Nov 29 (2-3), 1935.

WITT INFANT. (Holly Witt) A baby was born to Mr. and Mrs. Henry Witt last Saturday, but only lived a few hours. Burial was in the McGregor Cemetery by Lee Undertakers. The mother, who is quite ill, was taken to a Waco hospital, and is improving. McGregor Mirror: Dec. 6 (1-5), 1935.

JOHN BENJAMIN NOWLIN, age 55, died Tuesday at his home in Oglesby. He was born June 29, 1880, in Potts Camp, Mississippi, the son of John E. Nowlin and Sarah Annie Cox. Burial was in Post Oak Cemetery by Lee Undertakers after funeral services at the Primitive Baptist Church here at Old Salem. Survivors include his wife and five children. McGregor Mirror: Dec 6 (6-4), 1935/Lee Undertakers Records, 1935.

MRS. JOHN HAMILTON (Anna Oliver Hamilton), age 66, died at her home in McGregor Monday, December 2. She was born February 10, 1869, the daughter of Mr. Oliver and Smith Oliver, in Alabama and came to Texas when she was 2, settling in McGregor. She married John Hamilton at Eagle Springs in 1886 where they lived on the farm until moving into McGregor in 1919. Burial was in McGregor Cemetery by Amsler Funeral Home. Survivors inlcude two sons, Roy of Hewitt and Oliver of McGregor; two daughters, Mrs. A. E. Reynolds and Mrs. Albert Terry of McGregor. Her husband, John F. Hamilton, preceded her in death just four months ago. Three children also preceded her in death. McGregor Mirror: Dec 6 (8-5), 1935.

H. C. KILGORE, age 36, died in Austin December 4, 1935. He was born in Alabama. Lee Undertakers of McGregor was in charge of services. Lee Undertakers Records, 1935.

WILLIAM JACKSON, age 81, died December 11, 1935. He was born in Mansfield, Louisiana, October 4, 1854, the son of Wyet Jackson and Marie Louise Provent. Informant was Ella Jackson of Mound, Texas, his wife. Lee Undertakers Records, 1935.

FRANCES JANE JACKSON died December 25, 1936. She was born October 20, 1855, the daughter of _____ Alexander and _____ Robinson of Mississippi. Frances was the wife of J. A. Jackson. Informant was Miss May Jackson of McGregor. Burial was in Comanche Springs Cemetery by Amsler Funeral Home. Survivors include her husband; and five daughters, Miss Mittie Jackson, Miss May Jackson and Mrs. J. D. Poss, all of McGregor, Mrs. Frank Jenkins of Uvalde and Mrs. G. L. Alexander of Stephenville. Mrs. Jackson was married in Mississippi but had been a resident of McGregor for 33 years. Amsler Funeral Home Records, Book 2/McGregor Mirror: Jan 3 (1-3), 1936.

CHAPTER 2

GRISSOM W. LEE, prominent McGregor merchant, died suddenly Sunday, December 22, 1935, in Autaugaville, Alabama, the son of William Lee and Louise B. Hall. He was born January 24, 1873. In 1889, G. W., at age 16, became assistant to his father, William Lee, in the Lee Hardware Company. In July of 1936, he would have been working in the family business for 50 years. Mr. Lee was president of the First National Bank of McGregor, was a Mason, being a member of the McGregor Blue Lodge and the Karem Shrine on Waco. He was also one of the organizers of the Retail Merchants Association and one of the original members of the McGregor Rotary Club. Funeral services were conducted at his home. The Knights Templar escorted his body to the McGregor Cemetery where the Masonic fraternity committed his body to its last resting place. Survivors include his wife, Lena R. Lee (1878-1965); a daughter, Irene Lee; a son, G. W. Lee, Jr., all of McGregor; two sisters, Mrs. Eva Johnson of McGregor and Mrs. Eunice Johnson of Oglesby; and one brother, A. L. Lee of McGregor. McGregor Mirror: Jan 3 (1-1), 1936.

FRANCES ALEXANDER JACKSON of McGregor died at her home December 25, 1935. She is survived by her husband, Jacob Anderson Jackson (1854-1945); five daughters, Miss Mittie, Miss May, Mrs. J. D. Poss, all of McGregor, Mrs. Frank Jenkins of Uvalde, and Mrs. G. L. Alexander of Stephenville. Mr. and Mrs. Jackson were married in Mississippi but had lived in McGregor for 33 years. Burial was in Comanche Springs Cemetery by Amsler Funeral Home. Out of town relatives and friends were: Mr. and Mrs. L. E. King, Mr. R. L. Shannon, Mrs. Martha Thompson, all of Fort Worth, and Mrs. Michael Kelly of Waco. McGregor Mirror: Jan 3 (1-3), 1936.

GEORGE I. DRAPER died at his home at Mound, Sunday. Burial was in Davidson Cemetery by Lee Undertakers. He was a pioneer of Coryell County whose sudden death brought sorrow to all who knew him. Survivors include his wife; two sons, W. Guy Draper of McGregor and Claxton Draper of Fort Worth; five daughters, Mrs. W. S. Garnett of Big Spring, Mrs. Aubrey Davidson, Mrs. Clyde Childres and Miss Mona Draper, all of Mound, and Mrs. Quincy Davidson of Hamilton. McGregor Mirror: Jan 3 (1-3), 1936.

WILEY WATSON "WATT" CAUFIELD, age 75, a native of McLennan County and a member of a pioneer family, died suddenly Sunday, December 29, 1935, at his home eight miles southeast of McGregor. Burial was in Harris Creek Cemetery by Amsler Funeral Home. Mr. Caufield, son of the late Henry J. Caufield born in Alabama and Martha Jones born in Milam County, Texas, was born January 1, 1860, at the old Caufield Ranch and spent most of his life there. He married Miss McLennan on December 22, 1880. Survivors include his wife, Kate (1861-1957); two daughters, Mrs. W. T. Montgomery and Mrs. Elizabeth Armond of San Antonio; a sister, Mrs. Joe

Cavitt of McGregor; a brother, George Caufield of Borger; a granddaughter, Mrs. James Burwell of San Antonio; and a grandson, Watson Arnold of San Antonio; as well as a great granddaughter, Katherine McLennan Burwell of San Antonio. McGregor Mirror: Jan 3 (1-4), 1936.

EDNA PORTER BROWN, the daughter of Rev. J. M. Porter, died Monday in Temple. She was born in 1867 in Caldwell County, Texas. Her body was brought to McGregor for burial in McGregor Cemetery beside her husband, Dr. James Edwin Brown (1865-1916) by Amsler Funeral Home. Mrs. Brown had been making her home in Mart with her daughter, Mrs. Paul Beresford (Katherine Brown), but had been hospitalized in Temple. She is survived by three sons and two daughters, J. Edwin Brown of Amarillo, Dr. William Porter Brown of Fort Worth, Ben Brown of New York City, Mrs. Burbank Woodson of Temple and Mrs. Paul Beresford of Mart. Also surviving are three sisters and one brother, Mrs. R. L. McKnignt of Temple, Mrs. Marion Witt of McGregor, Mrs. Jesse B. Brown of Austin, Fred Porter of Temple. McGregor Mirror: Jan 3 (1-5), 1936.

MRS. M. M. VAUGHN, mother of Mrs. E. B. Gibson, died in her home in Pendleton last week. McGregor Mirror: Jan 3 (4-3), 1936.

ANDERSON INFANT. A baby daughter was born to Mr. and Mrs. Leonard Anderson on December 22, 1935, but lived only a few hours. Burial was in the Moody Cemetery. McGregor Mirror: Jan 3 (5-6), 1936.

MRS. MARY JACOBS died at the home of her daughter, Mrs. Ben Neff, in Dallas. Mrs. Jacobs, age 88, was a resident of Texas for 86 years. She came with her family, settling in Henderson, Texas, and later in Coryell County where she grew up. After her marriage to her husband, who served in the Confederacy, Mrs. Jacobs went west in the 1870's to Erath County which had just been formed, but had lived in Dallas since 1914. Burial was in Restland Memorial Park of Dallas. Survivors include three sons, W. F. Jacobs, J. W. Jacobs and J. S. Jacobs; two daughters, Mrs. Ione Neff and Mrs. Edith Reynolds, all of Dallas; one brother, M. V. Baugh of Rogers, Texas. McGregor Mirror: Jan 3 (8-2), 1936.

WILLIAM CLINTON DEW, age 40, died in a Waco hospital Saturday, January 2, 1936, of pneumonia. He was born December 15, 1896. Mr. Dew and his wife, who is the former Pearl Johnson, daughter of Mrs. Julius Johnson, lived about nine miles out McGregor on the Caufield Ranch. Burial was in Harris Creek Cemetery by Lee Undertakers. Survivors include his wife; one son, Kenneth Wayne Dew; his parents, Mr. and Mrs. William J. Dew. McGregor Mirror: Jan 8 (1-2), 1936.

ROBERT WILLIAM MONCRIEF, born in Waco on March 1, 1873, died at his home near Windsor, December 22, 1935. He had lived in that community for 45 years. On December 22, 1904, he married Fannie Lyon and they had 4 children, one having preceded him in death. Burial was in

DEATHS IN CENTRAL TEXAS, VOL. II

Evergreen Cemetery by Compton Funeral Home of Waco. Survivors include his wife; three daughters, Mrs. M. R. Dyess of McGregor, Miss Sallie Moncrief of Turnersville, Mrs. J. H. Dove (Betty Bob Dove) of Waco, and one brother, C. E. Moncrief of Fort Worth; three sisters, Mrs. C. S. Standefer of Godley, Mrs. R. D. Clark of Clifton, Mrs. R. M. Armstrong of Cleburne. McGregor Mirror: Jan 8 (2-5), 1936.

MR. NATION was well known in McGregor and carried mail between the Post Office and the depot. Five years ago he moved to Waco. Children in Waco knew him as "Uncle Charlie", having sold them ice cream for the past two summers. *Most of this obituary was missing. McGregor Mirror: Jan 8 (1-5), 1936.

ANNIE LAMMERT died of pneumonia in a Waco hospital Wednesday, January 6, 1936. She had been a resident of McGregor since coming here from Washington County 26 years ago with her parents, Henry and Louise Wiethorn. Funeral serviced were held at the Harmony Lutheran Church with burial in the McGregor Cemetery by Amsler Funeral Home. Survivors include her father, Mr. Henry Wiethorn; one sister, Mrs. Fred Witt; four sons, Edwin, Arnold, Lonnie and Willie Lammert; three daughters, Ruby, Ester and Anita; three brothers, Henry, Louis and Gus Wiethorn, all of McGregor. She was preceded in death by her husband, William Lammert (1884-1926), and one son who died in infancy. McGregor Mirror: Jan 8 (4-4), 1936.

J. T. FLETCHER died Sunday, December 27, 1935, from a broken hip he suffered in a fall earlier in the week. He was carried to a Waco hospital for treatment where he died. His body was brought back to McGregor and carried to the home of his son, L. P. Fletcher, where funeral services were held. Burial was in McGregor Cemetery by Lee Undertakers. Mr. Fletcher was born in Cumberland County, Kentucky, in September of 1850. He moved to Texas 14 years ago, making his home with his three sons. Survivors include three sons, L. P. Fletcher, J. N. Fletcher, and C. R. Fletcher, all of McGregor. McGregor Mirror: Jan 8 (4-4), 1936.

MRS. J. T. CHAMBLEE, age 61, died at the home of her daughter, Mrs. Tom Thurmond, four miles northeast of McGregor, Sunday. Burial was in Crawford Cemetery by Lee Undertakers. She was born October 2, 1875, in Shawnee, Georgia, and came to Texas in 1895. On September 25, 1898 she married Mr. Chamblee, who preceded her in death on January 2, 1929. Survivors include three daughters, Mrs. Thurmond, Mrs. Cousins and Mrs. Roy Culp, all of McGregor; three sons, Roger, Roland and Ralph Chamblee, all of McGregor; two sisters, Mrs. Ed Srader of Crawford, Mrs. R. C. Wolf of Joplin, Missouri; a brother, W. E. Matther of Denver, Colorado. McGregor Mirror: Jan 8 (5-1), 1936.

MELVIN HARRIS, 11 year old son of J. W. Harris, died accidentally in Greenwood on Saturday after Christmas. Melvin had made his home in Greenwood with his sister, Mrs. Bessie Stem. The accident occurred when he was playing ball with a group of boys and the ball lodged on a passing truck. Melvin climbed onto the rear of the truck to recover the ball just at the mment the truck drove onto a bridge. The approach to the bridge caved in and pinned Melvin beneath the truck, killing him instantly. McGregor Mirror: Jan 8 (5-1), 1936.

RILEY GIP CAMPBELL, age 63, died at his home Tuesday, December 22, 1935. He was born in 1873. He had worked at his barber shop in Oglesby for about 40 years. Burial was in Post Oak Cemetery by Amsler Funeral Home. Survivors include his wife, Tishey L. Campbell (1875-1954); three daughters, Mrs. V. L. Edwards of McGregor, Mrs. J. N. Powell of Wichita, Kansas, and Mrs. B. L. Haynes of Wichita Falls, Texas; two grandchildren, Mary Lanell and B. L. Haynes, Jr.; one brother, W. M. Campbell; four sisters, Mrs. Jim Whigam of Flat, Mrs. Jim Webster, Mrs. John Gossett and Mrs. Ellison Short, all of Gatesville. Pallbearers were his newphews, Floyd Campbell, Dick Whigham, Eddie Lawrence, Dick Thompson, Mark Short, Dr. D. C. Hamon and Paul Whigham. McGregor Mirror: Jan 8 (6-1), 1936.

CHARLES RAY HAMILTON. CARD OF THANKS: We wish to thank everyone for kind thoughts and deeds during the brief illness and death of our infant son, Charles Ray. Singed -- Mr. and Mrs. Oliver Hamilton and family. Burial was in McGregor Cemetery. McGregor Mirror: Jan 8 (8-1), 1936.

WILLIS JONES, brother-in-law of Mrs. Ben Jones, died at his home in Patterson, Texas, Tuesday. Mrs. Jones and her daughter, Mrs. Joe Harris, attended the funeral there on Thursday. McGregor Mirror: Jan 8 (8-4), 1936.

GORDON ALBERT DAVIS, who was born December 5, 1898, in Coryell County, Texas, accidently killed himself while hunting on his farm near Coryell City, Friday, January 10, 1936. He was crawling through a fence when his gun went off, shooting him through the heart. His body was discovered by several children returning from school. Bert Davis (his cousin) and Jeff Gill were the first to reach the scene. Burial was in Davidson Cemetery by Lee Undertakers of McGregor. Survivors include his wife, Ruth E. Davis; sons, Burl, Royce and Hubert Davis, all of Gatesville; his mother, Mrs. Albert P. Davis (Lottie M. Clowers) of Oglesby; three brothers, J. M. of Oglesby, H. D. of McGregor, and M. E. Davis of Dallas; a niece, Mrs. Raymond Barber of Waco. McGregor Mirror: Jan 17 (1-2)/(7-2), 1936.

WALTER KOEHLER, age 29, died January 18, 1936. He was born in Texas, the son of Will Koehler and Martha Willman. Informant was Hermina Koehler of Crawford. Walter died in the Prarie Chapel community. (Place of burial now mentioned.) Amsler Funeral Home Records, Book 2.

GEORGE PORTERFIELD died in Waco, Monday. Burial was in Moody Cemetery by Compton Funeral Home of Waco. Mr. Porterfield, age 4, had lived in the McGregor community many years ago. Survivors include four sons, all of Sherman and two daughters, Mrs. Bill Cagle of Houston and Mrs. Lee Wheat of Moody. He was an uncle of Mrs. Mary Meador of McGregor. Mrs. Meador and son, John Meador, attended the funeral. McGregor Mirror: Jan 17 (5-2), 1936.

MR. WARNICK. W. L. Warnick of Oglesby was called to Aquilla last week to attend the funeral of his youngest brother who had resided with another brother for several years. McGregor Mirror: Jan 17 (7-1), 1936.

ELVIN DOUGLAS ANDERSON, the two year old son of Mr. and Mrs. Clem Anderson, died Sunday, January 12, at their home near McGregor. He was born November 24, 1933. Survivors include his parents, Clem Anderson born in Tom Green County, Texas, and May Marsha Anderson born in Hill County, Texas; and a little brother and sister. Burial was in McGregor Cemetery by Amsler Funeral Home. McGregor Mirror: Jan 17 (7-6), 1936.

NANCY LOU BENNETT, five month old daughter of Mr. and Mrs. B. D. Bennett, died of pneumonia Tuesday, January 15. She was born in McGregor, August 6, 1935. Survivors include her parents, Mr. Bennett born in Coryell County, Texas, and Vera High Bennett born in Coryell County, Texas; brothers, Ray, Duane and Nathan; and sister, Mary Ann Bennett. Funeral Services were conducted at the home of her grandparents, Mr. and Mrs. B. F. High. Burial was in McGregor Cemetery by Amsler Funeral Home. McGregor Mirror: Jan 24 (2-5), 1936.

JOHN McCLINTOCK. Mrs. G. F. Adcock was in Haskell recently attending the funeral of her brother, John McClintock. McGregor Mirror: Jan 24 (4-1), 1936.

GRANDPA MOON. Mrs. I. T. Farmer and family of Comanche Springs community attended the funeral of Grandpa Moon at Eddy last Wednesday. McGregor Mirror: Jan 24 (5-4), 1936.

JOHN L. JENKINS. Mrs. G. F. Adcock, Mrs. J. C. Keltner and Raymond Keltner were in Temple Tuesday to attend the funeral of Mr. John L. Jenkins, age 5. Mrs. Adcock and Mrs. Keltner were nieces of Mr. Jenkins. McGregor Mirror: Jan 24 (5-6), 1936.

KROLLAGE INFANT. The infant son of Henry Krollage died shortly after birth on January 31, 1936. He was the son of Henry Krollage born in Robinson, McLennan County, Texas and Minnie Hodde Krollage born in Washington County, Texas. Burial was in McGregor Cemetery by Amsler Funeral Home. Amsler Funeral Home Records, Book 2.

JOHN THOMAS (collored) died February 13, 1936, at age 2. He was born in Mississippi in 1854 and married Nancy _____. His parents were _____ Thomas and Annie _____ both born in Mississippi. Burial was in the McGregor Cemetery by Amsler Funeral Home. Informant was H. C. Thomas of Oglesby. Amsler Funeral Home Records, Book 2.

A. L. DALTON. The Jones Hill community was saddened Friday when news spread that A. L. Dalton had passed on. Mr. Dalton was a brother-in-law of Mrs. Geroge Goode of Jones Hill. McGregor Mirror: Feb 2 (5-2), 1936.

WILLIAM RABBE of Prarie Chapel community died in a Waco hospital Wednesday, February 25, after being badly gored by a bull in his pasture the day before. He was born in Germany on June 20, 1859, 76 years ago, coming to America when he was a young boy. His mother was Miss Rohloff born in Germany. Burial was at Coryell City Lutheran Church Cemetery (St. John Lutheran Cemetery) by Amsler Funeral Home. Survivors include his wife, Ottilie Athelia Rabbe (1864-1938), and seven children. McGregor Mirror: Feb 28 (5-5), 1936.

MRS. JIM CARROLL was buried in Killeen this week. Charles Murphy, Mr. and Mr. Cyph Murphy, Mr. and Mrs. Ernest Murphy, Mr. and Mrs. E. C. Murphy, and Mr. and Mrs. Mack Reed attended the funeral of their sister and aunt. McGregor Mirror: Feb 28 (5-5), 1936.

REV. R. R. CROCKETT died in Groesbeck, February 14, 1936. Rev. Crockett was pastor in Comanche Spring community near McGregor for a short time and had held several revival meetings there in the past. McGregor Mirror: Feb 28 (8-6), 1936.

JASPER PERKINS died in Houston this past week. Grady Perkins of Oglesby was called to Houston to bury his youngest brother, Jasper Perkins, who died of a stroke of paralysis. McGregor Mirror: Mar 7 (6-2), 1936.

C. V. "LIN" HOWARD, age 67, died of pneumonia in Austin on February 29, 1936. Mr. Howard was a native of Coryell County, having been born October 1, 1868, on the Howard river farm near Eagle Springs. His parents were among the earliest of settlers in Coryell County, his father having a headright from the State and settling in the Eagle Springs community in 1842. Although Lin was never married, he had a splendid homestead. Rev. A. J. Mann of McGregor officiated the last rights at the home. Survivors include four brothers: Phil of Olney, Sam of Abilene, Harvey of La Rue and W. S. of Dallas. Burial was in Eagle Springs Cemetery beside his parents by Amsler Funeral Home. McGregor Mirror: Mar 7 (6-2/(7-2), 1936.

CARL C. HATTER, age 54, a Moody resident, was creamated in his car Monday night when it ran into a ditch five miles east of Moody. A negro found his body burned beyond recognition. Identification was made from his watch. Officers surmised that the car caught fire when Hatter lit a cigarette after the accident, probably igniting spilled gasoline. McGregor Mirror: Mar 20 (1-5), 1936.

ELMORE HARRIS, JR. , age 16, died Tuesday when the V-8 he was driving collided with a gravel truck near South Bosque. Others in the car were his father, Elmore Harris, H. D. Short and Wayne Shaffer of Hamilton. McGregor Mirror: Mar 20 (1-5), 1936.

J. G. WARREN, age 55, died Tuesday when the gravel truck he was driving collided with a V-8 driven by Elmore Harris, Jr. near South Bosque. McGregor Mirror: Mar 20 (1-5), 1936.

MRS. BEN R. WILSON, sister-in-law of Mr. and Mrs. Dick Lawson, died last Friday at her home in Verden, Oklahoma. McGregor Mirror: Mar 20 (4-6), 1936.

MARY A. SRADER, an 83 year old resident of Crawford, died at her home last Monday, March 30. She moved to the Crawford community from Arkansas with her parents, Mr. and Mrs. Sam Dosher, when 13 years of age. Mary was born May 13, 1852, in Missouri, the daughter of Sam Dosher and Sallie Russell, both born in Missouri. She was a charter member of the Shilo Baptist Church. Burial was in Crawford Cemetery by Amsler Funeral Home. Suriviors include her husband, William L. Srader (1848-1938); two sons, H. E. Srader of Crawford and S. L. Srader of Waco; one daughter, Mrs. J. D. Arrowood of Crawford. McGregor Mirror: Apr 3 (1-3), 1936.

MARTHA JANE INGRAM, 87 year old wife of H. C. Ingram, died at the home of her daughter, Mrs. Fannie McMullen in Oglesby, Tuesday, March 31, 1936. She was born January 29, 1848, in Arkansas, the daughter of Nathan A. Primm who was born in Alabama, and Frances Leggen who was born in Louisiana. Mrs. Ingram made her home in McGregor until several years ago whem she moved to Oglesby to be with her daughter. Burial was in Post Oak Cemetery by Lee Undertakers. Survivors include two daughters, Mrs. Fannie McMullen of Oglesby and Mrs. Tom Wood of Alvarado; grandchildren, Mrs. Jim McMullen of McGregor, Mrs. Cecil Cryer of Temple, Mrs. Sam Ward and Polk Ingram of Gatesville, Mrs. J. R. Watson of Smackover, Arkansas, Mrs. I. N. Green, Mrs. Cliff Lynch and Joe Travis McMullen of Oglesby and Mrs. Willie Bowden of Alvarado. McGregor Mirror: Apr 3 (1-5), 1936.

C. C. HIGH was buried in Union Cemetery near Durango last Sunday. Mr. High was an uncle of Mrs. A. L. Blanton, Mrs. Tap Wells and Mr. B. F. High, all of McGregor. McGregor Mirror: Apr 3 (5-2), 1936.

MRS. E. H. JOHNSON, who passes away in a Waco hopsital was buried in Post Oak Cemetery last week. She was well known and had many friends who are grieved because she was quite young. Oglesby News. CARD OF THANKS: signed by E. H. Johnson, Mrs. Oscar Stone and family, and Mother Johnson and family. McGregor Mirror: Apr 3 (6-1)/(8-6), 1936.

HENRY QUEBE, age 80, pioneer citizen and retired farmer of McGregor, died in a Waco hospital Wednesday, April 8. Mr. Quebe died of injuries suffered 10 days ago when he was struck by an automobile on the streets of McAllen, Texas. He was born April 24, 1856, at Whedem, Germany, but immigrated to Galveston, Texas, in September of 1871. He had made his home in McGregor for the past 52 years. On December 3, 1885, he married Miss Hulda Hueske (1862-1924) who preceded him in death 12 years ago. Mr. Quebe helped organize the building of the Sons of Herman Lodge and the Evangelical Lutheran Church in McGregor. Burial was in McGregor Cemetery by Amsler Funeral Home. Survivors include five sons and one daughter: W. F. Quebe of Waco, B. O. Quebe of Plainview, Henry Quebe, Jr., Gus L. Quebe and Fred C. Quebe of McGregor, and Mrs. Heinz Quebe of McGregor. McGregor Mirror: Apr (1-1), 1936.

MRS. J. D. FREEMAN, SR. died last Saturday. She came to McGregor 51 years ago with her husband. At the time they had been married six or seven years. Burial was in Crawford Cemetery beside other members of her family by Lee Undertakers. Survivors include her husband; sons, D. G. Freeman of Crawford, Roy of Alvarado, John and Tom Freeman of McGregor and Mrs. Ernest Clark of Memphis. McGregor Mirror: Apr 10 (1-5), 1936.

ANNIE IRENE DUNCAN died at her home near Pecan Grove Wednesday, April 8, of pneumonia. Funeral services were held a Pecan Grove church with burial in Post Oak Cemetery by Lee Undertakers. She was buried beside her husband, Walter Grover Duncan (1886-1930), who died several years ago. Mrs. Duncan was born in Holly Springs, Mississippi, on November 20, 1888, the daughter of R. L. Brinkley and Edna Wafford both born in Mississippi, but moved to Texas at the age of 3. She had lived in the Oglesby community since that time. Survivors include four daughters, Mrs. W. R. Berts, Miss Gladys, Miss Bonnie Jean and Miss Lola Murl; four sons, Volney, Spurgeon, Thermon and Riley; mother, Mrs. Bob Brinkley; eleven sisters, Mrs. J. D. Griffin of Oglesby, Mrs. Henry Evans of Houston, Mrs. Lother Rollins of Lahay, Mrs. Myrtle Hinton of Valley Mills, Mrs. Baybil Autrey of Longview, Mrs. Leon Etzell of Galveston, Mrs. Hugh Walker of Oglesby, Mrs. Ray Richard of Roby, Mrs. Earl Clayton of Nolan, Miss Fay Brinkley of Brady; three brothers, Clark of California, Bryan and Clyde of Santa Fe, New Mexico. McGregor Mirror: Apr 10 (5-6)/Apr 17 (6-2), 1936.

MRS. KELLUM. The Stockburger family of Oglesby was called to Jonesboro Tuesday to attend the funeral of Mrs. Kellum, the mother of Mrs. Robert Stockburger. Burial was in Jonesboro. McGregor Mirror: Apr 10 (6-2), 1936.

STONE FAMILY. G. C. Stone; his father, mother and brother, George Stone; and W. W. Stone attended the funeral of Mrs. W. J. Stone's mother at Belton, Wednesday, April 14, 1936. She was 86 years of age. Survivors include four daughters and three sons. Pallbearers were her grandsons. Her husband preceded her in death 17 years ago. They were married in 1869. McGregor Mirror: Apr 17 (4-6), 1936.

CHESTER C. HUTCHEON, city marshal of Merkel, was shot and killed Saturday when he attempted to arrest a suspect. Mrs. Mattie Fields and Miss Willie Darsey of McGregor were called to Merkel Sunday for the funeral. Mr. Hutcheon's wife is a daughter of Mr. Tom Darsey of Merkel and is a niece of Mrs. Fields and Miss Darsey of McGregor. McGregor Mirror: Apr 17 (4-5), 1936.

THERON SHOPE of Dalton, Gerogia, died this week. Mrs. Baxter Shope of New Braunfels and brother, Festus Shope of Oglesby, were called to Dalton for the funeral. Theron was editor of the Dalton Citizen for the past 33 years and was connected with Showalter Co. Publishers. Survivors include his wife; daughter, Helen; three brothers, S. F. Shope and Z. F. Shope of Oglesby and Baxter Shope of New Braunfels; and a sister, Mrs. John Hoover of Killeen. McGregor Mirror: Apr 17 (6-5), 1936.

DORA ISBILL WALTON died at her home near The Grove Tuesday, April 28, 1936. She was born in Jackson Parish, Louisiana, January 20, 1857, the daughter of Mr. Evans and Miss Pill, both born in Louisiana, and married almost 60 years ago. Eight children were born to them but only four survive, Mrs. Ralph McEntire of McGregor, Mrs. G. R. Wilson of Gatesville, Mrs. Miller Robinson of Abilene and Mrs. F. B. Walton of The Grove. Other survivors include a sister, Mrs. Cynthia Smith of Dallas; and a brother, Jim Evans of Goldthwaite. Burial was in Turnersville, Texas, by Amsler Fuenral Home. McGregor Mirror: May 1 (1-1), 1936.

RAYMOND BROWN died in Waco May 1, 1936. He was born March 9, 1897, in Crawford, the son of Jasper Brown who was born in Gerogia and _____ Pool who was born in Georgia. His wife was Ruby English Blanton. Mr. Brown drove a milk truck for Borden's Milk Company. The day of the wreck, Mr. Brown and two girls, Ruby Blanton and Glynda McNeil (his step-daughter) were riding in the milk truck when a truck loaded with hot asphalt skidded into them, splashing hot asphalt over the three occupants of the milk truck. Mr. Brown died instantly and the two girls died later in a Waco hospital. Survivors include his wife; two children, Ladene and Sammy Brown; his mother, Mrs. J. T. Brown of Houston; four sisters, Mrs. J. T. Compton of Crawford, Mrs. G. B. Wall of Hewitt, Mrs. A. J. Crowden and Mrs. R. T. Barnard of Houston; a brother, J. T. Brown of Houston. Burial was in Crawford by Amsler Funeral Home. Amlser Funeral Home Records, Book 2 / McGrgor Mirror: May 8, 1936.

RUBY RUTH BLANTON, age 17, died in Waco in a truck wreck on May 1, 1936. She was born June 8, 1918, in Collin County, Texas, the daughter of Jim Blanton who was born in McGregor and Hassie Pack who was born in Tennessee. Ruby died in the same accident as Raymond Brown and Glynda McNeil. Surviving Miss Blanton are her parents, Mr. and Mrs. Jim Blanton of Crawford; gour sisters, Mrs. Opal Christie, Miss Verne, Miss Mildred and Miss Wilma Blanton of Crawford; three brothers, Ray, Earl and Royce Blanton, all of Crawford. Burial was in Crawford Cemetery by Amsler Funeral Home. Amlser Funeral Home Records, Book 2 / McGregor Mirror: May 8, 1936.

GLYNDA McNEIL died in Waco in a truck wreck May 1, 1936. She was born August 15, 1915, in Pendleton, Texas, the daughter of G. R. McNeil who was born in Moody and Ruby English who was born in McGregor. She died in the same accident as Raymond Brown and Ruby Blanton. Miss McNeil was to have been married to Earl Drake on Saturday. Survivors include her mother, Mrs. Raymond Brown; a brother, Raymond McNeil; a step-sister, Ladene Brown; and a step-brother, Sammy Brown. Burial was in Crawford Cemetery by Amsler Fuenral Home. Amsler Funeral Home Records, Book 2/McGregor Mirror: May 8, 1936.

CECIL R. SPENCER, age 19, died at the home of his aunt, Mrs. Eph Murphy, Wednesday, Apri 29, of pneumonia. He was born February 5, 1916. Survivors include his aunt and uncle, Mr. and Mrs. Eph Murphy; grandparents, Mr. and Mrs. C. H. Murphy of Kopperl; a sister, Miss Louise Spencer; a half-sister, Miss Grace Allen, and another aunt and uncle, Mr. and Mrs. C. C. Whittenburg. His parents both preceded him in death. Burial was in McGregor Cemetery by Lee Underatakers. McGregor Mirror: May 1 (1-3), 1936.

J. E. LEONARD of McGregor died in an automobile accident Thursday. He was killed when the car he was driving crashed into a concrete culvert on Highway 7 about 8 miles east of McGrgor. After an inquest in Waco, the body was returned to McGregor by Lee Undertakers. Burial was in Lone Oak Cemetery in Hunt County, Texas. Mr. Leonard was born in Winn, Alabama, March 11, 1887, but had lived in McGregor for the past 25 years. During that time he was engaged in the blacksmith and machine shop business. Survivors include his wife; four daughters, Mrs. Wootson Johnson, Miss Lula, Miss Lillian and Midd Edith; twin sons, Earl and Ernest; his mother; a brother, Erby; sisters, Mrs. Gennie Cravey and Mrs. Mamie Pettus, all of Winn, Alabama, Mrs. Julian McCain of Sarah, Oklahoma, Mrs. Alice Pezan and Mrs. Maude Milstead of Jackson, Alabama; brothers, Curtis of Grove Hill, Alabama, Claude of Oak Hill, Alabama, and W. J. Leonard of Mercedes. McGregor Mirror: May 1 (5-1), 1936.

HENRIETTA MAKOWSKI, age 58, died in a Waco hospital Monday. Survivors include sisters, Mrs. Sophie Wehrmann and Mrs. Charles Wellmann of Eagle Springs community who attended the funeral in Meier, Texas, Wednesday. Other survivors include her husband, Rev. William Makowski, pastor of the Buckhorn Church below Neff Park; six sons and a daughter; two sisters, Mrs. Minnie Fischgrabe and Mrs. Lena Wiese of Moody; a brother, Fritz Wellmann of Moody. McGregor Mirror: May 1 (5-2), 1936.

WILLIAM AMTHOR died at his home in Waco, Saturday. Burial was in Oakwood Cemetery. Mr. Amthor was born in Colorado County, Texas, in 1849 and came to McGregor in 1884. He moved to Waco in 1907. A charter member of the McGregor Masonic Lodge, he was made a Mason at Brenham and at the time was considered the youngest Mason in Texas. Survivors include three sons, A. W. and Will H. Amthor of La Feria, and J. M. Amthor of San Saba; two daughters, Mrs. William Rathman of New Braunfels and Miss Bertha Amthor of Waco. McGregor Mirror: May 15 (1-1), 1936.

MARGARET LOU WALKER died at her home in Temple Tuesday. Mr. and Mrs. C. W. Mogle were called to Temple to attend the funeral of the thirteen month old daughter of Mr. and Mrs. J. W. Walker. Mrs. Walker is a niece of Mr. and Mrs. Mogle. McGregor Mirror: May 15 (3-4), 1936.

MRS. SAM H. AMSLER, JR. Sam Amsler received a message last Friday telling of the death of his daughter-in-law, Mrs. Sam H. Amsler, Jr., in Las Vegas, New Mexico. McGregor Mirror: May 15 (4-3), 1936.

BETTIE WRIGHT. Mr. and Mrs. Glenn Crain, Mrs. E. J. Thomason and Mrs. A. L. Lee attended the funeral of Mrs. Bettie Wright in Gatesville last Thursday morning. Mrs. Wright was a pioneer of Gatesville and Coryell County but had made her home in Amarillo with her daughter for several years. McGregor Mirror: May 15 (4-4), 1936.

SILAS MAGEE, age 25, died May 9, 1936. He had been living with Bro. Fairchild and his wife as one of the family at Hale Center near Plainview. He had been in poor health for several years. He would have graduated this school term at the end of the summer if he had lived. His body was brought to Oglesby by Ellis Fairchild, his boyhood companion. Survivors include his father; one brother, Jack; four sisters, Evelyn and Rosalyn (twins), Marcelle and Willie Mae. (Place of burial not mentioned.) McGregor Mirror: May 15 (7-1), 1936.

PRUDIE JIBS WALLACE, age 64, died Tuesday, May 12, 1936, at her home in Osage. She was born March 19, 1872, in Tennessee, the daughter of Jesse and Mary Wallace, and married Jeff Bland in 1892. After his death, she married Mr. J. F. Wallace, who had been her companion for 31 years. Funeral services were held at Osage Baptist Church with burial in Osage Cemetery by Lee Undertakers. Survivors include her husband, Jesse F. Wallace (1867-1954); two daughters, Miss Carrie and Miss Willie Bland; two sons, Elisha Wallace and Jesse Wallace; two sisters, Mrs. C. L. Thetford and Mrs. S. A. Comer of Purmela; a brother, T. N. Edwards of McGregor; nieces, Miss Joise Comer, Onietra Thetford, Bettie Sue Thetford, Ella Thetford, Millie Jack Jayroe, Mrs. Alice Buckner, Vella Chambers and Bonnie Morris. Pallbearers were her nephews, Lee, George and Foy Thetford, Jim and Mike Comer and Buster Morris. Mr. and Mrs. Fred Talley and Mrs. Lynn Donahoo and son, Bill, of Floresville, were among the out of town relatives. McGregor Mirror: May 15 (8-1), 1936.

CORA LEE BEATY died at her home Monday, May 11. Burial was in Comanche Springs Cemetery by Lee Undertakers. Mrs. Beaty had lived in this area most of her life. Survivors include her husband, Luther Lee Beaty (1887-1937); two daughters, Miss Carrie Lee Beaty and Miss Frances Beaty; two sons, Sam and John Beaty of McGregor; her father, J. H. Williams of McGregor; three sisters, Mrs. Ella Redman of Tennessee, Mrs. Willie Mitchell of Lorena, and Mrs. Sadie Parker of Waco; two brothers, Kirk and Felix Williams of Waco. McGregor Mirror: May 15 (8-6), 1936.

LOU M. ENGLAND died in a Temple hospital May 17. She was born in Columbus, Kentucky, August 5, 1862, and married Mr. Jerry England on January 20, 1880. He preceded her in death in 1922. Eight children were born to them, four girls and four boys. All are living except one son, Ivin, who passed away last year. Burial was in McGregor Cemetery by Lee Undertakers. Survivors include her children: Stanford and George of McGregor, Rolin of San Antonio, Mrs. Elmer Brown, Mrs. Ovater Hall, and Mrs. Roy Vowel of McGregor, Mrs. Byron Culperrer of Temple; one sister, Mrs. J. R. Breeding of McGregor; three half-sisters, Mrs. Harold Bakke of Temple, Mrs. Florence Whiteman of Austin, Mrs. Pearl Coker of Houston; two brothers, June McKinney of Waco and Bob McKinney of Texas City. McGregor Mirror: May 22 (1-1), 1936.

JONAS JONES, age 60, died at hishome near Crawford, Tuesday May 19, 1936. He was born in 1876 in Tennessee and at age 15 came to Texas. Burial was in Crawford Cemetery by Amsler Funeral Home. Mr. Jones was a farmer most of his life and was well known in Crawford and McGregor. Survivors include his wife, Emma C. Jones (1883-1961); four sons and six daughters. McGregor Mirror: May 22 (5-6), 1936.

FRIEDARIKE WENDT, age 61, died Monday, May 25, 1936. Mr. and Mrs. Wendt had made their home in the Mc Gregor community for more than 25 years, having come from Washington County, Texas. Burial was in the McGregor Cemetery by Amsler Funeral Home. Survivors include her husband, William Wendt (1872-1951); two sons, F. W. Wendt and Louie Wendt; three daughters, Mrs. W. G. Abel, Mrs. Fritz Fehler, and Miss Frieda Wendt, all of McGregor; one brother, H. C. Schulte of Crawford; her mother, Mrs. H. Schulte of McGregor. She was prededed in death by four children: Rev. John Wendt and three who died when quite young. McGregor Mirror: May 29 (1-1), 1936.

BRYANT. Mr. and Mrs. Oscar Bryant and children are in Arkansas where they were called on account of the death of his father. McGregor Mirror: May 29 (4-1), 1936.

MILDRED VENETA NELSON died in Waco May 28 at age 4. She was born in Waco, April 20, 1932, the daughter of F. D. Nelson who was born in Moody and Edith Prewitt who was born in Waco. Burial was in McGregor Cemetery by Amsler Funeral Home. CARD OF THANKS: thanks for the kind words and thoughts over the death of our little darling Mildred Veneta. Signed, Mr. and Mrs. F. D. Nelson. McGregor Mirror: Jun 5 (5-5), 1936.

JOE COLE (Colored) died in Waco, June 1, 1936. He was born August 17, 1896, in Beeville, Texas, the son of Joe Cole. Ida Cole was his wife. Burial was in McGregor Cemetery by Amsler Funeral Home. Amsler Funeral Home Records, Book 2, 1936.

HARRY M. WILLIAMS, age 77, died in Temple last Tuesday. He was the father of Robert H. Williams of McGregor. Burial was in Lorena Cemetery. He was born and raised in Lorena, his parents being pioneer settlers of McLennan County. The family had made their home in Waco for the past 7 years. Survivors include his wife; two sons, Robert of McGregor and Holvey Williams of Waco; a daughter, Mrs. Ewell Strong of Beaumont; a brother, Peeler Williams, and a sister, Mrs. Bettie Grey Robinson, both of Waco. McGregor Mirror: Jun 5 (3-3), 1936.

MRS. W. A. McCAULEY died at her home at Whitson last Monday. Burial was in Moody Cemetery. Mrs. McCauley was born in Covington, Tennessee, July 2, 1856, but for the past 30 years the family has lived at Whitson. She had been an invalid and confined to ther bed for 9 years. Survivors include her husband; son, Dr. E. R. McCauley of Moody; three daughters, Mrs. A. T. Nelson and Miss Nora McCauley of Whitson and Mrs. Curtis Ritchie of Gatesville. McGregor Mirror: Jun 19 (1-4), 1936.

ALBIN WEHRING, born June 21, 1872, in Washington County, Texas, the son of William Wehring who was born in Germany, died of a heart attack Tuesday, June 16, 1936, at his home seven miles southeast of McGregor. He was 64 years of age, having farmed in the McGregor area for over 30 years. Burial was in the McGregor Cemetery by Amsler Funeral Home. Survivors include his wife, Mary Wehring (1875-1941; three daughters, Miss Johanna Wehring, Miss Elsie Wehring and Mrs. Edwin Bishoff; two brothers, Ben and Henry Wehring of Washington County; two sisters, Mrs. W. C. Wiechart of Washington County, and Mrs. Fritz Brockschmidt of Port Arthur. McGregor Mirror: Jun 19 (1-5), 1936.

WILLIAM T. MILLER died in Crawford on June 26, 1936. He was born in Georgia, December 13, 1846, the son of John Miller who was born in Arkansas and Mandy Brazelton who was born in Georgia. Betty Jane Miller (1864-1956) is his wife. Informant was Roy B. Miller of Crawford. Burial was in Crawford Cemetery by Amsler Funeral Home. Amsler Funeral Home Records, Book 2, 1936.

HENRY FEHLER, age 61, died at his home last Saturday, June 20. He had been on the streets of McGregor in the late afternoon but died in his easy chair that evening. Mr. Fehler was born in Germany on March 9, 1875, and came to America when he was 24 years old. He lived in Washington County, Texas, nearly four years before coming to McGregor. Here he married Miss Emma Meiske, who survives him along with four daughters, Mrs. Louis Wiethorn, Mrs. Henry Schulte, Mrs. Herbert Luedeker of McGregor, and Mrs. Melvin Schutte of Moody; two sons, Ben and Herbert Fehler of McGregor; one brother, J. F. Fehler of McGregor and another brother living in Germany; and one sister in Poland. Mr. Fehler, the son of William Fehler and Sophie Rethmeier, both born in Germany, visited his old home in Germany last year. Burial was in McGregor Cemetery by Amsler Funeral Home. McGregor Mirror: Jun 26 (5-1), 1936.

MRS. CLARK ANDERSON died in Basdrop Sunday afternoon after an appendectomy. Clark Anderson of McGregor married Mrs. Anderson only a short time ago, their marriage having been kept a secret. She was a member of the faculty in the Stockdale Public Schools. Mrs. Anderson, the former Faye Jett, is survived by her husband; her parents, Rev. and Mrs. I. N. Jett of Smithville; two brothers, Paul N. Jett of Crosby and James P. Jett of Jonah. Funeral services were in Smithville with burial in Mission Burial Park in San Antonio. Mrs. John D. Anderson of McGregor attended the funeral. McGregor Mirror: Jun 26 (5-3), 1936.

MRS. E. O. SLOANE of Lodi, California, died last week. She was a sister of the late George W. Connally of McGregor. McGregor Mirror: Jul 3 (4-6), 1936.

NANCY C. McCORKLE died Monday, Jul7 6. She was before her marriage, Nancy Cleveland Johnson, and was born on July 8, 1890, in North Carolina. At age 3 she came to Texas and settled near Leon Junction. There she married John McCorkle on April 25, 1910. Burial was in Seaton Cemetery by Lee Undertakers. Pallbearers were her nephews, Ruben Fry, Ernest McCorkle, Otha McCorkle, Virgil Johnson, John Johnson, and Otto Sutton. Survivors include her husband, John W. McCorkle (1891-1960); two sons, Oscar and J. C. McCorkle; three sisters, Miss Etta Johnson and Mrs. Dora Sutton of Leon Junction, and Mrs. Zona Owens of McGregor; three brothers, Neal, Rob and Dolphius Johnson, all of Leon Junction. McGregor Mirror: Jul 10 (1-5), 1936.

OSCAR BENJAMIN "DOC" BROWN died at his home near Crawford last Sunday, July 5. He was born October 4, 1874, in Georgia and moved to Crawford when a young man. Mr. Brown was the son of Stephen Brown, born in Georgia. He never married but lived with a widowed sister, Mrs. Annie Hawkins, for a number of years. Burial was in Crawford Cemetery by Amsler Funeral Home. Survivors include three sisters and four brothers. McGregor Mirror: Jul 10 (4-2), 1936.

RUTH MARY REEDER, daughter of Mr. and Mrs. E. C. Reeder of Temple, died July 4, 1936, at the home of her grandmother, Mrs. J. A. Poe. The child and her mother were visiting Mrs. Poe when Ruth was milled when a mule she was riding became frightened and drug her to death. Lightening and thunder firghtened the animal. Burial was in Temple, Texas. Survivors include her parents, Mr. and Mrs. E. C. Reeder; a brother, Charles Richard Reeder of Temple; and her grandmother, Mrs. J. A. Poe. McGregor Mirror: Jul 10 (1-1), 1936.

RED KANADY. Jim Allen and Mrs. Allen went to Dallas Monday accompanied by Ernest Allen of Temple to attend the funeral of their brother-in-law, Red Kanady, who died of apoplexy. Burial was in Dallas. Oglesby News. McGregor Mirror: Jul 10 (7-3), 1936.

MABE NORTHAM. Mrs. Freeman Morgan and daughter, Ethel Mae and son, Lee Roy, were in Nolanville last Sunday where they attended the funeral of Mrs. Morgan's uncle, Mabe Northam. McGregor Mirror: Jul 10 (8-2), 1936.

JENNINGS BROWN, age 14, drown in the Bosque River, Sunday. The boy, son of Mr. and Mrs. A. Harley Brown, stepped into a deep hole on the river below Lake Waco Dam and could not swim. Virginia Nell Lewis, age 12, was able to dive for the boy but was unable to save him because of his weight and strength and his frantic struggling. Her mother, Mrs. G. A. Lewis, attempted to help her from shallow water but they were unable to save him. George W. Brown, his uncle, also helped search but the fire department rescue squad finally found his body. Though born in McGregor, the boy had been a resident of Waco for the past 8 years. Survivors include his parents; a sister, Anita; aunts, Mrs. George W. Brown and Mrs. Carrie Patton of Waco, and Mrs. D. M. Harbourgh and Mrs. R. A. Wilkerson of Dallas; uncles, George W. Brown of Waco and R. A. Wilkerson of Dallas. Six cousins acted as pallbearers: Jack and Mack Cawthorn, Howard Nation, Gene Stokes, Shelburn Land and Jimmy Edsall. McGregor Mirror: Jul 17 (1-1), 1936.

MORGAN CUMMINGS, age 80, died at the home of his daughter, Mrs. Tom Morgan, last Saturday, July 10. He was born in Arkansas on October 9, 1855, the son of Billy and Rebecca Cummings, and came to Texas in early life. On December 15, 1881, he married Mrs. Bell Brown (1861-1934), who preceded him in death. Burial was in Seaton Cemetery by Lee Undertakers. Pallbearers were grandsons. Survivors include his children: E. B. Cummings of Bay City, Mrs. Tom Norman, Mrs. Lawrence of Leon Junction, Mrs. Jim Robinson of Moody, Mrs. Ethel Marshall of Rosenburg, and Mrs. E. C. Murphy of McGregor; two brothers, Bob and Jess Cummings of Leon Junction. McGregor Mirror: Jul 17 (4-5), 1936.

LEE WHEAT of Moody, injured in an automobile collision in Waco, died in a Waco hospital Wednesday. Mr. and Mrs. Wheat were going north on highway 67 and a car occupied by Mr. and Mrs. W. A. Wonlard of Shreveport, Louisiana, were enroute home and headed east off highway 7. The two cars collided at the intersection. Mr. Wheat worked for the John Mann Grocery in McGregor as manager of the Moody store. At the time of the accident, he was on a ten day vacation. Burial was in Moody, Thursday. Survivors include his wife; a brother, J. V. Wheat of McGregor; two sisters, Mrs. Kate Porterfield and Mrs. Burl Hunt of Waco. McGregor Mirror: Jul 24 (1-2), 1936.

IRL PRITLE, formerly of McGregor, died Firday near Hico. He was returning from Cranfills Gap, and presumably a blowout in a tire caused his car to go into a ditch. He was dead when the body was discovered.

Burial was in Hico. Survivors include his wife, Sallie Bradshaw Pritle (the daughter of Mr. and Mrs. W. P. Bradshaw); two daughters, Miss Marie and Miss Peggy Pritle; his parents, Mr. and Mrs. M. S. Pritle, all of Hico; two brothers, Bert of Whichita Falls and Otis of the valley; one sister, Mrs. Owen Gogett of Hamilton. McGregor Mirror: Jul 24 (4-6), 1936.

MRS. A. CHRISTOPHERSON died at her home in Waco, Sunday. Burial was in McGregor Cemetery by Compton's Funeral Home of Waco. She lived in McGregor many years ago, where her husband followed the trade of shoemaking. McGregor Mirror: Jul 24 (5-1), 1936.

PIMENTO INFANT. The little babe of Mr. and Mrs. Coke Pimento died last week after a short illness. Burial was at Post Oak Cemetery. Oglesby News. McGregor Mirror: Jul 24 (7-3), 1936.

RICHARD OLIVER COUSINS died at the home of his son, M. H. Cousins, in McGregor Tuesday, July 21. He was born March 29, 1863, in Georgia, moving to Texas with his widowed mother when a mere boy. His father was killed in the Civil War. In November of 1889, Mr. Cousins married Miss Pattie Frances Clibourne of McGregor. Five sons were born to the couple, one having died in infancy. Survivors include his wife, Pattie F. Cousins (1866-1938); four sons, John and Marion of McGregor, Dick of Crawford and Will of Bryan; one sister, Mrs. Bettie Hancock of Lakeview; two brothers, C. L. of Hewitt and Willis G. Cousins of Kirkland, Texas. Burial was in Crawford Cemetery by Amsler Funeral Home. McGregor Mirror: Jul 24 (8-4), 1936.

MRS. O. D. BANKHEAD, age 28, died in a Waco hospital Tuesday, July 21. Her body was carried to the family home in Oglesby, and burial was in Post Oak Cemetery by Lee Undertakers. Survivors include her husband; her father and step-mother, Mr. and Mrs. W. A. McMullen; four sisters, Mrs. Willie (Odessa) Eary of Fort Worth, Mrs. M. L. (Gladys) Moore of Longview, Mrs. J. (Thelma) Terry and Miss Rozella McMullen of Oglesby; six brothers, Lloyd, Arthur, Paul, and Bill of Oglesby, R. T. of Beeville, and Jim McMullen of McGregor. McGregor Mirror: Jul 24 (8-5)/Jul 31 (7-1), 1936.

HITT INFANTS. McGregor friends sympathize with Mr. and Mrs. Aubrey Hitt of Cameron in the loss of their little twin sons, who were born in Cameron Saturday and lived only a short time. Burial was in the McGregor Cemetery, Sunday. McGregor Mirror: Aug 7 (4-5), 1936.

B. C. RIDDLE, age 35, died July 23, 1936. His life was cruely snatched away in a terrific boiler explosion which occurred at Mt. Vernon, Texas. Funeral services were at Oglesby with burial in Post Oak Cemetery by Wilkerson and Hatch Funeral Home of Waco. Pallbearers were uncles: W. B. Alexander of Temple, L. D. Alexander of Fort Worth, C. W. Alexander of Clovis, New Mexico and cousins, Allen Gallman of Longview, Clifford Gallman of Ruston, Louisiana, and L. C. Woods of

Oglesby. Survivors include two little motherless sons, Howard, age 11, and Bryan, age 6; his mother, Mrs. B. G. Yarborough of Waco; an adopted sister, Mrs. R. H. Cement of Dallas; his grandparents, Rev. and Mrs. W. Alexander of Oglesby. Mr. Riddle, who was born in 1901, lived with his grandparents from age 6 to age 15. McGregor Mirror: Aug 7 (7-1), 1936.

CALVIN E. NALER died in Crawford, July 31, 1936. He was born in Texas on February 21, 1886, the son of George D. Naler and Mary M. Naler, both born in Georgia. Informant was his wife, Zola Naler (1889-1955), who later married Benjamin R. Hay. Burial was in Crawford Cemetery by Amsler Funeral Home. Amsler Funeral Home Records, Book 2, 1936.

WILLIAM DOLPHUS ANDERSON, "Uncle B", died at his home in Crawford last Monday. He is survived by his wife, one daughter and three sons, all of Crawford. Other survivors include his brother, Mr. L. H. Anderson of Crawford. Mr. Anderson came to Crawford with his family from Louisiana in 1892. Burial was in Crawford Cemetery by Amsler Funeral Home. McGregor Mirror: Aug 14 (1-2), 1936.

ALEXA ALLEN LAWSON, age 67, died Saturday, August 15, 1936, at her home in Bremond. Her body was brought to McGregor by J. I. Riddle of Mexia for burial in the McGregor Cemetery by Amsler Funeral Home. Mrs. Lawson, who was born in 1869 in Bremond, Texas, was telephone operator in McGregor for the Santa Fe station many years before the railroads operated a joint office. She was married to Mr. Oliver Perry Lawson on Christmas Eve in 1892 at Lebanon, Missouri, where she had gone for the holidays to visit relatives. Mr. and Mrs. Lawson made their home in McGregor for many years and three children were born here. Two children died in infancy leaving the only surviving child, L. A. Lawson, a son. Her husband, Oliver Perry Lawson who was born in 1872 preceded her in death in 1932. Mr. Harry Lawson, an uncle, and Mrs. Lawson of San Antonio were present for the funeral. McGregor Mirror: Aug 21 (1-3), 1936.

ROGER JORDAN, age 37, died in Waco, August 13, 1936. He was born in Crawford, the son of J. J. Jordan. Burial was in Crawford Cemetery by Amsler Funeral Home. Amsler Funeral Homel Book 2, 1936.

SARA HORD. Mr. and Mrs. Carl Phelan were in Moody Thursday to attend the funeral of Mrs. Phelan's step-grandmother, Mrs. Sara Hord, who died Wednesday at the home of her daughter in Maypearl. McGregor Mirror: Aug 21 (5-2), 1936.

OTTO PENNINGTON, brother of Messrs. Oma and Vesta Pennington, died in a Temple hospital August 25, 1936. He was a resident of Killeen. Burial was in Gatesville. McGregor Mirror: Aug 28, 1936.

LULA ELIZABETH McENTIRE, age 69, died at her home in McGregor Wednesday, September 16, 1936. She was born July 2, 1867, in Whitfield

County, Georgia, the daughter of John Devault Grenhower and Mary Barnet. During the more than 40 years she and her husband had lived here, Mr. McEntire was in the grocery business. Survivors include her husband, Joseph R. McEntire (1864-1939); three children, Ralph and Mrs. Dan Harris of McGregor, and Mrs. Elva Wallace of Dallas. Burial was in Comanche Springs by Amsler Funeral Home with services conducted by Rev. A. J. Mann, who is a brother-in-law of the deceased. McGregor Mirror: Sep 18 (1-1), 1936.

J. S. SCARBOROUGH, age 78, died at his home in Kingsville, Texas, last week. Mrs. L. W. Stockburger of McGregor was his niece. Mr. Scarborough had been found dead in his home. McGregor Mirror: Sep 11 (7-2), 1936.

WALTER CONLEY died in Quanah. A message of his death was received by friends in McGregor Wednesday. Walter lived in McGregor as a boy, the son of Mr. and Mrs. N. C. Conley. Several months ago he was in Scott & White Hospital in Temple for treatment. Survivors include his wife, children, father, and two brothers. McGregor Mirror: Sep 18 (1-4), 1936.

MRS. L. C. CLARK died Friday. Burial was in Moody Cemetery. Jones Hill News. McGregor Mirror: Sep 25 (16-3), 1936.

SAMUEL C. "BOB" WALKER, age 65, died in Waco Thursday, October 8, 1936. Mr. and Mrs. Walker left McGregor that morning and were in a Waco department store when he suffered the heart attack. Death came before he could be rushed to the hospital. His body was returned to his home by Amsler Funeral Home, but funeral arrangements had not been made, pending word from the three children, Mrs. W. C. Corbett, Jr. of Houston, Robert Walker of California and Sidney Walker, who is in South America. Mr. Walker had for several months operated the Humble Service Station in McGregor. Known here as Bob, he was born in Georgia on April 25, 1871, the son of T. E. Walker and Florence Brown both born in Georgia, and came to Texas in 1883, locating near Crawford where he resided for a number of years. In 1889, he moved to McGregor where he engaged in the merchantile business. He managed the last congressional campaign for R. L. Henry of Waco and for some years after that date managed the state farms in Falls County. Survivors include his wife, Evelyn Barrett Walker (1872-1955); one daughter, Mrs. W. C. Corbett of Houston; two sons, Sidney of South America and Robert of California. One daughter, Mrs. Rosalie Stanworth, preceded him in death several years ago. Burial was in McGregor Cemetery by Amsler Funeral Home. McGregor Mirror: Oct 9 (1-3)/Oct 16 (1-3), 1936.

MRS. J. R. MARTIN died Monday near Waco in a car wreck. The impact killed her instantly. Her two daughters-in-law, Mrs. Weldon Martin and Mrs. Joe Martin, were injured when the crash of the two autos came. Funeral arrangements are not complete but will probably be in Gatesville. McGregor Mirror: Oct 9 (10-6), 1936.

FOSTER SMITH, nephew of Mr. and Mrs. Carl Mogle, died in Granger the first of this week. Funeral services were held in Granger Tuesday. McGregor Mirror: Oct 9 (4-3), 1936.

ARMSTRONG HILL of Columbia, Kentucky died October 6, 1936, at Russelville, Kentucky. He is the father of Mrs. Joe Yates of Comanche Springs. He and his wife and others were on their way to Texas when death came. Mrs. Yates left for Columbia Wednesday. McGregor Mirror: Oct 16 (13-4), 1936.

LOUISA SIMS (colored) died in McGregor on October 20, 1936, at age 65. Burial was in McGregor Cemetery by Amsler Funeral Home. Amsler Funeral Home Records, Book 2, 1936.

FRITZ W. JACOBS of Osage, age 56, was found dead last Friday pinned underneath his car in a small creek just west of McGregor. He evidently drowned when his car left the approach near a culvert. After an inquest held in McGregor, the coroner rendered his verdict, death by drowning. Mr. Jacobs, who was born in Germany on September 25, 1880, the son of August Jacobs and Frieda Schiltz, both born in Germany, and came to America when he was four years old. He resided first in Washington County, Texas, then moved with his family to Coryell County. Survivors include his wife, Anna Jacobs; three sons, Fritz, Lonnie and Willie; two daughters, Miss Claudine and Miss Hettie Jacobs; a brother, Henry Jacobs of Coryell City; two sisters, Mrs. W. Haack of Coryell City and Mrs. G. W. Lee, wife of Dr. Lee of Eagle Springs. Burial was in Coryell City by Amsler Fuenral Home. McGregor Mirror: Oct 23 (1-2), 1936.

J. O. CURRY, 82, prominent Killeen resident, died in Temple Monday. Mr. Curry was born in Alabama in 1853, and moved to Texas to settle in Coryell County. While living there he was a county commissioner for three terms. He moved to Killeen in 1917, where he was a stockholder and director of the First National Bank of Killeen. He was also mayor of Killeen for part of one term, resigning because of ill health. Survivors include his wife; three daughters, Miss Eva and Miss Izora Curry of Killeen and Mrs. Turk Brown of Gatesville; four sons, Dr. J. L. Curry of Belton, C. C. Curry of McGregor, J. M. Currry of Gatesville, and E. L. Curry of Florence; one brother, Jep Curry of Killeen. Burial was in Killeen. McGregor Mirror: Oct. 23 (1-3), 1936.

J. H. LINDSEY, age 66, longtime resident of McGregor, died Wednesday, October 28, 1936, at the home of her daughter, Mrs. E. L. White of Coleman, Texas. Since the death of her husband, some four years ago, she had been making her home with her daughter and her son in Dallas, Turner Lindsey. Two sons, Martin and Earl Lindsey, preceded her in death. She will be remembered here as the aunt of Mrs. John Freeman, Jr., and Mrs. F. O. Connally. Mrs. Lindsey was born in Georgia. Her body was transported to McGregor by Horn Funeral Home of Coleman with graveside services conducted by Amsler Funeral Home of McGregor. McGregor Mirror: Oct 30 (1-2), 1936.

ETHEL R. ROBINSON died at her home in Moody on October 22, 1936. She was born in 1887. Burial was in Seaton Cemetery by Denny & Witt Funeral Home of Moody. Survivors include her husband, James R. Robinson (1882-1963); two daughters, Mrs. Abbie Holland of Dallas and Mrs. Mark Huermann of Waco. Pallbearers were brothers-in-law, Will, Charlie and Ernest Robinson of Moody, Mr. Owens of Alverado, Ethel Marshall of Rosenburg and E. C. Murphy of McGregor. McGregor Mirror: Oct 30 (4-5), 1936.

MARVIN DEAN HAMILTON, four month old son of Mr. and Mrs. Sam Hamilton, died Sunday in a Waco hospital. Burial was in Osage Cemetery. Survivors include his parents; three brothers; one sister; grandparents, Mr. and Mrs. J. V. Daniel; one uncle, Claude Daniel of Coryell Church; two aunts, Mrs. Raymond Brown of Dallas and Mrs. Roy Cox of McGregor. McGregor Mirror: Oct 30 (6-5), 1936.

MARTHA ELLEN HUDSON, age 78, died at the home of Mr. Louis Eckols in McGregor on October 23, 1936. She was born in Ohio County, Kentucky, November 18, 1858, the daughter of Robert Hudson and _____ Bell, both born in Kentucky. She lived there until 1883 when she and her husband, J. H. Hudson, whom she married in 1874, moved to Texas to settle in Wise County. From there they moved to Grandview, Texas. To this union were born five daughters and one son. Three of her children and her husband preceded her in death. Survivors include Mrs. Oma Drake of Athens, Mrs. Annie Echols of McGregor, Mrs. R. L. Savely of Brandon. Burial was in Antioch Cemetery near Grandview. Pallbearers were her grandsons, Joe Hudson, Elbert Gann, Tom Blissett, Frank Hudson, Lewis White and Jim Page. McGregor Mirror: Oct 30 (8-1), 1936.

CHARLES BUNYAN MILLER died at his home near Crawford Sunday, November 1, 1936. Had he lived until the following Tuesday, he would have been 69 years old. His brother-in-law, Mr. Levi Glasgow of Oklahome, was visiting in preparation for the birthday when Mr. Miller died. Mr. Miller was born in Tennessee on November 3, 1868, the son of Thomas Hamilton Miller and Alpha Omega Cox, and came to Texas with his parents when three years of age. He settled on the ranch were he later died. Survivors include his wife, Mattie Glasgow Miller (1871-1940); two daughters, Mrs. S. M. Abbe of McGregor and Mrs. L. B. Fulp of Crawford. Burial was in Crawford Cemetery by Amsler Fuenral Home. McGregor Mirror: Nov 6 (1-1), 1936.

JOHN F. McDONALD, age 55, died in a Waco hospital Saturday. Burial was in the Ridge Park Cemetery in Hillsboro by Marshall & Marshall Funeral Home of Hillsboro. Mr. McDonald, a son of the late Mr. and Mrs. O. P. McDonald, was a native of Alabama and moved with the family to Hill County when 10 years old, living in Abbott and Hillsboro until ten years ago when he moved to McGregor. For eleven years he was connected with McDonald & Marshall Buick agency in Hillsboro. He was a member of a family of twelve children, and the third to pass away. Survivors include his wife, to whom he would have been married for 35 years on November 24, 1936; children, F. R. McDonald of Columbia, South Carolina, J. V. McDonald of Hillsboro, O. P. McDonald of Fort Worth, Jerry Ray McDonald of McGregor, Mrs. H. W. Anderson of Dallas, Mrs. Jack Cawthron of Waco, Mrs. Murry Blakeley of Gatesville and Miss Rose Mary McDonald of McGregor; four grand-daughters, Phoebe Jo, Barbara Ann and Martha Frances McDonald, and Carolyn Cawthron; one sister, Miss Dewey McDonald of Waco; brothers, Sam, Homer, Will, Cliff and Claud McDonald of Hillsboro, Doc of Abbott, Emmett and Clarence McDonald of Maypearl. McGregor Mirror: Nov 6 (5-3), 1936.

IVA PEARL POLSTON, Mrs. Jack Polston, age 22, died Friday in a Waco hospital. She was born in Zephyr, Texas, on February 24, 1914, and moved to McGregor several years ago with her parents. She married Jack Polston of McGregor on November 11, 1929, and they had two daughters. Survivors include her husband; two small daughters, Berniece and Gladys Polston; her parents, Mr. and Mrs. E. B. Beaty; four brothers, Nugent, Wayne, Otha and Eugene; two sisters, Norma and Joyce, all of Del Rio. Burial was in McGregor Cemetery. Funeral Services were in McGregor by Lee Undertakers. McGregor Mirror: Nov, 1936.

TOM MANNING, age 55, resident of McGregor since 1890, died in a Waco hospital Monday. He was born in 1881 and before moving to McGregor had resided in Medina County. Burial was in McGregor Cemetery by Lee Undertakers. Survivors include an only sister, Mrs. A. N. McGowen of McGregor. McGregor Mirror: Nov 13 (5-1), 1936.

ALICE SHIRLEY, age 47, died in a Waco hospital Monday, November 9, 1936. She was born February 20, 1889. The family lived on the J. N. Crain farm near Harris Creek. Burial was in Davidson Cemetery in Coryell County by Lee Undertakers. Survivors include her husband, Joel B. Shirley (1892-____); four children, Moxie, F. A., Ben and Leta Beth Shirley; six brothers, H. M., F. B., Lafayette, Elie, John and Easter Lam, all of Oglesby; three sisters, Mesdams J. L. Monney and George L. Draper, both of Oglesby and Miss Maggie Lam of Beaumont. McGregor Mirror: Nov 13 (5-4), 1936.

MRS. RICE ADKINS, age 49, died in a Waco hospital Monday of pneumonia. Survivors include her husband and loved ones. Burial was in Lott Cemetery by Compton Funeral Home of Waco. McGregor Mirror: Frv 4 (1-5), 1936.

JOHN CHIRSTIE, brother of Mary Fall, died in Garden City last Friday. Mrs. Fall and her son, Howard Fall of Cedar Lane, were called to Garden City last Friday because of the death. Mr. Christie, age 68, died November 27, 1936. He will be remembered by the old settlers here, having lived in the Comanche Springs neighborhood. Survivors include his wife; four nieces and a nephew, whom he raised; two sisters, Mrs. Mary Fall and Mrs. Frankie McBride of McGregor. McGregor Mirror: Dec 4 (4-2)/(6-6), 1936.

BENNETT. Ward was received in Comanche Springs Tuesday of the death of Mrs. H. W. Bennett's mother at Alma, Nebraska. She died Sunday. Rev. and Mrs. Bennett left Valley Mills Sunday for Alma but her mother passed away before they reached Nebraska. Mrs. Bennett's father died in January and they lost their infant daughter in August. McGregor Mirror: Dec 4 (8-3), 1936.

JOE BRUCE SCHEPERS, age 6, died Tuesday, December 8, 1936, of pneumonia. He was born in 1930, the son of J. Will Schepers and Ella Bruce Schepers. Burial was in McGregor Cemetery by Amsler Funeral Home. Survivors include his parents; a sister, Joan Schepers; his paternal grandmother, Mrs. Joe Schepers of McGregor; his maternal grandparents, Mr. and Mrs. E. T. Bruce of Bruceville. McGregor Mirror: Dec 11 (1-2), 1936.

SOPHIE WITTE, age 82, resident of McGregor since 1885, died at her home Tuesday, December 8, 1936. Her husband, Mr. F. Witte (1844-1923), preceded her in death twelve years ago. Mrs. Witte was born in Independence, Washington County, Texas, on March 19, 1854, the daughter of Henry Bockehman and Louise Halle, and married Mr. Witte at Berlin in 1873. Three children preceded her in death. Survivors include three sons, Fred, Willie, and Albert Witte, all of McGregor; five daughters, Mrs. Richard Amthor, Mrs. Ernest Luedtke, Mrs. Lewis Bischoff, Mrs. Walter Manske of McGregor, and MRs. P. Goglin of Brenham. Burial was in McGregor Cemetery by Amsler Funeral Home. McGregor Mirror: Dec 11 (1-3), 1936.

WILLIAM GEORGE HORNE died Thursday in Dallas. Burial was in Hillcrest Memorial Park by Weiland's Funeral Home. He was an old McGregor settler before moving to Dallas. He married a sister of the late J. P. Cunningham. Survivors include his wife; a son, Earl W. Horne; a daughter, Mrs. Vern Parsons, all of Dallas; six sisters; four brothers, including Bob Horne of McGregor and Sam Horne of Waco. McGregor Mirror: Dec 11 (6-3), 1936.

FRANCIS LYNCH lost his life when the bedding in which he slept was ignited. Mr. Lynch, age 37, was found dead in the city jail Thursday. He lived on the John D. Mann farm in Walker Harris community. City Marshall, Jim Williams, answered a call from a local cafe to come and take Mr. Lynch out of the place. Mr. Lynch was jailed and was alright at 12:30 o'clock but his body was found Thursday morning lying in the ashes of the bed. Burial will probably be in Moody Cemetery by Lee Undertakers. He was the son of Mrs. T. N. Lynch. Survivors include his mother; his wife; four children, Mrs. Weldon Martin of Oglesby, Mary Frances, Jeanette and Jack Lynch; five sisters, Mrs. Paul Brooks of Houston, Mrs. Henry Olson of Houston, Mrs. Audie Oliver, Mrs.

Leonard Anderson and Miss Margaret Lynch; three brothers, Morris of California, Gene of San Antonio, and Mick of McGregor. McGregor Mirror: Dec 18 (1-1), 1936.

FLORENCE BROWN, age 72, widow of the late Jason T. Brown, died at Crawford. Burial was in the Crawford Cemetery by Amsler Funeral Home. She died Wednesday, December 16, 1936, at the home of her daughter, Mrs. J. T. Compton in Crawford. Mrs. Brown had been a resident of Crawford for the past 40 years. Survivors include four daughters, Mrs. Compton, Mrs. A. J. Crowden and Mrs. R. F. Barnard of Houston, amd Mrs. G. B. Wall of Hewitt; one son, J. T. Brown of Houston; two sisters, Mrs. J. H. Buice of Waco and Mrs. Fannie Stone of Cummings, Georgia; three brothers, Jasper Pool of Hamilton, C. Pool of Buford, Gerogia, and W. N. Pool of Lawrenceville, Georgia. McGregor Mirror: Dec 18 (1-4), 1936.

JOHN FRANKS of Gatesville died Sunday. He was a brother-in-law of Mrs. Felix Collard of Oglesby. McGregor Mirror: Dec 18 (3-3), 1936.

CHAPTER 3

JAMES D. McCOLLUM, age 65, died at his home in Crawford Tuesday, January 12, 1937. He was born December 20, 1871, the son of Samuel McCollum and Elizabeth Armstrong. James came to Texas from Tennessee when he was 10 years old and had lived in the Crawford area for over 40 years. Mr. McCollum was engaged in the drug and banking business. Burial was in the Crawford Cemetery by Amsler Funeral Home. Survivors include his wife, Ida Garrett McCollum (born 9/27/1874); three sons, C. M. of Houston, O. H. of Hearne and James Alton McCollum of Dallas; one daughter, Mrs. W. H. Powers of Corpus Christi; one sister, Mrs. Sallie Standifer of Crawford and three brothers, Tom of Valley Mills, A. O. of Crawford and Dr. Charles McCollum of Fort Worth. McGregor Mirror: Jan 15 (1-1), 1937.

S. L. TATE died in Sweetwater, Tennessee, last Saturday. He had made his home in McGregor for 38 years before moving to Waco 5 years ago. Mr. Tate was employed at a Waco hospital. At the time of his death he had returned to his old home in Tennessee for a visit. Burial was in Tennessee. McGregor Mirror: Jan 15 (1-4), 1937.

L. N. CONNALLY, age 85, died Friday at the home of his daughter, Mrs. Ola Nichols, in Gillette, Wyoming. He had resided there since leaving Plainview about 18 months ago. Plainview had been his home for 27 years before moving to Wyoming. Burial was in Plainview. Mr. Connally was born October 24, 1851, in Georgia. He moved to Plainview many years ago from McGregor. The body came as far as Amarillo by train. Survivors include one daughter, Mrs. Nichols of Gillette, Wyoming; five sons, Leo Connally of Gillette, Ollie and Pled Connally of Plainview, Henry Connally of Hart, and Fred Connally of Happy. McGregor Mirror: Jan 22 (8-2), 1937.

JOHN W. HIGH, age 81, died in McGregor January 25, 1937. He was born in Arkansas June 25, 1855, the son of L. D. High and Betsie Blailock. His wife was Susie High. Burial was in McGregor Cemetery by Amsler Funeral Home. Informant was L. D. High, a son and Mrs. J. H. Beck of Marlow, Oklahoma, a daughter. Amsler Funeral Home Records, Book 2.

ALBERT FELT TERRY died in McGregor January 25, 1937. He was born in Hamilton, November 29, 1884, the son of Charles H. Terry who was born in Alabama and Laura Harrison who was born in Washington County, Texas. Mr. Terry was married to Annie (?) Hamilton Terry. Burial was in Coryell County. Amsler Funeral Home Records, Book 2.

MRS. JESSIE HEYMAN died last Friday, January 29, in a Fort Worth hospital. She was born April 30, 1882. Burial was in Crawford Cemetery by Compton's of Waco. She will be remembered here as Mrs.

Jesse Cooper, a sister-in-law of Dr. E. C. Kunz of McGregor. McGregor Mirror: Feb 5 (1-3), 1937.

WILLIAM L. DEDECK, 48, died at his home in Waco Sunday. Burial was in Oakwood Cemetery. Survivors include his wife; his mother, Mrs. M. L. Dedeck of Waco; a son, W. L., Jr. of Waco; three sisters, Mrs. R. Q. Moore of Waco, Mrs. G. C. Crump of Waco and Mrs. J. L. Spicer of Colorado, Texas; a brother, J. L. of Austin. McGregor Mirror: Feb 5 (2-8), 1937.

JOHN D. ANDERSON died in Robertson County, Texas last week. He was born May 15, 1879, the son of Low Anderson born in Mississippi. (Tombstone says he was born in 1880) John married Ione Clark Anderson (born 8/30/1887 - died 1/24/1971). The informant was Clark Anderson of Fredericksburg, Texas, and the funeral was ordered by Kathryn Anderson. Mrs. A. P. Anderson and her niece, Miss Morris Alexander of Temple, came to McGregor last Friday to attend the funeral. Amsler Funeral Home Records, Book 2/McGregor Mirror: Feb 5 (3-4), 1937.

J. A. MOTE, 88, died in Speegleville at the home of his daughter, Mrs. J. H. Youngblood, Saturday. Burial was in Moody Cemetery. Pallbearers were six grandsons, Ray Hatter, Lou Hatter, Orvid Youngblood, Morris Thomas, Moran Mote and Tommie Mote. Survivors include two daughters, Mrs. Youngblood and Mrs. L. W. Hatter of Spring Valley; four sons, John and Joe of Spring Valley, Bob of Moody and Whit of Tucson, Arizona. Mr. Mote had been a resident of McLennan County for over 50 years, residing in Moody and McGregor. McGregor Mirror: Feb 5 (3-5), 1937.

BOB REECE of Roswell, New Mexico, died Tuesday morning of a heart attack. At the time of his death he was 56. Jim Roach of McGregor left Wednesday for Roswell to attend the funeral. His mother, Mrs. B. G. Roach and sister, Mrs. H. R. Toutt, both of Meridian, were with Mr. Reece when he died. He was well known in McGregor, having lived here until about 3 years ago when he moved to New Mexico. Survivors include his mother, brother and sister mentioned above as well as another sister, Mrs. J. B. Taylor of McGregor and two more brothers, George Roach of Dallas and Lucian Roach of Englewood, California; a daughter, Mrs. Cleo Merchant of Santa Fe; and a son, Robert Reece of El Paso, Texas. McGregor Mirror: Feb 5 (4-4), 1937.

ROBERT LAWRENCE GREENHAW, son of Rev. and Mrs. Lawrence Greenhaw of Evant, died suddenly at their home about three weeks ago. Survivors include his parents; and one sister, Fern Virginia Greenhaw. Mrs. Greenhaw will be remembered in McGregor as Miss Virgie Davis. McGregor Mirror: Feb 12 (4-4), 1937.

JOHN L. EDWARDS, 84, was buried in Osage Cemetery last Saturday. He was born August 16, 1852. His wife was Sarah L. Edwards (Jan 5, 1876 - Nov 23, 1962). McGregor Mirror: Feb 12 (6-5), 1937

MARY E. MEADOR died at her home here Wednesday, February 17. She was born October 11, 1868, in Hollie Springs, Mississippi, the daughter of John D. Porterfield and Mary McFadden, both born in Mississippi. She came to Texas at the age of 5 and was married to W. S. Meador when she was 20 years old. He preceded her in death some 15 years ago. Burial was in Moody Cemetery beside her husband, W. S. Meador, by Amsler Funeral Home. Survivors include four daughters, Mrs. Myrtle Meador of Austin, Mrs. LaVerne Thompson of Waco, Mrs. Lorraine Sharp and Miss Cora Mae Meador of McGregor; four sons, John, Moran and Ernest of McGregor, and Duff Meador of Amarillo; one brother, Howard Porterfield of Roy, New Mexico. McGregor Mirror: Feb 19 (1-1), 1937.

S. ROSS CRAIN died last Friday, February 12, in Waco. He was born July 18, 1875. Mr. and Mrs. Crain had lived in McGregor until 12 years ago when they moved to Waco. Burial was in Harris Creek Cemetery by Clark's Undertakers. Pallbearers were four cousins, Watt, Riley and Glen Crain, Sam Horne, Dr. C. C. Lemly and Forest Walters. Survivors include his wife, Lena Crain (4/3/1877 - 11/17/1961); two daughters, Mrs. Ernest Lyons, Jr. and Miss Mavis Crain; a sister, Mrs. O. H. Minnis of McGregor; and two brothers, Charles Z. Crain of San Antonio and Joel N. Crain of Waco. McGregor Mirror: Feb 19 (1-2), 1937.

COLLEEN ALICE GRADY, age 6, died in a Waco hospital Friday, February 12, 1937. She was born May 14, 1930, the daughter of Edward L. Grady born in Gradyville, Kentucky and Jessie Brevillot who was born in Pasadena, California. She was the only child of Mr. and Mrs. Ed L. Grady. Burial was in Roselawn Cemetery in San Antonio by Amsler Funeral Home of McGregor. McGregor Mirror: Feb 19 (1-4), 1937.

BOB BRAZZIL died at his home in Herferd, Tuesday, February 9, 1937. He was reared near McGregor but left here some 35 years ago. Mr. Brazzil married Miss Marie Humphries of McGregor, who is a niece of Mr. and Mrs. Jim Grantham. Survivors include his wife; six children; two sisters, Mrs. John Ash of McGregor and Mrs. Mollie Williams of San Angelo. McGregor Mirror: Feb 19 (4-5), 1937.

HARVEY COX, age 29, died in a San Francisco hospital on February 8, 1937. Burial was in San Francisco. Mr. Cox, son of Mr. and Mrs. Richard Cox formerly of McGregor and Oglesby but now of Waco, left here for California about 7 years ago where he married and made his home. Survivors include his wife; three small children; his mother and father; two brothers, Joe of Belton and Dowd of Waco; three sisters, Mrs. Nellie Wiese of McGregor, Mrs. Ruby Climer of Mart and Mrs. Estelle Davidson of Houston. McGregor Mirror: Feb 19 (8-4), 1937.

NANCY CEFUS (colored) died February 21, 1937. She was born in 1891 in Eagle Lake, Texas, the daughter of Rufus and Sarah Long. Her husband was Ned Cefus. Burial was in McGregor Cemetery by Amsler Funeral Home. She had been working for Stanford England. Amsler Funeral Home

Records, Book 2.

OLIVER HOOD (colored), age 80, died February 28, 1937. He was born in Gonzales, Texas, August 17, 1856, the son of Isom Hood and Lucy Hood. He was found dead in McGregor on the H. H. Sanders Farm. Burial was in McGregor Cemetery by Amsler Funeral Home. Informant was Emma Canady of McGregor, a daughter. Amsler Funeral Home Records, Book 2.

LEE HARRIS, 24, was killed in an automobile accident near McGregor, Sunday. Funeral services were held Monday in Levita for Mr. Harris. He was the son of Mr. and Mrs. Tom R. Harris of Lavita and was born November 1, 1912, in Lavita. Survivors include his parents; brother, Melvin Harris of Pampa; two sisters, Ardine of Levita and Mrs. Lois Rankin of Abilene. Mr. Harris graduated from Levita High School in 1929, and since then had been associated with his father in business there. McGregor Mirror: Mar 5 (1-1), 1937.

WILLIAM MARION (BILL) WHEELER, 44, was killed instantly on his farm 6 miles west of Crawford, Tuesday, March 2, when he was cruched beneath a tractor which reared and fell over backward on him as he was trying to drive it out of a mudhole. He was born December 13, 1892 in Cummings, Georgia, the son of R. L. Wheeler and Emma Pilgram who was born in Illinois. Burial was in Ocee near Crawford by Amsler Funeral Home. (Funeral home records say he was buried in Osage Cemetery.) Survivors include his wife, Lula Allison Wheeler; seven children; brothers; two sisters; and his parents of Axtell. Informant was L. E. Wheeler of Waco. McGregor Mirror: Mar 5 (1-5), 1937.

OLA BRITTON RILEY died in a Waco hospital Tuesday. Burial was in McGregor Cemetery by Lee Undertakers. She was born 1899 in McGregor and married Marvin E. Riley March 10, 1922. Survivors include her husband, Melvin E. Riley (1896 -   ); four small children; her parents, Mr. and Mrs. W. J. Reed; five sisters, Mrs. Lena England of Waco, Mrs. Iva Nell McCorkel of Gatesville, Mesdames Cloree Anderson, Wilma Pomeranke, Oscar McCorkel and Miss Jessie Dimple Reed of McGregor; a brother, Jack Reed. McGregor Mirror: Mar 5 (5-3), 1937.

MARY B. WAGGONER died at the home of her son at Winters, California, Saturday, March 6, 1937. She was born in Mississippi, January 9, 1860, coming to Texas with her family when just a girl. Mary was the daughter of Wesley Kelly who was born in Mississippi and Elizabeth Higginbotham who was born in Virginia. She made her home in Salado for a number of years where she attended the old Salado College. She was married to James T. Waggoner who was born in Dyer County, Tennessee, January 29, 1856, and preceded her in death December 24, 1890. Survivors include her six children, Seymour Waggoner, Dr. Una Cary and Mrs. Lena Dunn of California, Mrs. C. B. Diltz of San Antonio, F. Waggoner of Hamilton and Willard Waggoner of Belen, New Mexico; a brother, Rev. J. W. Kelley of Goldthwaite; also three sisters. Burial was in McGregor Cemetery beside her husband by Amsler Funeral Home.

Pallbearers were R. J. Riley, Bud McAnnally, Jay Waggoner, James Rey of Hamilton and Cary and Theo Diltz of San Antonio. McGregor Mirror: Mar 12 (1-1), 1937.

THEODORE G. BROWN, 66, died Tuesday, March 9, 1937. He was born January 1, 1876. He was employed with the county on road work, and had reported for work as usual. Complaining of feeling badly, he was taken to the doctor's office where he died a few minutes after arriving. Mr. Brown had made Crawford his home for 25 years before he and his wife moved to McGregor several months ago. Burial was in Crawford Cemetery by Lee Undertakers. Survivors include his wife, Eva M. Brown (Oct 18, 1881 - Oct 16, 1971); three daughters, Mrs. D. H. Holmes, Mrs. Clifford Bennett and Mrs. Doyle Strickland, all of Crawford; two sons, C. D. Brown of Galveston and Ernest Brown of Crawford. McGregor Mirror: Mar 12 (1-4), 1937.

LEROY GILLILAND, JR., age 10 months, died at his home in Temple, March 5, 1937. He was born April 17, 1936. Burial was in McGregor Cemetery by Lee Undertakers. Survivors include the parents, Mr. and Mrs. L. R. Gilliland; four sisters, Grace, Mattie, Billie and Kathryn; one brother, Andrew; his grandparents, Mr. and Mrs. A. M. Polston of Oglesby and Mrs. C. C. Gilliland of McGregor. McGregor Mirror: Mar 12 (5-6), 1937.

SARAH ELIZABETH STONE, age 90, died at the home of her daughter in Eddy last Tuesday, March 22, 1937. She was born in Georgia, August 25, 1846, the daughter of W. L. and Phoebe Isbill, and married Mr. G. L. Stone there in 1868. After having moved to Arkansas and living there a few years the family moved to Grimes County, Texas, before moving to McGregor in 1889. Mr. Stone was one of the organizers in McGregor of the State Grange Fair. Mr. Stone (11/5/1849 - 11/8/1919) and four of their children preceded Mrs. Stone in death. Survivors include these children, Mr. W. J. Stone of McGregor, Mrs. Emma Smith of Ozarks, Arkansas, R. R. Stone of Corpus Christi, Mart C. Stone of North Zulch, Texas, and Mrs. Don Mansker of Eddy. Mrs. Stone had been blind for the past 22 years. Burial was in McGregor Cemetery by Amsler Funeral Home. Pallbearers were her six grandsons. McGregor Mirror: Mar 26 (1-4), 1937.

J. M. CROUCH, age 84, died at his home in Temple, Monday. He was born July 24, 1852, in Heard County, Georgia but came to Bell County, Texas at age 21. He was preceded in death by his wife and four daughters. Survivors include four sons, E. W. Crouch of McGregor, A. B. Crouch of Auckland, New Zealand, J. C. Crouch of Dallas, and Burl A. Crouch of Fort Worth. Burial was in Greathouse Cemetery. McGregor Mirror: Mar 26 (1-5), 1937.

KATE SANDERS ROSS died Easter Sunday, March 28, 1937. She was born in Barron County, Kentucky, November 28, 1865, the daughter of J. R. Sanders and _____ Hutchins, and was married there to Mr. W. W. Ross in 1884. Five children were born to this union, three having died before the family moved to Texas. One daughter, Mrs. Andy Hill, died in November 1933, and one daughter, Mrs. Earl Crain of California, now survivrs. Other survivors include her husband, W. W. Ross (2/19/1859 - 3/4/1939); one sister, Mrs. Sallie Renfro of Glasgow, Kentucky; three grandchildren. Mr. and Mrs. Ross, before coming to McGregor in 1911, lived in Fort Worth, moving there from Bowling Green, Kentucky. Mr. and Mrs. Ross and family have been residents of McGregor for more than 25 years. Burial was in McGregor Cemetery by Amsler Funeral Home. McGregor Mirror: Apr 2 (1-2), 1937.

JACOB HENRY SMITH died in a Waco hospital Wednesday, March 30, 1937. His body was brought back to McGregor by Lee Undertakers for burial in McGregor Cemetery. Mr. Smith was born in Atlanta, Georgia, February 24, 1875, but had lived in Texas since 1896. In 1901 he married Mrs. Gustine Hall. Survivors include his wife, Gustine Smith (12/17/1876 - 12/21/1943); son, Henry Smith; step-daughter, Mrs. A. W. Hering; two brothers who live in Atlanta; and one sister, Mrs. Fannie Smith of San Perlita, Texas. Having lived in McGregor for 40 years, he was for years a director of the First State Bank, and at the time of his death he was a wholesale agent for the Gulf Refining Co. and owned and operated the Texas Theatre. McGregor Mirror: Apr 2 (1-4), 1937.

W. A. McCAULEY, age 87, died at his home in Whitson nine miles south of McGregor, Friday, March 26. Burial was in Moody Cemetery. Mr. McCauley had lived in Whitson for the past 40 years and operated a store there for more than 28 years. Survivors include his children, Dr. E. R. McCauley, Mrs. A. T. Nelson and Miss Nora McCauley, all of Moody, and Mrs. Curtis Ritchie of Gatesville. Mr. McCauley's wife died in June of 1936. McGregor Mirror: Apr 2 (1-5), 1937.

NOBLE HARPER, brother of Mrs. John Montgomery of Comanche Spring, died Wednesday, March 24, in Houston. His body was brought to McGregor for burial in Flint Cemetery. Mr. Victor Harper of Oglesby was called to attend the funeral of his uncle, Noble Harper. McGregor Mirror: Apr 2 (2-6)/(7-3), 1937.

ELIZA LINDER, age 71, died in a Dallas hospital Tuesday, March 25th. Her body was brought to Temple by Lee Undertakers for burial in Temple. She was born in Tennessee, coming to Texas in early life. At the time of her death she was making her home with her daughter in Dallas. Survivors include several children including a son, John Linder of Moody. McGregor Mirror: Apr 2 (5-5), 1937.

T. J. RENFRO, 82, died at the home of his daughter, Mrs. Myrtle Locksby at Ackerly, Texas, Thursday, April 1. He was born in Georgia in 1855, came to Texas in early manhood, and lived in the McGregor community until 1925, when he moved to Tahoka. Since that time he has made his home in that part of the state. Burial was in Tahoka. Survivors include his wife; one daughter; two sons, Cal and Cliff Renfro of

McGregor; three grandsons, Lloyd Renfro, T. J. Renfro and Sid Blanton. McGregor Mirror: Apr 9 (5-4), 1937.

NELLIE CHESSER, 24, died of pneumonia on her 24th birthday, April 4, 1937. She was born April 4, 1913. Burial was in Post Oak Cemetery by Lee Undertakers. Survivors include her parents, Mr. and Mrs. Charlie Chesser; one brother, Earl Chesser of Oglesby; one sister, Mrs. J. T. Smith of Ebony, Texas, and several nieces and nephews. McGregor Mirror: Apr 9 (7-1), 1937.

WILL BEACHEM (Colored), died April 8, in McGregor at age 52. He was born in Mississippi March 4, 1885, the son of Alex Beachem. His wife was Minnie Beachem. Burial was in McGregor Cemetery by Amsler Funeral Home. Amsler Funeral Home Records, Book 2.

JOHN LACINA, 58, died of pneumonia in a Waco hoapital Monday, April 12, 1937. He was born in Washington County, Texas, February 5, 1879, the son of Frank and Mary Lucina who were born on Bohemia. He moved to Marlin then to McGregor. Mr. Lacina came to McGregor 25 years ago to take charge of the Lee Davis farm, which he operated for 20 years. For the past few years he and his family have lived near Clifton. Survivors include his wife, Bessie Perry Lacina; one daughter, Mrs. Maurice Jamieson of Clifton; one brother, Frank Lacina of Chilton; one sister, Mrs. Bud Johnson of Waco. Burial was in Comanche Springs Cemetery by Amsler Funeral Home with Masonic rights. McGregor Mirror: Apr 16 (1-2), 1937.

EDNA P. FISK died at her home in McGregor, Wednesday, April 14, 1937. She was born in Fayetteville, Tennessee, on June 6, 1866 (funeral home gives birth date June 6, 1870.), the daughter of Jeff Gilliland and Thlitha Rowe both born in Tennessee, and married Mr. B. D. Fisk (born 1860 - died 1941) on September 23, 1883. Ten children were born to them; five daughters Mrs. Almon McGaughey and Mrs. A. L. Tate of Quanah, Mrs. W. A. Johnson and Mrs. Jeff Simons of Waldon Arkansas, and Mrs. L. E. Mitchell of McGregor; five sons, G. G. Fisk of Fort Worth, Oscar Fisk, Alvin Fisk, Oliver Fisk and Ross Fisk of McGregor. Burial was in Blackfoot Cemetery (Davidson Cemetery) by Amsler Funeral Home. McGregor Mirror: Apr 16 (1-3), 1937.

FRANCIS JOSEPH COSGROVE died in Crawford April 15, 1937. He was born in Ireland October 26, 1861 (or 1863), the son of Patrick Cosgrove and Margaret Boyle. His wife was Sarah Shelby Cosgrove (1869 - 1949). Informant was Mrs. William Couch (Letha C. 1900 -) of Crawford. Burial was in Crawford Cemetery by Amsler Funeral Home. He was prededed in death by two sons, Jack Hall Cosgrove (8/22/1894 - 6/28/1896) and Frank Douglas Cosgrove (11/26/1896 - 11/29/1897) who are buried in Crawford Cemetery. Funeral Home Records, Book 2.

AGUSTA CORBELL, 82, widow of the late William Corbell, died at her home near Ocee, Wednesday, April 14. She was born November 21, 1854. Burial was in Crawford Cemetery. Pallbearers were six grandsons, Elmer Kunz, Dean Richards, Adolphus Borbell, Jr., Horace Corbell, Howard Kunz and A. W. Kunz. Survivors include one son, Adolphus Corbell of Ocee. Mrs. Corbell had been a resident of McLennan County for 65 years. McGregor Mirror: Apr 16 (4-4), 1937.

SUSAN R. SCOTT, age 78, died at her home near Eagle Springs, Wednesday, April 21, 1937. She was born February 10, 1861, in Louisiana, the daughter of Doc Franks who was born in Louisiana and Matilda Cummings who was born in Arkansas. She married Mr. F. M. Scott (born Aug 29, 1845 - died Dec 19, 1927) at Cold Springs, Coryell County, in 1882 and they moved at once to her present home. Her husband died in 1927 and two of her children have also preceded her in death. Survivors include her children, W. H. and Walter Scott of Garesville, Frank Scott of Moody, D. B. Scott of McGregor and Miss Emma Scott, Miss Ola Scott, Miss Mabel Scott and Miss Ethel Scott of McGregor, Mrs. Lucile Wheat of McGregor and Mrs. W. L. Bowlin of Gatesville; three half brothers, John L. Franks of San Antonio, George B. Franks of Mound and Milton Franks of Gatesville. Burial was in Eagle Springs Cemetery by Amsler Funeral Home. McGregor Mirror: Apr 23 (1-5), 1937.

LEONA L. CAMPBELL died April 21, 1937. She was born in Washington County, Arkansas, May 2, 1858, the daughter of Euso Mills and Margaret Robinson. Her husband was Thomas J. Campbell who was born in 1854 and died in 1923. Informant was Mrs. Andrew J. Hodges (Amanda E.) of Crawford. Burial was in Crawford Cemetery by Amsler Funeral Home. Amsler Funeral Home Records, Book 2.

LUKE JAYROE, age 58, died in Waco, April 21, 1937. He was born June 24, 1877, in Texas, the son of Robert Jayroe who was born in Alabama and Amanda Dean who was born in Mississippi. His wife was Mary Louise (Lula) Jayroe (2/7/1886 - 12/18/1964) and the informant was Carol Jayroe of Crawford. Burial was in Osage Cemetery by Amlser Funeral Home. Amsler Funeral Home Records, Book 2.

MARY ELEN WILLIAMS, 81, widow of the late Cooper Williams, died at her home in Lorena, Tuesday. Burial was in Lorena Cemetery. Survivors include three daughters, Mrs. W. P. Evans of Lorena, Mrs. W. W. Cox and Mrs. Agnes Barnes of Waco; two sons, V. W. Williams of Waco and J. C. Williams of McGregor; one sister, Mrs. Joe Osborn of Waco; one brother, W. H. Hays of Ojai, California. Mrs. Williams had resided in thes county for the past 74 years and had lived in Lorena for 37 years. McGregor Mirror: Apr 30 (1-3), 1937.

HENRY LIPPE, JR. The infant son of Fred Lippe and Emma Geltemeyer of McGregor died April 30, 1937. He was born April 29, 1937. Burial was in McGregor Cemetery by Amsler Funeral Home. Amsler Funeral Home Records, Book 2.

MRS. L. P. FLETCHER died Saturday. She was born near Columbia, Kentucky on November 22, 1884 and married Mr. Fletcher in 1897. Two children were born to them, Virgil L. (1898 -1919) and Bay Fletcher, the former dying in the cause of his country in 1919 and the latter now residing here with his parents. Burial was in McGreor Cemetery by Lee Undertakers. Survivors include her husband, L. P. Fletcher (1876 - 1957); her son, Bay Fletcher; and one grandson, Carrol Fletcher; her parents, Mr. and Mrs. D. H. Janes; one brother, Thomas Janes; three sisters, Mrs. Yeager Samson, Mrs. Gunderloy and Mrs. Otto Dickerson, all of Indianapolis, Ind. McGregor Mirror: May 7 (1-4), 1937.

KREYER. Mr. and Mrs. Alf H. Kreyer left Wednesday for Fort Scott, Kansas, where they were called on account of the sudden death of their sister-in-law. McGregor Mirror: May 14 (4-4), 1937.

JOSEPHINE WARREN (colored), age 49, died May 13, 1937. She was born July 27, 1887 in Bastrop County, Texas, the daughter of Washington Kemp and Lucy Willis Hood. Her husband was Isham Warren. Informant was Lucy Willis Hood. Burial was in McGregor Cemetery by Amsler Funeral Home. Amsler Funeral Home Records, Book 2.

MOSES WILLIAMS (colored), age 48, died in McGregor May 25, 1937. He was born in Halletsville, Texas February 16, 1889, the son of Jesse Williams who was born in Quero, Texas, and Julia Howard who was born in Mississippi. His wife was Delia Burks Williams. Burial was in McGregor Cemetery by Amsler Funeral Home. Informant was Nora Williams of McGregor. Others mentioned include Alanzo Williams of Dallas, Frilba Williams, James Williams of Waco, Mrs. Maggie Simpson of Houston, Walter Williams of Waco, and Valura Williams of Moody, Texas. Amsler Funeral Home Records, Book 2.

JIM F. ELLIS, 76, died Thursday, May 27, at his home. He was born October 6, 1860. Survivors include his wife, Maggie E. Ellis (2/17/1871 -2/14/1950), to whom he has been married 49 years; three sons, Lee of South Bosque, John of Edinburg and Arthur Ellis of Corpus Christi; three daughters, Mrs. John L. Bloodworth of Gatesville, Mrs. Charlie Howard and Miss Ora Mae Ellis of McGregor. Burial was today at Harris Creek Cemetery by Amsler Funeral Home. Mr. Ellis was born in October 1860, in Catoosa County, Georgia, the son of Mr. Ellis and _____ Daffron, and came to Texas at the age of 25. He had been a Mason since 1906. Out-of-town relatives and friends who attended the funeral include Mrs. E. B. Cass and Mrs. W. C. Torbett, nieces of Waco; Mrs. J. S. Petree and W. M. Riley, sister and brother of Mrs. Ellis, and quite a number from the State Training School in Gatesville. McGregor Mirror: May 28 (1-4)/Jun 4 (5-4), 1937.

NANNIE DOWIS, age 74, died at her home in Dallas Thursday, June 3, 1937. Burial was in Hillcrest Mausoleum with the Daylight Chapter of the Eastern Star services at the grave. Mrs. Dowis had formerly lived in McGregor. Survivors include her husband, W. J. Dowis; one son, Dr.

J. M. Dowis of Dallas; five brothers, Dr. C. M. Moore of Clifton, Joe Moore of Waco, R. P. Moore of Sipe Springs, Dr. Frank Moore of Houston, Hugh Moore of New Mexico; two sisters, Miss Ida Moore and Miss Mae Moore of McGregor. McGregor Mirror: Jun 11 (5-1), 1937.

EPP RUSH, age 34, who lived near Moody, was killed when the light truck he was driving was in a head-on collision with a heavy oil truck three miles north of Temple, Wednesday. Survivors include his wife; a daughter; his parents, Mr. and Mrs. J. A. Rush of Moody; two brothers, Walter and John Rush of Moody; two sisters, Mrs. J.A. McKamie of Moody and Mrs. Lucy Myers of Temple. (Place of burial not mentioned.) McGregor Mirror: Jun 18 (1-6), 1937.

ESTHER ANN SCHEPERS, age 91, died at the home of her son, J. W. Schepers in McGregor on June 17, 1937. She was born in Maryland, August 18, 1846, the eldest of several children. She was born August 18, 1846, the daughter of Sam Robertson and Eleanor Bounds, both born in Maryland. Her mother having died, Mrs. Schepers remained at the old home and helped rear the other children to maturity. She came to Texas in 1886, married Mr. Joseph G. Schepers (1852 - 1928) and they have lived in McGregor since that time. One son, J. W. Schepers, was born to this union and since her husband's death in 1928, Mrs. Schepers has made her home with her son. Burial was in McGregor Cemetery by Amsler Funeral Home. McGregor Mirror: Jun 25 (1-2), 1937.

WILEY M. DAILY died in a Waxahachie hospital last Thursday, June 17, 1937. He was born in 1880. The body was brought back to McGregor for burial in McGregor Cemetery by Lee Undertakers. Mr. Daily had lived in and near McGregor for many years, but left for California several months ago. While in California he became ill and returned to Waxahachie where he was a patient in the hospital for five weeks. Survivors include his wife; five children, Mrs. Herman Merten of McGregor, Mrs. Ruby Hemphill of Leonard, Mrs. Lovie Smith of Edgewood, New Mexico, Mrs. Ray Marr of Shallowater and B. C. Daily of Speegleville; five sisters, Mrs. A. A. Petty of Winsboro, Mrs. Frank Warren of Crawford, Mrs. Leslie Collard of Mesquite, Mesdames W. T. Cook and R. L. Mize of McGregor; two brothers, Henry and Marion Daily of Pittsburg, Texas. McGregor Mirror: Jun 25 (8-1), 1937.

MARY C. GILL, age 84, died at the home of her daughter, Mrs. E. E. Howard, Monday, July 5. She was born in Franklin, Georgia November 1, 1852. When she came to Texas she made her home with the late Mrs. Neff, mother of Pat M. Neff, and later with Mrs. John Day of Eagle Springs community. She spent some time in Alabama with her daughter, but returned to Texas about one and a half years ago. Survivors include three daughters, Mrs. K.A. Reed of McGregor, Mrs. E. E. Howard of Oglesby, and Mrs. R. P. Yates of Woodland, Alabama; two sons, Jim Gill of Maywood, California and Jeff Gill of Oglesby; three brothers, M. C. Kidd of Thorpe Springs, J. L. Kidd of Hico and Frank Kidd of Woodland, Alabama. Burial was in Eagle Springs Cemetery by Lee

Undertakers. McGregor Mirror: Jul 9 (6-1)/(8-1), 1937.

SYLVIA LOCKHART (colored) died last Saturday at age 86. She was born in Gonzales, Texas, in March of 1852, the daughter of _____ Williams who was born in Mississippi. Her husband was Odam Lockhart. She had lived in McGregor for almost fifty years. Burial was in McGregor Cemetery. Only one grandson, Frank Gant, and a niece survive her. McGregor Mirror: Jul 16 (1-4), 1937.

WILLIAM JASPER WELCH, age 73, died at his home in China Spring on July 6, 1937. He was born in 1863. Funeral services were held in Valley Mills with burial in Harris Creek Cemetery near McGregor. Until a few years ago, Mr. Welch lived in McGregor, coming here from North Carolina 30 years ago. Survivors include his wife, Sarah C. Welch (1868 - 1952); three daughters, Mrs. F. P. Branshaw of McGregor, Mrs. Thornton McGregor of Veribest, Texas, Mrs. Charlie Edmond of Crawford; three sons, John and Joe Welch of Crawford and Bryan Welch of China Spring. McGregor Mirror: Jul 16 (3-1), 1937.

CHARLES M. VANDIVER, died in the Old Confederate Home in Austin, Tuesday, July 20, 1937. He had lived in McGregor with his daughter, Mrs. A. E. Morris, until the family moved to Corsicana. Mr. Vandiver was born 90 years ago in Lawrence County, Tennessee, on February 17, 1847. He came to Texas in 1875 settling in the Hackney community most of his life. Mr. Vandiver spent 18 months in the service of his country, serving under General Forrest during the Civil War. He married Miss Jane Winters in 1867 and they had nine children. A son, Bill Vandiver, a daughter, Mrs. J. W. McKelvy and an infant preceded him in death and well as his wife who died November 19, 1923. Survivors include one son, George of Gatesville; five daughters, Mrs. W. L. McAda of Staley, Mrs. W. O. Evetts of Waco, Mrs. High Davis of Oglesby, Mrs, A. E. Dowler of Ponca City, Oklahoma, Mrs. A. E. Morris of Corsicana. Burial was in Blackfoot Cemetery (Davidson Cemetery) near Oglesby by Lee Undertakers. Six grandsons were pallbearers. McGregor Mirror: Jul 23 (1-2), 1937,

WILLIAM R. WALLACE died in a Waco hospital Wednesday, July 21, 1937. He was born July 13, 1862. "Uncle Bill", as he was affectionately known, was age 75 and had lived in McGregor for 41 years, coming here from Georgia with his wife. Burial was in McGregor Cemetery by Lee Undertakers. Survivors include his wife, Jo Ella Wallace (7/10/1862 - 2/13/1952); two nieces, Mrs. George Thomas of Oklahoma and Mrs. Smiley Wallace of Rome, Georgia who were reared his home; his children, Mrs. H. A. Holloway, Mrs. Lon Henry, Mrs. Jobe Wright, John Wallace, all of McGregor, Mrs. Louis Berry, Mrs. Bob Walker and Homer Wallace of Waco. One son, Jim Wallace preceded him in death several years ago. Other survivors include three brothers, Ike of Houston, Virgil and John of Rome, Georgia. McGregor Mirror: Jul 23 (1-6), 1937.

JOSEPH ELIJAH MOREHEAD died Friday, July 17, 1937, in a Temple hospital. He was born in Leon County, Texas, March 31, 1872, the son of Henry A. Moorehead and Columbia Sparks, both born in Mississippi but had lived in McGregor for over 30 years. For many years he was local manager for the Waco Packing Company of Waco, but the last few years were spent in the grocery business, associating himself in McGregor with his son-in-law, Johnnie Williams. Survivors include his wife, Millie Lucy Legg Moorehead (1879 - 1973); daughter, Mrs. Doris Williams; a granddaughter, Mary Anne Williams; five sisters, Mrs. Isla Dutton and Mrs. Emma Beckwith, both of California, Mrs. Travis W. Thames of Beaumont, Mrs. Horace Thompson of Lubbock and Mrs. Virginia Fowler of Oklahoma City. Burial was in McGregor Cemetery by Amsler Funeral Home. Informant was Miss Gladys Allen of Waco, a niece. Amsler Funeral Home Records, Book 2 / McGregor Mirror: Jul 23 (5-1), 1937.

WILLIAM LEE CONNALLY, age 72, died at his home in McGregor, Tuesday, July 27. He was born in Georgia August 31, 1864, the son of Tom G. Connally and Samantha Christian, both born in Georgia. He was well known here having held the office of public weigher in his precinct for 13 years. He came to Texas with his parents from Georgia at age 6, and after 2 years residence near Waco and Moody, made his home in the Comanche Spring community. Mr. Connally was the oldest child of one of the pioneer families of this area. Survivors include his wife, Julia Ann Cox Connally (2/24/1868 - 8/3/1942); three sons, Roy of Beaumont, Ernest of Midlothian and Chris of Palestine; five daughters, Mrs. G. D. Lewellen of Palinview, Mrs. C. W. Webb of Flomot, Mrs. Hunter Mann of Waco, Mrs. E. L. Cherry of Amarillo and Mrs. Jack Wardlaw of Plainview. Mr. and Mrs. Connally celebrated their 50th wedding anniversary last year. Other survivors include three brothers, Tom of Clarendon, Dr. H. F. and Clarence of Waco; and one sister, Mrs. T. W. Gaddy of Lorena. Burial was in Comanche Spring Cemetery by Amsler Funeral Home. McGregor Mirror: Jul 30 (1-6), 1937.

JOHN W. WRIGHT, 80, was buried at Post Oak Cemetery by Lee Undertakers after funeral services at Eagle Springs. He was a native Texan born in Anderson County and coming to this part of the state some 50 years ago, settling in the Eagle Springs community. Survivors include his wife; four children, Charlie of Moody, J. F. of Gatesville, Mrs. Lula Renfro of McGregor and Mrs. Bird Kane of Shreveport, Louisiana; six step-children, Jack, Charles and Clarence Carter of McGregor, Johnnie Carter of Moffatt, Mrs. Ida Lee Taylor of Belton, and Mrs. Addie Burch of Temple. McGregor Mirror: Aug 6 (1-5), 1937.

BERNICE PACK, 22, died in a Waco hospital, Thursday. Burial was in Speegleville Cemetery. Survivors include her husband, C. M. Pack of Waco; her parents, Mr. and Mrs. J. A. Gatlin of Waco; five sisters, Mrs. D. W. Welch, Mrs. N. T. Sharp, Miss Dorothy Gatlin and Miss Virginia Gatlin, all of Waco, Mrs. Ray Noland of Wink; five brothers, W. H. Gatlin and A. C. Gatlin of Austin, A. H. Gatlin of Abilene, E. W.

Gatlin of Waco and A. S. Gatlin of McGregor. McGregor Mirror: Aug 5 (3-4), 1937.

MRS. E. A. STURGES, daughter of Mrs. O. B. Gardner of McGregor, died at her home in Dallas last Saturday. She will be remembered here as Miss Althia Gardner of McGregor who was born and reared in South Bosque. They moved to McGregor when she was young where she attended school and graduated in 1910. She later worked at the local telephone office and taught school for several years. She married in 1915 and made her home since that time in Dallas. Survivors include her husband; three children, E. A. Sturges, Jr., Oliver Sturges and Miss Julia Sturges; her mother; one brother, Charlie Gardner; four sisters, Mrs. Laura Haley, Mrs. Margie Beebe, all of McGregor, Mrs. Mary Sales of Littlefield and Mrs. Ollie D. Allen of Oklahoma City. Burial was in Laurel Land Memorial Park in Dallas. McGregor Mirror: Aug 6 (5-1), 1937.

THOMAS H. PLACE died in his home in Crawford Monday, August 2, 1937. He was born in Mount Vernon, Illinois, February 28, 1869, and came to Texas when a lad. He was known as a successful driller of wells, having followed his work over a large part of central Texas. Survivors include his wife, Jessie Brittain Place (9/20/1875 - 3/29/1959); two sons, Brittain and Frank B. Place; one daughter, Mrs. Willis Naler, all of Crawford. Burial was in Crawford Cemetery by Amsler Funeral Home. McGregor Mirror: Aug 6 (5-6), 1937.

LONNIE B. CLOPP, 37, died at his home at Frost, Monday of last week. He was born in 1898. Survivors include his wife; two sons; his mother, Mrs. J. D. Clopp; two brothers, Henry and Walter Clopp; two sisters, Mrs. Ernest Bankhead of Rotan and Mrs. Earl Long of Tyler. Burial was in Post Oak Cemetery. McGregor Mirror: Aug 13 (7-1), 1937.

NANCY ELIZABETH MATTHEWS, 97, died at the home of her granddaughter, Mrs. Ben Templeton, Saturday, September 4, 1937. She was born in Alabama on March 19, 1840. Nancy was the daughter of Lahan and Rachael Thomas, coming to Texas in 1870. Two years later she settled in Hopkins County near Sulphur Springs. She was widowed in 1875. After her husband's death she taught school for a living. Survivors include one son, W. C. Matthews of Sulphur Springs, three children preceding her in death; two sisters, Mrs. Harris Ingram of Copperas Cove (age 86) and Mrs. Lattie Underwood of Ravenna (age 77). Burial was at Old Tarrant, Hopkins County, Sunday. Several of her ex-pupils were pallbearers. McGregor Mirror: Sep 10 (1-1), 1937.

D. A. FOX, 64, died at the home of his brother, L. C. Fox, three miles east of McGregor, Monday. Burial was in Batesville, Arkansas by Lee Undertakers of McGregor. Mr. Fox and his wife had been in Marlin for treatment and were visiting in the home of his brother when death came. Survivors include his wife; one brother, L. C. Fox and one brother of

Dallas; two daughters of San Antonio. McGregor Mirror: Sep 10 (1-4), 1937.

HOMAN ARBUCKLE, brother of Otho Arbuckle of McGregor, died in an oil field accident Saturday. Mr. Arbuckle made his home in McGregor until some 12 years ago when he moved to Monahans. McGregor Mirror: Sep 10 (4-5), 1937.

JAMES L. CAUDLE, 66, of Oglesby, died Thursday, September 2, 1937, in a Waco hospital. He was born August 11, 1871. Survivors include his wife, Nellie E. Caudle (Jun 29, 1876 -Jan 24, 1955); two daughters, Mrs. Walter Witte and Mrs. Marvin Rucker; his mother who resides in Gatesville; one brother, Louis Caudle of Houston; one sister, Mrs. Edgar Brittain of Pidcoke; an uncle, Mr. P. H. Herring of Prescott, Arkansas. Burial was in Post Oak Cemetery by Lee Undertakers. McGregor Mirror: Sep 10 (6-1), 1937.

BESSIE LANE WILLIAMS died at her home in Waco, Tuesday. Burial was in Comanche Springs Cemetery by Lee Undertakers. She had made her home in McGregor for many years before moving to Waco. Survivors include her husband, Kirk Williams of Waco; a son, Samuel of Waco; her father, J. W. Lane of McGregor; eight brothers, Robert Lane of Memphis, Tennessee, Samuel, Eddie, Fred and Paul Lane of Valley Mills, Roy, Jessie B., and Tommie D. Lane of McGregor; two sisters, Mrs. Frances Holt and Mrs. Charlie Walters, Jr., of McGregor. McGregor Mirror: Sep 3 (5-2), 1937.

DONALD BRUCE CLEMONS, little son of Mr. and Mrs. Wenford Clemons, died of burns from gas fumes. He was rushed to the Gatesville hospital but to no avail. Funeral services were held at Coryell Church. McGregor Mirror: Sep 3 (8-4), 1937. CARD OF THANKS: We deeply appreciate your kindness during the passing of our darling baby. Mr. and Mrs. Winford Clemons, Mr. and Mrs. W. H. Clemons, and Mr. and Mrs. W. D. Ray. McGregor Mirror: Sep 3 (8-6), 1937. Coryell Church Cemetery Records say Willie L. Clemons (Sep 23, 1936 - Aug 28, 1937).

CATHERINE WILHELMINA WILLMANN died September 6, 1937. She was born November 22, 1861, in Germany, the daughter of William Lehrman and Charlotte Meyer. Her husband was William Willmann, (Sep 13, 1857 - Jan 29 1932). Informant was Earnest Willman of Crawford. Burial was in St. John's Cemetery near Coryell City by Amsler Funeral Home. Amsler Funeral Home Records, Book 2.

DAN C. FREEMAN, son of Mr. J. D. Freeman, died at age 54, Sunday. He died at his home in Crawford following a heart attack. Burial was in Crawford Cemetery by Lee Undertakers beside his mother and a son. Survivors include his wife; one daughter, Mrs. Ola Mae Bunyard of Temple; his father, J. D. Freeman of McGregor; three brothers, John D. Freeman, Jr., and Tom of McGregor, and Roy Freeman of Alvarado; one sister, Mrs. E. C. Clark of Memphis, Texas. McGregor Mirror: Sep 17 (1-2), 1937.

HOWARD HORNBUCKLE, son-in-law of Mrs. Ben Jones, died at his home in Oklahoma City, Tuesday. Mrs. Jones and her daughter, Mrs. Joe Harris, left immediately for Oklahoma. Others from McGregor who attended the funeral were Miss Doi Evers and brother, Parke D. Evers, and C. F. Blake. The people of McGregor extend their sympathy to Mrs. Hornbuckle and her daughter, Bettie Jo. McGregor Mirror: Sep 17 (4-4), 1937.

J. LAYTON DORMAN died at his home in Meridian last Friday, September 17, 1937. Burial was in the Meridian Cemetery. Survivors include his wife, formerly Miss Myrtle Lee of McGregor; and a small son. McGregor Mirror: Sep 24 (5-1), 1937.

ELMER P. ELLIS, age 40, died in a Waco hospital Monday. Burial was in Oakwood Cemetery by Compton's Chapel with the American Legion in charge of services at the grave. Mr. Ellis had been employed as head engineer at the Mother Neff Park CCC Camp for several years. Survivors include his wife; two children, Bettie Jo and Wallace. McGregor Mirror: Oct 15 (5-6), 1937.

LUTHER LEE BEATY died in a auto accident last Saturday, October 16, 1937, when a car driven by W. H. Kruse ran into a ditch. He was born April 28, 1887. Other occupants were Mr. and Mrs. Sterling Poe. Mr. Beaty lived on the Mrs. J. C. Bivens place some three miles west of C. F. Luedtke corner. Burial was in Comanche Springs Cemetery by Lee Undertakers. Survivors include two sons, Sam of San Antonio and John Luther; two daughters, Carrie Lee and Frances of McGregor; two brothers, Walter of Oklahoma and Frank of McGregor. McGregor Mirror: Oct 22 (1-6), 1937.

ERNEST CHARLIE RABBE, age 36, died September 8, in Valley Mills. He was born in McLennan County, Texas, November 7, 1900, the son of William Rabbe and A. Rohloff. His wife was Clara Rabbe and informant was Wilma Dreyer. Burial was in St. John Lutheran Cemetery in Coryell City by Amsler Funeral Home. Amsler Funeral Home Records, Book 2.

ALBERT GEORGE SPENCER, 10 year old son of Mr. and Mrs. Frank Spencer, died in a Waco hospital Thursday, October 21, 1937. He died of tetanus resulting from having stuck two nails in his foot on Saturday. Amsler Funeral Home and Wilkerson-Hatch of Waco were in charge of the burial in McGregor Cemetery. Survivors include his parents, Frank H. Spencer and Terry Spencer; three brothers and two sisters; his two grandmothers, Mrs. Gid Bates and Mrs. A. F. Terry. McGregor Mirror: Oct 22 (5-3), 1937.

IRA HUNT, 46, died at his home in Bellvue last week. Mr. Foy Walker, Mrs. J. L. Mooney and son, William, from Oglesby, attended the funeral.

Survivors include his wife; two daughters; and one son. McGregor Mirror: Oct 29 (3-1), 1937.

JIM POWELL died suddenly in Cleburne while attending a ball game. Mr. Sam Powell and family went to Temple Sunday to attend the funeral. Jim Powell was his half-brother. McGregor Mirror: Oct 29 (3-2), 1937.

H. B. RHODES, 50, of Dallas, fell from the second floor of the King Hotel Saturday. Night Watchman, Felix High, was across the street in front of the Carey Cafe at the time and saw the man fall. After being given first aid he was rushed to a Waco hospital where he died. His body was shipped to Houston for burial where he is survived by his wife and one daughter. Mr. Rhodes was a Colonel in the Calvary of the U. S. Army Reserves and make his headquarters in Dallas. Recently he engaged in the oil business and was in McGregor looking after his interests in the test they are making for oil in this area. McGregor Mirror: Nov 5 (1-1), 1937.

ALICE BOYCE, 67, died in a Temple hospital Wednesday, November 3, 1937. Alice was born February 22, 1871. She was a native of McLennan County, spending most of her life near Moody. She and Mr. Boyce had made their home on their farm near Mother Neff Park for several years. Survivors include her husband, P. B. Boyce ; two sons, J. B. of McGregor and Frank of Louisiana; one daughter, Mrs. Louise Shaller of San Francisco; two step-sons, Tom Knowles of Pampa, Texas, and Claud Knowles of Napa, California. Other family mentioned was Claud K. Manley of Napa, California. Burial was in Moody Cemetery by Amsler Funeral Home. McGregor Mirror: Nov 5 (1-4), 1937 / Amsler Funeral Home Records, Book 2.

JAMES OBIE CLEMONS died in McGregor, November 15, 1937. He was born in Wilson County, Tennessee, March 11, 1876, the son of George Clemons and Florence Pollard, both born in Tennessee. His wife was Sallie Clemons. Informant was Mrs. Velma Smith of Buchanan Dam, Texas. Burial was in Osage Cemetery by Amsler Funeral Home. Pallbearers were Tom Clemons, Harris Clemons, George Clemons, Claud Knight, C. C. Curry and Winford Clemons. Amsler Funeral Home Records, Book 2.

LAWRENCE SANDERS died in McGregor November 20, 1937. He was born in Austin County, Texas, July 10, 1889, the son of William Sanders and Minnie Vahrenkamp. His wife was Henriette Fehler Sanders (Jun 16, 1890 - Mar 10, 1979). Informant was William Sanders of Crawford. Burial was in McGregor Cemetery by Amsler Funeral Home. Amsler Funeral Home, Book 2.

CHRISTINE SCHNEIDER, age 78, died Wednesday at the home of her daughter, Mrs. McDormett. Mrs. Schneider, a long time resident of The Grove, had been making her home with her daughter in recent years. Funeral services were in The Grove with burial in Lexington, Texas, by Lee Undertakers of McGregor. McGregor Mirror: Nov 20 (1-3), 1937.

W. M. KNOWD, Santa Fe trainmaster, whose home was in Temple, died Tuesday of a heart attack in Houston where he had gone to visit with his daughter. He had been with the Santa Fe for many years and visited in McGregor often. Funeral services were held in Temple with burial in Chicago. McGregor Mirror: Nov 20 (1-5), 1937.

VIRGE MOORE died at his home in Comanche County near Proctor. Mrs. Jennie Lou Ethridge of Oglesby is his daughter. Survivors include his wife and several children. Mrs. Ethridge, her family and Mrs. Nannie Rogers attended the funeral Sunday. McGregor Mirror: Nov 28 (8-3), 1937.

T. ADOLPHUS WELLS died in Hamilton, Texas, November 27, 1937. He was born in Georgia, November 8, 1851, the son of W. W. Wells and Mary Daugherty, both born in Georgia. His wife was Letitia Wells (11/15/1861 - 6/22/1957). Informant was T. E. Wells of McGregor. Burial was in Harris Creek Cemetery by Amsler Funeral Home. Amsler Funeral Home Records, Book 2.

BEN THOMAS died this week at his home in Lockney at age 84. Burial was Christmas day. Mr. Thomas lived south of McGregor for many years then moved to West Texas some 20 years ago. Survivors include five sons, Lucian, Arthur, Ivy, Hershel and Clarence Thomas. McGregor Mirror: Dec 31 (1-4), 1937.

MRS. LON HARDY died Friday. Her son, Mr. Jeff Hardy and her daughter, Mrs. Lonnie Matheson of Beaumont were in Oglesby with her at the time of her death. Burial was in Gatesville. Oglesby News. McGregor Mirror: Dec 31 (2-3), 1937.

MISS LAURA CAVITT. There were several from Oglesby who went to Gatesville Tuesday to attend the funeral of Miss Laura Cavitt, which was held at the First Baptist Church. Oglesby News. McGregor Mirror: Dec 31 (2-4), 1937.

MARY ESTHER WALKER died December 13, 1937. She was born November 7, 1869, in Georgia, the daughter of Daniel Low and Mary E. Cauley, both born in Georgia. Her husband was Joe T. Walker (1868 - 1949) of Crawford. Burial was in Crawford Cemetery by Amsler Funeral Home. Amsler Funeral Home Records, Book 2.

CHAPTER 4

HENRIETTA KOEHLER, age 68, died at her home in McGregor Monday, January 17, 1938. She was born in Germany on October 27, 1870, came to Texas in 1891, and soon afterward married Severin Koehler at McGregor. The family had made their home in the Prairie Chapel community near Crawford until about 3 years ago when Mrs. Koehler moved to McGregor. Her husband prededed her in death in 1929. Survivors include three sons, Adolf of McGregor, Ben of Osage, and Willie of Littlefield; two daughters, Mrs. Hennie Lander of Crawford and Mrs. Minnie Weschke of McGregor; one sister, Mrs. Will Peters of Washington County; two brothers, Fritz Lehrman of Coryell City and Christ Lehrman of Denton. Burial was at Coryell City by Amsler Funeral Home. McGregor Mirror: Jan 21 (1-3), 1938.

J. W. PERKINS died in Lubbock. He was the father of Grady Perkins of Oglesby. Oglesby News. McGregor Mirror: Jan 21 (6-3), 1938.

JOHN W. SHOFNER, age 84, died at the home of his son, Tom Shofner in Crawford last Saturday, January 15, 1938. He was born October 6, 1854, in Tennessee but had been a resident of Crawford for more than 41 years. Survivors include one son, Tom of Crawford; one daughter, Mrs. J. W. Gee of Waco. Burial was in Crawford Cemetery by Amsler Funeral Home. McGregor Mirror: Jan 21 (6-6), 1938.

DR. W. A. BUICE , age 53, died at his home in Santa Monica, California last Monday. Funeral services were held in Chelsea, Oklahoma, Thursday. Dr. Buice formerly lived in Waco, where he was a member of the faculty at Baylor University. Survivors include his wife; his parents, Mr. and Mrs. H. W. Buice of Waco; and ten brothers and sisters. He was a cousin of Mrs. Jessie Buice Chilcoat of McGregor. McGregor Mirror: Feb 11 (1-1), 1938.

MR. JOHN D. ARROWOOD died at his home near Crawford February 8, 1938. He was born in Georgia July 8, 1871, the son of Bartley Crowder Arrowood and Kathryn Arrowood, both born in Missouri. He came to Texas when 23 years old and has made his home near Crawford since that time. Survivors include his wife, Lila Bell Arrowood (1881 - 1952); two daughters, Mrs. Floyd Burks and Mrs. Jim Chandler of Crawford; and one brother of Georgia. Services were held at the Shiloh Baptist Church on Hog Creek. Burial was in Crawford Cemetery by Amsler Funeral Home. McGregor Mirror: Feb 11 (1-6), 1938.

ALBERT HENRY WITT died Wednesday, February 16, at the home of Gus Wiethorn near McGregor. Albert, age 27, who was born January 10, 1911, had lived most of his life with his grandfather, Henry Wiethorn, Sr. and with Gus Wiethorn. His mother, Frieda Weithorn Witt, died when he was only a year old. He was a member of the Harmony Playboys Orchestra and was employed on the A. W. Hering farm. Survivors inlcude his father and step-mother, Mr. and Mrs. Paul Witt; one half-sister, Mrs. Ernest Schwettmann of McGregor; three step-brothers, Ervin Vahrenkamp of Dallas, Marvin Vahrenkamp of McGregor and Herbert Vahrenkamp of Waco; his grandfather, Mr. Henry Wiethorn, Sr. of McGregor. Burial was in Crawford by Amsler Funeral Home after services at Harmony Lutheran Church in Crawford. McGregor Mirror: Feb 25 (1-3), 1938.

OTTILA RABBE died in Crawford, February 9, 1938. Ottila was born in Germany on April 6, 1864, child of Ludwig Rohloff and Caroline Nietzsehke. Burial was at St. John's Cemetery in Coryell City beside her husband, William Rabbe (1859 - 1936). Pallbearers were Charles Westerfeld, Charles Leizert, Marvin Dreyer, Herbert Dreyer, August Pietzsch and Robert Pietzsch. Others mentioned included Emil Rabbe of Crawford, Mrs. Ed Pietzsch of Waco, Mrs. Henry Dreyer of Reisel, Bill Rabbe of Haskell, Mrs. Otto Geibler of Valley Mills, Mrs. Ernest Rabbe of Coryell City and Miss Ella Rabbe of Crawford. Amsler Funeral Home Records, Book 2.

CHARLIE W. WALTER, age 68, a prominent farmer of this community for more than 50 years, died at his home near McGregor Tuesday, February 22, 1938. He was born in Missouri May 22, 1869, the son of William Walter and came to Texas when young, settling in Waco. He drove the first mule-drawn street cars in Waco and worked with Mr. Rigglesworth and other ranchers in the Middle Bosque community. He married Mary A. Plemons in 1894. Survivors include his wife, Mary A. Walter (1878 - 1955); seven daughters and five sons, Mrs. Nettie Westerfield, Mrs. M. F. Renfro of McGregor, Mrs. C. A. Smith of Clifton, Mrs. C. W. Nelson of Plainview, Mrs. Henry Roe of Oglesby, Miss Mattie Mae and Miss Helen Walter of McGregor, and Jim F. Walter of Lorena, Charlie, Jesse, John and Milton Walter of McGregor; two brothers, Fred and George Walter of Oglesby; and one sister Mrs. Emma Taylor. Burial was in Crawford Cemetery be Amsler Funeral Home. McGregor Mirror: Feb 25 (1-5), 1938.

R. L. FOX, 69, editor and publisher of the Moody Courier, died last Friday in a Waco hospital. Born in Tennessee, Mr. Fox had been a resident of Moody for 28 years. Funeral services were held Saturday at Moody. Survivors include a daughter, Miss Florine Fox; five sisters; and five brothers. McGregor Mirror: Feb 25 (1-6), 1938.

MR. SAFFLE. Mrs. R. C. Hodges, Oran Kilgore, Buster Morris and Rev. Ritchie were among those from McGregor who attended the funeral of Mr. Saffle in Waco last Saturday. McGregor Mirror: Feb 25 (4-4), 1938.

HOUSTON CROW, brother of Mrs. J. M. Webb died in De Leon last Saturday. Mr. and Mrs. J. M. Webb of McGregor were called to De Leon last Saturday on account of the death of Mrs. Webb,s brother. Funeral services were held there Sunday. McGregor Mirror: Feb 25 (4-4), 1938.

W. E. PARTLOW died at his home in Mount Salem, Texas, Wednesday. Mrs. Corrie Leache received a message Wednesday telling of the death of her cousin. She left Thursday to attend the funeral. McGregor Mirror: Feb 25 (4-4), 1938.

TOM B. BROCK, age 81, died Thursday, Februray 24, at his home south of Leon Junction. He was born in North Carolina on November 20, 1856, the son of Jacob Brock and when 3 years old moved to Texas. He moved to Coryell County from east Texas in 1870, settling near Leon Junction. In 1888 he married Elizabeth E. Hale (Sept. 27, 1865 - October 6, 1932). Survivors include three children, Jace Brock of Hamilton, Mrs. S. A. Whittenburg of Winters and Mrs. E. J. Evans of Leon Junction. Burial was in Seaton Cemetery by Amsler Funeral Home. McGregor Mirror: Mar 4 (5-3), 1938.

ETHEL PAULINE DAVIS was buried in McGregor Cemetery Tuesday. She met sudden death, along with her companion, Monday, when the car they were in struck a concrete abuttment of an underpass near Waco. A verdict of murder and suicide was returned by Justice Claude Segrest of Waco. McGregor Mirror: Mar 4, 1938.

RICHARD B. CORY, 23, was driving the car at the time of the accident. Segrest said his verdict was based on information obtained from sisters-in-law of the dead girl, Mrs. W. H. Davis and Mrs. R. E. Davis. The girl made her home with her brother, W. H. Davis in Waco. Mr. Cory lived at Orchard Lane near Waco. Cory was a carpenter and was said to have kept company with Miss Davis for two years. Besides his parents, he is survived by two sisters. Miss Davis is survived by her mother; six brothers and three sisters. For many years the Davis family lived on a farm northeast of McGregor before moving to Waco 15 years ago. McGregor Mirror: Mar 4 (8-3), 1938.

WILLIE HENSON, age 51, of Crawford, died in a Waco office building March 10, 1938. He was born in Ocee on September 27, 1886, the son of Columbus M. Henson and Symantha Elzada Srader and reared in Crawford. Willie was a mechanic by trade. He had been in the gin business with Mr. Kelling for a number of years, making his home with the Ed Srader family. Survivors include one son, Francis of New Mexico; sister, Mrs. Arthur Loper of Gatesville; and one brohter, Otis of Goose Creek. Burial was in Crawford Cemetery by Amsler Funeral Home. McGregor Mirror: Mar 18 (5-2), 1938.

JOHN DENSMAN, age 82, died at the home of his sister, Mrs. Mattie Erwin in DeLeon, Sunday. For many years he had made McGregor his home but left here 10 years ago for DeLeon. Survivors include his sister;

and a brother, D. M. Densman of Santa Anna, Texas. Burial was in McGregor Cemetery. McGregor Mirror: Mar 25 (1-2), 1938.

R. E. DUNCAN, age 74, died at the home of his daughter, Mrs. D. D. Dunn, in Cooper, Thursday. He was buried at Harris Creek Cemetery beside his wife who died in December of 1928. Since the death of his wife, Mr. Duncan had lived among his eight children: Mrs. D. D. Dunn of Cooper, Mrs. Ray Wayland of Alice, Mrs. Emmett Gray and Mrs. C. C. Arnold of Galveston, C. E. Duncan of Waco, Mrs. Paul Johnson, Elbert and Robert Duncan of McGregor; three sisters and one brother. McGregor Mirror: Mar 25 (1-4), 1938.

J. F. HANNAH, age 75, well known rancher and pioneer of McLennan County, died at his home in South Bosque, Monday. Burial was in Harris Creek Cemetery. Survivors include one son, Clytus Hannah of Galveston; one daughter, Connie Lee Hannah of South Bosque; one brother, L. P. Hannah of Waco. Mr. Hannah had lived at South Bosque for the past 70 years. McGregor Mirror: Mar 25 (1-5), 1938.

MERLE MOONEY, daughter of Oll Mooney, died in Floydada. Mr. John King and family left Oglesby Monday to attend the funeral. Mrs. N. B. Mooney, her grandmother, had the children several years. Miss Mooney was about age 16.
Mr. and Mrs. John King, Miss LaJuanah King and Elmo Montgomery went to Floydada on account of the death of Miss Merle Mooney, Mrs. King's niece, daughter of Oll Mooney. They formerly lived in Oglesby. Comanche Springs News/ Oglesby News. McGregor Mirror: Mar 25 (5-2)/ (8-3), 1938.

M. F. REED, was found dead on the porch of his home Friday. Mr. Reed had farmed in the McGregor community for 34 years. He was born September 26, 1877, at Cohutta, Georgia, and died April 1, 1938. Survivors include two brothers, Horace Reed of Clarendon, Texas, and Leonard Reed of DeQueen, Arkansas; four children, Mrs. Hal Hunter of Ranger, Glenn Reed of Stratford, Mack Reed of Breckenridge, and Warren Reed of McGregor. Burial was in McGregor Cemetery by Lee Undertakers. Pallbearers were C. C. Stone, Clay Chapman, N. R. Legg, M. B. Martin, L. P. Fletcher, and Jim Grantham, being the same pallbearers used at Mrs. Reed's funeral, November 27, 1937. McGregor Mirror: Apr 8 (1-1), 1938.

VERNON GRADY, age 39, died in San Fernando hospital in California. He was buried Thursday in Los Angeles. Mr. Grady once lived in McGregor. Survivors include his wife; daughter (age 11); his parents, Mr. and Mrs. D. A. Grady of McGregor; four brothers; and three sisters. McGregor Mirror: Apr 8 (5-1), 1938.

ROSEANN ABBE, age 86, was born October 27, 1851 in Monroe, Louisiana and died at her home near McGregor Sunday, April 3, 1938. Mr. and Mrs. Abbe moved to Texas from Louisiana, settling in Navarro County then moving to McLennan County in 1901. They have made their home in the Middle Bosque community since that time. Mrs. Abbe was preceded in death by her husband, Mr. S. G. Abbe, who died in 1923. Survivors include seven children, Mrs. Frank Reed of McGregor, Mrs. W. M. Thompson of Ropeville, Mrs. G. W. Dunson of Waco, Mrs. A. D. Smith of Mont Belvieu, Texas, Will Abbe of Crawford, George and Milford Abbe of McGregor. Burial was in Crawford Cemetery by Amsler Funeral Home. Paulbearers were Aruld Reed, Alvin Smith, Kelton, Cecil, Wingred and Jack Dunson, all grandsons of Mrs. Abbe. McGregor Mirror: Apr 8 (5-6), 1938.

WILLIAM BUCK, age 74, was found dead near his home Wednesday, April 6, 1938. He had walked to look over his fields and when he did not return a search was started. Burial was in McGregor Cemetery by Amsler Funeral Home. William was born September 8, 1863, in Oglesby, Texas, the son of William and Anne (Peterson) Buck. Survivors include his wife, Minnie Heckman Buck, and a large family. McGregor Mirror: Apr 8 (8-2), 1938.

JENNIE WOODS, 79, died at her home in Waco Saturday. She was the widow of the late L. A. Woods, who died seven years ago. Survivors include one son, L. C. Woods of Oglesby; two daughters, Mrs. M. A. Jones of Lubbock and Miss Nora Woods of Waco; two granddaughters, Miss Ione Jones of Lubbock and Mrs. Richmond Chunn of Waco; two brothers, J. M. Crawford and E. D. Crawford; three sisters, Mrs. Sallie Crump, Mrs. Sue Crumley of Austin and Mrs. Mack Kraft of Saint Louis. Burial was in Post Oak Cemetery by Lee Undertakers. McGregor Mirror: Apr 15 (3-1), 1938.

EMMA ALICE ALEXANDER, wife of White Alexander of Oglesby, died Friday, April 15, 1938. She was born February 9, 1859, in Russellville, Georgia, the daughter of Jackson Jones and Annie Smith. She married White Alexander in September of 1878 and to this union eight children were born. One son died in infancy and another son, John T. Alexander, died in June of 1922. Emma spent her life in Georgia and Louisiana until moving to Milam County, Texas, about 44 years ago. She has lived in Coryell County for the past 35 years. Burial was in Post Oak Cemetery by Lee Undertakers. Survivors include one brother, Rev. R. B. Jones of Winfield, Texas, a niece, Mrs. Clyde McMinn of Meridian, Mississippi; two nephews, Rob Gallman and Allen Gallman of Longview; her husband, White Alexander; her children, Mrs. B. G. Yarborough of Waco, W. B. Alexander of Temple, L. D. Alexander of Fort Worth, C. W. Alexander of Clovis, New Mexico, Mrs. Georgia Collard of Oglesby and Mrs. A. P. Anderson of Temple; her grandchildren, Morris and Henry Alexander of Temple, Harrell A. Collard of Brownwood, Jo Anne Alexander of Clovis, New Mexico, Mrs. Ruth Clements of Dallas; three great-grandchildren, Howard Riddle of Oglesby, Bryan Riddle of Waco and Dolores Clements of Dallas; her brothers and sisters, Rev. R. B. Jones of Winfield, Homer Jones of Lizella, Georgia, C. L. Jones of Madill, Oklahoma, Mrs. Lizzie Ballew of Los Angeles, California, Mrs. Clara

Gallman of Ruston, Louisiana. McGregor Mirror: Apr 22 (3-5), 1938.

LORENE ROSE MASSIRER, age 8 months, died in Waco on April 22, 1938. She was born in Oglesby on August 19, 1937, the daughter of Walter and Hattie Martha Massirer. Burial was in Prairie Chapel Cemetery by Amsler Funeral Home. Amsler Funeral Home Records, Book 2.

MARY ANN TANNER, 87, died at the home of her daughter, Mrs. J. F. Herring in Waco, Thursday, April 28, 1938. Burial was in McGregor Cemetery. Survivors include three daughters, Mrs. Drury Week and Mrs. A. L. Jameson of Meridian and Mrs. J. F. Herring of Waco; three sons, J. W. N. Tanner of Waco, J. W. Tanner of Waco and George Adams of Ferris. Mrs. Tanner was born in Chapel Hill, South Carolina, May 11, 1850, and came to Texas with her parents at age 1, settling in Freestone County. When McGregor was laid out as a town in 1882, she and her husband purchased lots and moved here in 1883. Mr. Tanner died here some 22 years ago, after which Mrs. Tanner moved to Meridian and then to Waco. McGregor Mirror: May 6 (1-3), 1938.

MARTIN. During the electrical storm here last Saturday, lightning struck and instantly killed a negro girl, age 15. She and her father, Harry Martin, were standing on the front porch of their home when the accidnet occurred. Martin was knocked down by the shock, but was able to arise immediately. The daughter was given immediate artificial respiration, but the shock was too much for her and she never did regain consciousness. CARD OF THANKS: We appreciate all kindnesses shown us at the death of our daughter and sister who was a victim of a stroke of lightning. Signed: Rev. and Mrs. H. L. Martin, Mrs. Atha B. Chandler, Mrs. Deoras Washington, Mrs. Zella M. Rogers, Mrs. Lillie G. Perry, H. L. Martin, Jr., R. J. Martin, Marcia V. Martin. McGregor Mirror: May 13 (1-4)/ (8-4), 1938.

MRS. RICHARD O. COUSINS died at the home of her son, M. H. Cousins in Waco, Friday, April 29, 1938. Burial was in Crawford Cemetery by Amsler Funeral Home. Mrs. Cousins, formerly Miss Pattie Frances Claiborne, was born in Farmersville, Virginia, on October 26, 1866, the daughter of G. W. Claiborne and Bettie Ann (Rice) Claiborne and came to Texas in 1889. She married R. O. Cousins (Mar. 29, 1863 - July 21, 1936) who preceded her in death about 2 years ago. Survivors include four sons, W. T. Bryan, J. H. McGregor, D. C. Crawford and M. H. Crawford of Waco. McGregor Mirror: May 13 (3-5), 1938.

WILLIAM H. REED, 74, died at his home at Windsor, about seven miles northeast of McGregor, Sunday. Burial was in Crawford Cemetery. Survivors include his wife; four daughters, Mrs. J. B. Draughon and Mrs. Myrtle Sandel of Windsor, Mrs. J. A. Burt of Comanche and Mrs. Opal Smith of Waco; three sons, Frank of Windsor, George and Wallace Reed of Waco. Mr. Reed was been a resident of Windsor for the past 30 years, having been in the mercantile business there until 2 years ago when he retired because of poor health. He had lived in Texas for 43 years, settling in McGregor before moving to Windsor. McGregor Mirror: May 20 (5-3), 1938.

W. A. PUTMAN, 64, died at his home in Oglesby Sunday. He was born November 27, 1874, in Lexington, Tennessee, the son of Frank Putman and Missy Estus, both born in Tennessee. At the time of his death he was sitting on the front porch in his chair preparing the program for the Sunday evening program at church. Burial was in Post Oak Cemetery by Lee Undertakers. Survivors include his wife; and one daughter, Mrs. W. C. Layne of Oglesby; one brother and one sister who reside in Tennessee. McGregor Mirror: May 20 (8-3), 1938.

MEREDITY N. ROACH, 62, died at the home of his brother, J. B. Roach, four miles southeast of McGregor, Wednesday. Survivors include two sons, Olis Roach of Troy and Ernest Roach of Eddy; two daughters, Mrs. Curtis Johnson and Mrs. Andrew Smith of Bruceville; two brothers, W. K. Roach of Beggs, Oklahoma and J. B. Roach of McGregor; two sisters, Miss Lear Roach of Emond, Oklahoma, and Mrs. A. L. (Lizzie) Hartman of McGregor. Burial was in Old Perry Cemetery Thursday by Lee Undertakers. McGregor Mirror: May 27 (1-2), 1938.

SALLIE HANNA died in Waco on June 2, 1938. She was born in Tennessee on August 23, 1849, the daughter of T. A. Mangum. She was married to Sam Hanna who preceded her in death. Informant was H. G. Mooney of Waco. Burial was in the McGregor Cemetery by Amsler Funeral Home. She was recipient of a Confederate Widows Pension #43946. Amsler Funeral Home Records, Book 2.

C. G. BRANUM, cousin of Mrs. M. L. Jordan of Oglesby, was buried in Moody Sunday. Had he lived until July, he would have been 91 years old. McGregor Mirror: May 27 (8-3), 1938.

ROBERT GLENN HOWARD, 18, was fatally injured when the truck in which he was riding overturned about five miles northwest of the CCC Camp at Mother Neff Park. Funeral services for the young man, son of C. E. and Lillie Howard of Waco, were held Friday with burial in Rosemound Cemetery. He was born in Tokio, Texas, October 5, 1918 and died May 26, 1938. Survivors include his parents; seven brothers, and five sisters. McGregor Mirror: June 3 (4-5), 1938.

RUFUS WILLIAM SUMMERS died at his home Wednesday. He had lived in McGregor for the past 28 years. Survivors include his wife; nine children, Guy, Amos, Jack and Dock Summers and Mrs. Oscar Bryant of McGregor, Mrs. Katie Honeycutt of Waco, Roy of Statesville, N.C., Pete and Grover of Burlington, N.C.; two brothers and four sisters. Burial was today in the McGregor Cemetery by Lee Undertakers. McGregor Mirror: June 10 (1-2), 1938.

DR. DAVID C. HOMAN, 55, was shot to death Saturday, June 4, at his home in Oglesby. He was born December 1, 1882 in Leon Junction, the son of

James Fred Homan born in New York and Sarah Campbell. Mrs. Alice Homan, his wife, was accused of the slaying in a complaint signed by Sheriff Joe White of Coryell County before Justice of the Peace, M. V. Dalton, at Oglesby. She was released on a $2,000.00 bond to await the action of the Grand Jury. Dr. Homan had been practicing medicine in this area for over 25 years. He died of a charge of shot, which entered the body just above the heart from a 12-gage single barrel shotgun. Burial was in Post Oak Cemetery near Oglesby, Sunday. Survivors include his wife; two sons, Fred of Oglesby and C. D. of Houston; three brothers, Willie and Dewey of Gatesville, Walter of Oklahoma; two sisters, Mrs. Aubrey Brazzil of Flat and Miss Maude Homan of Oklahoma. McGregor Mirror: June 10 (1-6)/(8-2), 1938.

SALLIE EMMA FORD, 78, died at her home in Eagle Springs, nine miles southwest of McGregor, Tuesday. Burial was in Eagle Springs Cemetery (Coryell County) beside her husband, R. S. Ford, who preceded her in death 18 years ago. Mrs. Ford was a pioneer of the Eagle Springs community, having moved to Texas in 1882 from Morgan County, Alabama, settling in Eagle Springs for the past 56 years. She was born February 11, 1860, the daughter of W. J. Owens and Emma Sandlin. Survivors include one sister of Colorado Springs, Colorado; four sons, R. D. Ford of Walnut Springs, Claud Ford of Gatesville, Owen Ford of McGregor and Henry Ford of Wickett; and one daughter, Mrs. R. V. Sullins of Moody. McGregor Mirror: June 10 (4-5), 1938.

E. A. CHAPIN, 45, died Sunday at his home in Waco. Burial was in Eagle Springs Cemetery in Coryell County. Survivors include his wife; his father, C. N. Chapin of McGregor; one daughter, Mrs. Troy Armes of Waco; six brothers, Cecil Chapin of McGregor, Elbert Chapin of Prairie Hill, Hugh Chapin and Joe Chapin of Waco, Brady Chapin of Houston and Ross Chapin of Longview; two sisters, Mrs. Myrtle Sims of Moody and Mrs. Earnest Meador of McGregor. Mr. Chapin was born in Eagle Springs and had lived in Waco for the pase 28 years. He was connected with Cameron Company until recently. McGregor Mirror: June 10 (4-6), 1938.

JOHN N. ROGERS, 68, died in a Waco hospital Saturday. Burial was in Rosemound Cemetery in Waco by Wilkerson-Hatch Funeral Home. Mr. Rogers, born in Tennessee, came to McGregor to make his home for many years until moving to Waco 13 years ago. He was chief engineer at Hillcrest Memorial Hospital at the time of his death. Survivors include his wife; two daughters, Mrs. D. S. Covey of Waco and Mrs. L. E. Shelby of Dallas; one son, Joe M. Rogers of Idabell, Oklahoma; two brothers, W. G. Rogers of Kansas City, Missouri, and Arthur Rogers of Whitehall, Illinois; and one grandson. McGregor Mirror: June 10 (4-4), 1938.

FRANK NORMAN BROACH, a retired attorney, died in Crawford June 10, 1938. He was born in Camden, ARkansas, February 6, 1856, the son of B. Broach born in Tennessee and Caroline Lightfoot born in Arkansas. His wife, Kate Walter Broach (1858 - 1932) preceded him in death.

Informant was Mrs. R. S. McDaniel of Yellowpine, Texas. Burial was in Crawford Cemetery beside his wife. Amsler Funeral Home Records, Book 2.

EMMA SIEWERT, 89, died Saturday, June 18, at the home of her daughter, Mrs. Paul Rinehart, four miles east of McGregor. She had made her home with her daughter for the past 8 years. Survivors include four daughters, Mrs. Paul Rinehart, Mrs. Martha Austin of Dallas, Mrs. A. F. Banke of Corpus Christi and Miss Annie Siewert of Waco. Mrs. Siewert, daughter of Wilhelm Kintzel and Caroline Pape, was born in Berlin, Germany on November 7, 1848, coming to America when a young woman and living for some time in Gayette County, Texas. Burial was in McGregor Cemetery beside her husband, Fred Siewert (Nov 23, 1843 - Jan 19, 1931), by Amsler Funeral Home. McGregor Mirror: June 24 (1-2), 1938.

FLORENCE ANN PORTERFIELD, age 83, died Saturday, June 25, 1938, in McGregor. She was the wife of Frank M. Porterfield who died in 1914. Florence was born in Mississippi and orphaned as a small girl. She then went to live in Pine Bluff, Arkansas and married Frank Porterfield in 1872. They moved to Caddo Peak, Johnson County, Texas, in a two-horse wagon. Later they moved to McGregor. She was the mother of 11 children, two of whom died in infancy and two as adults. Survivors include 7 children, O. R. Porterfield of Galveston, Mrs. I. T. Jones of Plant City, Florida, Mrs. Emma Smith of McGregor, Mrs. Dora Gilmore of Lyford, Texas, Mrs. Etta Young of Bakersfield, California, Mrs. Hazel Fore of Corpus Christi, Henry Porterfield of Bakersfield, California; one brother, H. L. Moffitt of Austin, Texas (age 88). McGregor Mirror: Jul 1 (8-4), 1938.

MOLLIE RIDDLE SURRATT, 85, the second white child born in Waco, died at Seymour last night at the home of her daughter, Mrs. O. S. Moillett. Burial was in Seymour. Mrs. Surratt was the daughter of Dr. and Mrs. J. J. Riddle the former pioneer doctor and preacher of central Texas who came here in 1851 from Mississippi. She was reared in Waco, Mount Calm and Bosqueville during the stirring reconstruction period. In 1873 she was married to J. P. Surratt, a young Waco attorney. The lived in and around Waco until he died in 1890. For the past 17 years she had lived with her daughter in Seymour. Survivors include five children, J. E. Surratt of Dallas, J. P. Surratt of Phoeniz, Arizona, Mesdams O. S. Moillett and O. C. Harrison of Seymour and Mrs. E. W. Crouch of McGregor. Mrs. Surratt was a member of the Daughters of the American Revolution. McGregor Mirror: June 24 (15), 1938.

E. B. NOLAND. Mr. and Mrs. M. V. Dalton of Oglesby went to Hico Saturday to attend the funeral of Mr. E. B. Noland, a brother of Mrs. Dalton. He died suddenly at his home, having only been sick for a few hours. McGregor Mirror: June 24 (5-1), 1938.

JAMES M. LONG (Uncle Jim) died Thursday, June 23, in Austin. Mr. Long made his home in McGregor with his sister, Mrs. Lillie Christie, for many years. Miss Nellie Christie, who is spending the summer here in McGregor, attended the funeral Friday in Round Rock. McGregor Mirror: Jul 1 (1-5), 1938.

JONAS BRADSHAW died last Friday, July 1, at his home four miles west of McGregor, where he had been living for 52 years. Burial was in Comanche Springs Cemetery by Amsler Funeral Home. Mr. Bradshaw was born in North Mississippi, August 14, 1870 but came to Texas in 1884 with his parents, O. P. Bradshaw born in North Carolina and Shara Malinda Cox born in Georgia. After two years in Ellis County, he moved to his present location where he resided until his death. On March 15, 1907, he married Miss Annie Anthon (Dec 11, 1875 - Aug 17, 1956). To this union were born four children, Price of Beaumont, Mrs. P. W. Horner of Poplar Bluff, Missouri, Mrs. Vesta Pennington and Jonas Bradshaw, Jr. of McGregor, all of whom were present when he passed away. Other survivors include one small grand-daughter, Frances Ann of Beaumont; three brothers, W. P. and Joe Bradshaw of McGregor and Dick Bradshaw of Ennis. McGregor Mirror: Jul 8 (1-1), 1938.

I. W. WALLACE, 72, of Houston, died Sunday night while on duty as night watchman at the Houston Y.W.C.A. Mr. Wallace, who was a brother of the late Bill Wallace of McGregor, made his home in McGregor until moving to Houston about 20 years ago. Those from McGregor who attended the funeral in Houston, Tuesday, were Mrs. Bill Wallace, Mr. and Mrs. H. A. Holloway, Mrs. Carl Duncan, Mrs. Jobe Wright and daughters, Mrs. V. G. Rich and Miss Kathleen and Miss Helen Wright, and Mrs. Wallace Wright and son. McGregor Mirror: Jul 8 (1-6), 1938.

BETTIE MARIE BUCKBEE, 4, daughter of Mr. and Mrs. Tom Buckbee of McFarland, California, died Firday. Mrs. Buckbee will be remembered in McGregor as Miss Mildred Cannon, daughter of Mr. and Mrs. J. L. Cannon. Friends here extend sympathy to the parents and small sister, who will miss little Bettie Marie. Mrs. Ed Mertins of McGregor was a aunt of Bettie Marie. McGregor Mirror: Jul 15 (1-2), 1938.

DORIS SMITH, 32, died Wednesday in a Waco hospital. Mrs. Smith and her husband, Ira Lee Smith, had made their home in McGregor for the past 6 or 7 years. They lived on the Robinson Ranch for several years and for the past three years had made their home on the John Mann farm near McGregor. Survivors incluide five children, Roberta, Alonzo, Mary, Charlie Lee and Iva Lee, all of McGregor; three sisters and one brother, Mary Lee Johnson of Waco, H. B. Barnum of Waxahachie, Mozzell Hornbeak of Pitcher, Oklahoma and Katie Warlick of Longview. Burial was in McGregor Cemetery by Lee Undertakers. Pallbearers were nephews, C. W., Clifford, and Roy Johnson, Willie Fisher, H. B. Barnum and Ervin Wickliffe. McGregor Mirror: Jul 22 (4-5), 1938.

EDWIN O. ANDERSON, age 58, died in Oklahoma City, Oklahoma, July 10, 1938. He was born July 12, 1880, the son of Lewis H. Anderson and Nancy

Sims. Edwin served in the military with the 410 RES LABOR BN QMC. He was buried beside his infant son who died Nov. 16, 1917. Burial was in Crawford Cemetery. His wife was Minnie A. Anderson (Lawrence) who died in 1968. Amsler Funeral Home Records, Book 2.

EMILY O. McWILLIAMS (MRS. W. A. McWILLIAMS), 76, died Wednesday, July 20. The family had lived in Plainview for several years until moving back to McGregor recently. They bought the A. E. Morris residence where they lived together with their daughter, Mrs. John Westerfield and family. She was born in Ripley, Mississippi, the daughter of Isaac Newton Cox and Nancy Elizabeth Deshaungh. Survivors include her husband, Lonnie (W. A.) McWilliams (Oct 7, 1856 - Apr 30, 1947); children, Walter McWilliams of White Flat, Texas, Mrs. Wash Dalton, Joe McWilliams of Plainview, Jess McWilliams of Speegleville, Mrs. Tom Wells of Lockney, Mrs. John Westerfield of McGregor and Tommie McWilliams of Waco. She is also survived by three sisters, Mrs. Will Morris of Baytown, Mrs. Lynn Buckner of Roscoe and Mrs. Lee Connally of McGregor; four brothers, Joe, John and W. C. Cox of McGregor and O. N. cox of Dallas. Burial was in McGregor Cemetery by Amsler Funeral Home and pallbearers were grandsons, Joe Westerfield, Roger Shamblee, Layton McWilliams, Tommy McWilliams, Jr., Burnice Dalton and Connally Allen. McGregor Mirror: Jul 22 (5-5), 1938.

MRS. WILL WALTERS, 62, died Monday at the home of her son, John Walters. Burial was in Harris Creek Cemetery by Lee Undertakers. The family was well known in McGregor, having once lived on the Caufield Ranch. For the past several years she had been making her home with her son in Speegleville. Survivors include her children, John Walters of Speegleville, Mrs. Ralph Reneau of Waco and Garland Walters of McGregor; one sister, Mrs. Oscar Nance of Florida. McGregor Mirror: Aug 5 (1-2), 1938.

JUANITA JO WATERS, age 1, died in Waco on August 8, 1938. She was born June 19, 1937, the daughter of Jack H. Waters. Burial was in McGregor Cemetery by Amsler Funeral Home. Amsler Funeral Home Records, Book 2.

PEARL D. PLEMONS died July 24, 1938, in Ocee at age 45. Burial was in Crawford Cemetery by Amsler Funeral Home. Amsler Funeral Home Records, Book 2.

MAILON A. BRACKNEY, 28, died Tuesday at his home in Waco. Burial was in Comanche Spring Cemetery just west of McGregor. McGregor Mirror: Aug 5 (1-3), 1938.

WILMA LEE DILLARD, 39, died in a Dallas hospital Wednesday. Funeral serviced were in Dallas with burial in McGregor Cemetery. She was the daughter of Mr. and Mrs. George Dillard and was born in McGregor. Her parents preceded her in death several years ago. Survivors include two brothers, Tom Dillard and Frank Barrett, both of Dallas. McGregor Mirror: Aug 5 (1-5), 1938.

MRS. WILL R. GREEN died at her home in El Paso Wednesday, July 28th. Burial was in the Station Creek Cemetery in Coryell County by Lee Undertakers. Mrs. Green who before marriage was Kate Johnson, was born in Lockhart, Texas, March 1, 1854. When about 12 years old, she moved to Coryell County. In 1874 she married Will R. Green who preceded her in death about 61 years ago. She was also preceded in death by a son, W. A. Green, who died 4 years ago. Survivors include a daughter, Mrs. Norton of El Paso; two sisters, Mrs. Mattie Compton and Mrs. Nora Martin of Fort Worth; one brother, Harry Johnson of Oglesby and three grandchildren. McGregor Mirror: Aug 5 (3-1), 1938.

BERNICE BATES, 9, daughter of Mr. and Mrs. Lee Bates, died. Burial was in Post Oak Cemetery by Lee Undertakers. McGregor Mirror: Aug 5 (3-3), 1938.

AGNES JOHNSON died in Waco August 8, 1938. She was born in Denmark March 14, 1880, the duaghter of Mr. and Mrs. Christiansen. Informant was Mrs. Edwin B. Kirk of McGregor. Burial was in McGregor Cemetery beside her husband, C. Julius Johnson (Jan 1, 1867 - Feb 18, 1934), by Amsler Funeral Home. Amsler Funeral Home Records, Book 2.

SALLIE PETERSON died in Arlington and burial was in McGregor Cemetery August 13, beside her husband, C. J. Peterson (Feb 28, 1858 - Mar 4, 1905) by Amsler Funeral Home. Mrs. Peterson, the daughter of Mr. and Mrs. Beal, had resided in the Masonic Home at Arlington for a number of years. Survivors include one sister, Mrs. Kate Perkins of McGregor. McGregor Mirror: Aug 19 (1-3), 1938.

MRS. HENRY FLACK, 74, died at the home of her daughter, Dr. Minnie B. Smith, in Cleburne, Thursday. Funeral services were held in Waco with burial in Comanche Springs Cemetery near Oglesby. Mr. and Mrs. Flack were residents of McGregor for many years before moving to Waco, where Mr. Flack died in 1921. Survivors include a daughter, Dr. Minnie B. Smith; a brother, Reece Evans of Dawson and three grandchildren. McGregor Mirror: Aug 19 (1-19), 1938.

MRS. BOB MERRITT, sister of the late B. A. McKelvain, died at her home in Dallas. Funeral services were in Dallas with burial in Post Oak Cemetery in Coryell County. Mrs. N. A. McKelvain and daughter, Miss Isla, could not be present. Mrs. Merritt was an aunt of Mr. Jim McKelvain of Oglesby. McGregor Mirror: Aug 19 (7-3), 1938.

JACOB OSCEOLA PECK, age 67, died in Crawford. He was born in Tennessee, the son of William Osceola Peck and Sarah Elizabeth Fouts. His ex-wife was Minnie Belle Whitlock. Informant was O. (A?) T. Peck of Crawford. Burial was in Crawford Cemetery by Amsler Funeral Home. Amsler Funeral Home Records, Book 2.

MRS. EUGENE HIGHSMITH, 56, died at her home Sunday. Burial was in Harris Creek Cemetery by Lee Undertakers. Survivors include her husband; one son, Vernon Highsmith; tow sisters, Mrs. John Fegette of McGregor and Mrs. Ramsey Alexander of Oglesby; one brother, Sturgeon Duncan of McGregor. McGregor Mirror: Aug 26 (1-3), 1938.

DOLLY LANE CAMPBELL died Saturday, August 27, at her home seven miles northwest of McGregor. Burial was in McGregor Cemetery. Mrs. Campbell was born in Milam County, January 15, 1876, and married William Thomas Campbell in 1894. Three daughters and two sons were born to this union. Mr. Campbell preceded her in death 31 years ago and a daughter, Mrs. Lula Anderson, died in 1932; one son Cullen, who served in WWI, died in 1924. Survivors include two daughters, Mrs. Reva Burton of McGregor and Mrs. Meda Lee of Brownwood; one son, R. T. Campbell of Waco; five brothers and four sisters. McGregor Mirror: Sep 2 (4-2), 1938.

MRS. L. P. COOPER, 75, died Sunday at the home of her daughter, Mrs. Ernest Holbrook. Burial was in McGregor Cemetery by Lee Undertakers. Mrs. Cooper was the mother of nine children, A. D. and Walter Cooper of McGregor, Preston Cooper of Waco, Mrs. Ernest Holbrook, Mrs. M. E. Mize and Mrs. J. M. Mize , all of McGregor, Mrs. W. C. Odell of Waco, Mrs. E. R. Breeding of Abilene and Mrs. Frank Chamblee of Crawford; several brothers and sisters in Oklahoma and Georgia. McGregor Mirror: Sep 2 (4-3), 1938.

CHARLES WILLIAM HOWE, 83, died at his home near Neff Park on August 26. He was one of the early settlers of that community having lived on his farm for 50 years. He was born in Illinois, September 4, 1855, the son of Thomas Howe and _____ Bayborn and came to Texas from Illinois at age 17, settling near Flat. Survivors include his wife, Amanda Stevens; four sons, A. R. and A. W. of Goldsmith, Texas, Riley W. of Crane, Texas, and L. B. of Moody; four daughters, Mrs. L. H. Hare of Gladewater, Mrs. R. C. Hare and Mrs. J. R. Glass of Overton, Mrs. J. M. Glass of Moody. Burial was in Flint Creek Cemetery by Amsler Funeral Home. McGregor Mirror: Sep 2 (5-5), 1938.

HENRY JACKSON BRINKLEY died September 1, 1938, at his home near Oglesby. He was 72 at the time of his death. He was born March 30, 1866 in Marshall County, Misissippi, the son of George Daniel Brinkley born in England and Caroline Marsh born in Cold Spring, Mississippi. Survivors include his wife, six sons and two daughters. The sons include Lee of Hamilton, Cliff of Gatesville, Bill of Moody, Kelly of Fort Worth, Jesse of Moody and Austin of Fort Worth, Mrs. Rivers Bankhurst of Belton and Mrs. Lillie McClinton of Oglesby. Burial was in Post Oak Cemetery by Lee Undertakers. McGregor Mirror: Sep 9 (6-4), 1938.

MRS. T. T. HAMBLEN, 78, died at her home in McGregor Thursday. Burial was today in Harris Creek Cemetery by Amsler Funeral Home. She and her husband had lived in this community for over 50 years. Survivors include her husband; five children, Mrs. S. A. Stebbins of Wichita, Kansas, Mrs. G. C. Brock of Abilene, A. L. Hamblen of Berkley, California, T. T. Hamblen of Fort Worth and Mrs. Albert Connally of McGregor. McGregor Mirror: Sep 16 (1-4), 1938.

JAMES McKINNEY (Negro), age 27, died in a Waco hospital Sunday as a result of a gun shot wound received around 2:00 a.m. L. E. Elliott, another Negro, was taken into custody for the shooting. Both men were from McGregor. McGregor Mirror: Sep 16 (1-5), 1938.

MRS. ROY J. COX was buried in Osage Cemetery last week. The family lived in Oglesby several years before moving to Livingston. She is survived by her husband and children. McGregor Mirror: Sep 16 (3-4)/(8-3), 1938.

SARAH FRY, 72, died at her home in Beaumont Saturday. Mr. H. E. Hackney of McGregor was called to Beaumont on account of the death of his sister. Burial was Monday in Beaumont. McGregor Mirror: Sep 30 (1-3), 1938.

CHARLES REDDING SEARCEY died Thursday at his home in Oglesby. He was born in Macon, Georgia, on September 25, 1869, the son of James Hunt Searcy and Sarah Searcy and would have been 79 years old on the 25th of September, had he lived until Sunday. Survivors include his wife; seven sons and two daughters, Ware of McGregor, Jim, Lawton, Dot, Henry and Arthur of Oglesby and C. B. of Rosebud, Mrs. Floyd Campbell of Hamilton and Mrs. Jim Morris of Oglesby; one brother, Henry of Forsyth, Georgia. His seven sons were pallbearers and burial was in Post Oak Cemetery by Lee Undertakers. McGregor Mirror: Sep 30 (3-1), 1938.

MARY MILDRED MANSKER, 84, died at her home in Waco, Saturday. Burial was in Perry Cemetery by Compton Funeral Home of Waco. Survivors include four daughters, Mrs. Nannie Jackson of Cleburne, Daisy Mansker of Wiiner, Mrs. C. C. Welch of McGregor and Mrs. Addie Chapin of Waco; three sons, Tom and Joe Mansker of McGregor and Don Mansker of Eddy. McGregor Mirror: Oct 28 (5-6), 1938.

DR. GEORGE W. LEE of Eagle Springs community was found dead in his car near his home Tuesday, November 1, 1938. He had been dead several hours from a heart attack or stroke, from all appearances. He had been a practicing physician in Coryell City before moving to Eagle Springs to engage in farming and ranching. He moved to Texas from Georgia when a boy, having been born in Georgia in 1874. Survivors include his wife; six children, Mrs. Mamie Burkney of San Antonio, C. R. Lee of Waco, L. A. Lee of Beaumont, G. W. Lee, Jr. of Washington, Homer and Josephine Lee, who are at home with their mother; one brother, W. J. Lee of Rockdale and two sisters, Mrs. James McMillan of Thorndale and Mrs. L. Gilchrist of Houston. Burial was in Comanche Spring Cemetery by Amsler Funeral Home. McGregor Mirror: Nov 4 (4-4), 1938.

MRS. O. E. THOMAS, sister of Mrs. F. M. Lyon, died in Austin, Saturday. Mr. and Mrs. F. M. Lyon and son, Louie, were called to Austin for the funeral and burial in Oakwood Cemetery in Austin. She will be remembered here as the former Miss Agnes Clark. Survivors include her husband; three daughters and two sons; two sisters, Mrs. Lyon of McGregor and Mrs. H. P. Cavaness of Tahoka; two brothers, J. S. Clark of Mt. Calm and R. D. Clark of Clifton. McGregor Mirror: Nov 4 (5-2), 1938.

W. L. (UNCLE BILLY) SRADER, 90, died at the home of his daughter, Mrs. J. B. Arrowood near Crawford, Monday, October 31, 1938. He had been a citizen of Crawford for 84 years and was a charter member of Shilo Baptist Church. Mr. Srader was born in Nacogdoches and moved to Shilo on Hog Creek when 4 years old. Survivors include two sons, S. L. Srader of Waco and H. E. Srader of Crawford; one daughter, Mrs. J. B. Arrowood of Crawford. Pallbearers were six grandsons. Burial was in Crawford Cemetery by Amsler Funeral Home. McGregor Mirror: Nov 4 (5-4), 1938.

J. E. TAYLOR, brother of Reb. W. C. Taylor of Oglesby, died in Hewitt. He had been living in Rosenburg. The funeral was in Hewitt with burial in Stanford Chapel. Miss Ora Graham and Mrs. Blonde Powell accompanied Rev. Taylor and attended the funeral. McGregor Mirror: Nov 4 (7-3), 1938.

MRS. S. K. LINDSEY, 81, died Monday at the home of her daughter, Mrs. D. H. Lynn in McGregor. Mrs. Lindsey and her husband, Mr. S. K. Lindsey, were among the earliest settlers in McGregor, having married in Milam Conty and moving to Comanche Springs in 1884. Soon after that time they moved to McGregor where Mr. Lindsey was a peace officer for many years. He was City Secretary for some time and died in 1918. Three children having died in infancy, Mrs. Lindsey is survived by five children, Mrs. D. H. Lynn of McGregor, Mrs. J. R. Burleson and Miss Wilma Lindsey of Fort Worth, J. S. Lindsey of Waco and Mrs. Ernest Howard of Portland, Oregon. Burial was in McGregor Cemetery by Amsler Funeral Home. McGregor Mirror: Nov 11 (1-2), 1938.

PAUL ENGLAND died Wednesday in the Nix Hospital in San Antonio. Paul was 35 years old, the son of Mr. and Mrs. Stanford England and was born in McGergor where he attended school and played football. Survivors include his wife, Isla Webb England; one son, Billie; his parents, Mr. and Mrs. England. Burial was this morning in McGregor Cemetery by Lee Undertakers. McGregor Mirror: Nov 11 (1-5), 1938.

WILLIAM THORPE ATKINS, 38, died at his home in McGregor Sunday. Burial was in McGregor Cemetery by Lee Undertakers. Survivors include his wife; two sons, Billie and Jerry; two daughters, Owana and Bonnie June; his parents, Mrs. and Mrs. George Atkins of Plainview; three brothers,

Junius, Charlie and Jack of Plainview; three sisters, Mrs. Jimmie Frye and Mrs. Robert Jefferies of Plainview and Mrs. Bill Holbrook of McGregor. McGregor Mirror: Nov 18 (1-4), 1938.

MRS. W. R. HARRISON, 82, died at the family home in Crawford Thursday, November 10, 1938. Burial was in Crawford Cemetery by Amsler Funeral Home. Mrs. Harrison came to Texas from Tennessee 54 years ago, settling near Crawford. Survivors include her husband; five sons and three daughters. One son, Horace Harrison, resides in McGregor. McGregor Mirror: Nov 18 (4-4), 1938.

T. G. BEERWINKLE died in a Temple hospital Saturday. Burial was in Buckhorn Cemetery by Denny and Witt of Moody. Mr. Beerwinkle was born in Austin County November 30, 1905, the son of Mr. and Mrs. Fritz Beerwinkle. He married Miss Irene Wiese on December 17, 1930, and had lived most of his life in the Buckhorn community. Survivors include his wife; mother; one brother; and three sisters. McGregor Mirror: Nov 18 (5-1), 1938.

MRS. JIM DAMON died at her home in Crawford Tuesday. Survivors include her husband and three children. She was born in Crawford and spent her life there. Burial was in Crawford Cemetery by Amsler Funeral Home. McGregor Mirror: Nov 18 (5-6), 1938.

TRENA JUNE LOFLAND, infant daughter of Mr. and Mrs. Pierce Lofland, was born November 13, 1938. She was buried in the Gatesville Cemetery this week. McGregor Mirror: Nov 25 (1-2), 1938.

A. P. ANDERSON died at his home in Temple Sunday. Burial was in Cold Springs, the family home. Survivors include his wife; four sisters, Mrs. Harriet Harris of Waco, Mrs. Maude Harrell of Arlington, Mesdames Alice Trapp and Arthur Matthews of Gatesville; two brothers, Arnett of Richmond and Ed of Sherman. Mrs. John D. Anderson of McGregor, a sister-in-law, and daughter, Anna Frances of Waco, attended the funeral. McGregor Mirror: Nov 25 (4-4), 1938.

BEN CULPEPPER, 53, died at the home of his daughter, Mrs. Earl Graham, in McGregor, Saturday, from paralysis caused by a stroke suffered earlier in the day. Burial was in Eagle Springs Cemetery by Lee Undertakers. Survivors include two daughters; two sons; his mother; a brother, E. A. Culpepper; three sisters, Miss Freddie and Miss Margie Culpepper of Eagle Springs, and Mrs. Ollie Mann of Waco. McGregor Mirror: Nov 25 (4-6), 1938.

SIM SHEPPARD, brother of Mrs. A. L. Lee, died Thursday in Mineral Wells, where he had gone for a few days rest. Mrs. Lee left for Lawton, Oklahoma to attend the funeral. Mr. Sheppard had been elected Sheriff of his county at the last election. Survivors include his wife; son, Craig; three brothers, John of Los Angeles, Bob of Winters, Ross of Winters; three sisters, Mrs. W. R. Moncrief and Mrs. Alma

Echols of Waco and Mrs. A. L. Lee of McGregor. McGregor Mirror: Nov 25 (5-3), 1938.

WILLIAM RAYMOND WIBLE died Tuesday, November 15, in a Houston hospital. His uncle, Mr. Dave Bright, also Mr. and Mrs. L. D. Alexander and Dr. and Mrs. Doud Wible (aunts and uncles) were with him at the time of death. The body, accompanied by his uncle, Dave Bright, was brought to Waco, his home. Burial was in Post Oak Cemetery near Oglesby. Mr. Wible, age 22, was the son of Claud Wible and India Collard Wible, deceased. He was born at Oglesby. His father died when he was 2 and his mother died when he was 8. After his mother's death he moved from Oglesby to Waco to live with his Uncle, D. E. Bright. He graduated from Waco High School and was attending State University. Survivors include his sister, Mrs. Hobert Howell. Wilkerson-Hatch of Waco was in charge of the funeral. McGregor Mirror: Nov 25 (7-3), 1938.

ALICE ANN SCOTT, baby daughter of Mr. and Mrs. Crawford Scott of Gatesville, died in a Temple hospital Monday. Burial was in Gatesville. Mrs. Scott, a niece of Mrs. J. F. Cass of McGregor, will be remembered here as Miss Ethel Routh. McGregor Mirror: Dec 2 (4-6), 1938.

SARAH MELVINA PENNINGTON LEWIS, age 80, was born in northern Georgia March 11, 1858, and died November 21, 1938. She was the daughter of C. P. Pennington and Nancy Jones, both born in Georgia. When a child she moved to Upsher County, Texas, later moving to Oglesby, Coryell County, Texas. On February 18, 1875, she married M. J. Lewis and eight children were born to the union. Freddie and Frankie, twin boys, died in infancy. Those who survivor are, R. S. Lewis of Oglesby, P. P. Lewis of Quanah, Mrs. C. S. Tucker of Gatesville, Mrs. E. W. Strickland of Gustine, Mrs. O. F. Peterson of Ft. Worth and Mrs. Cecil Graham of Oglesby. Her husband preceded her in death some 15 years ago. Burial was in Post Oak Cemetery by Lee Undertakers. McGregor Mirror: Dec 2 (6-2), 1938.

CHAPTER 5

BERTHA QUEBE, age 40, after an illness of three years, died at the family home near McGregor on January 1, 1939. She was born September 30, 1898, the daughhter of F. Vahrenkamp and Sophie Wedeking. Survivors include her husband, Henry A. Quebe (Feb 14, 1892-Feb 8, 1958); three daughters, Helen, Hazel and Mildred Ann; her mother, Mrs. F. Vahrenkamp of McGregor; five brothers, H. A. of Fort Worth, Ed of Bryan, Fred H. and Otto of McGregor, and F. Will Vahrenkamp of Waco; two sisters, Mrs. C. W. Kestler of Waco and Mrs. H. C. Lehde of Navasota. Mrs. Quebe was born and raised near McGregor. Burial was in McGregor Cemetery by Amsler Funeral Home. McGregor Mirror: Jan 6 (1-6), 1939.

MINERVA I. NUNLEY, age 79, died at her home west of Crawford January 1, 1939. She was born March 23, 1858 in Tennessee the, the daughter of John Whitlock and Minerva Ann Brown. She is survived by three sons, Tally, John and Wesley; three daughters, Mrs. Ira Holt, Mrs. Kelton and Mrs. Edwards; her husband, W. B. Nunley, preceded her in death about 10 years ago. Burial was in Coryell Church Cemetery by Amsler Funeral Home. McGregor Mirror: Jan 6 (5-2), 1939.
CARD OF THANKS: We are grateful for your help during the illness and death of our dear mother. Signed: J. W. Nunley, Tallie Nunley and wife, Wesley Nunley and wife, Mr. and Mrs. E. S. Kelton, Mr. and Mrs. W. B. Edwards, Mr. and Mrs. I. G. Holt, and grandchildren. McGregor Mirror: Jan 6 (4-5), 1939.

HESSIE PHILLIPS, age 67, died at the home of her son, L. L. Phillips near Hewitt on December 21, 1938. Mrs. Phillips made many friends in McGregor during her short stay here and she was active in religious and social activities of Pecan Grove and Osage. Burial was in Osage Cemetery beside her husband, A. L. Phillips (Apr 10, 1871-Dec 11, 1915). Her grandsons were pallbearers. Lee Undertakers was in charge of services. McGregor Mirror: Jan 6 (4-6), 1939.

LESTER J. MARSHALL, age 57, McLennan County farmer who dropped dead of heart failure in a field near his home in New Hope, was buried in the McGregor Cemetery Thursday. He had lived on the Brown Ranch near McGregor for many years before moving to the New Hope community four years ago. Survivors include his wife, Mollie Marshall (1882-? *buried in Fort Worth); a daughter, Mrs. Ed Holbrook of Wink, Texas; a brother, Tom Marshall of Waco, and several half-brothers and sisters. McGregor Mirror: Jan 6 (8-6), 1939.

JOHN GONZALES who lived on the farm of Mrs. J. L. Caudle accidently shot himself during the holidays. He was carried to a Waco hospital where he died Monday. OGLESBY NEWS. McGregor Mirror: Jan 13 (6-2), 1939.

MRS. L. D. HIGH, age 54, died in a Waco hospital Tuesday from complications of surgery done Monday. Burial was in a Waco cemetery. Mrs. High and her husband had been living near McGregor for about four years, moving here from Waco. Survivors include her husband; a brother, Houston Wade of Dallas; two sisters, Mrs. Bessie Ditto of Frost and Mrs. Minnie Graves of Amherst; three sons, J. R. and R. C., both of McGregor, and J. D. High of Waco; two daughters, Mrs. Vivian Frances of Waco and Mrs. Vernice Ferguson of McGregor; and nine grandchildren. McGregor Mirror: Jan 13 (4-4), 1939.

WALKER INFANT. The infant son of Mr. and Mrs. George Walker died in a Waco hospital on January 4, 1939. Burial was in Crawford Cemetery. Survivors include the parents; two sisters, Janelle and Nadine; and three brothers, Elma, Dan and G. B. Walker. McGregor Mirror: Jan 20 (1-1), 1939.

MR. JIM STEWART of Leon Junction was buried Thursday in Comanche Spring Cemetery beside his wife, Mary M. Stewart (Jun 13, 1884-Feb 11, 1914), who passed away 28 years ago. Mr. Stewart died suddenly Wednesday of last week. They were relatives of the Sutton brothers who formerly lived in McGregor. McGregor Mirror: Jan 20 (5-6), 1939.

JENKINS. Mrs. T. H. Jenkins and children, Doris and Harold, went of Bridgeport Sunday to attend the funeral of her grandfather which was held there Sunday. His death occurred at his home in Pueblo, Colorado. McGregor Mirror: Feb 3 (1-3), 1939.

REUBIN DEJERNETT, son of Mrs. C. R. DeJernett of Dallas, died last week while visiting his grandmother, Mrs. M. L. Jordan and aunt, Mrs. Guy W. Draper. Reubin became ill and was taken to a Waco hospital but died Saturday. Burial was in Dallas in Laurel Cemetery. Those attending the funeral included Mr. and Mrs. Guy W. Draper of Temple, Mrs. M. L. Jordan of Oglesby, Mr. and Mrs. Noah Graham of Waco, Dr. and Mrs. Doug Jordan of Brady, Wendell Jordan, Jr. of Temple, Mrs. Mayme Jordan and daughter, Louise, and Dr. and Mrs. DeJernett, all of Commerce. McGregor Mirror: Feb 3 (8-1), 1939.

SAM SMITH OXFORD died in Crawford February 9, 1939. He was born December 29, 1858, in Georgia, the son of Jeremiah Oxford and Frances Oxford. His wife was Sarah E. Tarpley. Informant was Mrs. Howser of Crawford. Burial was in Prairie View Cemetery 5 miles Northwest of Turnersville. Amsler Funeral Home Records, Book 2.

JOSEPH R. MCENTIRE died at his home Friday, February 3, 1939. He was born on July 23, 1864, near Spring Place, Georgia, and was married to Lula Elizabeth Isenhour on December 28, 1886. They celebrated their golden wedding anniversary before she preceded him in death on September 16, 1936. They came to Texas in 1894 and had lived in the McGregor area for 44 years, being in the grocery business here some 32 years. Funeral services were held by his brother-in-law, Rev. A. J.

Mann, at the family home with burial in Comanche Spring Cemetery by Lee Undertakers. Survivors include two daughters, Mrs. Elver Wallace of Dallas and Mrs. Dan Harris of McGregor; one son, Ralph D. McEntire of McGregor; two brothers, H. B. McEntire of Chattanooga, Tennessee, and G. A. McEntire of Waco. Among out-of-town relatives who were here to attend the funeral were Mrs. Nora Curb and son, Byron, and Miss Mamie Womack of Merkle; Mrs. Cleo Summers and Mrs. O. C. Ewing of Abilene; Mrs. Ocoee Kellen of houston; Mrs. Elva Wallace and daughters, Kathleen and Lula Beth, and son, Joe, of Dallas; Mr. and Mrs. Bill Butler of Dallas; Mr. and Mrs. George McEntire and son, Ernest, of Waco; and Mr. and Mrs. Wayne Mann of Taylor. McGregor Mirror: Feb 10 (1-1)/(4-5), 1939.

JAMES JOSHUA JORDAN, age 76, died at his home in Crawford on February 5, 1939. James was born in 1862, the son of James M. Jordon and Sarah Gober. He was a successful farmer in the Crawford community, having moved there from Belgren, Alabama, in 1910. He was public weigher for two terms in Crawford. Survivors include his wife, Emma Dobbs Jordan (1864-1950); six children, Mrs. T. M. Dowis of Mercedes, Mrs. A. B. Bunch of Mission, Mrs. Lovie Compton of Waco, Mrs. R. W. Bennett of Cameron, Mrs. D. L. Langston of Cisco, Mrs. J. A. Lusk of Temple; one son, C. T. Jordan of Crawford; three brothers, A. A. Jordan of New London, Texas, and two who live in Alabama. Burial was in Crawford Cemetery by Amsler Funeral Home. McGregor Mirror: Feb 10 (1-6), 1939.

OTTO H. LUEDKE died on his 76th birthday, January 28, 1939. He had lived on a farm five miles east of McGregor for two years moving there from Riesel, Texas. He had lived in Riesel for 18 years, moving there from Washington County, Texas, where he was born January 8, 1863. Survivors include his wife, Augusta Luedke; four sons, Paul and Henry of Reisel, William and Walter of McGregor; four daughters, Mrs. Lillie Bargas of Riesel, Mrs. Mary Pundt of China Springs, Mrs. Emma Haferkamp of Houston, and Mrs. Mada Stinke of Mart; two brothers, Dan Luedke of Caldwell and Herman Luedtke of Navasota; one sister, Mrs. Dora Silhiemer of Gay Hill. Burial was in Riesel by Amsler Funeral Home. McGregor Mirror: Feb 10 (4-6), 1939.

MAMIE C. SMITH, age 64, died at her home Sunday. She was born in 1874. Burial was in McGregor Cemetery by Lee Undertakers. Survivors include six children: Mary, Addie, Mae, Harold and Calvin of McGregor and Floyd and Ellis Smith of Houston; four sisters, Mrs. B. P. Ramsey and Miss Lela Kelso of Gatesville, Mrs. F. E. Campbell of Flat, and Mrs. Marvin Williamson of Pidcoke; four brothers, Frank and Walter Kelso of Gatesville, Jim of Dallas, and P. G. Kelso of Mercedes. McGregor Mirror: Feb 17 (1-5), 1939.

J. S. KILGORE of Mexia died at his home Wednesday. Burial was in Mexia Cemetery. The Kilgore family was well known in McGregor. They had lived on the Caufield ranch nine miles southeast of McGregor until last year. Survivors include his wife; two daughters, Miss Lottie Kilgore and Mrs. Edwin Larson of Mexia; three sons, Ralph of Rosebud, Glenn of McGregor and Granville Kilgore of Mexia. McGregor Mirror: Feb 17 (4-4), 1939.

HUGH EDMON HACKNEY, known in McGregor as Doc Hackney, died at his home Saturday, March 11, 1939. He was born in Alabama september 5, 1864, the son of W. W. Hackney and Louisa M. Reeves. He came to Texas when a lad, locating on Coryell Creek in Coryell County at a spot known as Hackney. From there he moved to McGregor in 1883, one year after the sale of McGregor's original lots. He helped organize the Methodist Church in McGregor, was a member of the Grand Lodge of the Knights of Pythias in Texas for 41 years being director of the Pythian Home at Weatherford. He also held office as a school trustee in McGregor for several terms, having taught school himself for a time. His wife, Mary Loretz Hackney, preceded him in death in 1931. Survivors include two sons, W. L. (Loretz) Hackney of Memphis, Tennessee and Hoyle E. Hackney of McGregor. Burial was in McGregor Cemetery by Amsler Funeral Home. McGregor Mirror: Mar 17 (1-5), 1939.

LYCURGUS CALDWELL was born January 29, 1860, in Helena, Arkansas, the son of George Caldwell born in Pennsylvania and Narcissus Hartin born in Mississippi. He died March 3, 1939, at his home in Crawford at age 78. He had been a resident of Crawford for 45 years, having moved there from Mississippi. Survivors include his wife, Margaret Susan Foster; nine children, George and Ralph Caldwell of Crawford, Frank and Mrs. George Reed of Waco, Mrs. Ernest Hill of Amarillo, Harry Caldwell of Oklahoma City, Mrs. John Mitchell of Dallas, Bill Caldwell of Monahan and Mrs. Julius Fulp of Highlands. Burial was in Crawford Cemetery. Amsler Funeral Home Records, Book 2.

W. W. ROSS, 80, died March 4, 1939, in McGregor. He was born in Kentucky February 19, 1859, the son of Henry Ross and Mandy McKinney both born in Kentucky. He and his family came to McGregor from Kentucky in 1910. Mr. Ross married Kate Sanders who preceded him in death 2 years ago. Burial was in McGregor Cemetery by Amsler Funeral Home. Four children also preceded him in death, Mrs. Andy Hill and three children who died in Kentucky at an earlier date. Survivors include one child, Mrs. E. N. Crain of Hollywood, California; three grandchildren; one brother, J. C. Ross of Bonham; one sister, Mrs. Nannie Jenkins of Moody. Amsler Funeral Home Records, Book 2.

FRANCES ANN BURTON, 77, died at her home in Crawford Sunday, March 12, 1939. She was born September 24, 1863. Funeral services were held at Coryell Church by Lee Undertakers. Survivors include her husband, M. W. Burton; five daughters, Mrs. Della Atkins of Waco, Mrs. Emma Hambrick of McGregor, Mrs. Lena Swafford of Corsicana, Mrs. Annie Adcock of Memphis and Mrs. Ethel Adcock of Eddy; three sons, Lee Burton of Waco, L. V. Burton of Oglesby, and Luther Burton of McGregor. McGregor Mirror: Mar 17 (4-6), 1939.

M. F. COLE, age 82, died at his home in McGregor Sunday. Burial was in Post Oak Cemetery near Oglesby by Lee Undertakers. Survivors include his widow; two daughters, Mrs. E. S. Tolliver of McGregor and Mrs. M. V. Bartek of Waco; a son, Ben Cole; and a step-son, Albert Minnix, both of McGregor. Mr. Cole had been living in McGregor for a number of years moving here from Coryell County where he had been a resident for over 50 years. McGregor Mirror: Mar 17 (5-5), 1939.

CORA POLLARD, collored, who had lived in McGregor for 41 years, died at the home of her daughter, Rebecca Flewellen, Monday, March 13, 1939. Burial was in McGregor Cemetery. Aunt Cora served as a nurse to mothers and new born babes. McGregor Mirror: Mar 17 (7-6), 1939.

GEORGE A. VANDIVER died March 11, 1939, at the home of his daughter, Mrs. Sam Jones. He was born in Mississippi in 1869 but came to Texas as a young man settling on Coryell Creek near the present site of Hackney Methodist Church. Survivors include 12 children: Charles, Homer, Tad and High Dave Vandiver of Oglesby, George Vandiver of Turnersville, Allen and Walter Vandiver of Gatesville, Lonnie Vandiver of El Paso, Mrs. Sam Jones, Mrs. Jim Brown and Mrs. Jim Simmons of Gatesville, and Mrs. Arthur Mooney of El Campo; five sisters, and 24 grandchildren. Oglesby News. McGregor Mirror: Mar 17 (8-1), 1939.

CHARLES B. GRAHAM died at his home near Oglesby Wednesday. Burial was in Post Oak Cemetery by Lee Undertakers. His grandsons were pallbearers. Mr. Graham or Uncle Charlie, age 92, had lived near Oglesby for 58 years. He was born in Booneville, Missouri, October 25, 1846. On January 14, 1875, he married Frances Gentry. Survivors include his wife; eight children, Mrs. Maggie Searcy, Mrs. Blonde Powell, Miss Ora Graham of Oglesby, Mrs. Lee Ellis of South Bosque, C. W. Graham, H. B. Graham, Cecil Graham of Oglesby, and W. N. Graham of Waco. Mr. Graham helped build the First Methodist Church in Oglesby and was a charter member of that church. McGregor Mirror: Mar 24 (1-5)/Mar 31 (8-3), 1939.

NANCY CAROLINE MITCHELL, age 71, died March 19, 1939, at her home near McGregor. She was born in Arkansas May 26, 1867, the daughter of John Morrison, and married Mr. E. C. Mitchell at age 21. They had resided in Texas for the past 30 years, the last 20 near McGregor. Survivors include her husband, Elibe C. Mitchell (Nov 24, 1856-Jan 19, 1954); seven daughters, Miss Vergie Mitchell of McGregor, Mrs. J. H. Cook of Waco, Mrs. W. M. Fowler of Hillsboro, Mrs. J. F. Walter of Lorena, Mrs. T. P. Ingram, Mrs. J. A. Pettigrew and Mrs. W. C. Davis of Louisiana; two sons, Garland Mitchell and Bryan Mitchell of La Porte, Texas; four brothers, Johnnie and Henry Morrison of Arkansas, Thomas and Dave Morrison of Oklahoma; four sisters, Mrs. Jim Butler, Mrs. Sarah Mitchell, Mrs. Mary Ann Rainbolt and Mrs. Ben Silton, all of Oklahoma. Burial was in McGregor Cemetery by Amsler Funeral Home. Pallbearers were grandsons: J. B. Cook, Henry Doyle Cook, L. D. Cook,

Wiley Earl Fowler, Jennings B. Cook and Marion Cook. McGregor Mirror: Mar 24 (8-6), 1939.

HENRY FRANK JENKINS, 58, died at his home in Ballinger March 23, 1939. Burial was in Ballinger Cemetery. In 1924 he married Uda Vee Jackson of McGregor. Survivors include his wife, Uda Vee; three sons, Duane, John David and Paul Jenkins; one daughter, Gloria; a sister, Mrs. J. C. Keltner of McGregor. Mr. Jenkins who was born near McGregor had made McGregor his home until some 15 years ago when he moved to Uvalde. A few years ago he moved to Ballinger. Those attending the funeral from McGregor were Mr. and Mrs. J. C. Keltner, Raymond Keltner, Mrs. J. D. Poss and Miss Mae Jackson. McGregor Mirror: Mar 31 (4-3), 1939.

GEORGE DIXON NALER died March 29, 1939, in Crawford. He was born March 28, 1864 in Cleveland, Tennessee, the son of Tom Naler and Sallie Cox Naler, both born in Redclay, Georgia. Burial was in Crawford Cemetery. His wife was Sallie Worthy Naler. Informant was Willis Naler. Amsler Funeral Home Records, Book 2.

MARY S. ADCOCK died in a Waco hospital Sunday. Burial was in McGregor Cemetery by Lee Undertakers. Mrs. Adcock, 59, was born in Alabama in 1881, but came to Texas with her parents, settling near McGregor. After her marriage she and her husband made their home on a farm near McGregor. Survivors include her husband, George F. Adcock (1872-1961); two daughters, Mrs. D. B. Rhea of McGregor and Mrs. P. D. Dawson of Lorena; six sons, Jimmy of Memphis, Texas, Albert of Eddy, Clyde of Honolulu, Roy of Lee, New Mexico, Hubert of Deadwood, South Dakota, and Jesse B. of McGregor.; three sisters, Mrs. S. J. Anderson of Old Glory, Mrs. F. M. Short of Henrietta and Mrs. Roxie McGregor of Benjamin; four brothers, C. A. McClintock of Stamford, E. E. McClintock of Brownfield, George and Johnnie McClintock of Refugio. McGregor Mirror: Apr 7 (5-2), 1939.

MARY A. HORNE died at her home April 11, 1939. She was born on April 23, 1861, in Georgia and came to Texas at age 21 with her mother, Mrs. Shan Connally. In 1882 she married Mr. R. A. Horne and they had lived in McGregor for 52 years. Survivors include her husband, R. A. Horne; two sons, Roy of Dennison and R. N. of Elk, New Mexico; two daughters, Mrs. Stanford England of McGregor and Mrs. C. L. Warren of Separ, New Mexico. Burial was in Horne Cemetery by Amsler Funeral Home. Pallbearerd were Horace Harris, Tom and Gid Smith, Tom, Grover and Naler Connally. McGregor Mirror: Apr 28 (5-2), 1939.

HENRY R. BOYD, 54, died Monday in a Gatesville hospital. Burial was in Osage Cemetery by Lee Undertakers beside his wife Bertie Ward Boyd (1888-1926). Mr. Boyd was an employee of the Gatesville training school for the past 9 years and had lived in Coryell County all his life. Surivovrs include two daughters, Miss Laurine and Miss Wilma Boyd of Gatesville, one son, Howard Boyd of Gatesville; three sisters, Mrs. Charity Simmons and Miss Minnie Boyd of Oglesby and Mrs. Emma

Rittan of Swenson; five brothers, Claude Boyd and Tom Boyd of Oglesby, Fred Boyd of Gatesville, Pitson Boyd of Dallas and Summer Boyd of Bartlett. McGregor Mirror: Apr 28 (8-2), 1939.

J. HENRY HACKFELD, 85, died in a Waco hospital Saturday, May 6, 1939. He was born in Germany February 15, 1854, the son of J. H. Hackfeld and first came to Columbus, Colorado County, Texas, in 1881. For 27 years he had lived in McLennan County, making his home near McGregor for the past 15 years. Survivors include his wife, Bertha M. Schroeder Hackfeld (1865-1939); four sons, F. W. of Orange, Henry F. of San Antonio, Emil H. and Otto H. Hackfeld of McGregor; four daughters, Mrs. Martha Brown of Porers, Texas, Mrs. Joe J. Jarrett of Stephenville, Mrs. F. H. Fehler of Clifton and Mrs. W. G. Hueske of McGregor. Burial was in McGregor Cemetery by Amsler Funeral Home. McGregor Mirror: May 12 (1-4), 1939.

NEWT CRAIN, brother of Glen Crain of McGregor, died in a Marshall hospital Sunday. He was born in South Bosque but for the past 20 years he had made his home in Big Spring. Burial was in Big Spring. Survivors include his wife and two daughters; three brothers, Glen Crain of McGregor, Watt Crain of Waco and Joel Crain of Mounds, Oklahoma; one sister, Mrs. Sally Haley of South Bosque. McGregor Mirror: May 19 (1-3), 1939.

FRANK S. PEEL, 75, died Tuesday in Gatesville. Burial was in the Masonic Cemetery in Gatesville. He was born in Desha, Arkansas, July 5, 1863. He later moved to McGregor and remained several years before moving to Gatesville where he has been living for the past 40 years. He married Mary Bradley Ryan, who preceded him in death about 5 years ago. Survivors include one brother, S. W. (Dick) Peel of Desha, Arkansas and one step-son, Joyce Ryan of Gatesville. McGregor Mirror: May 19 (3-2), 1939.

J. R. CAMPBELL, who has been living in the county home in Waco for the past 6 years, died Tuesday. Burial was in Waco. Survivors include a brother, E. K. Campbell of McGregor. At one time Mr. Campbell lived near McGregor. McGregor Mirror: May 26 (1-4), 1939.

FRITZ WILLMANN, 46, died in a Waco hospital May 25, 1939. He was born in McGregor May 14, 1893, the son of W. Willman and Minnie Lehrman, but had lived most of his life in the Crawford community. Survivors include his wife, Lena Willman ; two daughters, Mrs. Lonnie Sandhoff and Miss Minnie Willmann; two sons, Albert and Tilbert Willmann; one sister, Mrs. Will Koehler; and three brothers, Henry, Willie and Ernest Willmann. Burial was in the Coryell City Lutheran Church Cemetery by Amsler Funeral Home. McGregor Mirror: Jun 2 (5-1), 1939.

LOUISE HERING, 80, who was born December 2, 1858, died at her home Saturday, May 27, 1939. She died of pneumonia after suffering a stroke. Burial was in McGregor Cemetery by Lee Undertakrs. Grandsons were pallbearers. Her husband, C. G. Hering (May 7, 1857-May 28, 1919) died 20 years to the day before her. They were married December 12, 1878. To them were born twelve children, five daughters and seven sons, all living except two sons who died in infancy. Survivors include the following children: Mrs. R. Scheele, Mrs. Fred Witte, Mrs. John Scruggs, Mrs. Fred Wiese, all of McGregor, and Mrs. Nettie La Fitte of Shreveport, Louisiana, Bob Hering of New Braunfels, Luther, Albert, Jim and Charlie Hering, all of McGregor; two sisters, Mrs. Fred Bockelmann of Welcome and Mrs. Sophie Otto of Needville. McGregor Mirror: Jun 2 (5-4), 1939.

JEFF MURRAY, 77, died at his home in Moody Monday, May 29, 1939. He was born March 2, 1861. Burial was in McGregor Cemetery by Moody Undertakers. Survivors include three daughters and two sons. His wife, Florence Mathews Murray (Apr 9, 1870-Jun 25, 1905), preceded him in death. McGregor Mirror: Jun 2 (8-5), 1939.

TINY YOUNG BANNISTER, 82, died Tuesday, June 13, 1939. He was born February 13, 1857 in Marrietta, Cobb County, Georgia but for the past 45 years had been a resident of the Oglesby area. On August 14, 1874, he married Martha Emma Wise of Marrietta. On December 9, 1894, they left Georgia for Texas. Burial was in Post Oak Cemetery by Lee Undertakers. Grandchildren acted as pallbearers. Survivors include his wife, Martha Emma Bannister (1860-1953); four sons, Dr. C. D. of Marrietta, Georgia, Prof. M. L. (Luther) Bannister of Waco, W. T. and T. R. Bannister of Oglesby; a daughter, Mrs. Clara Harrison of Dallas. Two children preceded him in death, Dr. J. M. Bannister who died 5 years ago at Snyder, Texas, and Mrs. W. A. Simmons. McGregor Mirror: Jun 16 (8-3)/(8-4), 1939.

HENRIETTA MEISKE, 84, died at her home in McGregor June 16, 1939. She was born December 26, 1854 in Germany, the daughter of William Vahrenkamp and Caroline Hueske. For 50 years the family had lived here, her husband predeceasing her some 10 years ago. When 17 she emmigrated from Germany with her mother, Mrs. Carolina Vahrenkamp and settled in Washington County, Texas in 1871. In 1875 she married Mr. William Meiske (Dec 10, 1852-Mar 25, 1929), and to this union nine children were born, two of whom preceded her in death. Survivors include seven daughters, Mrs. E. Luedeker, Mrs. Henry Fehler, Mrs. William Wiese, Mrs. F. W. Wendt of McGregor, Mrs. Charles Mattlage of Crawford, Mrs. H. F. Meyer and Mrs. Will Krempin of Taylor. Burial was in McGregor Cemetery by Amsler Funeral Home. Pallbearers were J. F. Fehler, William Wendt, H. C. Fehler, Ernest Luedtke, Frank Hodel and Will Koehler. McGregor Mirror: Jun 23 (1-3), 1939.

JOE J. MILLER died in Houston at the home of his father-in-law, J. M. Harding, Tuesday. He was an employee of the McGregor Mirror for several years, leaving here fifteen years ago for Fort Worth where he worked for the Star Telegram. Survivors include his wife; a son, James

B. Miller; father, T. C. Miller, all of Fort Worth; two brothers, T. A. Miller of Charleston, Virginia, E. O. Miller of Chima Spring; two sisters, Miss Emma Miller and Mrs. Jeff D. Ray of Fort Worth. McGregor Mirror: Jul 14 (4-4), 1939.

MRS. SUMMERS. Mr. R. C. Summers, carrier of route one out of McGregor, received word Tuesday of the death of his mother. Mrs. Summers, age 75, died in Corsicana. Burial was in Zion Rest Cemetery near Corsicana. Survivors include R. C. Summers of McGregor, J. S. Summers of Wortham and T. F. Summers of Stephenville. McGregor Mirror: Jul 14 (5-6), 1939.

ALFRED L. BURKS, brother of Mrs. J. B. Chilcoat of McGregor, died Saturday July 9, 1939, at his home near Ocee. He was born August 2, 1884. Burial was in the Crawford Cemetery beside his wife, Ollie O. Burks (Feb 5, 1879-Jun 22, 1934). McGregor Mirror: Jul 14 (5-5), 1939.

LOUIE H. REYNOLDS, 52, died at his home near Moody Saturday. Burial was by Lee Undertakers. Survivors include his wife; four sons, Bill, Frank, Ora and Airel Raynolds; three daughters, Hazel Nell Reynolds, Mrs. Webb McCarter of Moody and Mrs. Alsteen Hefft of McGregor; four grandchildren, a foster father, John A. Morris of Moody; a sister, Mrs. E. C. Cook of Shreveport, Louisiana; and a half-brother, Alcus Turnage of Arkansas. Jul 21 (7-5), 1939.

CICERO JUDSON JOHNSON, the youngest son of Mr. and Mrs. Isham Johnson, was born April 5, 1865, and died July 14, 1939, at the home of his brother, W. C. Johnson in Oglesby. He was born in Coryell Church but had resided in Oglesby most of his life. Burial was at Coryell Church Cemetery with six friends of long standing as pallbearers. Survivors include his brother, W. C. Johnson; four nephews; and one niece. McGregor Mirror: Jul 14 (8-2), 1939.

ANNA BELLE ARMSTRONG, 42, died at the home of her sister, Mrs. Ethel Richardson Friday. Burial was in Crawford Cemetery by Lee Undertakers. Mrs. Armstrong died in a Waco hospital. Survivors include one sister, Mrs. Richardson; two brothers, Hubert Kilpatrick of Lincoln, Nebraska and E. R. Kilpatrick of Crawford. McGregor Mirror: Aug 11 (5-2), 1939.

SALLIE MOONEY was born January 27, 1858, and died August 5, 1939, at the age of 81. She was the tenth child of Mr.and Mrs. I. L. Dishough. She was born in Holly Springs, Mississippi, and in 1875 married C. D. Mooney. To this union thirteen children were born, two of who , along with her husband, preceded her in death. She is survived by the following children, Will of Houston, Arthur of El Campo, Jess and Mrs. Alice Homan of Oglesby, Mrs. Jennie Cox of McGregor, Mrs. Daisy Whigham of McAllen, Mrs. Effie Bankhead of Lovington, New Mexico, Mrs. Clay Tyson of Fort Worth, Mrs. Grace Hunt of Bellevue, Mrs. Agnes Whitlock of Dallas, Mrs. Ruby Walker of Oglesby. In the fall of 1891, Mr. and

Mrs. Mooney with their eight children moved from Mississippi to Texas, settling at Oglesby. Burial was in Post Oak Cemetery by Lee Undertakers. McGregor Mirror: Aug 11 (8-2), 1939.

MARY LOU WHILDEN was born Mary Lou Walker at Oglesby, Texas, July 21, 1902, and died August 2, 1939, at age 37. She was the seventh child of Mr. and Mrs. W. F. Walker. Fourteen years ago she married Homa Whilden of Oglesby and they had two children, W. H., Jr. and Ruth. Mrs. Whilden is survived by her husband; two children; her father and mother; three brothers, Jim, Foy and Hugh; five sisters, Mrs. Tom Fowler, Mrs. Wes Davis, Mrs. George Griffin, Mrs. Dick Ethridge and Mrs. Robert Green. Burial was in Post Oak Cemetery by Clark's Funeral Home of Waco. Oglesby News. McGregor Mirror: Aug 11 (8-3), 1939.

AMELIA CORNELIA BATES, 80, died at her home at Leon Junction, Tuesday, August 15, 1939. Burial was in Seaton Cemetery by Lee Undertakers. Mrs. Bates had lived in the Leon Junction community for over 31 years. Seven children survive, Marion and Burrews Bates of Leon Junction, Mrs. Mattie Henager of Leon Junction, Mrs. Molly Chamblee of Lewis Colorade, Mrs. Lizzie Kirk of Elm Mott, Will Bates of Cortez, Colorado, Lee Bates and Mrs. Lena Fields of Oglesby. McGregor Mirror: Aug 18 (8-5), 1939.

MRS. S. C. ANTHON, 85, died at her home in Uvalde, Tuesday. The family lived west of McGregor until moving to Uvalde 25 years ago. Mrs. Bloomer Ramsey and Mrs. Annie Bradshaw of McGregor and their brother, Rufus Anthon of Waco, left Sunday for Uvalde for the funeral. Survivors include five daughters, Mrs. Bloomer Ramsey, Mrs. Annie Bradshaw, Mrs. Carrie Chilcoat of Dallas, Miss Mamie and Miss Florence Anthon of Uvalde; three sons, Rufus Anthon of McGregor, Garland and John Anthon of Uvalde. McGregor Mirror: Sep 8 (1-6), 1939.

ANDREW J. HODGES, 78, died at his home in Crawford Thursday, August 31, 1939. He was born May 12, 1861, in Illinois, the son of Creed Clay Hodges and Caroline Gray Hodges, but came to Texas as a young man. Survivors include his wife, Amanda Elizabeth Hodges (Dec 25, 1874-Feb 25, 1965); five children, E. G. Hodges of Denton, Mrs. Gene Thomas of Mart, Mrs. Johnny Nelson and Miss Norma, Miss Ona and Miss Willie Mae Hodges of Crawford. Burial was in Crawford Cemetery by Amsler Funeral Home. McGregor Mirror: Sep 8 (5-3), 1939.

BEN J. BROWN, age 38, died in a fatal automobile accident near Taft on Saturday, September 9, 1939. He had been practicing law at Rockport for the past two years. He attended McGregor schools and after finishing law school at the State University he practiced law in Houston and New York City. Mr. Brown married in New York 5 years ago but for the past two years had been making his home in Rockport, Texas. Burial was in McGregor Cemetery beside his parents, James E. Brown and Edna Porter Brown, and other relatives. Amsler Funeral Home and Pace Funeral Home of Temple were in charge of services. Survivors include his wife; two brothers, Edwin of Amarillo and Dr. Porter Brown of Fort Worth; two sisters, Mrs. Paul Beresford of Mart and Mrs. Dr. Burbank Woodson of Temple. McGregor Mirror: Sep 15 (5-3), 1939.

BOB ROBERTS, 66, who was born in 1873, died at his home in McGregor Sunday. Burial was in McGregor Cemetery by Lee Undertakers. Survivors include his wife; two daughters, Miss Mary Roberts of Waco and Mrs. Carrol Wood of Cameron; a son, Henry Roberts of Brownwood. Mr. Roberts had been a resident of McGregor for 26 years, being employed as section foreman for the Santa Fe Railway. He retired 2 years ago after 35 years of service with the railroad. McGregor Mirror: Sep 15 (5-4), 1939.

MARTHA JANE BRAZIEL, age 65, died at her home in Shreveport, Louisiana, Sunday, September 17, 1939. She was born October 4, 1874. Burial was in McGregor Cemetery by Lee Undertakers. Survivors include two daughters, Mrs. Alma Caldwell of Lake Charles, Louisiana, Mrs. W. W. Lanch of Shreveport, Louisiana; a son, Herbert Braziel of Longview, Texas; two sisters, Mrs. Arthur Porterfield and Mrs. Tom Mansker of McGregor; three brothers, John Scruggs of McGregor, Charlie of Valley Mills and Tom Scruggs of Wichita Falls. Mrs. Braziel was a native of McGregor, living here until 13 years ago when the family moved to Waco then a short while afterwards to Shreveport. McGregor Mirror: Sep 22 (5-2), 1939.

BERTHA M. HACKFELD, age 74, died at her home near McGregor Monday, September 25, 1939. She was born February 22, 1865 in Oldenburg, Germany, the daughter of D. H. Schroeder and Margaret Merks, and came to America when 17 years old. Soon after arrival in Brooklyn she moved to Texas and married J. Henry Hackfeld in 1884 at Sublime, Texas. They made their home near McGregor for 30 years. Mr. Hackfeld (1854-1939) preceded her in death last May. Three children also preceded her in death. Burial was in McGregor Cemetery by Amsler Funeral Home. Survivors include four sons, F. W. of Orange Grove, Texas, Henry F. of San Antonio, Emil H. and Otto H. of McGregor; four daughters, Mrs. Martha Brown of Porters, Texas, Mrs. Joe Jarrett of Stephenville, Mrs. F. H. Fehler of Clifton and Mrs. W. G. Hueske of McGregor. McGregor Mirror: Sep 29 (1-4), 1939.

MARY ELLEN CLINE HARRIS died September 29, 1939. She was born in Alabama May 29, 1857. Her husband who died September 17, 1900, at age 69, was Wootson D. Harris, a Confederate soldier from Arkansas. Burial was in McGregor Cemetery by Amsler Funeral Home. Pallbearers were grandsons.

WILLIAM W. MAGEE, a well known resident of Oglesby for 35 years, died at his home Thursday. He was born in 1878. Burial will be today in Post Oak Cemetery beside his wife, Stella Floy Magee (1887-1930), by Lee Undertakers. Survivors include four daughters, Rosalyn, Evelyn,

Marcelle and Willie Mae; a son, Jack Magee of Houston. McGregor Mirror: Sep 29 (5-2), 1939.

FRANKLIN PERRY BRADSHAW fell into a well and drowned October 9, 1939. He was born in McGregor February 20, 1887, the son of Joe S. Bradshaw and Sarah Cox, both born in Mississippi. Burial was in Comanche Springs Cemetery. Survivors include his wife, Etta Lynch Bradshaw; one daughter, Mrs. Winn Butler of Crawford; his parents, Mr. and Mrs. J. S. Bradshaw; five brothers, Luit, Howe, Link, Grady and Joe; and two sisters, Mrs. Mae Crain and Mrs. E. G. Able of McGregor. Amsler Funeral Home Records, Book 2.

WILLIAM WALDO CAMERON, age 61, died of a heart attack Monday while testifying in a law suit in the 74th District Court in Waco. Burial was in a Waco cemetery. He was the millionaire president of one of Texas' largest lumber concerns. McGregor Mirror: Oct 20 (5-6), 1939.

HOWELL C. WILLS, 80, died October 25, 1939. He was born in Georgia, September 12, 1859. Mr. Wills died in a Terrell Hospital. Informant was Mrs. Black of Crawford. Burial was in Crawford Cemetery by Amsler Funeral Home. Amsler Funeral Home Records, Book 2.

MRS. EVERETT COLE died at her home at Pilot Point, near Gainsville. She was a sister of Mrs. George W. Russell and an aunt of Mrs. E. C. Kinz of McGregor. McGregor Mirror: Oct 27 (4-2), 1939.

ORVILLE S. POTTER was buried in Oakwood Cemetery in Waco Sunday by Wilkerson-Hatch Funeral Home. Mr. Potter, age 69, had made his home with his daughter, Mrs. Oliver Winchell, since the death of his wife in 1935. He died Saturday, November 4, 1939. Survivors include his two children, Margaret Winchell and Jerry Potter. McGregor Mirror: Nov 10 (1-2), 1939.

MRS. ARTHUR JOHNSON died at her home in Stephenville last Firday. Her body was brought to Moody for burial in the family burial ground. Survivors include her husband; two sons; two sisters, Mrs. Asa Cantwell of Fort Worth and Mrs. Marion Beesley of Houston; two brothers, W. A. Vowel of Copperas Cove and L. C. Vowel of McGregor. McGregor Mirror: Nov 17 (4-2), 1939.

A. G. (ALEX) ARMSTRONG, age 70, died at his home in Crawford Sunday, Noverber 12, 1939. He was born June 17, 1869, the son of Alfred M. Armstrong and Mary Elizabeth Grimes. Burial was in Crawford Cemetery. Mr. Amstrong at the time of his death was Justice-of-the-Peace in his precinct and at one time was Postmaster of Crawford. Survivors include his wife, Willie Alvira Crouch; a daughter and a son, Jack Armstrong of Sweetwater. McGregor Mirror: Nov 17 (5-5), 1939.

FRANK E. GRAHAM, 50, was found dead by his wife Tuesday, November 21, 1939. He was born September 15, 1885. Burial was in McGregor Cemetery by Lee Undertakers. Survivors include his wife; two sons; six brothers, Will, Arch, Tom, Mack, Lane and Dr. Emmett Graham; two sisters, Mrs. Richard Dyess and Mrs. John Freeman, Jr. McGregor Mirror: Nov 24 (1-1), 1939.

MRS. E. W. CULBRETH, mother of Mrs. D. W. Jones of Oglesby, died at her home in Statesville, North Carolina, Saturday, November 11, 1939. Burial ws in Oakwood Cemetery in Statesville. Survivors include daughters, Mrs. D. W. Jones of Oglesby and Mrs. Jesse M. Brown of Madison, North Carolina; five sons, E. E. and Homer Culbreth of Raleigh, North Carolina, W. G. Culbreth of West Hollywood, California, Frank Culbreth of Statesville and J. K. Culbreth of Palatka, Florida. Mrs. Culbreth was born in Randolph County, N. C. on January 11, 1855, and after her marriage moved to Statesville. Mr. Culbreth preceded her in death in 1926. McGregor Mirror: Nov 24 (8-4), 1939.

GUS W. THOMPSON, age 28, was killed in a tractor accident at Redding, California on November 30, 1939. He was operator of a bulldozer tractor when he stopped to help out another worker with car trouble. Mr. Thompson was born March 1, 1911, in Arcadia, Florida, and became acquainted in McGregor while doing road work here a few years ago. He was married in McGregor to Juanita Hunter, who survives him. A two year old daughter also survives. Other survivors include his father; eight brothers; and four sisters of Archdia, Florida. His body was shipped to McGregor by train and the funeral was held in the home of Mr. and Mrs. R. T. Hunter. Burial was in McGregor Cemetery by Amlser Funeral Home. McGregor Mirror: Dec 8 (1-6), 1939.

CHAPTER 6

ELLA L. BLANTON of Houston, died Sunday. January 7, 1940, at the home of her daughter, Mrs. Willie Barron of Tyler. Burial was in the McGregor Cemetery by Amsler Funeral Home. Mrs. Blanton was born near Friend, Nebraska, April 17, 1868, and came to Texas in 1883, settling 8 miles south of McGregor. She married George W. Blanton in 1886 and they made their home near McGregor until they moved to Tyler in 1922 where Mr. Blanton died on November 22, 1922. Survivors include six daughters, Mrs. Willie Barron of Tyler, Mrs. Ruby Duncan, Mrs. Leone Penito, Mrs. Lillian Williamson, all of Houston, Mrs. Glen Bolger of Mercedes and Mrs. A. B. Cloud of Cisco; two sons, James Blanton of Crawford and George Blanton of Houston; three sisters, Mrs. Z. G. Allen of McGregor, Mrs. Mary Merideth of Lincoln, Nebraska, and Mrs. Nellie Adams of Dallas; four brothers, John M. Simmons of Wichita Falls, Texas, W. A. Simmons of Wynwood, Oklahoma, Robert J. Simmons of Waco and Frank E. Simmons of Oglesby. McGregor Mirror: Jan 12 (1-3), 1940.

MARTHA LOU ELLA "MATTIE" GLASGOW MILLER, age 68, died Sunday, January 21, 1940, in a Waco hospital. Her clothing caught fire the day before from an open door on a wood heater. Mrs. Miller had just moved from McGregor ten months ago to a farm adjoining her daughter, Mrs. S. M. Abbe, near McGregor. She was born February 11. 1871, in Comanche Springs, Texas, February 11, 1871, before McGregor was founded. Mrs. Miller was the daughter of W. T. Glasgow and Minerva Jane Burns, both born in Tennessee. She was preceded in death by her husband, Bunyan (C. B.) Miller, (1867-1936) three years ago. Survivors include two daughters, Mrs. S. M. Abbe and Mrs. L. B. Fulp of McGregor; two brothers, Levi and J. L. Glasgow of Eric, Oklahoma; four sisters, Mrs. T. J. Wood of Sweetwater, Mrs. Betty Sanford of Brownwood, Mrs. Ada Lee White of Houston, and Mrs. R. W. Sales of McGregor. Burial was in Crawford Cemetery by Amsler Funeral Home. McGregor Mirror: Jan 26 (1-1), 1940.

MELTON THOMPSON of Waco was buried in Gatesville Sunday. Mr. Thompson was a brother of Dick Thompson of Oglesby. Friends and relatives from Oglesby who attended the funeral included Walter (Dick) Thompson, J. R. Thompson, Clifford Green and daughter, Janelle, R. D. Edwards and Davis Ray, F. B. Lam, Joe Draper, Rannel Graves, Mittie Lawrence, Stella Graves, T. O. Humpries, Savoy Lawrence, J. C. Fox, Earl Huddleston, Joel Shirley and Miss Wanda Humphries. McGregor Mirror: Jan 26 (8-4), 1940.

HENRY FRANKLIN KING, age 66, died Thursday at his home. He was born December 4, 1873, in Coryell County near Gatesville and had lived in that county all his life. Henry was the son of Leon King and Sarah Williams , both born in Mississippi. Mr. King married Miss Katie Caufield November 3, 1901. Survivors include his wife; three daughters, Mrs. Victor Green of Mound, Miss Mary Kathryn King, (third daughter not named); three sons, Henry Leon King of Waco, Quince and Luther King of Oglesby; a brother, Tilman King of Gatesville; four sisters, Mrs. George Flowers of Gatesville, Mrs. Will Bray of Valley Mills, Mrs. Belle Prince of Lawton Oklahoma and Mrs. V. A. Adkins of Breckenridge. Burial was in Davidson Cemetery. McGregor Mirror: Jan 26 (8-5), 1940.

SARAH NOWLIN, sister of Mrs. Glen Crain, died at her home in Lewisville, Texas, last week. McGregor Mirror: Feb 2 (1-5), 1940.

TINSLEY WADE DOTY, age 57, died at his home on the Compton ranch seven miles north of Crawford Thursday, February 1, 1940. He was born in Missouri on August 16, 1881, the son of Harlon and Sarah Doty. Survivors include his wife, Lula E. Doty (1883-1965); three sons; two daughters; three brothers; and one sister. Burial was in Crawford Cemetery by Amsler Funeral Home. McGregor Mirror: Feb 9 (1-2), 1940.

LONNIE S. HERRING, age 27, as buried in Oakwood Cemetery in Waco Thursday by Wilkerson-Hatch Funeral Home. He had been to Comfort, Texas, on a business trip and was returning to Waco when he was involved in an accident near Leon Springs, 17 miles from San Antonio. The driver of the truck received only minor injuries in the head-on collision. Mr. Herring was the son of Jim Herring and the nephew of Charlie Herring of McGregor. Lonnie was married to Mildred Herster. Survivors include his wife; his parents, Mr. and Mrs. Luther Herring of Waco; one brother, C. F. Herring of Austin; and several aunts and uncles in McGregor. McGregor Mirror: Feb 9 (1-6), 1940.

LUTHER MILTON HENSON, age 57, died at his home on the Felix Morris old place Wednesday, February 7, 1940. He was born January 26, 1883 in Mississiippi, the son of H. W. Henson and Missoura Brinkley. Burial was Wednesday afternoon in Post Oak Cemetery by Lee Undertakers. He had lived in the Oglesby area for over 35 years. Survivors include his wife; five sons; and six daughters. McGregor Mirror: Feb 9 (8-1), 1940.

FRANCES ELLIOTT was buried in Meridian Sunday. She had lived in Oglesby with her daughter, Mrs. J. E. Huddleston, for the past few years. At the time of her death, she was with her daughter, Mrs. Williams of Buckholts. Survivors include two daughters, Mrs. Williams of Buckholts and Mrs. Huddleston of Oglesby; one son, Carl Elliott of Los Angeles, California. McGregor Mirror: Feb 16 (8-2), 1940.

ALMA J. MEADOWS (MRS. JOHN M. MEADOWS), age 49, died at her home near Ocee Wednesday, February 21, 1940. She was born September 18, 1890, in Bosque County, the daughter of T. G. Foss and Bertha Marie Boarsdatter who was born in Norway. Mrs. Meadows and her husband, Johnn M. Meadows (1884-1948) made their home on the farm near Ocee for the past several years. Survivors include one daughter, Annie Mae (age 10); her mother, Mrs. T. G. Foss; two sisters, Mrs. J. S. Bekkelund and Miss Hilda Foss; two brothers, Tom and Selvern Foss, all of Crawford. Mrs. Meadows was the daughter of Swedish immigrants, T. G. Foss and Bertha Marie Boardsdatter. Funeral services were at the home of her brother, Mr. Tom Foss, near Crawford where her mother (age 83) also resides. Burial was in the Crawford Cemetery by Amsler Funeral Home. Pallbearers were Ben, Sam and Harvey Meadows, C. Glaze, Johnnie and Willie Nelson. McGregor Mirror: Feb 23 (5-5), 1940.

DR. O. O. GAIN, a Dublin physician, died in an automobile accident Tuesday. J. H. Gain, band instructor in McGrgor schools, was summoned to Dublin Tuesday on account of the death of his father. The accident occurred on a narrow bridge six miles west of DeLeon when a tank truck for the R. B. Oil Company of Stephenville and Dr. Gain's car collided. Gasoline from the loaded tanker burned the occupants of both vehicles. Dr. Gain was removed from the burned wreckage of his car two hours later. His watch had stopped at 11:05 a.m. He was on his way to Blackwell Sanitarium to perform an operation. Burial was in Dublin. McGregor Mirror: Mar 1 (1-4), 1940.

MRS. M. E. GREGERY, age 88, died Saturday in a Waco hospital. Burial was in Bosqueville Cemetery. Survivors include two daughters, Mrs. Eula Driscal and Miss Virginia Gregery of Waco; and a sister, Mrs. O. B. Gardner of McGregor. McGregor Mirror: Mar 1 (4-1), 1940.

MISS OPAL GRISSOM, age 21, died at the home of her father, W. J. Young in Crews. Mrs. J. C. Keltner of McGregor received a message last week telling of the death. Miss Grissom visited many times in the home of the Keltners and the home of Mrs. Susie West. McGregor Mirror: Mar 1 (4-5), 1940.

MR. N. H. McBRIDE, father-in-law of Mrs. Frankie McBride of McGregor, died Tuesday at him home in Bullsgap, Tennessee. McGregor Mirror: Mar 1 (4-6), 1940.

THOMAS TILGHMAN HAMBLEN, age 82, died at the home of Lon Henry of McGregor on Tuesday, February 27, 1940. He had retired from business in McGregor some nine years ago. His wife, Emily J. Hamblen, preceded him in death less than two years ago. Mr. Hamblen was born in Rogersville, Tennessee, on August 22, 1857, the son of William D. Hamblen and Rachel Lawhuer, both born in Tennessee. When first coming to Texas, he located in Marble Falls where he married Emily Josephine Luckie in 1879. In 1884 they moved to McLennan County settling first in Moody then in McGregor. Survivors include three daughters, Mrs. Rose Stebbins of Wichita, Kansas, Mrs. Olivia Brock of Abilene and Mrs. Irene Connally of McGregor; two sons, Arthur L. Hamblen of Napa County Veterans Home, California and Theodore "Ted" Hamblen of Fort Worth. Burial was in Harris Creek Cemetery beside his wife, Emily (1860-1938) by Amsler Funeral Home. McGregor Mirror: Mar 1 (5-2),

1940.

FRITZ BARTLES, age 75, died at his home in McGregor Tuesday, February 27, 1940. He was born July 7, 1865. Burial was in McGregor Cemetery by Lee Undertakers. Mr. Bartles was born July 7, 1865, a native of the United States but his parents were from Germany. He had lived in this community for over 50 years. Survivors include his wife, Louise (1877-1959); seven children, Frederick, Walter, Herman, Albert and Hardy Bartles, Mrs. Elmer Sowders and Mrs. Doris Muegge, all of McGregor. McGregor Mirror: Mar 1 (5-5), 1936.

FANNY HOY, mother of Jim Hoy of McGregor, died at age 87 at the home of her daughter Sunday, February 18, 1940. She died in Gradyville, Kentucky and was buried in the Smith Cemetery. Mrs. Hoy had made her home in McGregor at one time with her son, Jim Hoy. Survivors include one son, Jim Hoy of McGregor; and two daughters, Mrs. Perry Smith of Gradyville, Kentucky and Mrs. Elmer Keen of Columbia, Kentucky. McGregor Mirror: Mar 1 (5-6), 1940.

WILLIAM ALBERT MATTHEW, ag 48, of Waco, died in a Waco hospital Wednesday, February 27, 1940. He was born September 10, 1890, in Smith County, Texas. Lee Undertakers was in charge of the funeral with burial in the McGregor Cemetery. Survivors include four daughters, Miss Laura Lee and Maude Matthews of Waco, Mrs. Frank Buckner of Waco and Mrs. Marvin Holt of McGregor; three sons, Woodrow, W. A., Jr., and Victor Paul Matthews, all of Waco. McGregor Mirror: Mar 1 (5-6), 1940.

CHARLES VERNON CASTLEMAN, age 46, died Monday, March 4, 1940. He was born July 12, 1893, in Coryell County, Texas, the son of R. H. Castleman (born in Texas) and Olive Wood (born in Kentucky). He was thrown from a horse Thursday of last week in the White Hall Community and was taken to the home of his sister, Mrs. Ed Brittain near Osage where he never regained consciousness. Survivors include seven sisters and three brothers. Burial was in McGregor Cemetery by Scott's Funeral Home of Gatesville. McGregor Mirror: Mar 8 (1-4), 1940.

ANNIE CAVITT, age 68, died at her home in San Marcos Tuesday, March 5, 1940. Burial was in McGregor Cemetery by Amsler Funeral Home. She was born on May 12, 1874, near Kosse in Limestone County, Texas, and married Mr. S. A. "Bud" Cavitt in 1888. Survivors include four of their eight children, two boys and two girls. Mr. and Mrs. Cavitt had lived in McGregor for some thirty years. After leaving McGregor they lived in Corsicana for a time and later moved to San Marcos so that their daughter, Mrs. Louise Boulin, might continue her education there. McGregor Mirror: Mar 8 (1-6), 1940.

R. A. (WREN) WELLS died Thursday at his home in Speegleville. Burial was in Speegleville Cemetery. Mr. Wells, at one time, made McGregor his home. Survivors include his wife; one daughter, Mrs. Otto Stewart of Angleton; one son, Clydus Wells of Fort Worth; his mother, Mrs. T.

A. Wells of Hamilton; two sisters, Mrs. P. P. Stewart of McGregor, and Mrs. Len Dalton of Hamilton; two brothers, Tom Wells of Lockney and T. E. Wells of McGregor. McGregor Mirror: Mar 8 (5-6), 1940.

CARL WIESE, age 79, died at his home near McGregor March 15, 1940. He was born in Whedem, Germany on February 7, 1861, coming to America at age 9 settling in Washington County, Texas. Carl was the son of Carl Wiese and Wilhelmine Meyer. In 1885 he married Miss Louise Wehmeyer in Prairie Hill. The family moved to Coryell County before settling in McGregor in 1915. Survivors include his wife, Louise (1865-1951); three sons, William Wiese of Tivoli, Texas, Fred and Ben of McGregor; two daughters, Mrs. Ed Weiss of McGregor and Miss Anna Wiese, at home with her mother. Burial was in McGregor Cemetery by Amsler Funeral Home. McGrgor Mirror: Mar 22 (5-3), 1940.

MRS. J. L. HAWKINS, age 67, died March 27, 1940. She was born in Florence, Williamson County, Texas, January 14, 1873, the daughter of G. W. Wright and _____ Connally, both born in Alabama. Burial was in Old Perry Cemetery near Moody. Survivors include her husband; two sons, Lum C. Hawkins of McGregor and Ernest R. Hawkins of McGregor; two brothers, George Wright and Elam Wright; two sisters, Mrs. Mandie Butler and Mrs. Ava Williams of Mullin, Texas.

JOHN EARL FARROW, age 19, of Itasca, died of electric burns Saturday. He had fallen into live wires while working on a rural electrical administration project between Lorena and Bruceville. Burial was in Itasca Cemetery. Survivors include his parents, Mr. and Mrs. E. D. Farrow; a brother Billy Jean Farrow; three aunts, Mrs. Donna McMahon of Itasca, Mrs. Julia Patterson of Memphis, Tennessee, and Mrs. Will of North Carolina. Mr. Farrow was making his home in McGregor at the time of the accident. He was employed by McLennan County Electric Cooperative and had been for around a month. McGregor Mirror: Apr 5 (5-3), 1940.

R. DEAN WHITE, age 28, of Leon Junction was killed Tuesday when the truck he was driving went to the bottom of the Leon River when a bridge gave away. Scott Funeral Home of Gatesville was in charge of funeral arrangements. He was returning from west Texas with a load of seed when the bridge gave way. His body was discovered early Wednesday morning by a bread truck driver who was making his morning rounds. McGregor Mirror: Apr 19 (1-4), 1940.

HERSHEL HUGH GOFF, age 52, died at his home Thursday, April 18, 1940. He was born October 15, 1887 in Pendleton, Texas, the son of L. P. Goff and Sarah Brim. Survivors include his wife, Olivia; two sons, L. P. Goff and Cecil Goff; three sisters, Mrs. Jack Malott of Meridian, Mrs. Bettie Manning of Brownwood and Mrs. G. H. Cook of California; one brother, Will Goff of Louisiana. Burial was in Moody Cemetery by Amsler Funeral Home. McGregor Mirror: Apr 26 (4-2), 1940.

JOSEPHINE BUBERT, age 90, died at her home in McGregor Friday, April 19, 1940. She was born June 21, 1849, at Frelsburg, Colorado County, Texas, the daughter of Mr. and Mrs. Frank Henneke. In 1873 she married Henry H. Bubert at Frelsburg and five children were born to them. Two of those died in childhood. In 1888 the family moved to Taylor, Texas, and after twelve years settled in McGregor. Mrs. Bubert's husband died in 1906 but she continued to make her home here with her son Leo Bubert. Survivors include three children, Leo Bubert of McGregor, Henry Bubert of Hamilton and Mrs. Laura Jechke of Bartlett; two brothers, Frank Henneke and Conrad Henneke of New Ulm, Texas; two sisters, Mrs. Bertha Hewitt of San Antonio and Mrs. Eleanora Stelea of East Bernard, Texas. Burial was in the McGregor Cemetery by Amsler Fuenral Home. Pallbearers were six grandsons, Mac, Elmer, Henry and Hubert Bubert, Willie Jechke and Walter Jechke. McGregor Mirror: Apr 26 (5-3), 1940.

HENRIETTA NIEMEIER, wife of C. Niemeier, died at the family home near Coryell City, Tuesday, April 23, 1940. She was born in Germany June 16, 1859 but for 48 years had lived in Coryell City, Texas. Henrietta was the daughter of Nagel Niemeier and Miss Berminghouse. Survivors include her aging husband, Carl Niemeier; four sons, Will of McGregor, Charlie of Crawford and Ernest and Henry of Coryell City; five daughters, Mrs. Henry Gohlke, Mrs. Fred Haferkamp, Mrs. Ella Loesch, Mrs. Bill Gohlke and Miss Minnie Niemeier. Burial was in Coryell City Lutheran Cemetery by Amsler Funeral Home. Pallbearers were Albert, Willis and Herbert Niemeier, Walter and Raymond Gohlke and Edgar Haferkamp. McGregor Mirror: Apr 26 (5-4), 1940.

FREDERICK FOOTE, SR. April 23, 1940 at Turnersville. He was age 88 and had lived in Coryell County, Texas, for 77 years. He married Mary Ann Young December 31, 1885, who died June 18, 1936. F. M. Lyon and R. H. Alexander of McGregor attended the funeral in Turnersville Wednesday of last week. Burial was in Turnersville Cemetery beside his wife. McGregor Mirror: Apr 26 (4-6), 1940.

W. S. HANOVER died at Wheelock last Thursday, April 27, 1940. W. S. was born November 25, 1888. He was the father of W. V. Hanover of McGregor. Mr. and Mrs. W. V. Hanover and daughters, Miss Anne Hanover and Mrs. Henry Smith and son Volney of McGregor attended the funeral. Others attending the funeral were J. F. Cavitt and John Montgomery. McGregor Mirror: Apr 26 (4-6), 1940.

OSCAR CARL HESSE died at his home Saturday, April 27, 1940. He was born near Aquilla, in Hill County, Texas, November 25, 1888, and lived there until 1911 when he moved to the McGregor community. Oscar was the son of E. W. Hesse and Ernestine Maunger, both born in Germany. In 1911 he was married to Miss Emile Lorenz. Survivors include his wife, Emma Hesse; five daughters, Mr. H. C. Schwettmann, Ernestine, Gertrude, Elsie and Myrtle Hesse; one son, Richard Hesse, all of McGregor; one brother, Max R. Hesse of West. Burial was in McGregor

Cemetery by Amsler Funeral Home. McGregor Mirror: Apr 26 (5-4), 1940.

EMIE KELM died May 2, 1940, at age 75. He was born in Germany on October 2, 1964, to Martine Kelm and Wilhima Schultz. Informant was Otto Kelm, a nephew. Survivors include a nephew, Otto Kelm; a sister, Mrs. Adolph Hueske; a sister-in-law, Mrs. Emma Kelm; nieces, Artelia Zacharias, Neta, Erna and Frieda Hueske. Emie Kelm was a single man at the time of his death. Burial was in McGregor Cemetery by Amsler Funeral Home. Pallbearers were nephews, Alfred, Walter and Otto Kelm, Julius Zacharias, Albert and Richard Kelm. Amsler Funeral Home, Book #3.

CHARLES JEFFERSON BOTKINS died at his home in the Flat community Monday, May 10, 1940. Burial was in Hubbard Cemetery near Flat by Lee Undertakers. Mr. Botkins, age 66, was born in Illinois but had lived in Flat for 30 years. Survivors include his wife; two sons, B. B. and P. J. Botkins, both of Flat; five daughters, Miss Jessie Bell Botkins, Mrs. Ollie Ingram of Flat, Mrs. Bessie Thompson and Mrs. Olene Copeland of Grove, and Mrs. Rubye Smith of Killeen. McGregor Mirror: May 10 (4-2), 1940.

ANNA MARIE LEUBNER, mother of Mrs. B. F. Dodson of McGregor, died in Dallas Friday at age 75. Burial was in Dallas. Mr. and Mrs. Dodson and daughters, Mrs. Price Cook and Miss Ramona Dodson, attended the funeral. Mrs. Leubner was the wife of the late F. W. Leubner. Survivors include Mrs. Dodson; four other daughters including Mrs. W. M. Cook of Boyd (formerlay of McGregor); three sons; one brother and three sisters. McGregor Mirror: May 17 (4-3), 1940.

J. E. CLAYBROOK, father of Mrs. T. N. Winston, died at his home in Steiner Sunday. Burial was in Steiner Monday afternoon. McGregor Mirror: May 17 (5-4), 1940.

MRS. O. F. HERING, age 73. died at her home in Mart Tuesday, May 21, 1940. Mrs. Hering formerly lived in McGregor. Survivors include her husband; six daughters, Mrs. Will Schroeder and Mrs. Albert Witte of McGregor, Mrs. R. L. Franke of Austin, Mrs. O. L. Barnhart of Fort Worth, Mrs. Knox Kelly of Gatesville and Miss Pearl Hering of Mart; five sons, Leo Hering of Riesel, Otto of Waco, Ben of Gatesville, Henry and Edd of Ben Hur; three brothers and three sisters. Others attending the funeral from McGregor were Mr. and Mrs. Fred Witte and daughter, Mrs. Hoyle Hackney, Mr. and Mrs. Rudolph Scheele, Mr. and Mrs. Fred Witte, Mrs. Albert Hering, Mrs. John Scruggs, Mr. and Mrs. Charlie Schroeder, Mrs. William Schroeder, Mr. and Mrs. Fred Vahrenkamp, Mr. and Mrs. E. R. Luedtke, Mrs. Willie Witte, Mrs. Louis Bishop, Mrs. Paul W. Stewart and daughter, Katherine. McGregor Mirror: May 31 (6-3), 1940.

MRS. ADDIE BAKER, age 88, died at the home of her daughter, Miss Helen Baker, in Temple last Friday, May 24, 1940. She had lived in Temple for the pase 26 years and would have been 89 years old on June 11 of this year. Burial was in Eddy Cemetery. Survivors include the son, W. S. Baker of McGregor and four other children, Mrs. J. C. Maxwell of Waco, Mrs. J. O. Hagler of Buckholts, Wellor Baker and Miss Helen Baker of Temple. McGregor Mirror: May 31 (7-1), 1940.

AUDRE DIAZ died June 2, 1940, in McGregor on the E. R. Luedtke farm. Informants were Ben and George Diaz. Burial was in McGregor Cemetery. Asmler Funeral Home, Book #3.

EVERETT E. BOULDIN, brother of Mr. E. E. Bouldin of McGregor, was buried in Pendleton Cemetery Thursday. He died in a Temple hospital after a brief illness. McGregor Mirror: June 7 (4-3), 1940.

J. R. CHILCOAT, brother-in-law of Mrs. Bloomer Ramsey of Comanche Springs, was buried in Longview recently. He formerly lived in Comanche Springs but had been a resident of Dallas for a number of years. McGregor Mirror: Jun 7 (5-4), 1940.

JOSEPH H. GOODE, age 67, died in a Waco hospital Tuesday. He was the son of Robert Goode. Burial was in Moody Cemetery by Lee Undertakers. Survivors include his wife; two daughters, Mrs. Leola Stephens of Tyler and Mrs. Pearl Newman of McGregor. McGregor Mirror: Jun 14 (1-5), 1940.

NAOMI C. GARRET (Mrs. M. M. Garret) of Crawford died Monday, June 10, 1940, at age 85. Naomi was born December 10, 1855, the daughter of J. M. Ramsey. She had made her home recently with her daughter, Mrs. Ida McCollum, of Crawford. Survivors include one daughter, Ida McCollum of Crawford; four sons, D. M. Garret of Crawford, G. W. Garret of Winnsboro, C. M. Garret of Fort Worth and M. C. Garret of Houston. Burial was in The Crawford Cemetery beside Manning M. Garret (1852-1923) by Amsler Funeral Home. McGregor Mirror: Jun 14 (5-6), 1940.

MARY "MOLLIE" ELIZABETH BICKEL died at the home of her daughter, Mrs. Homer Ruff, Thursday, June 20, 1940. She was born in Karnes County, Texas, September 2, 1865, the daughter of Gideon Pace and _____ Mauhler. but moved to McLennan County at age 6. Survivors include her husband, John Frederick Bickel (1859-1944); five children, F. E. Bickel, Mrs. H. W. Ruff and Miss Kate Bickel of McGregor, Mrs. O. G. Horne and Mrs. Wendell Bray of Waco; two brothers, Mr. W. D. Pace of McGregor and Mr. Charles Zipper of Waco. Burial was in Harris Creek Cemetery by Amsler Funeral Home. McGregor Mirror: Jun 21 (1-4), 1940.

CLARENCE C. WHITTENBURG, age 49, died at Legion, Texas, at Veteran's Hospital Tuesday, June 18, 1940. He was well known in McGregor, having moved here from Waco 9 years ago. He was born in San Antonio June 3, 1891, but spent most of his life in Coryell City. In 1916 he married Lenora Murphy and to this marriage were born two daughters, Waldean and Mary Alice. Mr. Whittenburg enlisted in the army in 1917, saw service in France with the A. E. F. with Battery B, 132nd Field Artillery, 36th Division. Survivors include his wife; two daughters; his father, Mr. Louis Whittenburg; two brothers, Willie of Abilene and Earl of Leon Junction; three sisters, Mrs. Otis Penny of Flat, Mrs. Mildred Price of Gatesville, Mrs. Vera Coahogon of Leon Junction; one sister-in-law, Mrs. Frank Whittenburg of Leon Junction. Burial was in McGregor Cemetery by Amsler Funeral Home. McGregor Mirror: Jun 21 (4-1), 1940.

WILLIAM SAMUAL PATTON, age 80, died Monday, June 24, 1940, at the home of his son in Crawford. He was born in Watertown, Tennessee February 19, 1860, the son of E. and Malinda Patton but had lived most of his life in Coryell County near Osage. Mr. Patton's wife, Martha J. (1863-1935) preceded him in death some 5 years ago and his is survived by three sons, W. E. Patton and E. R. Patton of Crawford, and Arp Patton of Willow, Oklahoma. Burial was in Osage Cemetery by Amsler Funeral Home. McGregor Mirror: Jun 28 (5-3), 1940.

FRED W. KALSCHEUER, age 21, died in a Waco hospital Saturday, June 29, 1940. He was born February 27, 1919, the son of Fred W. Kalscheuer and Hattie Rachuy. Burial was in McGregor Cemetery by Lee Undertakers. He was well known in McGregor where he attended high school. After graduation in 1937, he attended Baylor University for one year until ill health prevented him from continuing. Survivors include his mother and foster father, Mr. and Mrs. Albert M. Stolz of McGregor; a brother, Hans Kalscheuer of Fort Worth. McGregor Mirror: Jul 5 (1-1), 1940.

MRS. MORGAN BAKER of Waxahachie died Monday of injuries suffered in an automobile accident near Waco that occurred Thursday of last week. Rev. and Mrs. Baker were returning home after a visit with their son, Professor Paul Baker of Baylor drama department in Waco. Rev. Baker received only minor bruises. Burial was in Waxahachie. Rev. Baker was known in McGregor, having been pastor of the Comanche Springs and McGregor Presbyterian churches. McGregor Mirror: Jul 5 (4-4), 1940.

TOM NEWTON ALEXANDER, 64, died in a Temple hospital Tuesday, July 9, 1940. Tom was born August 25, 1875, the son on John Newton Alexander and Mary Patterson. He was a brother of Mrs. Morgan Fegette and Mrs. Ed Anderson of McGregor. Funeral services were conducted at the home of his brother, John M. Alexander, in Moody with burial in Naylor Cemetery by Lee Undertakers. Mr. Alexander was a native of Moody, having lived there all his life. Survivors include his four brothers, Judge James P. Alexander of Waco, R. H. Alexander of Oglesby, Paul Alexander of Moody, F. W. Alexander of Albany; five sisters, Mrs. J. W. Baggett of Waco, Mrs. J. W. McGregor of Moody, Mrs. Ruth Gipe of Weslaco and two sisters here; three sons, Clifford, Jack and Weldon, all of Moody; two daughters, Miss Mary Alexander and Mrs. Bill Permenter of Moody. McGregor Mirror: Jul 5 (5-6), 1940.

ROY EARL WEISS, age 11, was killed in an automobile accident in Lancaster, Texas, July 28, 1940. He was born February 11, 1929, the son of Ernest Weiss and Olge Hoppe. Roy was asleep in the back seat of the auto when the accident happened. He was an enthusiastic horseman and had participated in the recent Rodeo in McGregor. He is survived by his parents; and one sister, Joyce Weiss, age 6. Burial was in McGregor Cemetery by Amsler Funeral Home. McGregor Mirror: Aug 3 (1-2), 1940.

MARTHA RAGSDALE, age 83, died at the home of her daughter, Mrs. H. M. Handley of McGregor, Thursday, July 11, 1940. Burial was in Clifton by Connally Funeral Home of Waco. Mrs. Ragsdale, who had been residing in McGregor with her daughter for the past 5 years, was born June 29, 1857 in Bosque County, Texas. On April 5, 1879, she married John Ragsdale who preceded her in death. She is survived by four daughters, Mrs. H. M. Handley of McGregor, Mrs. L. L. Cutbirth of Abilene, Mrs. G. C. Richards of Corsicana and Mrs. J. G. Bekken of Waco; one son, W. T. Ragsdale of Clifton. McGregor Mirror: Jul 19 (7-3), 1940.

CARLTON A. DIBBLE of Madison, Conn. died on July 8, 1940, at age 85. Burial was in West Cemetery in Madison by Swan Funeral Home. Mr. Dibble was born May 26, in Westbrook, Conn. but came to Texas at age 12. He had lived in and around McGregor for 40 years engaging in railroad and carpenter work. In 1907 he left McGregor to return to Madison, Conn. Survivors include his wife, Mrs. Addelia Dibble of Madison; a daughter, Mrs. W. R. Cole of McGregor; a son, Sam B. Dibble of Terre Haute, Ind.; a sister, Mrs. Addie Everett of Huntington, West Virginia. McGregor Mirror: Aug 3 (4-2), 1940.

PAUL ELEMIAL FARMER, age 33, died in a Waco hospital Thursday, August 1, 1940. He was born March 25, 1907, the son of Stephen Douglas Farmer and Sarah Creekmore. Burial was in Crawford Cemetery by Lee Undertakers. He was a single man at the time of his death. Survivors include six sisters, Flora Lee, Lizzie Jeter, Jessie Mote and Velma Merritt, all of Waco, and Eve Brown and Lucy Dawson, both of McGregor; one brother, Henry Farmer of Waco. McGregor Mirror: Aug 3 (4-3), 1940.

ARNOLD E. HENAGER, age 25, died Monday, July 29, 1940. He was born November 7, 1914, the son of Guy M. Henager and Sybil Springfield. Arnold was accidently run over by a truck while engaged in his regular duties on road work. He was employed at Stinnett, Texas, by Cage Brothers road contractors where he had been employed for 5 years. Survivors include his wife; one child, Lawanda (age 5); his parents; four sisters, Mrs. Paul Clendenen, Mrs. Woodward Oswald, Dorothy and Ruth Henegar; one brother, Wayne Henegar. His body arrived by train and burial was in Harris Creek Cemetery by Amsler Funeral Home. Pallbearers were all brother-in-laws, Woodrow Oswald, Paul Clendenen, Cody Byford, Leroy Terry, Ted Patterson and Herman Fewell. McGregor Mirror: Aug 3 (4-5), 1940.

MRS. BETTY GOODE died in Hamilton Tuesday, June 12, 1940. She lived in Moody but had been visiting in Hamilton at the time of her death. Burial was in Moody Cemetery by Lee Undertakers. Survivors include her two daughters, Mrs. Leola Stephens of Tyler and Mrs. Pearl Newman of McGregor. McGregor Mirror: Aug 3 (8-3), 1940.

IDA FORD OGLESBY, 62, died Tuesday, July 30, 1940, in Waco. She was born January 30, 1878. Burial was in Crawford Cemetery beside her husband, Frank Oglesby (1870-1920), by Lee Undertakers. Mrs. Oglesby had lived in McGregor for many years before moving to Waco some ten years ago. Survivors include there daughters, Mrs. L. D. Skelton of Waco, Mrs. Ada England and Mrs. Charles Walters of McGregor; one son, Ford Oglesby of Shreveport, Louisiana. Pallbearers were eight grandsons, C. F. Blake, Jiggs Blake, Sonny Walters, Paul Skelton, Jim Skelton, Noll Sloan, Bill McMullen and J. E. Easter. McGregor Mirror: Aug 3 (8-4), 1940.

P. E. JONES, resident of Oglesby for 37 years, died August 1, 1940, in a Waco hospital at age 77. Mr. Jones, a native of North Carolina, was born October 15, 1862. Survivers include three daughters, Miss Eulalia Jones of Oglesby, Mrs. Robert Stiles of Wheeler, Mrs. A. E. McGinty of Liberty; two brothers, O. F. Jones, Sr. and D. W. Jones of Oglesby; one sister, Mrs. J. J. Jones of Fairy. Burial was in Post Oak Cemetery beside his wife, Martha Jones, who died December 7, 1934. McGregor Mirror: Aug 9 (8-1), 1940.

HENRY F. WIESE, 73, died Tuesday, August 20, 1940, at his home near Ocee. Burial was in McGregor Cemetery. Survivors include his wife, Hulda Wiese (1871-1964); four daughters, Mrs. Hulda Goessler of Washington, Texas, Mrs. Malinda Vonruth of Moody, Mrs. Addler of Crawford and Lydia Smith of Gatesville; seven sons, Fred Wiese of Bruceville, Otto Wiese and Will Wiese of Moody, Henry Wiese of Washington, Texas, Carl Wiese of Brenham, Robert Wiese of McGregor and Walter Wiese of Crawford. McGregor Mirror: Aug 23 (4-2), 1940.

HENRY BROCKERMEYER, 70, died at his home near McGregor on August 16, 1940. He was born in Germany, the son of William H. Brockermeyer. Since coming to McGregor from Washington County, Texas, several years ago, Mr. Brockermeier and his family farmed in this area. Survivors include his wife, Minnie; children, Mrs. Sophie Mutscher of Giddings, Henry Brockermeyer of Washington, Texas, Robert and Carl of Brenham, Lillie, Reinhardt, Albert and Fred Brockermeyer of McGregor. Burial was in the McGregor Cemetery by Amsler Funeral Home. McGregor Mirror: Aug 23 (4-5), 1940.

JOHN C. REYNOLDS, 72, president of the First National Bank at Moody, died in Long Beach, California, Wednesday, where he was spending his vacation. He was born in Moody and had been connected with the bank for 42 year, serving as president for the last 32 years. Survivors include two daughters, Mrs. Ford Bingham of Lubbock and Mrs. Michael Maryosip of Temple; two half-sisters, Mrs. C. O. Jones and Mrs. Jennie Cates of Moody; two half-brothers, Will Neely of Dallas and Robert Neely of San Angelo. Burial was near Moody. McGregor Mirror: Aug 30 (1-3), 1940.

MRS. PAUL BELL died in Bastrop Monday. Mrs. Bell and her husband had served as Mexican missonaries for the past 27 years. Mrs. T. H. Jenkins, Mrs. B. J. Allen, Mrs. Lee Williams, Mrs. Lonnie Webb, Mrs. Stanley Cook and Mrs. Butler, all of McGregor, attended the funeral of Mrs. Jenkin's aunt in Bastrop. McGregor Mirror: Aug 30 (5-1), 1940.

ORVIL GEE was killed in a gas explosion last week. Mrs. W. R. Cavitt, Mr. and Mrs. Jack Huddleston, Mr. and Mrs. Jack White were called to Wichita Falls last week-end to attend the funeral. Mr. Gee was a brother-in-law of Mrs. Huddleston and Mr. White of Oglesby. McGregor Mirror: Aug 30 (8-5), 1940.

ERVIN SLESS, age 25, died in a Waco hospital this morning. He was born In 1914 in Prairie Chapel community and had for many years been a member of the Coryell City Lutheran Church. Survivors include his parents, Mr. and Mrs. George Sless of Prairie Chapel; four sisters, Mrs. James Bullington and Mrs. Herbert Mattiza of Hamilton, Mrs. Edwin Schrader of Coryell City and Mrs. Fred Kasting of Roswell, New Mexico; several uncles and aunts; and his grandparents. Burial was in the Lutheran Cemetery in Coryell City by Amsler Funeral Home. McGregor Mirror: Sept 6 (1-3), 1940.

W. N. CLAWSON, 69, a native of the Flat community died Monday. He had eaten a hardy dinner, complained of feeling ill and died a short time later. Survivors include his wife; four daughters, Mrs. W. C. Colvin of Rockdale, Mrs. W. E. Crow of Olney, Mrs. Paul Blanchard of Flat and Mrs. Bruce Kearney of Leon Junction; four sons, Leonard and Edwin Clawson of Flat, Ernest and Ivy Clawson of Dallas. Burial was in Flint Creek Cemetery by Lee Undertakers. McGregor Mirror: Sept 6 (1-6), 1940.

MRS. TOM CROSS, 63, of Dallas, died Wednesday at her home. Mrs. Cross and her family had made McGregor their home until about 10 years ago, when she moved to Dallas. Survivors include three daughters, Mrs. E C. McEver of Waco, Mrs. R. M. Toler of Amarillo and Miss Tommie Cross of Dallas; two sons, James and Lloyd Cross of Waco; nine grandchildren; three sisters, Mrs. Ola Cox of Abilene, Mrs. Joe Cox of Mercury and Mrs. Billie Cox of McGreor. Burial was in Restland Memorial Park in Dallas by Guardian Funeral Chapel. McGregor Mirror: Sep 6 (5-4), 1940.

FANNIE HARLAN RUSSELL, 67, died Friday, September 11, 1940. Burial was in Crawford Cemetery by Lee Undertakers. Survivors include her husband, Robert R. Russell (1869-1957); three daughters, Mrs. Mack

Plemons of Crawford, Mrs. W. R. White of Oklahoma City and Mrs. O. B. Plemons of McGregor; one son, W. G. Russell of McGregor; several brothers and sisters including Mrs. Newt Mobley of McGregor. Mrs. Russell had lived in the McGregor community for 44 years. McGregor Mirror: Sep 13 (4-3), 1940.

GEORGE COFFELT died Friday of last week at his near Walnut Spring. Burial was in Walnut Spring Cemetery. Mr. Coffelt and his brothers once were leading merchants in McGregor both in the dry goods and grocery business. Mr. Coffelt left McGregor some 20 years ago, moving to Walnut Springs. Survivors include his immediate family; brothers, L. Coffelt of Waco and Robert of California, as well as, several sisters. McGregor Mirror: Sep 13 (4-6), 1940.

J. W. RICHARDSON, Cotton Belt Agent in Oglesby, died Saturday of a heart attack. He had just left the Post Office and was in front of the D. W. Jones store when stricken. Burial was in Kerns. Survivors include his wife; one son and; one daughter, all of Austin. McGregor Mirror: Sep 13 (8-3), 1940.

MRS. JIM JOHNSON died near Buffalo Sunday. Mr. and Mrs. Park Hambrick and son, Ray, Mrs. Talley Nunley and Mrs. Dwain Eupham and little daughter, Billie Helen, attended the funeral of their aunt in Buffalo. McGregor Mirror: Sep 13 (8-6), 1940.

W. J. EVERS, 68, died in an Austin hospital Tuesday following a stroke of paralysis a week before. Mr. Evers had interest in the Evers Drug Store in McGregor before moving to Brady 19 years ago. For the past 16 years he has made his home in Austin. Funeral services were at the University Presbyterian Church in Austin with burial in the Oakwood Cemetery. Survivors include his wife; two sons, Courtney and John Lawrence Evers, both of Austin; two daughters, Mrs. F. Birch Wallace of San Antonio and Miss Christine Evers of Baltimore, Maryland; three sisters, Mrs. C. Kowierschke of Castell, Mrs. W. L. McKelvey of Houston, Mrs. George Schuessler of Llano; three brothers, F. J. Evers of Castell, H. P. Evers of Berady and M. H. Evers of McGregor. McGergor Mirror: Sep 20 (5-3), 1940.

JERRY M. SPARKS, 49, died in McGregor last Friday of a heart attack. Burial was in Old Perry cemetery near Moody. Survivors include his wife; one son, Clarence Sparks; three sisters, Mrs. Lora Smith of Waco, Mrs. Rene Witt of Speegleville and Mrs. Artie Smith of Victoria; a brother, Amos Sparks of Victoria. McGregor Mirror: Sep 20 (5-4), 1940.

GEORGE F. ASH, 63, died Wednesday, September 25, 1940. He was born in Georgia February 29, 1877, the son of John Ash and Margaret McEver. Burial was in McGregor Cemetery by Lee Undertakers. Mr. Ash had lived in Mcgregor for 53 years. Survivors include his wife. Effie (1889-1941); two duaghters, Mrs. T. K. Bond of McGregor, and Mrs. H. P.

Robinson of San Antonio; two sons, Joe Ash and Buster Ash of McGregor; two sisters, Mrs. D. P. Davenport of Stanford, Texas and Mrs. J. J. Frady of McGregor; three brothers, John and Jim Ash of McGregor, and Mat Ash of Tyler. McGregor Mirror: Sep 27 (5-2), 1940.

JOE ED SIMS of Whitney died last Sunday. Four years ago he married Helen Harper of McGregor. Mr. Sims, age 30, was engaged in the grocery business and farming-ranching. Survivors include his wife, Helen; a young daughter; and an infant son; one brother, Harry Sims; and his mother, Mrs. J. C. Sims, all of Whitney. Burial was in Bethel Cemetery of Whitney by Marshall & Marshall Funeral Home of Hillsboro. McGregor residents attending the funeral were his mother, Mrs. L. Harper, the brother and three sisters of Mrs. Sims, Mr. and Mrs. Hoyle Hackney, Mr. and Mrs. Walter Amsler, Mrs. Robert Williams, Martha Williams, Mrs. Tom Freeman and John R. Grantham, Jr. McGregor Mirror: Oct 4 (1-2), 1940.

DONNIE IDELLA LEAMONS, age 19, died September 26, 1940, at the family home near McGregor. She was born in McGregor, February 23, 1921, the daughter of Oliver and Stella Hamilton. Survivors include her husband, Mr. Shearman Leamons; a young daughter, Nancy Jo Leamons; two brothers, W. J. and Jean Hamilton of McGregor; two sisters, Mrs. Virginia Potter of Hearne, Texas, and Miss Opal Hamilton of McGregor; her parents, Mr. and Mrs. Oliver Hamilton of McGregor. Burial was in McGregor Cemetery by Amsler Funeral Home. McGregor Mirror: Oct 4 (4-5), 1940.

JOHN WILLIAM STAPP died at Legion, Texas, October 12, 1940. Burial was in Oglesby in Post Oak Cemtery by Lee Undertakers. Mr. Stpp was born near McGregor in 1893 and for the past 20 years had been a citizen of Oglesby. He served in the 143rd Field Artillery, 90th Division in World War I, and was in the army of occupation in Germany after the war. In 1929, he married Miss Hazel Howland of Paul Valley, Oklahoma. Survivors include his wife; and several brothers and sisters. Oglesby News mentioned the following relatives: Mrs. John W. Stapp, F. M. Stapp of Clifton, Mr. and Mrs. Ed Stapp of Clifton, Mrs. Anna Stapp of Clifton, Mr. and Mrs. A. D. Binns of Moody, Mr. and Mrs. Frank Simmons of Oglesby, Mr. and Mrs. G. Stapp of Pauls Valley, Oklahoma, Mr. and Mrs. Jim Stapp of Waco, and Mr. and Mrs. Darrel High of Sweetwater. McGregor Mirror: Oct 18 (8-6)\Oct 25 (8-2), 1940.

INEZ WEST, 49, of Gatesville met instant death in an automobile accident four miles east of McGregor. She was accompanying her brother, A. B. Gage, to Waco, where he lived. Burial was in Gatesville where she had lived for the past 28 years. Survivors include her mother, Mrs. G. W. S. Gage of Gatesville; one daughter, Mrs. Neal Chapman of Carlsbad, New Mexico; four sisters, Mrs. R. E. West of Gatesville, Mrs. Allen Weaver of Los Angeles, Mrs. David Sakuth of Los Angeles, and Mrs. Ray Pearson of Merysville, California; six brothers. McGregor Mirror: Oct 25 (1-5), 1940.

DEATHS IN CENTRAL TEXAS, VOL. II

WILLIAM RICE HARRISON, 80, died at his home in Crawford, Thursday. Burial was in Crawford Cemetery beside his wife, Darthulia, who died in 1938. Amsler Funeral Home was in charge of burial. Mr. Harrison had lived near Crawford for 50 years, coming there from Tennessee. Survivors include five sons, Will of Frost, Clarence of Boyd, Homer, Horace, Harlan of Crawford; three daughters, Mrs. Frank Merritt and Mrs. Ben Nail of Crawford, and Mrs. Alice Elliott of Waco. McGregor Mirror: Oct 25 (4-6), 1940.

OSCAR DAVIS, brother of Mrs. J. W. Louterback of McGregor, received word of the death of her brother Monday. He died at his home in Bremerton, Washington, on October 27, 1940. Burial was in Bremerton, Washington. The Davis family left McGregor 10 years ago, but while they resided here, Mrs. Davis operated a beauty shop. Survivors include his wife; three sons of Bremerton; sister, Mrs. J. W. Loutherback of McGregor; four brothers, John Davis of Plainview, Claude Davis of Childress, Charlie Davis of Le Leon and Cecil Fleet of Oklahoma City. McGregor Mirror: Nov 8 (8-8), 1940.

T. S. SALES, son-in-law of Mrs. O. B. Gardner of McGregor, died Saturday in a Littlefield hospital. Burial was in Littlefield cemetery with Masonic services. Mr. Sales a former resident of McGregor married Mary Gardner in April of 1913 and they lived here until 1925 when they moved to Littltfield. While a resident of Littlefield, Mr. Sales served as Mayor, President of the Rotary Club and President of the Chamber of Commerce. For the past 2 years he had been operating a portable roller rink, traveling over West Texas. Survivors include his wife; two sisters, Mrs. J. C. McDaniel and Mrs. T. C. Coates of Waco; two brothers, Gordon Sales of Waco and R. W. Sales of McGregor. McGregor Mirror: Nov 15 (1-2), 1940.

RUFUS RICHARD ROE, 82, died Wednesday, November 5, 1940, in a Waco hospital. Mr. Roe had lived in the Coryell County area for 65 years. Survivors include his wife; and J. W. Roe, H. C. Roe of Oglesby, A. L. Roe of McGregor, S. M. Roe of Crawford, R. Q. Roe of Gatesville, Mrs. Annie Boyd of Gatesville, Mr. Les Mosely and Mrs. J. W. Clark of Waco, and Mrs. C. A. Vandiver of Oglesby. Pallbearers were six grandsons: J. W. Clark, Wayne Boyd, Edward Roe, George Vandiver, Claud Boyd and Ralph Roe. Burial was in Osage Cemetery beside Della E. Roe (1869-1932) by Lee Undertakers. McGregor Mirror: Nov 15 (8-4), 1940.

MARY JANE GLAZIER, 87, died November 18, 1940, at the home of her daughter, Mrs. Doshey Strickland, in Crawford. She was born August 31, 1853, in Alabama but had lived in Coryell County and Crawford for many years. Burial was in Crawford Cemetery beside J. A. Glazier (1848-1928) by Amsler Funeral Home. Survivors include three daughters, Mrs. Doshey Strickland of Crawford, Mrs. Dovey Noland of Hico and Mrs. Maggie Allison of Dallas; one sister, Mrs. Annie Edmondson of Quanah. Pallbearers were grandsons. McGreor Mirror: Nov 22 (8-2), 1940.

W. J. HIGH, 66, died at his home in Moody, Monday. Burial was in Old Perry Cemetery by Denny and Witt Funeral Home. Survivors include his wife; a son, Darrell of Caldwell; a daughter, Mrs. W. A. Moores of Lafayette, Louisiana; five brothers, B. F. of McGregor, Rev. J. F. High of Elmdorff, T. J. High of Walters, Oklahoma, J. L. High of Moody and W. L. High of Carlsbad, New Mexico; three sisters, T. E. Wells and Mrs. Chester Blanton of McGregor and Mrs. C. L. Larkins of Findlay, Oklahoma. McGregor Mirror: Dec 13 (4-1), 1940.

WILLIAM SCHMALRIEDE, age 75, died at his home near McGregor Saturday, December 7, 1940. He was born in Germany February 10, 1865, the son of Fred Schmalriede and Henrietta Loesch, and came to America at age 17, settling in Cincinitti, Ohio. Two years later he moved to Washington County, Texas, then in 1893, he settled in McGregor. He married Emma Springmann in Burlin, Texas, in 1896. Survivors include his wife; three sisters, Mrs. W. M. Kokemor of Brenham, Mrs. Louise Headt of Needville and Mrs. Carolyn Koester of Houston; three sons, Ted, Walter and Ben of McGregor; four daughters, Mrs. Henry Wiethorn, Mrs. Alvin Muegge, Mrs. E. A. Scott, all of McGregor, and Mrs. Willie Horn of Bryan. One son, Eldon, preceded him in death in 1922. Burial was in McGregor Cemetery by Amsler Funeral Home. McGregor Mirror: Dec 13 (5-4), 1940.

J. C. MORRIS, age 73, died at his home in Bosque County Friday, December 13, 1940. He was born in Tennessee November 28, 1867, the son of John Morris and Azoline Allen, both born in Tennessee, but moved to Whitehall near Waco in 1900. Since last February Mr. Morris had been living in Bosque County near Valley Mills. Burial was in McGregor Cemetery by Amsler Funeral Home beside his wife who preceded him in death on August 19, 1933. Survivors include one sister, Mrs. John Seleman of Waco; two brothers, Jack Morris of Houston and Jerry Morris of Oakland, California; one son, Miller Morris and one grandson, Miller Morris, Jr. of Waco. McGregor Mirror: Dec 20 (4-6), 1940.

CHAPTER 7

FREDERICK WILLIAM BISCHOFF died at his home near McGregor December 31, 1940. He was born in Germany in 1862, and came to America at age 7, settling in Brenham. After he married the family moved to Bartlett, then Copperas Cove, Salado and in 1914 to McGregor. He was preceded in death by four infant children, one daughter, Mrs. Ernest Wiese in 1918 and his wife in 1935. Survivors include one daughter, Mrs. Ben Wiese and four sons, Fred, Herman, Louis and Edwin (all of McGregor) and one sister, Mrs. Annie Fickle of Waco. Burial was in Buckhorn Cemetery by Amsler Funeral Home. McGregor Mirror: Jan 3 (4-1), 1941.

DAVIS W. STOCKBURGER, county school superintendent of Coryell County, died in a Temple hospital Wednesday, January 1, 1941. He had been associated with the schools for 30 years. Mr. Stockburger, who was unmarried, was born and reared in Coryell County near the Mound community on November 6, 1884 He graduated from Oglesby High School, attended North Texas State Teachers College and the University of Texas. Survivors include five brothers, Charlie F. and Garner Stockburger of Austin, R. A. of Gatesville, and John A. and Leonard W. of Oglesby; three sisters, Miss Ida Stockburger, post-mistress of Oglesby, Miss Edith, also of Oglesby, and Mrs. Owen (Winnie) Parker of Port Arther; a sister-in-law, Mrs. Clarence Stockburger, the widow of a former Coryell County Clerk; one nephew, Lobert Stockburger of Gatesville. Burial was in Post Oak Cemetery. McGregor Mirror: Jan 3 (8-3)/(8-3), 1941.

G. N. CARNES, known as Nick, died in a Waco hospital Sunday, December 29, 1940. He was born and reared a few miles south of Oglesby on the farm which his father acquired from the State of Texas. He never married and his later years were spent in blindness. He had prepared his own grave valt beside those of his parents and according to his own arrangements was laid away by the hands of a few friends. Burial was by Amsler Funeral Home. Present at the burial was a niece, Mrs. Leornard Ivy and her daughter of Pecan Grove. McGregor Mirror: Jan 3 (8-5), 1941.

SARAH ANN NEELY, age 82, died January 1, 1941. She was born June 25, 1858 in Tennessee, the daughter of John Tucker. Informant was Effie Neely. Burial was in Osage Cemetery. Coryell County Death Records.

MRS. J. C. DALY died in Amarillo Saturday, December 28, 1940. Funeral services were held in Channing, Texas. Mrs. Daly, formerly Miss Maggie Sparks, was born August 26, 1876, in McGregor, the daughter of H. A. and Laura Sparks. On January 6, 1896, she married Joseph Charles Daly, Sr. at McGregor. Three children were born to them, Russell, Edna and Joseph, Jr. Russell died in 1901 at age 14 months. The family moved to Childress in 1900 then to Channing in 1902. McGregor Mirror: Jan 10 (5-2), 1941.

TOM KING, brother of John King who lives west of McGregor, died at his home in Santa Monica, California, Wednesday, at age 48. Burial was in Santa Monica. Mr. King was born in the Comanche Springs community near McGregor. He was a veteran of World War I and upon his return from France, located in California. Besides his brother here, he is survived by his widow and one child; also a sister, Mrs. Frank Thwing of Quanah. McGregor Mirror: Jan 10 (8-2), 1941.

HURL CROUCH, age 29, died at the home of his parents, Mr. and Mrs. T. N. Nelson, near Waco on Thursday, January 9, 1941. He was born in 1911. Hurl was born in 1911. He died of pneumonia but had suffered of infantile paralysis since early infancy. Burial was in Osage Cemetery. Survivors include his mother and step-father, Mr. and Mrs. T. N. Nelson; twin brother, Earl Crouch of Waco; two step brothers, Leroy Nelson and Ernest Nelson of Houston; three sisters, Mrs. Walter Mize of McGregor, Mrs. Jesse Aars of Corpus Christi, and Mrs. Sloan Allen of Clifton. McGregor Mirror: Jan 17 (4-3), 1941.

MRS. ELMO WALDROP, wife of the vice-president of the Farmer's Bank in Meridian, was killed in an auto accident Sunday. Burial was in Meridian Cemetery, Tuesday. She was well known in McGregor, being born and reared here, and was the daughter of Mr. and Mrs. H. T. Grantham who moved from McGregor to Clifton a few years ago. Mr. and Mrs. John Grantham of McGregor attended the funeral. McGregor Mirror: Jan 24 (1-5), 1941.

JOHN HENRY WILLIAMS (UNCLE JACK), age 83, died in a Waco hospital Tuesday, January 21, 1941, from injuries suffered from falling down an elevator shaft in a Waco hotel. Uncle Jack had gone to Waco that morning to visit his son, A. K. "Kirk" Williams. J. H. was born in Georgia on November 25, 1857, but moved to Texas with his wife in 1878. Survivors include one son, Kirk; two daughters, Mrs. Willie Mitchell and Mrs. W. P. Parker of Waco; one daughter, Mrs. Ella Redmon of McMinnville, Tennessee; one half-brother, R. A. Smith of Gustine, Texas. Burial was in Comanche Springs Cemetery by Asler Funeral Home. McGregor Mirror: Jan 24 (1-6), 1941.

JOHN COOK, brother of A. F. Cook of McGregor, age 78, died in Eagle Springs, Oregan on Saturday, January 11, 1941. Burial was in Dublin, Texas, in Greenwood Cemetery. Survivors include six brothers, Ben Cook of Hutchison, Kansas, Tom Cook of Alice, Texas, N. J. Cook of Athens, Texas, Will Cook of Dublin, Texas, Charlie Cook of Morgan and A. F. Cook of McGregor; two sisters, Mrs. Callie Hackney of Rule, Texas and Mrs. Hub Spears of Temple, Texas; and two daughters. McGregor Mirror: Jan 24 (4-1), 1941.

MRS. ED WALKER, age 76, died in Austin Saturday. Burial was in Oakwood Cemetery in Austin, with nephews as pallbearers. She is survived by two daughters, Mrs. Fred Porter of Austin and Mrs. J. C. Hines of

Waskom, Texas; four grandchildren; and one brother, A. A. McNiel of Valley Mills. Mrs. Walker, a resident of McGregor for 38 years, had been living with daughters since the death of her husband some 8 years ago. McGregor Mirror: Jan 24 (5-3), 1941.

LOUISE RASCHKE, age 43, died Saturday at the home of her father, Oscar Hoppe near Coryell Church 8 miles northwest of McGregor. Burial was in Coryell Church Cemetery by Lee Funeral Home. Survivors include one daughter, Miss Estelle Raschke; a son, George Raschke, Jr.; her father, Oscar Hoppe; six sisters, Mrs. Bertha Schroeder of Sagerton, Mrs. Gladys Doty of Crawford, Mrs. Clara Edmonds of Oglesby, Mrs. Lydia Wells of Austin, Mrs. Gertrude Syler and Miss Erma Hoppe of McGregor; four brothers, Oscar D. Hoppe, Jr., of Sagerton, Walter Hoppe of Gatesville, Mark Hoppe of Clifton and Carl Hoppe of Anton. McGregor Mirror: Jan 24 (7-5), 1941.

MARY WEHRING. age 65, died January 24, 1941, in McGregor. She was born May 9, 1875, in William Penn, Texas, to Fritz Lueckemeyer and Mary Hueven Khaka of Germany. She married Mr. Alvin Wehring (Jun 21, 1872-Jun 16, 1936). Survivors include three sons, Ben, Walter and Herbert Wehring; three daughters, Johanna and Elsie Wehring and Mrs. Edwin Bischoff of McGregor; two sisters and four brothers. Mr. and Mrs. Wehring had lived in McGregor since 1905. Burial was in McGregor Cemetery by Amsler Funeral Home. Informant was Walter Wehring of McGregor. Amsler Funeral Home Records, Book #3 & McGregor Mirror: Jan 31 (8-4), 1941.

JOE M. COX, died at his home in McGregor, Saturday, January 25, 1941. Burial was in Parklawn Cemetery in Waco by Lee Undertakers. Mr. Cox is survived by his wife; three brothers, W. C. Cox and John D. Cox of McGregor, Otis Cox of Dallas; three sisters, Mrs. Betty Morris and Mrs. Dorea Buckner of Plainview and Mrs. Lee Connally of McGregor. He was born in Mississippi, December 27, 1870 but had lived in McGregor for the past 60 years. At the time of his death he was operating a shoe repair business. McGregor Mirror: Jan 31 (3-6), 1941.

B. D. FISK died at the home of his son, Alvin Fisk, in McGregor on January 30, 1941. About 47 years earlier Mr. Fisk and his family moved from Alabama to Texas. His wife, Edna P. Fisk (1866-1937), preceeded him in death some 4 years ago. Survivors include five sons, Gilbert Fisk of Fort Worth, Oscar Fisk of Gatesville, Ross Fisk of Carlsbad, Texas, Alvin Fisk and Oliver Fisk of McGregor; five daughters, Mrs. Almon McGaughy and Mrs. A. L. Tate of Quanah, Mrs. W. A. Johnson and Mrs. Jeff Simmons of Waldon, Arkansas and Mrs. L. E. Mitchell of McGregor. Burial was in Blackfoot Cemetery (Davidson Cemetery) beside his wife by Amsler Funeral Home. McGregor Mirror: Jan 31 (4-3), 1941.

VESTA EDNA GAGE MILES, mother of Arthur Cooper, died Sunday January 26, 1941, in a Waco hospital at age 56. She was born April 15, 1884, in Eastland County, Texas, the daughter of Robert Gage and Emma Tennessee

Bishop. Survivors include her husband, Sam Miles (1879-1962); one son, Sam Miles of Waco; two daughters, Mrs. Noah Cooper and Mrs. A. R. Cooper of Houston. Burial was in Comanche Springs Cemetery by Amsler Funeral Home. McGregor Mirror: Jan 31 (5-2)/(8-6), 1941

A. J. HICKERSON died in Temple last Saturday at the home of his daughter, Mrs. Joe O'Conner. He was well known in McGregor having engaged in the milling business here for many years before moving to Temple. A. J., age 80, was born near Valley Mills on February 17, 1860, and resided in Bell County until 1912. He married Miss Mollie Hill in 1883. His wife preceded him in death on May 30, 1923, as did an infant daughter and another daughter, Mrs. R. S. Dennis of Muleshoe. Survivors include three sons, Lee Hickerson of Corpus Christi, Jack Hickerson of Washington, D. C., and Cicero Hickerson of Mineral Wells; three daughters, Mrs. Joe O'Conner of Temple, Mrs. Ruby McElroy of Mexia, and Miss Mary Bell Hickerson of Corpus Christi; five brothers, L. R. Hickerson of Waco, Tom of Rosebud, Wash of Tahoka, H. C. of Canyon and Buck Hickerson of Crawford; four sisters, Mrs. Johm Lowe of Carlton, Mrs. A. L. Farris of Denton, Miss Emma Hickerson and Miss Mattie Hickerson of McGregor; seven grandchildren and two great-grandchildren. Burial was in Temple. McGregor Mirror: Feb 7 (1-5), 1941.

SOPHIE WEHRMAN, nee Wellmann, of Eagle Springs died at age 58 on February 1, 1941. She was born January 28, 1883, in Germany but came to Brenham, Texas, as age 4 years. Sophie was the daughter of Frederick Wellman and Eilhelminia Holle. In 1911 she moved with her mother to Moody, Texas. On October 24, 1912 she married Fred Wehrman and to this union were born two children. Survivors include her husband; one son, Henry Wehrman; one daughter, Mrs. Raymond Goodwin; one grandson, Kenneth Goodwin, all of Eagle Springs; two sisters, Mrs. Charlie Wiese and Mrs. Fritz Fischgrabe; two brothers, Fritz Wellmann and Charlie Wellmann of Moody; one half-brother, Henry of Houston; one half-sister, Mrs. Louise Seybold of St. Louis, Missouri. One sister, Mrs. Heneritta Makowski preceded her in death on April 20, 1936. Burial was in Buckhorn Cemetery by Lee Undertakers. Pallbearers were nephews, Henry Wellmann, Ernest Fischgrabe, Walter and Gilbert Wiese and Roy Wellmann, all of Moody, and Milton Makowski of Waco. McGregor Mirror: Feb 7 (5-1), 1941.

MRS. JOHN MASSIRER, age 53, died near Prairie Chapel on Saturday, February 1, 1941. She is survived by her husband; sons, Walter, Herbert, Louis; one daughter, Miss Ella Massirer, all of Crawford; two sisters, Mrs. Minnie Fischer of Buckholtz and Mrs. Frank Lander of Bynum; two brothers, Jake Freyer of Oklahoma and Martin Freyer of Oglesby. Mrs. Masssirer was born in Austria but came to America with her family when just a girl. They settled near Coryell City where she has resided since. Burial was in Prairie Chapel Cemetery by Amsler Funeral Home. McGregor Mirror: Feb 7 (5-6), 1941.

MR. CHLOMA M. WEEKLEY, formerly of McGregor, died at his home in Athens, Texas, Wednesday. He married Miss Vallie Black of McGregor, the daughter of Dr. and Mrs. W. T. Black. Survivors include his wife; one daughter, Mrs. H. T. Torrence of Waco; two brothers, John M. Weekley of Ennis and Pat Weekley of Dallas; five sisters, Mrs. W. F. Rogers of Quanah, Mrs. Iva W. Bradford of Dallas, Mrs. Emma W. Pace of Dallas, Mrs. Allie Prentice of Arlington and Mrs. H. A. Meyer of Sealy. McGregor Mirror: Feb 14 (1-4), 1941.

ERNEST WRIGHT died in Waxahachie at the home of his daughter, Mrs. Howard Gibson. He was born in Lovelady, Texas on September 27, 1873 and married Miss Hattie Scully in McGregor in 1900. Mr. Wright had a grocery business in McGregor for many years. Burial was in McGregor by Amsler Funeral Home. Survivors include his wife; two children, Mrs. Howard Gibson of Waxahachie and Fred H. Wright of Dallas; three sisters, Mrs. J. E. Boyd of Hillsboro, Miss Mary Wright and Miss Bettie Wright of Waco. McGregor Mirror: Feb 21 (4-1), 1941.

JOHN NOLAN, nephew of Emma Arp of Comanche Springs, died in an airplane accident in Ardmore, Oklahoma last Friday. Those attending the funeral in Oklahoma included Emma Arp, Lottie White of Waco, Joe Draper, Don Nolan and Wayne Arp. McGregor Mirror: Feb 21 (8-3)/(8-5), 1941.

MRS. H. RABBE, age 71, died at her home in Coryell City Monday. Burial was in Paririe Chapel Cemetery. Survivors include five daughters, Mrs. Charles Westerfield of Crawford, Mrs. Ernest Westerfield of Crawford, Mrs. Hubert Gohlke of Coryell City, Mrs. John Bohne of Valley Mills, and Mrs. Albert Weiss of Gatesville; three sons, W. L. Rabbe of Coryell City, W. W. Rabbe of Gatesville and Wallace Rabbe of Crawford. McGregor Mirror: Feb 28 (4-2), 1941.

NANCY REBECCA KATHRYN "KATE" STONE RUCKER, wife of Tom Rucker, died Wednesday, February 19, 1941. Burial was in Post Oak Cemetery by Lee Undertakers. She was born April 1, 1879 at Holly Springs, Mississippi. She came to Oglesby, Texas as a child and has resided there since that time. Nancy married Thomas P. Rucker on November 8, 1896. Survivors include her husband, Tom Rucker (Nov 6, 1874-Jun 4, 1948); two children, Mrs. James Walker and Marvin Rucker; five grand-children, Mrs. Anthony Griffin and Marie Walker of Austin, Mrs. Jim Searcy, Billy Parks and Jimmie Walker; a great-granson, Graham Searcy of Oglesby; five sisters, Mrs. Charles Coleman of Oglesby, Mrs. Irma Crouch of Wichita Falls, Miss Eva Stone of Montgomery, Alabama, Mrs. Jessie Pruitt of Hamilton, Mrs. Jack Meyers of Sinton; two brothers, J. L. Stone of Weslaco and Earl Stone of Hamilton. McGregor Mirror: Feb 28 (8-4), 1941.

MRS. H. C. ADAMS, who died at the home of her parents, Mr. and Mrs. George Miller of Gatesville, on February 28, 1941. Burial was in Gatesville by Lee Undertakers. Survivors include her husband; a daughter, Sandra Sue Adams; two brothers, Francis and Jim Miller of

Gateville; three sisters, Mrs. Madge Patterson and Mrs. Elmo Washburn of Gatesville and Mrs. Ted Pollard of Oglesby. Mrs. Adams was a daughter-in-law of Mrs. Sallie Adams of McGregor and a sister-in-law of Mrs. Bay Fletcher and Donald Adams of McGregor. McGregor Mirror: Mar 7 (4-2), 1941.

THEODORE T. HAMBLIN, age 42, died in McGregor at the home of his sister, Mrs. Irene Connally Friday, February 28, 1941. Burial was in Harris Creek Cemetery by Lee Undertakers. Survivors include three sisters, Irene Connally, Mrs. Rosa Stebbins of Wichita, Kansas and Mrs. Ollie Brock of Abilene; a brother, A. L. Hamblin of California. Mr. Hamblin was born in 1899. He attended high school in McGregor and A. M. College. He was also a World War I veteran. For the past few years he had been making his home in Fort Worth where he worked for the T & P Railroad as a landscape engineer. McGregor Mirror: Mar 7 (4-5), 1941.

JOHN NEWTON DAVIS, age 75, died in Dallas on February 24, 1941. He was superintendent of McGregor schools 45 years ago but moved to Hico where he was head of schools for may years. His death was the result of an auto accident last October. Survivors include two daughters and three sons. McGregor Mirror: Mar 7 (4-6), 1941.

PETER C. "PETE" MARTIN, age 71, died at his home at Pecan Grove in Coryell County on March 1, 1941. Burial was in Davidson Cemetery by Lee Undertakers. Six brothers were pallbearers. Survivors include his widow, Clara Martin (1874-1967); five sons, Othar, Byron, Joe, P. C. Jr., and Bruns; one daughter, Mrs. Paul Edmondson of Hamilton; eight brothers, F. L. Martin of Hamlin, F. M. Martin of Dallas, S. W. Martin of Hamilton, G. C. Martin and P. H. Martin of Gatesville, B. A. Martin and J. R. Martin of Pecan Grove and M. B. Martin of McGregor; four sisters, Mrs. A. T. Jones, Mrs. E. A. Perry and Mrs. Johnnie Johnson of Hamilton, and Mrs. G. W. Lee, Sr., of McGregor. McGregor Mirror: Mar 7 (8-3), 1941.

SOPHIE LANDER, age 70, died at the family home near Osage on Wednesday, March 12, 1941. She was born July 12, 1870 in Austria and came to America in 1901, locating near Crawford. Survivors include her husband, Frank P. Lander (Dec 24, 1864-Apr 6, 1958); three sons, Joe, Frank and Arnold Lander; four daughters, Mrs. Addelia Gauer, Mrs. Lena Willman, Miss Minnie and Miss Frieda Lander of Crawford; three nephews, nine grandchildren and one great-grandchild. Burial was in Coryell City Lutheran Cemetery by Amsler Funeral Home. McGregor Mirror: Mar 14 (5-3), 1941.

FREDERICK WILL VAHRENKAMP, age 62, died at his home in Waco on Saturday, March 8, 1941. Burial was in Rosemound Cemetery by Clark Funeral Home of Waco. Survivors include his wife; four daughters, Miss Lillie and Miss Bernice Vahrenkamp of Waco, Mrs. Frank Carruth of Waco, Mrs. Paul W. Stewart of McGregor; one son, Will Vahrenkamp, Jr.; three grandchildren; four brothers, Otto and F. H. of McGregor, H. A. of Fort Worth, E. C. of Bryan; two sisters, Mrs. H. C. Lehde of Old Washington and Mrs. C. W. Kestler of Waco; his mother, Mrs. Sophie Vahrenkamp of Waco. Mr. Vahrenkamp once owned a grocery store in McGregor but moved to Waco nine years ago. McGregor Mirror: Mar 14 (8-2), 1941.

MARY BADGER BLAILOCK, age 66, died Monday in Austin. Burial was in Oakwood Cemetery in Waco. Mrs. Blailock was born in Gonzales and married Dr. Harry F. Blailock in 1900 near Marble Falls. Dr. Blailock practiced medicine in McGregor and Waco at the time of his death. Mrs. Blailock moved to Dallas in 1924 but for the last 4 years had resided in Austin. Survivors include one daughter, Mrs. Badger Reed of Austin; one son, Russell Blailock of Dallas; a brother, R. T. Badger of Austin; a sister-in-law, Mrs. Frank Connally of Waco; and one granddaughter. McGregor Mirror: Mar 21 (5-4), 1941.

ARTHUR LEE CLUCK died Wednesday March 26, 1941 when struck by a car while walking along the Waco-Temple highway. Burial was in Comanche Springs Cemetery by Lee Undertakers. Mr. Cluck, age 25, was born May 21, 1918, the son of Mr. and Mrs. W. L. Cluck who live on the John Bennett farm north of McGregor. He had recently returned home from Springerville, Arizona, where he had been with a CCC camp. Survivors include his parents; two brothers, Rev. Charlie Cluck of Maybank and Sam Cluck of Hewitt; five sisters, Mrs. Jewel Lane of Speegleville, Mrs. Travis Evetts of The Grove, Miss Johnnie, Miss Frankie and Miss Mildred Cluck of McGregor. McGregor Mirror: Mar 28 (1-3), 1941.

EFFIE ASH, age 50, died Monday, April 7, 1941 at her home in McGregor. Burial was in McGregor Cemetery by Asmler Funeral Home. Mrs. Ash was born in Murray County, Georgia, November 15, 1890, and came to Texas as a small child with her parents, Joe J. Frady and Carrie Naler of Georgia. Her husband, George Ash, preceded her in death on September 25, 1940. Survivors include two daughters, Mrs. T. K. Bond of McGregor and Mrs. H. P. Robinson of San Antonio; two sons, Joe and Buster Ash of McGregor; her father, J. J. Frady of McGregor; three brothers, Howard of Waco, Gordon and Price Frady of McGregor; six sisters, Mrs. Mattie Davidson and Mrs. Lillie Dunn of Robinsonville, Mrs. Addie Davis of Ocee, Mrs. Mary Pauk of Waco, Mrs. Carl McMurtry of Amarillo and Miss Esther Frady of McGregor. McGregor Mirror: Apr 11 (8-1), 1941.

WILLIE EDWARD COX, age 42, of Austin, died April 4, 1941, of injuries suffered in an automobile accident a few days previous. Burial was in Coryell Church Cemetery by Lee Undertakers. Mr. Cox was a native of McLennan County but had been a resident of Austin for the past year, engaged in the contracting business. Survivors include his wife; three daughters, Mrs. Robuck of Houston, Mrs. Wener of Jonesboro and Doris of Austin; one son, Keith of Austin; his father of Floydada; two brothers, Alsie of Oglesby and Wess of Austin; one sister, Mrs. Annie Mae Smith. McGregor Mirror: Apr 11 (8-3), 1941.

WILLIAN MARION CAMPBELL of Waco died Wednesday, April 16, 1941. William was born February 12, 1867. He was a former resident of Oglesby and had been a Central Texas resident for 74 years. Burial was in Post Oak Cemtery near Oglesby by Lee Undertakers. Survivors include his wife, Eula V. Campbell (Sep 1, 1872-Sep 10, 1965); one daughter, Mrs. Murl Lamb of Fort Worth, and Floyd Campbell of Hamilton. McGregor Mirror: Apr 18 (8-4), 1941.

SPEIGHT JACKMAN, son of Mr. and Mrs. Loy Jackman of Hillsboro, died Wednesday in Waco as a result of injuries suffered in a motorcycle accident last Sunday. He was well known in McGregor, being the grandson of the late Mr. and Mrs. Don Speight. Survivors include two aunts, Mrs. H. H. Hudson and Mr. R. M. Harris; cousins, Mr. and Mrs. John Hugh Hudson, all of McGregor. Speight was a native of Hill County, attending Hillsboro schools and college. During the past year he assisted in teaching civil aeronautical class at Clifton College. It was one of his ambitions to work for one of the new Texas airplane plants. Burial in Hillsboro. McGregor Mirror: Apr 25 (1-3), 1941.

ERNEST BICKEL, age 73, died in Waco Saturday, April 19, 1941. Mr. Bickel was a well known farmer in McGregor who came to this country from Baden, Germany at the age of 26 years. He was born April 6, 1868 in Germany, the son of F. Jacob Bickel and Anna Marie Ricklin. Burial was in Harris Creek Cemetery by Amsler Funeral Home. Survivors include one brother, J. F. "Fritz" Bickel; a nephew, Pat Bickel; four nieces, Mrs. Homer Ruff and Miss Kate Bickel of South Bosque, Mrs. O. G. Horne and Mrs. Wendell Bray of Waco. McGregor Mirror: Apr 25 (8-2), 1941.

GEORGE VANDIVER died in at his home in Liberty. It was only a little over a week ago that his twin brother, Jim Vandiver, died suddenly at his home in Houston. Mrs. Sam Davis and son, Elvin Davis of McGregor, learned of the death of Mrs. Davis' brother Wednesday. Burial was in Liberty. McGregor Mirror: May 9 (4-4) 1941.

ROBERT SCOTT JOHNSON died at the home of his granddaughter, Mrs. Roy Culp, near McGregor Saturday, May 3, 1941. He was past 90 years old. He married his wife, Venice, on August 30, 1925. Mr. Johnson was born in Texas on October 5, 1850 to Mr. and Mrs. N. J. Johnson of North Carolina. He moved from Coryell County to McGregor about 29 years ago. He was preceded in death by his wife, Venice Johnson, two sons and two daughters. Survivors include five daughers, Mrs. Ola Culp and Mrs. Ernest Hodges of McGregor, Mrs. N. J. Lamb of Taylor, Mrs. W. P. Stewart of Texarkana and Mrs. T. J. McKee of Waco. Burial was in Comanche Springs Cemetery by Amsler Funeral Home. Pallbrearers were grandsons. McGregor Mirror: May 9 (4-6), 1941.

B. F. DODSON, age 57, died Friday, May 2, 1941, at his home in McGregor. He had been employed by Lee Hardware for the past 14 years. He left work in good health Friday but died in his sleep that evening.

Survivors include his wife; three daughters, Mrs. T. R. Wright of El Paso, Mrs. Price Cook and Miss Ramona Dodson of McGregor; two brothers, Lee Dodson of Post and Wiley Dodson of Houston; two sisters, Mrs. Charlie McCullough of Kopperl and Mrs. Robert Lee of Flat. Burial was in Rosemound Cemetery in Waco by Lee Undertakers. McGregor Mirror: May 9 (5-1), 1941.

WILLIAM L. MORRIS, pioneer resident of McGregor, died at the home of his daughter, Mrs. Harry Sanders, Thursday, May 1, 1941. He was born near Camden, Arkansas on October 18, 1852, and at the time of his death was 88 years old. Following the Civil War, Mr. Morris came to Texas settling near Cameron, Texas. Later the family moved to Oglesby where he married Miss Nancy Adaline Watkins, who preceded him in death in December of 1919. Survivors include six children, Mrs. Ada Scruggs, Mrs. Harry Sanders, L. P. Morris, C. A. Morris, and J. E. Morris, all of McGregor, and R. C. Morris of Sebastion, Texas. Burial was in McGregor Cemetery by Lee Undertakers. McGregor Mirror: May 9 (5-4), 1941.

J. H. "UNCLE DON" BLOUNT, former resident of Oglesby, died in Lockney, Texas, April 8, 1941, at age 87 years. He was born near Holly Springs, Mississippi on July 15, 1853, but came to Oglesby in 1894. He and his brother, Andrew Blount, farmed in Oglesby until 1906 when they moved to Lockney. Mr. Blount was never married. McGregor Mirror: May 9 (8-6), 1941.

MRS. W. D. LAWRENCE died in Austin Saturday, May 10, 1941. Burial was in Old Perry Cemetery near Moody by Lee Undertakers. Pallbearers were five nephews, Willard, Virgil, Jack and Joe Henry Polston, Andrew Gilliland and Ott Sutton. Mrs. Lawrence, formerly Annie Polston, was born near Ogleby in 1904 and at the time of her death was 37 years old. In 1923 she married W. D. Lawrence and seven children were born to them. Two children preceded her in death. Survivors include her husband; five children, Lucy, Irene, Lavon, Joyce Dean, Shirley Ann and Carl O'Danial Polston; her parents, Mr. and Mrs. A. M. Polston of Temple; one sister, Mrs. Roy Gilliland of Temple; six brothers, Bill and Jesse Polston of McGregor, Elijah Polston of Waco, Scott Polston of Oglesby, Joe and Jim Polston of Temple. McGregor Mirror: May 16 (8-2), 1941.

MRS. SAM BRANDES, age 53, died at her home in Temple, Wednesday. Survivors include her husband; three children, Edward, Irene and Catherine Alice Brandes of Temple; her father, C. F. Luedtke of McGregor; three brothers, Earnest Luedtke of McGregor, Ed. Luedtke of Houston and Charlie Luedtke of Pflugerville; four sisters, Mrs. Ben Brandes of Plainview, Miss Bertha Luedtke of Waco, Mrs. Gus Amthor of Waco and Miss Elsie Luedtke of Taylor. Burial was in Hillcrest Cemetery in Temple. Mrs. Brandes was born in Washington County, Texas on August 26, 1888 and had lived in Temple for the past 21 years. McGregor Mirror: May 23 (8-1), 1941.

DEATHS IN CENTRAL TEXAS, VOL. II

HENRIETTA MUEGGE, age 64, died at her home five miles north of McGregor Friday, May 23, 1941. Burial was in McGregor Cemetery by Lee Undertakers. Six grandsons were pallbearers: Lonnie Muegge, Alton Muegge, William Brinkmeyer, Albert Lippe, Edwin Lippe and Walter Boemer. Mrs. Muegge who was born June 27, 1877, had been a resident of this community for 34 years. Survivors include her husband, August Muegge (May 17, 1859-Sep 30, 1949); five sons, Albert, Fred and Lonnie of McGregor, Alvin of Valley Mills, Gayheart of Sagerton; three daughters, Mrs. Emma Weiss of Cranfills Gap, Mrs. Charles Brinkmeyer of Brenham and Mrs. Henry Lippi of McGregor. McGregor Mirror: May 30 (4-1), 1941.

MR. C. NIEMEIER, age 81, died at his home near Coryell City on Thursday, May 22, 1941. His wife, H. Niemeier (Jun 16, 1859-Apr 23, 1940)preceded him in death just 13 months ago. Mr. Niemeier was born on November 28, 1859, in Germany and came to America in 1892, first locating in Washington County then moving to McGregor. Soon after moving to McGregor he moved to his farm near Coryell City where he has resided for 42 years. Survivors include four sons, Will of McGregor, Charlie of Crawford, Ernest and Henry of Coryell City; five daughters, Miss Minnie Niemeier, Mrs. Henry Gohlke, Mrs. Fred Haferkamp, Mrs. Eldor Loesch and Mrs. Bill Gholke, all of the Coryell City community. Burial was in Coryell City Lutheran Cemetery by Amsler Funeral Home. McGregor Mirror: May 30 (4-3), 1941.

ELLA TOWNSEND BAKER, age 72, died at her home near McGregor Tuesday, May 27, 1941. Survivors include two sons, Meritt Townsend of Oklahoma and Richard Townsend of Lorena; one daughter, Mrs. Luther Hering of Waco. Mrs. Baker was born April 22, 1868, in Baton Rouge, Louisiana, the daughter of Willford Wise, and married M. F. Townsend in 1885. In 1906 she married J. T. Baker (Jul 11, 1859-Feb 28, 1929) and for the past 35 years had made her home in McLennan County. Burial was in McGregor Cemetery with Amsler Funeral Home in charge of the funeral. McGregor Mirror: May 30 (8-1), 1941.

LENORA "NORA" BELLE (Smith) GILLILAND, age 70, died in her home in McGregor, Monday, June 2, 1941. She was born on January 16, 1871 in Illinois, the daughter of John Smith and Mary Stout. She and a baby sister were orphaned at the ages of 2 and 4, after which they were brought to Adair County, Missouri. At age 16 Nora married Columbus Gilliland in Missouri in 1887. They moved to Texas soon after their marriage and moved to McGregor in 1913. Mr. Gilliland died November 22, 1933, at the age of 84. He was born January 16, 1839. Survivors include her sister, Mrs. Bina Stull of Elmer, Missouri; seven children, Mrs. Lizzie Polston, Mrs. Lucy Polston and Miss Belle Gilliland, all of McGregor, Burges Gilliland, Less Gilliland of McGregor, Roy Gilliland of Temple and William Gilliland of Dallas. One child preceded her in death. Burial was in McGregor Cemetery beside her husband, by Amsler Funeral Home. McGregor Mirror: Jun 6 (5-3), 1941.

DEATHS IN CENTRAL TEXAS, VOL. II

G. C. CLEMENTS, died Wednesday at the home of his daughter, Mrs. J. Wesley Clements, in Stephenville, Texas. Burial was in Naylor Cemetery in Moody, Texas, after funeral services in Stephenville. Survivors include his wife of Houston; four sons, Olen of New York City, Glen of Galveston, Manning of Fort Worth and Roy Clements of McGregor; three daughters, Mrs. J. Wesley Clements of Stephenville (wife of the Mayor of Stephenville), Mrs. Maxine Himes of Houston and Mrs. Gertrude Oliver of California. McGregor Mirror: Jun 6 (5-4), 1941.

MRS. FRANK (Robbecke) SMITH, age 68, died at her home in McGregor Saturday, May 31, 1941. Burial was in McGregor Cemetery by Compton's Funeral Home of Waco. She was born in Moulton, Texas, and later moved to McGregor. She was well known here as Mrs. Joe Culpepper. Waco has been her home for the past 25 years. Survivors include three sons, J. B. Culpepper of Temple, A. L. Culpepper of Corte Maderia, California and Donnell Culpepper of Long Beach, California; and a niece, Mrs. Ollie Mann of Waco. McGregor Mirror: Jun 6 (5-6), 1941.

MRS. PAUL GARRETT, age 61, died in McGregor Monday. Burial was in McGregor Cemetery by Lee Undertakers. Survivors include her husband; two daughters, Mrs. Mike Brennan of Austin and Mrs. K. A. Allen of McGregor; two sons, Jack and Bob Garrett of McGregor; two sisters, Mrs. George Caufield of Phillips, Texas and Mrs. Fred Gamble of Dallas; one brother, Earl Crain of California. Amoung those from out of town who attended the funeral were Mr. and Mrs. Tom Garrett of Richland Springs, Mrs. Con Blanchard of Mound, Mrs. J. N. Crain, Mrs. Fred Gamble and Mrs. J. W. King, all of Dallas, Mr. and Mrs. George Caufield and son, George, Jr. of Borger, Mrs. Roy Jacobs, Mr. and Mrs. Watt Crain, Mr. Walter Dossett, and Mrs. Sally Haley, all of Waco, and Mrs. Bassel Blanton of Temple. McGregor Mirror: Jun 13 (5-4), 1941.

CLEO WHITLOCK of Dallas was killed in an auto accident in Waxahachie last week. Friends of Mrs. W. C. Cox of Comanche Springs sympathize with her on account of the serious condition of her sister, Mrs. Cleo Whitlock, and the death of her brother-in-Law, Cleo Whitlock. McGregor Mirror: Jun 13 (8-2), 1941.

RUTH ANN REEVES, infant daughter of Mr. and Mrs. E. W. Reeves of McGregor, died suddenly June 17, 1941. She was born 9 months ago on September 10, 1940, the daughter of E. W. Reeves and Ora Farris. She had been well on her way to recovery from the operation she underwent at Dallas when but a tiny baby. Burial was in McGregor Cemetery by Amsler Funeral Home. McGregor Mirror: Jun 20 (4-2), 1941.

MRS. B. E. (EL) DALTON died at her home in Merkel last Friday. burial was in Merkel. Mr. and Mrs. Dalton made there home in McGregor many years ago. McGregor Mirror: Jun 20 (4-5), 1941.

MRS. MARIA PERALES, 20 year old Mexican woman, was fatally burned Sunday, June 22, 1941. The stove in her home on the Holley Haynes farm exploded while she was building a fire. She died in a Waco hospital. Burial was in McGregor Cemetery by Lee Undertakers. Survivors inlcude her husband; a one year old daughter; her parents; three sisters and six brothers. Desidero Castillo, father of the woman, suffered severe burns while rescuing his daughter from the flaming house. McGregor Mirror: Jun 27 (8-1), 1941.

ELVENA "VENIE" EVETTS, age 62, wife of Samuel Henry Evetts, died last Saturday, June 28, 1941, at her home three miles southeast of McGregor. Burial was in McGregor Cemetery by Lee Undertakers. Survivors include her husband, Sam Evetts (Sep 29, 1875-Nov 24, 1950); three daughters, Mrs. Ollie Sheffield of Houston, Mrs. Nora Cooper and Miss Hazel Evetts of McGregor; three sons, W. M. Evetts and Elmer Dean Evetts of Houston, and Frank Evetts of McGregor; three sisters, Mrs. Ida White of Fort Worth, Mrs. Theo McFatrick of Antlers, Oklahoma, and Mrs. Nettie Rose of Durant, Oklahoma; a brother, Elmer Mitchell of Houston. Five other brothers also survive. Mr. and Mrs. Evetts had been married over 40 years. McGregor Mirror: Jul 4 (7-4), 1941.

ADDIE R. COLE. age 78, died at her home in Vernon, Texas on Monday, July 7. 1941. Her body was brought to McGregor for burial in Coryell Church Cemetery by Smith Funeral Home. Pallbearers were nephews, Tull, Parker and Paul Johnson, E. J. Thomason, Earl and Quince Meritt and Carlos Kirby. Survivors include her husband, Alexander "Alix" Cole (Oct 9, 1863-Jan 25, 1953); three sons, Harry of Vernon, Joe and Clyde of San Antonio; three daughters, Edna Lynn of Vernon, Gracie Louise of California and Mrs. Ruby Archer of Amarillo; and a brother, Sam Allen of Waco. The Cole family lived in McGregor for many years but since 1906 they had lived in Hardeman County. McGregor Mirror: Jul 11 (5-6), 1941.

WILLIAM WALTER EMBRY, age 80, died at his home in Ballinger, Texas, Tuesday. He moved from Runnels County from McGregor some 35 years ago. Survivors include his wife; a son, W. H. Embry of Ballinger; a brother, J. M. Embry of Quanah and three grandchildren. Burial was in Evergreen Cemtetery by Agnew Funeral Home. Miss Una Kinnamon, his niece, Mrs. Ben Jones and W. A. Hamilton of McGregor attended the funeral. McGregor Mirror: Jun 20 (4-5)\Jul 11 (6-6), 1941.

G. R. WALTON died Thursday, July 3, 1941, at the home of his daughter, Mrs. R. D. McEntire in McGregor. He had lived near The Grove for 39 years where he was engaged in farming and ranching. Since the death of his wife some five years ago, he had made his home with his daughter. Mr. Walton was born in Sedalia, Missouri, January 23, 1856. He came to Texas in 1876 and married Dora Isabelle Evans in Nararro County, Texas. Survivors include four daughters, Mrs. R. D. McEntire, Mrs. F. R. Wilson of Gatesville, Mrs. Miller Robinson of Abilene and Mrs. T. B. Walton of The Grove; and a sister, Mrs. Laura Barnes of Columbia, Missouri. Burial was in Turnersville Cemetery by Lee Undertakers. McGregor Mirror: Jul 11 (8-1), 1941.

RICHARD MORRIS ELMS died at his home in McGregor Monday, July 21, 1941. He was born in Arkansas in 1857, the son of Samuel Elms and Lorettie Johnson, and came to Texas with his father's family in 1878. Mr. Elms had lived in McGregor for the past 59 years. Survivors include his wife, Ursie P. Elms (1880-1972); three sons, H. L. Elms of Shreveport, Louisiana, Morris Elms of San Antonio, Grady Elms of College Station; one step-son, Chester Cook of Shreveport; three grandchildren, Gus and Anna Lee Cook and Little Richard Elms. Burial was in Harris Creek Cemetery by Amsler Funeral Home. McGregor Mirror: Jul 25 (8-2), 1941.

JAMES EDWIN BROWN, age 51, was buried last Monday by Wilkerson-Hatch Funeral Home. Edwin was well known in McGregor as vice-president of the First National Bank of McGregor. In the latter days of WWI he had become a volunteer student in the officers' training camp in the Field Artillery at Camp Haylor in Kentucky. For the past few years Edwin had lived in Amarillo doing field supervisory work for the Federal Farm Credit set-up. He had given up his work when he became a sufferer with a brain tumor and for the past three months he was a patient in the Veteran's Hospital in Waco, where he passed away Sunday, July 27, 1941. He was the son of J. E. Brown and Edna Porter. Survivors include his wife, Dorothy Brown; three daughters, Dorothy, Virginia and Betty; one brother, Dr. Porter Brown of Fort Worth; two sisters, Mrs. Paul C. Beresford of Mart and Mrs. W. B. Woodson of Temple. Burial was in McGregor Cemetery beside his father and mother by Amsler Funeral Home. McGregor Mirror: Aug 1 (4-6), 1941.

JAMES LAWS CANNON died at the home of his son, Lois Cannon, in Waco, Fridy, July 25, 1941. Burial was in McGregor Cemetery by Lee Undertakers. Mr. Cannon had lived in McGregor all his life. At the time of his death, which occurred on his birthday, he had reached age 62, having been born in Moody on July 25, 1879. Survivors include his wife, Ethel Parsons (Jun 16, 1884-Sep 13, 1962); five daughters, Mrs. Ed Mertins of McGregor, Mrs. C. W. Cash of Meridian, Mrs. Tom Buckbee of McFarland, Colorado, Mrs. Mamie Hurlock and Miss Leita Fay Cannon of Dallas; three sons, Jay and Ovie Cannon of McGregor and Lois Cannon of Waco; two sisters, Mrs. B. F. High and Mrs. Emma Stone of McGregor; two brothers, Watt Cannon and Will Cannon of Kopperl. James and Ethel married on November 18, 1900. McGregor Mirror: Aug 1 (8-4), 1941.

GUENTHER A. SCHWARZ, age 32, superintendent of the public school in Mason, Texas, and coach of the Mason High football team for six years (1934-1940) died Tuesday, July 22, 1941. Death occurred in San Antonio. Burial was in Gooch Cemetery near St. Paul Lutheran Church in Mason, Texas. Survivors include his wife; two children, Peggy age 5 and Teddy age 4; his parents, Rev. and Mrs. M. J. Schwarz of Mason and a brother, Helmuth of Austin. McGregor Mirror: Aug 1 (8-6), 1941.

EBEN R. KILPATRICK, JR., age 49, died Sunday, August 3, 1941, at a Waco hospital. He was born February 1, 1892, and had been a resident of Crawford for several years. For the past few years had served as night watchman. Eben was an ex-service man, having served in the U. S. Army in San Domingo for a time and later in France as a member of the U. S. Marine Corps. Survivors include his wife; children, Lorraine, Mary Frances, James Hubert, Mildred and Billy Baker of Crawford and one son, Robert, of Randolf Field. Burial was in Crawford Cemetery by Amsler Funeral Home. McGergor Mirror: Aug 8 (4-4), 1941.

WILLIAM BEN PLEMONS, age 74, died at his home on route 4, McGregor, on Sunday, August 9, 1941. Burial was in Rosemound Cemetery in Waco. Survivors include his wife; four sons, C. T. of Dalworth Park, J. T. of McGregor, O. B. of McGregor and L. H. of Waco; four daughters, Mrs. E. H. Hunter of Fort Worth, Mrs. J. Lances of Fort Worth, Mrs. Otis Parker of Waco and Mrs. Bruns Martin of Oglesby; two brothers, G. W. Plemons of Crawford and R. H. Plemons of McGregor; two sisters, Mrs. G. W. Pack of Ocee and Mrs. C. W. Walters of McGregor. Pallbearers were Evett Plemons, Vernon Plemons, Walter Plemons, Harrell Plemons, Johnnie Walters and Lilburn Pack. McGregor Mirror: Aug 15 (6-6), 1941.

T. W. STUBBLEFIELD, age 90, died at the home of his daughter, Mrs. J. W. Blewett of Moody, Monday, August 19, 1941. He was born March 12, 1851. Burial was in McGregor Cemetery. He was a native of Tennessee but in 1890 moved to McGregor where he was in the grocery business until 1920, when he retired. Survivors include his wife; two daughters, Mrs. Blewett of Moody and Mrs. W. W. Roberts of Norwood, Colorado; two sons, Albert Stubblefield of Waco and Ray Stubblefield of Dallas; four sisters and six grandchildren. Pallbearers were Cecil Stubblefield of Hillsboro; Bert and Ray Ford of Austin, Wesley Ford of Teague, I. N. McDonald of Strawn and Bryan Stubblefield of Waco. McGregor Mirror: Aug 22 (4-3), 1941.

DR. JAMES W. CONLEY, age 57, died in Wichita Falls following an operation of a few days ago. He was born and reared in McGregor. Dr. Conley served as a captain in WWI, returning to settle in Quanah, Texas, where he practiced medicine since 1924. Burial was in Quanah. Survivors include his wife; one daughter, Gail; his father, N. C. Conley; and one brother, C. G. Conley, postmaster of Quanah. McGregor Mirror: Aug 22 (4-4), 1941.

LUCY E. BURLESON, former resident of Coryell Church Community, died at the home of her son, J. A. Burleson, in Lubbock, Monday, August 18, 1941. She was born on December 26, 1851. She married J. M. Burleson (Mar 24, 1849-Feb 7, 1901). Burial was at Coryell Church by Amsler Funeral Home. Survivors include two sons, J. R. Burleson of Fort Worth and J. A. Burleson of Lubbock; a step-daughter, Mrs. M. C. Herman of O'Donnel, Texas. Mrs. Burleson was born in Mississippi in 1851, but came to Texas with her parents in 1858. Ten years later the family moved to Coryell Church. For the past twenty years she had been making her home with her son in Lubbock. McGregor Mirror: Aug 22 (4-6), 1941.

JAMES FENO JONES of West Columbia, Texas, was killed Saturday night August 23, 1941, in an auto accident. The accident occurred on highway 317 between Moody and McGregor. Burial was in Post Oak Cemtery by Lee Undertakers. Mr. Jones was born January 1, 1909, in Gatesville, Texas. He married Leola Humphries on March 19, 1932. Survivors include his wife; a daughter, Marylyn Kay; his father and mother, Mr. and Mrs. J. E. Jones of Gatesville; five brothers, Herschell and F. T. of Gatesville, Harry of McAllen, Ray of Texas City and Lynn of Waco; three sisters, Miss Reva Jones and Mrs. Don Adams of Gatesville and Mrs. Leo Domstead of McAllen. McGregor Mirror: Aug 29 (1-6), 1941.

HERBERT LUEDEKER, age 20, died in a Waco hospital Tuesday, August 26, 1941. He was born in McLennan County, Texas, on November 5, 1920. Survivors include his parents, Willie and Annie (Witt) Luedeker; two brothers, Edgar and Harold; one sister, Lillian, all of McGregor; his grandparents, Mrs. E. Luedeker and Mr. and Mrs. A. F. Witt of McGregor. Burial was in McGregor Cemetery by Amsler Funeral Home. McGregor Mirror: Aug 29 (5-2), 1941.

TOM BROWNING, a resident of Leon Junction, died at his home Monday. Burial was in Seaton Cemetery by Lee Undertakes. Mr. Browning had lived in Leon Junction for over 40 years. Survivors include his wife; seven sons, Jess of Keene, Dick of Mound, Calvin, Fred, Ben, Raymond and Jack of Leon Valley. McGregor Mirror: Aug 29 (5-4), 1941.

JAMES DANIEL GRANTHAM died suddenly of a heart attack Sunday at his home in McGregor. Burial was in McGregor Cemetery by Lee Undertakers. Jim was born February 14, 1870 in Navarro County near Corsicana, Texas. He moved to McGregor when a young man and has lived in that community for the past 55 years. For the past 49 years he had been engaged in the gin business. Mr. Granham married Mary Ella Misely of McGregor on December 23, 1892. Survivors include his wife; two sons, Harry of Houston and Lloyd of Cordon, Ohio; three daughters, Mrs. George Breeding of Moody, Mrs. Frank Carr of Cloudcroft, New Mexico, and Mrs. Clyde Barton of Kermit, Texas; brothers, Will of Corsicana, Luther of Arkansas, Hiram of Clifton, Nathan and John of McGregor; one sister, Mrs. E. C. Huckabee of Corsicana. McGregor Mirror: Sep 12 (4-2), 1941.

MRS. M. L. BAGGETT, age 35, died at the family home in Stampede Valley Saturday, September 6, 1941. She is survived by her husband; one daughter, Ella Faye; her parents, Mr. and Mrs. H. C. Nelson; two sisters and five brothers, one of her brothers being F. D. Nelson of McGregor. Burial was in Buckhorn Cemetery by Amsler Funeral Home. McGregor Mirror: Sep 12 (5-2), 1941.

MR. COLLINS of Jonesboro died Sunday, August 31, 1941. Mrs. Vera Collins and son of Comanche Springs attended the funeral. Mr. Collins and family formerly lived in Comanche Springs. McGregor Mirror: Sep 12 (8-3), 1941.

FRED CHRISTIAN WEHRMAN died at his home near Eagle Springs last Friday, September 12, 1941. He was born in Germany on November 20, 1872 but had lived in Eagle Springs for the last 28 years. His wife preceded his in death about a year ago. Survivors include two children, Henry Wehrman and Mrs. Clara Goodwin. Burial was in Buckhorn Cemetery by Lee Undertakers. McGregor Mirror: Sep 19 (5-1), 1941.

HENRY WIETHORN, SR., age 81, died at the home of his son, Gus Wiethorn, near McGregor on Sunday, September 21, 1941. He was born January 16, 1860, in Germany and came to America at age 21, locating first in Washington County. From there he came to McGregor in 1910, where he engaged in farming. His wife, Louise Wiethorn (Jul 18, 1864-Feb 16, 1926) preceded him in death several years ago and for the past few years he had made his home with his son, Gus. Survivors include three sons, Henry, Louis and Gus; one daughter, Mrs. Fred Witt, all of McGregor; one brother, William Wiethorn of Brenham. Burial was in McGregor Cemetery by Amsler Funeral Home. McGregor MirrorL Sep 26 (4-2), 1941.

EMMA (Wiethorn) WITT, age 41, died in McGregor on September 30, 1941. She was born in Washington County, Texas, June 22, 1920, the daughter of Henry Wiethorn, Sr. and Louise Knippel. She was the wife of Fred Witt of McGregor. Burial was in McGregor Cemtery by Amsler Funeral Home. Amsler Funeral Home Records.

DR. ALLEN JOHNSON of San Antonio died at his home Monday. Mr. and Mrs. Tull Johnson, Mr. and Mrs. Buddy Johnson, Mrs. Will Johnson and Mrs. Park Johnson, Mr. and Mrs. Jesse Murphy of Comanche Springs attended the funeral in San Antonio. Dr. Johnson had formerly lived in McGregor. Survivors include his father, W. C. Johnson of Oglesby; brothers, Tull, Paul and Parker Johnson; one sister, Mrs. J. A. Murphy of Big Springs. McGregor Mirror: Oct 17 (8-3)\(8-6), 1941.

PEGGY SUE BASS, age 3, died in McGregor on November 13, 1941. She was born in McGregor November 19, 1937, the daughter of W. J. Bass and Ruby Riley Bass. Informant was Ella Bass of McGregor. Burial was in McGregor Cemtery by Amsler Funeral Home. Her uncles, Richard, Herman, Cohen and Trav Bass were pallbearers. Survivors include her parents; two sisters and three brothers. Amsler Funeral Home Records. McGregor MIrror: Nov 21 (8-6), 1941.

ROBERT WILLIAM WRYE, age 75, died at his home at Station Creek, near McGregor, November 18, 1941. He was born in Muscatine, Iowa, but was in business in Dallas before moving to Station Creek some 22 years ago. At one time he held an appointment as a United States Marshall.

Survivors include his wife; five daughters, Mrs. Rosa Handlin, Mrs. Hazel DeBorde, Mrs. Daisy McGuire of Dallas, Mrs. Allie Boltinghouse of Burnett and Miss Myrtle Wrye of McGregor; one son, Garland F. Wrye of Dallas. Burial was in Evergreen Cemetery by Amsler Funeral Home. McGregor Mirror: Nov 21, 1941.

NORMA KNIGHT died Friday following an automobile accident near Hillsboro on Wednesday, November 19, 1941, which killed three other people. Burial was in Rosemound Cemetery in Waco by Lee Undertakers following funeral services at Coryell Baptist Church. Double services for BONNIE NELL BOSTIK and MARY INEZ COULTER, also killed in the same accident, were held in Moody on Friday. The third victim, BILL EVANS of Denton, was buried in Denton. Norma was survived by her parents, Mr. and Mrs. Claude Knight; a sister, Mrs. Rolland Bell of La Grange. McGregor Mirror: Nov 28 (3-4), 1941.

REV. D. H. BEEBE, son-in-law of Mrs. O. B. Gardner of McGregor, died in Lawton, Oklahoma, Sunday. Burial was in Lawton City Cemetery by Ritters Funeral Home of Lawton. Survivors include his wife, Marjorie Gardner Beebe, formerly of McGregor; a sister who lives in Denver, Colorado. Mrs. Laura Haley of McGregor and Mrs. Mary Sales of Midland, sisters of Mrs. Beebe, attended the funeral. McGregor Mirror: Dec 5 (5-4), 1941.

EMMETT T. BARNARD, age 66, died in a Waco hospital Sunday, November 30, 1941. He had lived around McGregor for over 40 years. For the past 8 years the family had made their home near The Grove where he was engaged in farming. Survivors include his wife; two daughters, Mrs. Butler Westerfield of Wichita Falls and Mrs. Jake Canough of Livingston, Texas; one son, Doyle Barnard of The Grove. Several brothers and sisters also survive. Burial was in Flint Cemetery by Lee Undertakers. McGregor Mirror: Dec 5 (8-1), 1941.

CHARLES W. MARSHALL, age 33, died in a Waco hospital Friday, December 6, 1941. Burial was in McGregor Cemetery by Lee Undertakers. Survivors include his wife, Beatrice Marshall; two sons, C. W. and Melvin Doyle Marshall; a daughter, Loyce Beth Marshall; five sisters and four brothers, Mrs. Guy Summers and Mrs. Joe Lechler of McGregor, Mrs. John Hendrix, Dorothy and Louise Marshall of Waco, Lester and Glenn Marshall of Waco, Roy Marshall of El Paso, Loy Marshall of San Antonio. McGregor Mirror: Dec 12 (4-2), 1941.

MRS. BERT DAVIS died at her home near Arnett Sunday, November 23, 1941. Burial was in Blackfoot Cemetery by Scott Funeral Home in Gatesville. Mrs. Davis had lived most of her life around Oglesby, only having moved to Arnett some 2 years ago. Survivors include her husband; one son, Bertrum Davis; mother; two sisters; a brother. Pallbearers were brothers-in-law. McGregor Mirror: Dec 12 (8-4), 1941.

MARY KIRKPATRICK, age 83, died at her home in Fayettville, Arkansas. She was the mother of Mrs. John Grantham of McGregor and had lived here about 40 years ago. Survivors include three daughters, Mrs. John Grantham of McGregor, Mrs. Dwight Moffett and Mrs. C. J. Davis of Sumers, Arkansas; one son, I. J. Kirkpatrick of Fayettville, Arkansas; eight grand-children and twelve great-grand-children. McGregor Mirror: Dec 19 (8-2), 1941.

CHAPTER 8

CARL HORSTMANN died Wednesday, March 18, 1942, in McGregor at age 69. He was born in Germany February 2, 1873, the son of William Horstmann and _____ Buschmeier of Germany. Survivors include his wife; one son, Fritz Horstmann of McGregor; one daughter, Mrs. Dick Brauer of Needland, Texas; seven grandchildren; one sister in Germany. He was preceded in death by one child which died in infancy and his first wife, Charlotte Hodde, who died in February of 1933. After the death of his first wife, he married Mrs. Eliza Schutt of Philadelphia. Mr. Horstmann was born in Germany and when 17 years old came to New York City where he worked for 2 years before moving to Illinois. Two years later he moved to Washington County, Texas, then 5 years later, in 1901, he moved to McGregor. Burial was in McGregor Cemetery by Amsler Funeral Home. Cemetery records show him buried beside Caroline Horstmann (Sep 30, 1871-Feb 2, 1933). Amsler Funeral Home, Book 3.

RAMONA DIAZ, age 4, died February 5, 1942, in McGregor. She was born in McGregor on August 31, 1937, the daughter of Ben Diaz born in Lockhart, Texas and Margaret Gonzales born in San Marcos, Texas. Burial was in McGregor Cemtery by Amsler Funeral Home. Amsler Funeral Home Records, Book 3.

JUAN DIAZ, age 8, died April 11, 1942, in a Waco hospital. He was born May 10, 1935, in Austin, the son of Ben Diaz and Margaret Gonzales. Burial was in McGregor Cemtery by Amsler Funeral Home. Amsler Funeral Home Records, Book 3.

JOHN COOPER WILLIAMS, age 45, died in a Temple hospital, Tuesday, April 21, 1942. He was born August 20, 1896, in Lorena, Texas, the son of Cooper Williams and Mary Ellen Hayes. He had been in the gin business in Lorena for several years. For the past 8 years he had also been in the grocery business in McGregor. Survivors include his wife, Doris Morehead Crouch Williams; one daughter, Mary Ann Williams; three sisters, Mrs. Walter Evans of Lorena, Mrs. Agnes Barnes and Mrs. W. W. Cox of Waco; one brother, Mr. Van Wood Williams of Calvert; one nephew, Lee Vaughn Williams of Knoxville, Tennessee. Burial was in McGregor Cemetery by Amsler Funeral Home. Amsler Funeral Home Records, Book 3.

C. F. LUEDTKE, age 83, died April 23, 1942, in Waco. He was born March 4, 1859. Burial was in McGregor Cemetery by Wilkerson-Hatch Funeral Home of Waco, beside Emma Luedtke (1866-1928). Amsler Funeral Home Records, Book 3.

REV. HANS ERIC KRAUSE, age 53, died June 10, 1942, in a Waco hospital. He was born in Minden, Germany November 23, 1887, the son of Lothur Krause and Lydia Krause. He was a Lutheran minister married to Ella Sophia Heinsohn (Oct 30, 1884-Aug 27, 1964). Burial was in McGregor Cemtery by Amsler Funeral Home. Amsler Funeral Home Records, Book 3.

THOMAS LEE ALLISON, age 75, died June 17, 1942, in McGregor. He was born in Kingsville, Texas on September 23, 1866, the son of Jay Allison and Sarah McPeak. Informant was Mrs. R. W. Chambers, daughter, of Austin. Burial was in McGregor Cemtery by Amsler Fuenral Home, beside Mary Ellen Allison (Jul 4, 1875-Nov 4, 1961). Amsler Funeral Home Records, Book 3.

MRS. CORRIE LEACHE, age 73, died in McGregor on July 16, 1942. She was born in Talladega County, Alabama on August 18, 1868, the daughter of Rev. T. G. Sammons born in Tennessee and Eluira DeShazo born in Alabama. In 1883 she came to McGregor with her parents and in 1893 married C. Lytton Leache. Mr. Leache preceded her in death many years ago. Seven children were born to them, the oldest C. Lytton, Jr. died in 1918 and left a son who now lives in Crawford. Survivors include his children, Mrs. Corrie Henderson of Essex, Missouri, J. W. Leache of Willmington, California, Mrs. R. B. Russell of McGregor, J. D. Leache of Mt. Vernon, Ohio, Lieut. F. S. Leache of Galveston and Edd Leache of McGregor who is now in the Army stationed at Sheppard Field in the Air Corps. Burial was in McGregor Cemetery by Amsler Funeral Home. Amsler Funeral Home Records. Book 3.

JULIA ANN ARRIE CONNALLY, age 74, died August 3, 1942, in a Waco hospital. She was born in Georgia on February 23, 1868, the daughter of I. N. "Newt" Cox and D. E. Chamins. Burial was in Comanche Springs Cemetery by Amsler Funeral Home beside her husband, William Lee Connally (Aug 31, 1864-Jul 27, 1937). She was born in Georgia but moved to Texas when a child. The family lived in Comanche Springs community for may years and there she married Lee Connally, who preceded her in death 5 years ago. Survivors include three sons and five daughters, Roy of Beaumont, Ernest of Memphis, Texas, and Chris Connally of Palestine, Mrs. G. D. Lewellyn of Plainview, Mrs. C. W. Webb of Flomont, Mrs. E. L. Cherry of Amarillo, Mrs. Jack Wardlow of El Paso and Mrs. Hunter Mann of Waco; three brothers and two sisters, W. C. and John D. Cox of McGregor, Otis Cox of Dallas, Mrs. Will Morris of Gatesville and Mrs. Len Buckner of Roscoe. Amsler Funeral Home Records, Book 3.

OTTO HERMON HUESKE, age 78, died near his home in McGregor, Monday August, 9, 1942. He had been a resident of this area for 56 years. He was born in Germany on July 24, 1864, the son of August Hueske and Amelia Gramunder. Otto came to Texas at age 18 and lived in Washington County for 4 years before moving to McGregor. Survivors include his wife, Tischer Hueske; three sons, W. G. "Will" Hueske and Bed Hueske of McGregor and Ed Hueske of Beasley, Texas; two daughters, Mrs. Ernest Brandes and Mrs. W. H. Becker of McGregor; one borther, Adolf Hueske of Waco. Burial was in McGregor Cemtery by Amsler Funeral Home, beside Emma Hueske (Oct 17, 1873-Jun 30, 1972). Amsler Funeral Home Records, Book 3.

DEATHS IN CENTRAL TEXAS, VOL. II

ORA EDNA REEVES, age 38, died August 9, 1942, at the home of Mr. and Mrs. Ed Reeves. She was born in Oklahoma on February 1, 1904, the daughter of J. F. Farris and Edna Pearl Jones. She is survived by her husband, E. W. Reeves; five children, Cledyth "Pat", A. C., Roland, Farris Dale and John E. Reeves; her father, J. F. Farris of Hood River, Oregon; two sisters, Mrs. L. A. Mooney of Hood River, Mrs. C. A. Pinkley of Amarillo; six brothers, Fred L. Farris of Causey, New Mexico, W. E. Farris of Hood River, C. L. Farris of U. S. Navy at Norfolk, Virginia, Frank Farris of Hood River, R. A. Farris of Beaumont and Leon Farris of U. S. Navy at Pearl Harbor. Burial was in McGregor Cemetery by Amsler Funeral Home. Amsler Funeral Home Records, Book 3.

ROBERT FRED BROCKERMEYER of Brenham, age 46, died on August 13, 1942, in a Navasota hospital. He was born in William Penn, Texas on October 6, 1895, the son of Henry W. Brockermeyer and and Minnie Weise. He was a storekeeper. Survivors include his wife and seven year old daughter, Dorothy Mae Brockermeyer; his mother; five brothers, Henry and Carl of Washington County, Texas, Reinhardt and Albert of McGregor, Fred of Greenville; two sisters, Mrs. Sophie Mutscher of Giddings and Miss Lillie Brockermeyer of McGregor. He moved to McGregor from Washington County in 1923 and married Ruth Willingham of McGregor in 1934. In May of 1916 he volunteered for service in the U. S. Army and served on the Mexican bourder as a corporal in the Second Texas Infantry. He also served overseas in the 36th Division in WWI. Burial was in McGregor Cemetery by Scott Funeral Home of Navasota and Amsler Funeral Home of McGregor. Amsler Funeral Home Records, Book 3.

JOHN A. ROACH, age 64, died in McGregor on September 14, 1942. He was born April 21, 1878, in Gradyville, Kentucky, the son of Martin W. Roach and Nan England. He had been employed as a guard with the Bluebonnet Ordnance Plant since last March. Mr. Roach moved here from Kentucky many years ago. For a few years he and his father operated a grocery here. Survivors include his wife, Eliza (1887-1964); one daughter, Mrs. John Hunnicutt of Waco; three sons, Clarence A. of McGregor, John Calvin of Waco and Frank Thompson Roach of U. S. Army Camp Edwards, Mass; four sisters, Mrs. W. T. Montgomery of Fort Worth, Mrs. Gove Stevens of Roby, Mrs. Cal Stevens and Mrs. June McKinney of Moody. Burial was in McGregor Cemetery by Amsler Funeral Home. Amsler Funeral Home Records, Book 3.

JAMES HENRY OLIVER, age 73, died Tuesday, November 3, 1942, in McGregor. He was born in MIssissippi on November 3, 1869, the son of John Oliver and Haley Smith. When he was 5 years old the family moved from Mississippi to McLennan County and watched the start of McGregor. Mr. Oliver married Alice Elizabeth Bishop 52 years ago at old Bishop near McGregor. Survivors include his wife, Alice (Nov 6, 1872-Feb 9, 1949); three daughters, Mrs. Mamie Goff and Mrs. Joe Mansker of McGregor and Mrs. Bob Safley of Belton; two sons, Audie Oliver of McGregor and L. J. Oliver of Waco; three brothers, Lee Oliver of Muleshoe, Texas, Will Oliver and Lewis Oliver of Cleburne; three sisters, Mrs. Henrietta Prince of Fort Worth, Mrs. Ella Wright and Mrs. Wilder Morris of Cleburne. Burial was in McGregor Cemetery by Amsler Funeral Home. Amlser Funeral Home Records, Book 3.

JOHN W. WRIGHT, age 69, died in California on November 6, 1942. He was born in Hot Springs, Arkansas on July 12, 1873, the son of Sam Wright and Anna Hall, both born in MIssissippi. Mr. Wright's body was shipped to McGregor for burial in Harris Creek Cemetery by Amsler Funeral Home of McGregor. He moved to McGregor in 1889, having resided here for 48 years before moving to California some 5 years ago, where he had been engaged in the building and construction business. Mr. Wright was preceded in death by his wife, Lee Wright. Survivors include one daughter, Mrs. Harvey Cline of Roscoe, California; three sons, Johnnie Lee Wright of San Francisco, Marvin Wright of Los Angeles and Roy Wright of Gardens, California; four brohters, Will Wright of Meridian, Jobe Wright of McGregor, Sam Wright of Plainview, and Henry Wright of Lamesa; one sister, Mrs. Mary Wright of Wheeler, Texas. Amsler Funeral Home Records, Book 3.

NANNIE R. TUBBS, age 73, died at the home of her son, W. T. Tubbs in McGregor on December 29, 1942. She was born in Mississippi on December 9, 1869, the daughter of Jack Walker and Ann Murry. Mrs. Tubbs had been a resident of McGregor for many years, coming here with her parents from Mississippi. Some years ago she lost her only son, Jimmie Millender, from accidental burns. She is survived by her step-son, W. T. Tubbs; one step-grandson, Lee Smith, of McGregor; two brothers, George Walker of McGregor and Frank Walker of Waco. Burial was in McGregor Cemetery by Amsler Funeral Home. Amsler Funeral Home Records, Book 3.

CHAPTER 9

FAYE J. HAYNES, age 44, died Monday, January 4, 1943. He was born November 15, 1898, the son of the late, Mr. and Mrs. W. L. Haynes, pioneers of McGregor. Survivors include his wife; a son in Louisiana and a step-son, Dick Richards, of McGregor; seven brothers, Roy of Gastland, Missouri, Wheeler of Oxnard, California, Don, Grady and Bonnie L. of Wichita Falls, Ira and Holly Haynes of McGregor. He was preceded in death by one sister, Mrs. R. E. Henry. Burial was in McGregor Cemetery by Lee Undertakers. McGregor Mirror: Jan 8 (4-1). 1943.

NANNIE R. TUBBS, age 73, died at the home of her son, W. T. Tubbs, in McGregor on December 29, 1943. She was born on December 9, 1869, in Mississippi but came to Texas with her father, Jack Walker. Survivors include her step-son, W. T. Tubbs; one step-grandson, Lee Smith, both of McGregor; two brothers, George Walker of McGregor and Frank Walker of Waco. Her only son, Jimmie Millender (1890-1917), died on September 3, 1917, of burns received in an accident. Burial was in McGregor Cemetery by Amsler Funeral Home. McGregor Mirror: Jan 8 (2-5), 1943.

ROY ROACH died in a Waco hospital Monday, January 4, 1943. He came to this community from Kentucky 55 years ago when he was 9 years of age. He had been a businessman in McGregor and a farmer in this area. Survivors include his wife; one son, Elmore of Richmond, Virgnina; one daughter, Mrs. Paul Isbill of Pelham, New York; two grandchildren, Miss Eleanor Roach and Paula Isbill; three sisters, Mrs. A. M. Howard of Waco, Mrs. J. W. Hendrick of Winters, Mrs. Della Sparks of Bryan; one brother, F. M. Roach of McGregor; one half-brother, C. W. England of Humble, Texas. Burial was in Old Perry Cemetery by Amsler Funeral Home. McGregor Mirror: Jan 8 (7-2), 1943.

JAMES ANDERSON MORRIS was born in Oglesby on September 24, 1898. He married Annie Lee Searcy on August 30, 1919. Survivors incude his wife, Annie Morris; two sons, Searcy Lee of Waco and Jack of Oglesby; his parents, Mr. and Mrs. Felix Morris of Oglesby; one brother, F. A. Morris of Oglesby; one sister, Mrs. Gertrude Donaldson of McGregor. Two children preceded him in death. He had been a stock farmer for many years and at the time of his death he was employed by Montgomery Ward in Waco. Mr. Morris died at his home in Oglesby Friday, December 11, 1942. Burial was in Post Oak Cemetery near Oglesby. McGregor Mirror: Jan 8 (6-2), 1943.

MR. MORRIS. Mr. and Mrs. Buster Morris and Arward Tomlinson were called to Ballinger, Texas, Christmas because of the death of Mr. Morris's father who died December 24, 1942. McGregor Mirror: Jan 8 (8-3), 1943.

MRS. J. V. WHEAT died in a Waco hospital Sunday after suffering a heart attack on the street in McGregor. She was born in Kentucky on September 1, 1881 and moved to this county in 1914. Survivors include her husband, whom she married on August 14, 1897; three children, Paul of Waco, Edwin and Billy Wheat of McGregor. Burial was in Moody Cemtery by Lee Undertakers. McGregor Mirror: Jan 29 (4-3), 1943.

MRS. D. M. BOSTIK, age 86, died at her home in Moody Tuesday, January 26, 1943. Burial was in Moody Cemetery by Lee Undertakers. Survivors include three sons, John G. Bostik, B. J. Bostik and S. P. Bostik; one daughter, Mrs. Mertie Patrick. McGregor Mirro: Jan 29 (4-3), 1943.

JAMES MADISON DAVIS died near Oglesby on Monday, January 25, 1943. He was born in Coryell County and married Jessie Foster on October 16, 1917. Survivors include his wife; two children, Elizabeth Jo Davis and Sgt. J. M. Davis, Jr. of Camp Edwards, Mass.; his mother, Mrs. A. P. Davis of Oglesby; two brothers, H. D. Davis of McGregor and Marvin E. Davis of Dallas; one niece, Mrs. Raymond C. Barber; four nephews, Lieut. H. L. Davis, Sgt. B. A. Davis of Camp Edwards, Sgt. Hupert Davis of Tampa, Florida and Cadet Royce Davis of officers training school in Florida. Burial was in Davidson Cemetery by Lee Undertakers. McGregor Mirror: Jan 29 (5-3), 1943.

GRADY HALL, JR. died in a Waco hospital Friday. He was born on July 29, 1941. Burial was in Post Oak Cemetery by Lee Undertakers. Survivors include his parents, Mr. and Mrs. Grady Hall; a seven year old sister; and his grandparents, Mr. and Mrs. Harry Hall of McGregor and Mr. and Mrs. Luther Kinsey of Oglesby. McGregor Mirror: Jan 29 (8-2), 1943.

EDNA AUGUSTA BRINKLEY died at her home in Oglesby on January 23, 1943. She was born in Ashland, Mississippi on November 20, 1872 but had lived in Oglesby for over 50 years. Burial was in Post Oak Cemetery by Lee Undertakers. Mrs. Brinkley was laid to rest beside her deceased husband, Robert Brinkley (1864-1919). Survivors include Mrs. Jim Griffin of Oglesby, Mrs. R. L. Roland of Trent, Mrs. Roy Hinton of Hearne, Mrs. Henry Evans of Waco, Mrs. S. P. Autry of Longview, Mrs. Earl Clayton of Sweetwater, Mrs. Charles DeWitt of Clifton, Arizona, Mrs. Henry Butts of Big Spring, Mrs. Hugh Walker of Oglesby, Mrs. Sam Matthews, Jr. of Tuscon, Arizona, Clark Brinkley of Berkeley, California, Bryan Brinkley of Los Angeles and Clyde Brinkley of Avalon, California. McGregor Mirror: Jan 29 (8-4), 1943.

JAMES DOUGLAS DAWSON, only son of Mrs. and Mrs. Frank Dawson, was killed in action on January 25, 1943. He was a radioman, third class in the U. S. Navy. "Nubbin", as he was called here, had been in the service for 2 years. J. D. Graduated from McGregor High School with the class on 1938 and was co-captain and quarterback of the 1937 football squad. If he had lived until March 29, he would have been 21 years old. Survivors include his parents; four sisters, Mrs. Leitha

Meador of McGregor, Mrs. Isla Blackburn, Mrs. Frankie Lee of San Angelo and Bobbie Lou Dawson of Mcgregor. (Picture included). McGregor Mirror: Feb 6 (1-3), 1943.

ELMO ROUTH was buried in Moody Saturday. He lived in McGregor a number of years ago when he owned the ice plant. He died Friday in Gatesville where he had been living since leaving McGregor. McGregor Mirror: Feb 6 (3-3), 1943.

MARY E. CRENSHAW (Mrs. D. M. Crenshaw), age 92, died at her home in McGregor Tuesday, February 9, 1943. She was born in Chapel Hill, Texas on September 26, 1850, but had lived in McLennan County for 63 years. She was the daughter of James W. Miller and Elizabeth Walker born in Bowling Green, Kentucky. The family had made their home in McGregor since 1921. Survivors include one son, Boss Crenshaw; two daughters, Mrs. J. E. Slight of Temple and Mrs. L. C. Cox of McGregor. Burial was in McGregor Cemetery by Amsler Funeral Home. Pallbearers were L. C. Fox, J. E. Slight, Miller Morris, Jay Martin, Dan Harris and J. H. Youngblood. McGregor Mirror: Feb 12 (5-6), 1943.

MR. J. H. CLEMENTS, age 78, died in a Temple hospital last Friday. Burial was in Copperas Cove, Texas. Mr. Clements had lived in Copperas Cove for over 50 years. He is the father of Lonnie Clements of McGregor. Survivors include three daughters, Mrs. W. A. Hazelwood of Newark, Mrs. R. C. Shoffer of Houston and Mrs. G. B. Henson of Copperas Cove; four sons, Dr. J. W. Clements of Texarkana, Dr. C. C. Clements of Groesbeck, Dr. E. R. Clements of Houston, and Lonnie Clements of McGregor. McGregor Mirror: Feb 19 (5-4), 1943.

JAMES ARTHUR CRELIA, age 32, died of pneumonia at the Army Station Hospital at Karnes Field, Utah, Saturday February 13, 1943. He was born June 16, 1910 in Weatherford, Texas, the son of James A. Crelia and Rosa Crelia, but had lived in McGregor for several years. About 5 years ago he married Eula Mae Ash. Survivors include his wife, Lula Mae Crelia; his parents, Mr. and Mrs. J. A. Crelia; four brothers, Clyde, Lester and Leslie of McGregor and Hoyt Crelia of Gatesville; three sisters, Mrs. Herman Gunter of Midland, Mrs. Monroe Wilson of Stamford and Mrs. Clyde Chaney of El Paso. Burial was in McGregor Cemetery by Amsler Funeral Home. McGregor Mirror: Feb 19 (8-3), 1943.

H. A. PERMENTER, age 69, was found dead in a well three miles north of Moody last Friday. It was reported that he went to the well with a mule-drawn sled and a barrel to haul water. He apparently became overbalanced and fell into the well. Burial was in Moody Cemetery by Lee Undertakers. Survivors include five sons, W. H. Permenter of Moody, B. J. of Eddy, Woodrow of the U. S. Army, Winnon and Armond of McGregor; six daughters, Mrs. Ivy Nelson of Clayton of New Mexico, Mrs. R. N. McIlhaney of Bartlett, Mrs. Dennis Kelley of Pendleton, Mrs. A. P. Prince of Troy, Miss Rena Permeter and Miss Luella Permeter of McGregor. McGregor Mirror: Feb 27 (4-4), 1943.

T. B. BATES, age 54, died at his home in Leon Junction on February 13, 1943. Burial was in Seaton Cemetery by Lee Undertakers. Survivors include his wife; two sons, Roy of Pecan Grove and Charles of Leon Junction; four sisters, Mrs. Molly Chablee of Cortez, Colorado, Mrs. E. M. Kirk of Waco, Mrs. Lena Fields of Moshein, Mrs. Mattie Henegar of Leon Junction; three brothers, Marion of Leon Junction, Will of Cortez, Colorado and Lee Bates of Oglesby. McGregor Mirror: Feb 27 (5-2), 1943.

ANNA BLANCO died March 4, 1943, in a Waco hospital at age 1. She was born May 1, 1941 in Crawford to F. Blanco and Jewel Gonzales of Devine. Informant was Feodono Blanco, her father. Burial was in City Cemetery by Amsler Funeral Home. Amsler Funeral Home Records, 1943.

ROBERT L. SMITH, age 71, resident of South Bosque for 50 years, died at his home Monday, March 8, 1943. He was born on October 21, 1871, the son of J. H. Smith (1825-1914). Survivors include his brother, J. H. Smith of Hamilton; two sisters, Mrs. R. H. Threat of McGregor, Mrs. W. E. Sikes of Tahoka. Mr. Smith was a native of Alabama. Burial was in Harris Creek Cemetery. Pallbearers were Roy and Clinton Sikes, Ralph Buice, Lee Ellis, Joe McFall and Raymond Darden. McGregor Mirror: Mar 12 (5-2), 1943.

ARTHUR L. TIPTON, age 29, was burned to death Monday March 1, 1943, near Raymondville. He was born on August 8, 1913. Burial was in McGregor Cemetery by Amsler Funeral Home. Arthur and his brother-in-law, Alvis D. Strickland, lost their lives when the gasoline truck Strickland was operating caught fire. Survivors include his wife; two children; his parents; two sisters; and one brother. McGregor Mirror: Mar 12 (5-3), 1943.

MARTIN CRAIN, age 75, died at the home of his daughter in Waco Friday, March 5, 1943. He was born on July 21, 1868, in Tennessee but came to Texas with his father's family when he was young. The family settled in Coryell County and had made their home in the Coryell Church community for many years. Survivors include his wife; two sons, Lawton of U. S. Naval Training Station at San Diego, Joe Crain of Coryell Church; one daughter, Mrs. M. M. Dickerson of Waco; one brother, George Crain; one sister, Delia Crain of Coryell Church. Burial was in Coryell Church Cemetery by Amsler Funeral Home. McGregor Mirror: Mar 12 (5-6), 1934.

LEONCE LEFEURE CUENOD (Mrs. Paul C. Cuenod) died at the family home in McGregor Sunday, March 14, 1943. She was born in Reims, France on June 28, 1869 but came to America at age 12 with her parents, Eugene Lefevre and Clara Lelong, who were part of a Franco-American colony, organized in Paris. The group first located near Weatherford, Texas, in 1881. Several years later the family moved to Galveston. There Leonce Lefevre met and married Paul C. Cuenod on August 4, 1898. Survivors include her husband, Paul C. Cuenod; one daughter, Maud Cuenod of Canyon, Texas; two sons, Henry of McGregor and Cpl. Eugene C. Cuenod of Army Air Base, Casper, Wyoming. Burial was in McGregor Cemetery by Amsler Funeral Home. Mr. and Mrs. Cuenod were merchants in McGregor for many years. Out-of-town attendants at the funeral included Mr. and Mrs. Marion E. Parrott of Rosenberg, Texas; Mr. W. E. Parrott of Houston; Dr. E. M. Cuenod and daughter, Louanne Cuenod of Houston; Mr. Lucien C. Cuenod and Mrs. Rene G. Cuenod of Galveston; Mrs. Elliot Ernst and Miss Ellen B. Cuenod of Dickinson; Mr. and Mrs. H. B. Gibbs and daughter, Peggy Gibbs of San Antonio; Miss Megda P. Cuenod and Miss Eula Gill of Austin; Bess T. Couch, Anne Johnson and Vida H. Dunbar; Mrs. Max Touchon, Mrs. Anna Heid, Mrs. Eva Neville and Mrs. A. O. Locke of Fort Worth; Miss Elizabeth Booton and Mr. B. W. Johnson of Dallas; Mr. and Mrs. Edwin Kirk and Mr. and Mrs. John E. Skinner of Waco. McGregor Mirror: Mar 19 (4-3), 1943.

LT. E. S. MOORES, flight instructor of Jackson Field, Mississippi, husband of Euna Lee High Moores and son-in-law of the late Jerry High and wife of Moody was killed in an air crash March 16, 1943. Burial was in Fort Worth, Texas. Survivors include his wife; one daughter, Mrs. Bus Fleming of Tulsa, Oklahoma; one granddaughter, Billie Fleming. Lieut. Moores was a nephew of Mrs. Tap Wells of McGregor. McGregor Mirror: Mar 19 (5-1), 1943.

JERRY DALE ANDERSON, infant son of Mr. and Mrs. Clem Anderson, died in a Waco hospital Friday, March 19, 1943. He was age 11 months. Jerry was born April 20, 1942, the son of Clem Floyd Anderson and M. Marsh. Survivors include his parents; two sisters, Jo Anne and Wynell; two brothers, Floyd and Donald Ray. Burial was in McGregor Cemetery by Amsler Funeral Home. McGregor Mirror: Mar 26 (5-1), 1943.

J. W. LANE, age 73, died Monday at the home of his daughter, Mrs. Frances Holt, in McGregor. Burial was in Comanche Springs Cemetery by Lee Undertakers. Survivors include two daughters, Mrs. Charlie Walters of Crawford and Mrs. Frances Holt of McGregor; seven sons, Robert Lane of Memphis, Tennessee, Eddie of Muleshoe, Jesse B. of Crawford, Fred in service in North Africa, Tommie D. and Roy Lane of McGregor, and Paul Lane of Mart; one sister, Mrs. Sam Clabaugh of Seymour, Tennessee. Mr. Lane had been a farmer in the McGregor area for over 37 years. McGregor Mirror: Apr 2 (4-6), 1943.

WILLIAM G. HUESKE, age 45, died at his home near McGregor, Thursday, April 8, 1943. He was born in McGregor in January 20, 1898, the son of Otto Hueske and Emma Tischler. Survivors include his wife, Pauline Hackfeld Hueske; one daughter, Leona; one son, Clayton; his mother, Mrs. Otto Hueske of McGregor; two brothers, Ben of McGregor, Edd of Beasley, Texas; two sisters, Mrs. Ernest Brandes and Mrs. W. H. Becker of McGregor. Burial was in McGregor Cemetery by Amsler Funeral Home. McGregor Mirror: Apr 9 (4-4), 1943.

MRS. M. J. LONG, age 90, died Thursday. "Grandma Long", as she was known, was a pioneer of McGregor. Burial was in Comanche Springs Cemetery by Lee Undertakers. McGregor Mirror: May 14 (1-5), 1943.

WILLIAM FRANCIS WALKER, age 80, died in a Waco hospital Saturday. Burial was in McGregor Cemetery. Mr. Walker was born in 1863 in Mississippi but had lived in McLennan County for 70 years. Survivors include his wife, Edna E. Walker (1868-1950); four sons, R. J. Walker of Rosenthal, S. E. Walker, F. C. Walker and A. J. Walker of Waco; one brother, George Walker of McGregor. McGregor Mirror: May 14 (6-6), 1943.

ALBERT JONES, age 74, died in McGregor on June 15, 1943. He was born September 15, 1868 in Georgia, the son of Robert Jones. He was born in Georgia but settled on the Caufield Ranch in McLennan County before moving to McGregor. Survivors include his wife, Nannie Dell "Della" Jones, (1872-1956); two sons, Robert Jones of McGregor and Clydus Jones, a private in the U. S. Army; two daughters, Mrs. Pearl Richardson of Dallas and Mrs. Grace Echart of Crawford; two sisters, Mrs. Emma Johnson of Houston and Mrs. Eliza Webb of Knox City, Texas; three brothers, Tom of Vernon, Henry of Roswell, New Mexico and Frank of Houston; two granddaughters, Kathleen Smiley and Doris Richardson; one great-granddaughter, Delores Ann. Burial was in McGregor Cemetery by Amsler Funeral Home. Amsler funeral Home Records, 1943.

AGAPITO A. GONZALES died June 23, 1943 in Oglesby, Texas, at age 69. She was born in Mexico on July 26, 1873, the daughter of C. Alvarado. Burial was in McGregor Cemetery by Amsler Funeral Home. She lived on the John F. Bennett farm near McGregor. Informant was Andores A. Gonzales. Amsler Funeral Home Records, 1943.

EMIL HACKFELD, age 53, was killed in a head-on auto collision Monday, June 21, 1943. Mr. Hackfeld, who was driving a car pulling a trailer, was killed instantly. W. L. Bradshaw, son of Link Bradshaw, formerly of McGregor, suffered injuries in the accident. Mr. Hackfeld was born in Sublime, Texas, on November 6, 1888, but moved to West, Texas as a child. He was the son of J. H. Hackfeld and Bertha Schroeder. In 1912 he moved to Roscoe, Texas, where he married Clara Anna Zetzmann. They moved to Osage after the marriage and in 1923 moved to McGregor. Survivors include his wife; three sons, W. H. of Orange Grove, Texas, Henry F. of San Antonio and Otto of McGregor; four sisters, Mrs. Martha Brown of Porters, Texas, Mrs. Joe J. Jarrett of Stevensville, Mrs. F. H. Fehler of Clifton and Mrs. W. G. Hueske of McGregor. Burial was in McGregor Cemetery by Amsler Funeral Home. McGregor Mirror: Jun 25 (1-4)\(8-7), 1943.

WALTER HOPPE was born in Thorndale, Milam County, Texas on January 15, 1902. Some 14 years ago he married Miss Doty of Osage. He died Thursday, June 17, 1943, in a Waco hospital. Burial was in McGregor

Cemetery by Amsler Funeral Home. Survivors include his wife, Doty Hoppe; five children, Walter Hoppe, Jr., Oscar Tinsley Hoppe, Alvin Edgar Hoppe, Robert Leroy Hoppe and Elizabeth Louise Hoppe; his father, Oscar Hoppe; three brothers, Oscar D. Hoppe of Sagerton, Texas, Mark H. Hoppe, U. S. Army in Oregon, and Carl H. Hoppe of Littlefield; six sisters, Mrs. Bertha Schroeder of The Grove, Mrs. Gertrude Syler of McGregor, Mrs. Gladys Doty and Mrs. Clara Edmonds of Coryell Church, Mrs. Lydia Wells of Austin and Mrs. Erma Hoppe of McGregor. McGregor Mirror: Jun 25 (8-8) 1943.

DR. WILLIAM PRICE CONNALLY, well known pioneer physician, died Sunday, July 11, 1943. He was age 73, having been born on January 29, 1871. His office was located on the second floor of the First National Bank building. He wore a long Santa like beard and always dressed in Black or navy suits. A string tie was also part of his dress. Dr. Connally always sat squat in a chair with his feet in the seat. He was a WWI Captain in the medical corps. Two of his sons graduated from West Point. Burial was in McGregor Cemetery by Lee Undertakers. Survivors include his wife, Gerturde Wallace Connally (1875-1961); children, Lt. Col. Price Connally, who is overseas with the staff of General MacArthur, Capt. Lanham Connally of Massachusetts, and Mrs. H. F. Houston of Kilgore; two brothers, Ben Connally of Lorena and Nep Connally of the panhandle. McGregor Mirror: Jul 16 (1-2)\ Jul 26 (1-1), 1943.

DONALD RAY ZIMMERMAN, age 4, died in a Waco hospital Saturday July 17, 1943. Donald was born June 20, 1939. He was carried to the hospital only a few hours before suffering from loss of blood from a small wound on the finger. Survivors include his parents, H. Olin Zimmerman and Katie Wallman Zimmerman; one brother; and one sister; grandparents on both sides of the family. Informant was his grandfather, C. E. Zimmerman of McGregor. Burial was in McGregor Cemetery by Amsler Funeral Home. Pallbearers were W. R. and D. L. Zimmerman, S. T. Webb and G. G. Morgan. McGregor Mirror: Jul 23 (4-2), 1943.

JESS KIRBY, age 89, died at his home in Oglesby Wednesday. Burial was in Osage Cemetery by Lee Undertakers. Survivors include five daughters, Mrs. A. A. Foster of Winters, Mrs. T. A. Coffman of Wingate, Mrs. Bertha Miller and Mrs. Ada Hackfeld of San Antonio, Mrs. Curte Bennett of Oglesby; one son, C. L. Kirby of Gatesville. Mr. Kirby had lived in Oglesby since he was a child. McGregor Mirror: Jul 23 (8-5), 1943.

MRS. W. P. PLEDGER died at the home of her daughter, Mrs. Edgar Isbill, Friday. Lee Undertakers conveyed her body to Hallsville, her former home, where it lay in state for several hours. Burial was in the Hallsville Cemetery beside her deceased husband, Rev. W. P. Pledger, who died 17 years ago. Survivors include two children, Mrs. Edgar Isbill of McGregor and Mrs. E. R. Norman of Killeen; five grandchildren, Dawn and Jack Isbill, Mrs. John Mack Alexander, Sarah

Hane and Marky Norman; four sisters; three brothers. One sister, Mrs. Gertie B. Harris and a sister-in-law, Mrs. Billy Bolding, both of Hallsville, were in McGregor at the time Mrs. Pledger died. McGregor Mirror: Jul 30 (5-5), 1943.

JOE BOB CLEARMAN, age 14, was killed last Friday, January 26, 1943, in a accident while helping unload pipe at North Camp Hood. He was born January 7, 1929. Burial was in Osage Cemetery by Lee Undertakers. Survivors include his parents, Mr. and Mrs. A. Jake Clearman; four sisters and four brothers, Mrs. R. T. McMullin of Oglesby, Miss Mary Lou Clearman of Oglesby, Mrs. L. L. Slaughter of Douglas, Arizona, Mrs. Fred Stoermer of Waco, Ray Clearman of Waco, Jack Clearman of U. S. Army Air Corps, Billie Clearman of U. S. Army and Phillip Clearman of Oglesby. McGregor Mirror: Jul 30 (8-6), 1943.

SARAH JANE "SALLIE" HOFFMAN, mother of Mrs. John D. Mann, Mrs. G. W. Searcy and Charlie Hoffman, died Thursday, August 5, 1943 at age 85. She had lived in Valley Mills until the death of her husband some 13 years ago. At the time of her heath she was making her home with her daughter, Mrs. G. W. Searcy in McGregor. Burial was in Odell Cemetery near Valley Mills by Lee Undertakers. Survivors include her children Mrs. John D. Mann, Mrs. G. W. Search and Charlie Hoffmann of McGregor and Mrs. J. V. Cagle of Houston. McGregor Mirror: Aug 6 (2-2)\Aug 13 (5-5), 1943.

NATHAN ED JAYROE, age 71, died suddenly of a heart attack at his home in Osage Friday, August 20, 1943. He was born on September 17, 1871, in Coryell County, Texas, and served several terms as Road Commissioner of his precinct. Survivors include his wife, Clara V. Jayroe (1881-1974); three daughters, Mrs. Lillian Sadler of Dallas, Mrs. Eddie Lee Petree of Gatesville and Mrs. Elsie Anderson of Osage; five sons, Coxswain Louis E. Jayroe of the U. S. Navy in Dallas, Carl R. Jayroe of Waco, Cpl. Harold Wayne Jayroe of U. S. Army overseas, Sgt. Alton Herbert Jayroe of U. S. Army at Fort Knox, Kentucky and Pfc. John Robert Jayroe of U. S. Army in California; one sister, Mrs. T. S. Whitlock of Mart; two brothers, W. T. Jayroe of Sentinel, Oklahoma and Sherrill Jayroe of Osage. Burial was in Osage Cemetery by Amsler Funeral Home. Pallbearers were Earl Huddleston, Earl Merritt, Wesley Jayroe, Carroll Jayroe, Bill Edwards and Talmage Whitlock. McGregor Mirror: Aug 27 (4-4), 1943.

LT. ROYCE O. DAVIS, son of the late Gordon A. Davis and Mrs. Ruth Schomell, was killed in a plane accident at the Army Air Field in Pocatello, Idaho. He was born June 10, 1919 and died August 14, 1943. At the time of his death he was serving with the 453rd Bomb Group. Burial was Sunday in Davidson Cemetery by Lee Undertakers. McGregor Mirror: Aug 27 (8-4), 1943.

SAM E. HORNE, age 75, died in a local hospital Tuesday. Burial was in Rosemound Cemetery by Compton's Funeral Chapel in Waco. Mr. Horne was born in McGregor but had lived in Waco for 20 years. Survivors include his wife; three daughters, Miss Flora Horne of Waco, Mrs. Lucian W. Roach of Inglewood, California, Miss Annie B. Horne of Los Angeles; three sons, H. E. Horne of Norco, California, Cpl. Jack T. Horne of Camp Barkeley; three borthers, R. A. Horne of McGregor, Tom Horne of Bay City, Cliff Horne of Plainview; six sisters, Mrs. Jim Hay of Waco, Mrs. H. A. Campbell of Waco, Mrs. Mack Harris of Los Angeles, Mrs. C. E. Harris of Plainview, Mrs. R. E. Jones of Olney, Mrs. D. C. Smith of Hamilton; five grandchildren. Pallbearers were six nephews. McGregor Mirror: Sep 3 (4-3), 1943.

CHARLIE WITT died Sunday. Charlie was born in 1875. He had lived near Comanche Springs until about 2 years when he moved to McGregor. Survivors include his wife, Emma Witt (1880-1962); four daughters, Mrs. Minnie Wiethorn, Mrs. Matilda Hicks, Mrs. Joanna Mattiza, all of McGregor and Mrs. Lillie Springman of Waco; six sons, Bill and Paul of McGregor, Rudolph of Houston, Otto and Charlie of Fort Worth, and Eddie Witt who is at camp in Abilene; three brothers; and one sister. Burial was in McGregor Cemetery by Lee Undertakers. McGregor Mirror: Sep 3 (4-1), 1943.

SARAH J. WEBB, age 67, died a Levelland hospital Sunday, September 5, 1943. She was born near Oxford, Mississippi and came to Texas, locating near Jonesboro. At age 22 she married John Mac Webb (1871-1950), making their home in Mosheim then moving DeLeon, Texas. Mr. and Mrs. Webb moved to McGregor in 1918. About 1 year ago Mrs. Webb moved to Levelland to be near her daughter, Mrs. Train Robertson. Survivors include her husband; one son, Lois Webb of Altus, Oklahoma; one daughter, Mrs. Train Robertson of Levelland; three grandsons, Jim Robertson of A & M College, Phil and John Dale Webb of Altus; four brothers, George Crow of DeLeon, J. F. Crow and Bunion Crow of Dallas, Jess Crow of Memphis, Tennessee; three sisters, Mrs. W. G. Kimble of DeLeon, Mrs. Vennie Young of Dallas and Mrs. Annie Neely of Fort Worth. One daughter died in infancy and one son, Earl Webb, died at McGregor in 1931. Burial was in McGregor Cemetery by Amsler Funeral Home. McGregor Mirror: Sep 10 (4-3), 1943.

PHILLIP MASSIRER, age 62, died in Clifton Monday, September 6, 1943. Burial was in Prairie Chapel Cemetery by Lee Undertakers. Mr. Massirer was born in Austria but had been living in the Prairie Chapel community for many years. Survivors include his wife; two children, Hattie and Lillian Mae; four borthers, Adam and George of Crawford, John of Oglesby and Jacob of Waco. McGregor Mirror: Sep 10 (5-5), 1943.

MRS. R. L. NEWMAN, age 48, died Tuesday, September 7, 1943. Burial was in Moody Cemetery by Denny & Witt. Survivors include her husband, R. L. Newman of Moody, one daughter, Mrs. John F. Scruggs, Jr. of McGregor; two sons, Jack and Billy Newman of the U. S. Army; one sister, Mrs. L. N. Newman of Moody; one brother, Claude Pierce of Waco. McGregor Mirror: Sep 17 (5-3), 1943.

JOE M. EMBRY, age 77, died in Quanah Friday September 10, 1943. His wife and eight children were all at his bedside when the end came. Mr. and Mrs. Embry lived in McGregor for many years but moved to Quanah in 1923. Mrs. Embry was the oldest daughter of the late Mr. and Mrs. C. L. Ramsey. McGregor Mirror: Sep 17 (5-4), 1943.

MRS. VIC COMPTON, age 79, died in the home of her daughter, Mrs. Lillie Robinett in Crawford on Monday. Burial was at Compton Cemetery by Lee Undertakers. Survivors include one daughter, Mrs. Charlie Richardson; one son, P. O. Compton of Crawford. McGregor Mirror: Sep 24 (8-6), 1943.

SHIRLEY BYFORD, age 48, died suddenly Monday, October 11, 1943. He was born in Texas on September 18, 1895, the son of J. P. Byford and Mary Alice Cooper. At the time of his death he was employed as a guard at the Bluebonnet Ordnance plant at McGregor. He served as a sergeant with the 360th Inf., 90th Div. in the U. S. Army in France during World War I. Survivors include his wife, Annie Mary Byford; three daughters, Mrs. Evelyn Pfieffer, Mary and Betty Byford of McGregor; two sons, W. O. Byford of McGregor and Av. Cadet Burnard Byford of Lancaster, California; his mother, Mrs. J. P. Byford of Waco; three sisters, Mrs. Montie Andrews and Miss Winnie Byford of Waco, Mrs. Ella Newberry of Waco; three brothers, Cody of Waco, Gaston of McGregor and Corporal A. B. Byford of Wilmington, Delaware. Burial was in McGregor Cemetery by Amsler Funeral Home. McGregor Mirror: Oct 15 (8-2), 1943.

L. H. "UNCLE LOUIS" ANDERSON, age 93, died Tuesday in Crawford at the home of his daughter, Mrs. John Noland. He had been a resident of Crawford for 63 years. Survivors include one son, L. L. Anderson of Crawford; two daughters, Mrs. John Noland of Crawford and Mrs. W. W. Tubb of Dallas; two sisters, Mrs. Marshall Hodnet of Verda, Louisiana and Mrs. Witt Chaldler of Dypring, Louisiana; four half-brothers, Rev. Jasper Brown, Albert Brown, Hayne Brown and Ira Brown, all of Dypring, Louisiana. Burial was in Compton Cemetery by Amsler Funeral Home. He was laid to rest beside his wife who died some 14 years ago. McGregor Mirror: Oct 22 (4-5), 1943.

ROBERT VAN CLEARMAN, age 88, died at his home in Osage Tuesday, October 19, 1943. He was born on September 8, 1855. Burial was in Osage Cemetery by Lee Undertakers. He was a pioneer of that community, having lived there for over 45 years. Survivors include his wife, Lucinda Clearman (1855-1946); six daughters, Mrs. J. B. Swift, Mrs. Creassie Jayroe of Osage, Mrs. Fannie Hallmark of Beaumont, Mrs. Mollie Kirk of Waco, Mrs. Corrie Griffith of Luders, Mrs. Winnie Robinson of Oglesby; four sons, Henry of Bangs, Jake of Oglesby, Sam of Denton and Bob of Dallas. McGregor Mirror: Oct 22 (5-5), 1943.

WILLIAM DIXON PACE, age 80, died Friday, October 15, 1943, in a Temple hospital. William was born on October 30, 1862. He had lived in

McGregor for over 50 years. Survivors include his wife, Mary Frances Pace (1868-1955); three children, Mrs. W. C. Kolb of Waco, Mrs. F. E. Baldridge of Temple and E. R. Pace of McGregor; one grandson, Russell Pace, now stationed in North Africa. Burial was in McGregor Cemetery. McGregor Mirror: Oct 22 (5-6), 1943.

WALTER COOPER died in a West Coast hospital this week. Mr. Cooper, age 63, formerly farmed in this area for more than 40 years. He was a brother to Mrs. Melvin Mize, Mrs. Ernest Holbrook and Mrs. Haggard Janes. McGregor Mirror: Oct 29 (8-3), 1943.

ERNEST FERRIS HOLLINGSWORTH, age 25, was killed Wednesday when he ran head-on into a gasoline tramsport truck. He was riding a motorcycle at the time of the accident. Apparently he was on his way back to Fort Hood where he was a T-5 in the Army. Next of kin presumably lived at Spicewood, Texas. McGregor Mirror: Nov 12 (1-1), 1943.

ROBERT SAMUEL SNIDER, SR., age 46, died at his home in Crawford Friday, November 19, 1943. He was born in Georgetown, Texas on August 10, 1897. Survivors include his wife, Florence Snider; two daughters, Jewel Dean and Mildred Snider; four sons, Robert Samuel Snider, Jr., Eugene Snider, Jim Snider and Billy Ray Snider, all of Crawford; one brother, Cecil Snider of Gatesville; one sister, Catherine Snider of Flat, Texas; three half-brothers, Atlas Brown of McAllen, John and Jesse Brown of Flat; mother and step-father, Mrs. and Mrs. B. M. Brown of Flat; three half-sisters, Mrs. Ada Healer of Roby, Mrs. Mattie Fisher of McAllen and Mrs. Onavea Fisher of Bay City. Burial was in Crawford Cemetery by Amsler Funeral Home. McGregor Mirror: Nov 26 (4-2), 1943.

THOMAS TED ARNOLD was killed in action this week. Ted was a member of the 1941 graduating class in McGregor. He joined the air forces in November of 1942 and had been stationed in England at Chipping Warden as a radioman on a bomber. Ted, age 19, was born in 1924, the son of Mr. and Mrs. Tom W. Arnold of McGregor. Burial was in McGregor Cemetery. McGregor Mirror: Dec 3 (1-1), 1943.

OSCAR McCULLUM, age 76, died at his home in Crawford November 27, 1943. In 1882 the family moved form Coryell City to Tennessee but moved back to Texas a few years later, settling in Crawford. He and his brother had been in the drugstore business for many years. In later years, Mr. McCullum operated a bank in Crawford. Survivors include three children, Gussie Hickerson of Crawford, Mrs. B. J. Moore of Port Lavaca and Ray R. Brown of Houston; two sisters, Mrs. Sallie Standifer of Dallas, Mrs. Mecca Meeks of Slaton; two brothers, M. A. McCollum of Waco and Dr. C. H. McCollum of Fort Worth. Burial was in Crawford Cemetery by Amsler Funeral Home. McGregor Mirror: Dec 3 (4-4), 1943.

MINNIE RICHTER, age 84, died at her home near Coryell City on November 25, 1943. She was born on November 9, 1859, in Germany but came to

America at an early age. The family first settled in Austin County, then Washington County and in 1907 settled in Coryell County, Texas. Survivors include four sons, Fritz, Otto and Albert Richter of Coryell City and Willie Niemeier of McGregor; six daughters, Mrs. Otto Schrader of Osage, Mrs. Ernest Symank and Mrs. Willie Symank of Mosheim, Mrs. John Symank of Coryell City, Mrs. Theo. Schaefer of Bleirvesville in Travis County, Texas, and Mrs. Henry Schneider of Austin; one sister, Mrs. Fritz Buth of Coryell City. Burial was in Coryell City Cemetery (St. John Lutheran) by Amsler Funeral Home. She was laid to rest beside her husband, Carl Richter (1854-1940). McGregor Mirror: Dec 3 (5-6), 1943.

CHARLOTTE BUTH died at the home of her daughter, Mrs. Robert Newman at Coryell City Wednesday, December 8, 1943. Burial was in Coryell City Cemetery (St. John Lutheran) by Amsler Funeral Home beside her husband, Friedrich Buth (1848-1932)who preceded her in death 11 years ago. Mrs. Buth had lived in the Coryell City community for 65 years. Survivors include nine children. McGregor Mirror: Dec 10 (5-5), 1943.

AGNES LOESCH, age 67, died at the family home in Prairie Chapel Tuesday, December 7, 1943. She was born on August 6, 1876, in Washington County, Texas, but moved to Coryell City. Survivors include her husband, Otto Loesch (1874-1949); four sons, Elder and O. C. of Prarie Chapel, Cpl. Ernest Loesch of Hammond Field, Louisiana and Erwin Loesch of the U. S. Navy; one daughter, Mrs. Ernest Wilman of Crawford.; two brothers and four sisters of Washington County. Burial was in Coryell City Cemetery (St. John Lutheran) by Amsler Funeral Home. McGregor Mirror: Dec 10 (8-6), 1943.

CHAPTER 10

W. H. BRASWELL was shot and killed during a robbery attempt Saturday. He was the owner and operator of the Hiway Grille in McGregor. Burial was in Gainesville. Survivors include his wife; one daughter, Mrs. Charles Blassingame of Fort Worth; his mother, Mrs. B. M. Seagraves of Denison; one sister, Mrs. H. L. Cowsert of Waco; one brother, J. A. Braswell of Dennison; and one grandchild. Mr. and Mrs. Braswell had only been in McGregor for a few short months. McGregor Mirror: Jan 7 (1-3), 1944.

WILLIAM EARL McMAHAN, age 42, was fataly shot in a local cafe Saturday, December 25, 1943. The shooting was the result of an argument between Mr. McMahan and Earl Farmer. Earl was born in Victoria, Texas, on December 16, 1901, the son of H. McMahan and P. Hays. Burial was in McGregor Cemetery by Amsler Funeral Home. Survivors include his wife, Doris McMahan; one son; and one daughter; two brothers, Dave and Bert McMahan of McGregor. A new baby was born to Mrs. McMahan on New Year's Day. McGregor Mirror: Jan 7 (4-2), 1944.

RETA MAXWELL, age 51, died in McGregor Sunday, January 2, 1944. He had been working at the Bluebonnet Ordnance Plant for about a year, living on a farm south of Oglesby. Reta moved to this area from San Marcos some 12 years ago. Survivors include his wife; two daughters, Mrs. Everett Hamilton and Eleanor Jeanette Maxwell; three sons, Reta Melvin Maxwell, Joseph Simpson Maxwell and Paul Maxwell, all of Oglesby. Burial was in San Marcus by Rogers Funeral Home. McGregor Mirror: Jan 7 (4-4), 1944.

REBECCA MUNIZ died January 2, 1944, in Oglesby at age 26. She was born in Mexico on February 7, 1917, the daughter of Joe Perales and Concepcion Navarro. Informant was her husband, Miguel Muniz. Burial was in McGregor Cemetery. Amsler Funeral Home Records, Book #3.

J. E. CLONCH, age 83, died at his home in Waco on December 28, 1943. Burial was in Rosemound Cemetery. Mr. Clonch was well known in McGregor, having owned the local water company for a number of years. He had loved to Waco some 13 years ago. Survivors include his wife, Mrs. Ella S. Clonch; three daughters, Mrs. W. B. Packingham of Crosby, Mrs. A. W. Billingsly of Big Lake and Miss Mae Clonch of Waco; one son, Morgan Clonch of McGregor. McGregor Mirror: Jan 7 (7-6), 1944.

WILLIAM C. NAYLOR, age 79, died Saturday, December 25, 1943, at his home in Speegleville. Burial was in the Speegleville Cemetery. When Lake Waco was built, his body was relocated in Chapel Hill Cemetery. He had been married for 51 years. Survivors include his wife; five sons, Ennis, W. William and Dewey of Speegleville, Sam of Dallas, Cecil of Temple; five daughters, Miss Mae of Speegleville, Mrs. W. A. Fletcher of Moody, Mrs. Bill Bowdoin of Speegleville, Mrs. A. F.

Stanford of China Springs and Mrs. Collin Brooks of Speegleville. McGregor Mirror: Jan 7 (8-4), 1944.

MRS. WILLIAM C. NAYLOR died December 31, 1943, just one week after the death of her husband. She was laid to rest beside her husband in the Speegleville Cemetery and relocated to Chapel Hill Cemetery when Lake Waco was built. McGregor Mirror: Jan 7 (8-4), 1944.

JAMES MARSHALL CROUCH, age 41, died on January 12, 1944, in a highway accident near Burleson, Texas. Mr. Crouch was fixing a flat tire when a car sideswiped him in a blinding sleet and rain storm. He had been on his way to Fort Worth to attend a State Grain Dealer's Association meeting. Marshall died on the way to the hospital. He was born on June 9, 1902, the son of Mr. E. W. Crouch and Pearl Surratt. After attending Baylor University, Marshall had been associated with his father and younger brother in the milling and grain business. Survivors include his wife, Rachel Brown Crouch (1898-1981); two children, Carolyn and Marsh; his parents, Mr. and Mrs. E. W. Crouch; brother, Halbert Crouch. Burial was in McGregor Cemetery by Amsler Funeral Home. McGregor Mirror: Jan 14 (1-3), 1944.

MARY JOSEPHINE RICHARDSON, age 91, died at the home of her son, Claud Richardson in Crawford on Monday, January 10, 1944. She had been a resident of Crawford for the past 50 years. Survivors include four daughters, Mrs. Bertha Compton of Crawford, Mrs. Frank L. Compton, Mrs. J. N. Cagle, Mrs. J. L. Miles, all of Valley Mills; three sons, W. O. Richardson of Walters, Oklahoma, Charles and Claud Richardson of Crawford; one sister, Mrs. John Hargett of Russelville, Alabama. Burial was in Compton Cemetery by Amsler Funeral Home. McGregor Mirror: Jan 14 (8-3), 1944.

DOROTHEA MORRIS ROBERTS, born on January 9, 1925, and her three month old daughter were killed in a train accident in Novice, Texas, Thursday, January 13, 1944. She was the wife of Jack Grimes Roberts. Dorothea, age 18, and her daughter, Bonita Madge Roberts, born October 21, 1943, were on their way to San Diego, California, where Mr. Roberts is stationed in the U. S. Navy. Burial was in Davidson Cemetery west of Oglesby by Lee Undertakers. McGergor Mirror: Jan 21 (1-1), 1944.

WILLIAM SANDERS, age 82, died at his home near Crawford Sunday, January 16, 1944. He had been a resident of Coryell County and Crawford for 31 years, moving here from Scurry County. William was a native of Texas, having been born on August 4, 1861, in Washington County. William was the son of Fred Sanders and Martha Seiss Sanders. Survivors include his wife, Minnie Vahrenkamp (1863-1955); four sons, Otto, Bill, John and Fred Sanders, all of Crawford; one daughter, Miss Bertha Sanders. Four children preceded Mr. Sanders in death. Burial was in McGregor Cemetery by Amsler Funeral Home. McGergor Mirror: Jan 21 (4-1), 1944.

MRS. JOE S. BRADSHAW, age 81, died at the family home near McGregor on January 18, 1944. She was born in Mississippi on March 18, 1862, the daughter of D. B. Cox and Irene Blackard. Mr. and Mrs. Bradshaw were married in Mississippi, their native state, and moved to McGregor 46 years ago. Survivors include her husband, Joe S. Bradshaw; two daughters, Mrs. Mae Crain and Mrs. Irene Able of McGregor; five sons, Luit and Joe of McGregor, Howe of California, Link of Waco and Grady of Mission, Texas. Two children preceded her in death, an infant and one son, Frank Bradshaw, who died in 1939. Burial was in Comanche Springs Cemetery by Amsler Funeral Home. McGregor Mirror: Jan 21 (4-3), 1944.

MILLIE POLLY, aged negress died Wednesday. She claimed to be 111 years old, the oldest resident McGregor had ever known. She was born in Mississippi, but came to McGregor before the town was founded. Nine children were born to her. Seven of those children survive her, six boys and one girl. Bertie Polly, her daughter-in-law, who lived next door cared for Millie in her later years. Burial was in McGregor Cemetery. McGregor Mirror: Jan 21 (4-5), 1944.

JOHN ROBERT LYNCH, age 75, died at his home in Jonesboro January 17, 1944. Burial was in Post Oak Cemetery by Lee Undertakers. Mr. Lynch had lived in Coryell County many years before moving to Jonesboro 6 years ago. Survivors include his wife; daughters, Mrs. Tom Tidsdale of Hope, Arkansas, Mrs. Arthur Brewer of Pearl, Mrs. Otto Stricker of Jonesboro, Mrs. Albert Stricker of Tulsa, Oklahoma, Mrs. Lena Donoho of Tulsa, Oklahoma; seven sons, John R. of Dallas, Frank R. of Valley Mills, William D., Jessie, Allard and Herbert, all in the armed forces. McGregor Mirror: Jan 21 (8-3), 1944.

LEWIS J. GARTMAN, age 59, died in an auto accident in McGregor Tuesday. His body was taken to Goldthwaite where he was one of the city's leading businessmen. He had been returning from Marlin where he had carried his wife for treatment when the accident happened. McGregor Mirror: Jan 28 (1-3), 1944.

PAUL CLIFFORD JONES died at his home at Flat, Sunday, where he had lived for 50 years. Survivors include his wife; and one son, Johnny B. Jones. Burial was in Gatesville Cemetery by Lee Undertakers of McGregor. McGregor Mirror: Jan 28 (5-2), 1944.

THOMAS ALLEN BROWN, 9 month old son of Mr. and Mrs. Roy A. Brown, died at a Waco hospital Saturday, January 22, 1944. Mr. and Mrs. Brown had moved to McGregor when the Bluebonnet Ordnance Plant began operation and Mr. Brown is employed as a guard at the plant. Survivors include his parents, Mr. and Mrs. Roy A. Brown; one brother; and two sisters. Burial was in Fletcher Cemetery in Coryell County, by Amsler Funeral Home. McGregor Mirror: Jan 28 (5-2), 1944.

JIMMIE D. ROBINSON, age 32, died at his home near Crawford on January 26, 1944. He had been a resident of Crawford for the past 17 years, moving there from Leon Junction. Survivors include his wife; three sons, Donald McCall, Darrell and Jimmie Dale Robinson, all of Crawford; his parents, Mr. and Mrs. Walter Robinson of Leon Junction; four brothers, Walter Lee of Pyote Army Air Base, Raymond of U. S. Army in England, Billie of U. S. Army in Italy and Phillip in Camp Leonard Wood, Missouri; three sisters, Mrs. F. H. Ross of Mobile, Alabama, Mrs. E. R. Haney of Dayton, Ohio and Mrs. Jesse H. Lockwood of Leon Junction. Burial was in Crawford Cemetery by Amsler Funeral Home. McGregor Mirror: Jan 28 (5-3), 1944.

JOSEPH DOUGLAS NEAGLE, age 78, died at his home in Oglesby Sunday, January 30, 1944. Burial was in Post Oak Cemetery by Lee Undertakers. Mr. Neagle was born in North Carolina on June 29, 1865, but had lived in Oglesby for the past 45 years. Survivors include his wife, India Neagle (1880-1965); four sons, D. M. Walter of Oglesby, Emmett of Moody, John R. of the U. S. Army in Arkansas; one daughter, Mrs. D. G. Dotson of Douglas, Arizona. McGregor Mirror: Feb 4 (5-3), 1944.

MRS. B. KAELIN, age 87, died at her home in McGregor Wednesday, February 2, 1944. She was born in Einsideln, Switzerland on July 4, 1856, the daughter of Mr. and Mrs. Berchler and married Mr. Jacob Kaelin before coming to America. Mr. and Mrs. Kaelin purchased land when the original lots were sold in McGregor in 1882. Mr. Kaelin preceded her in death in 1890. Survivors include two sons, Amil of McGregor and Jake of Houston; one daughter, Miss Mary Kaelin of Houston. Burial was in McGregor Cemetery by Amsler Funeral Home. McGregor Mirror: Feb 4 (8-5), 1944.

NORETO PIRES, age 5, was killed when an auto driven by a Camp Hood soldier hit him Monday. He was pronounced dead at a Waco hospital. The accident happened one mile west of the Oglesby cut-off. McGregor Mirror: Feb 4 (8-6), 1944.

HAMILTON MORGAN BAKER, formerly known in McGregor as "Uncle Hamp", was born December 11, 1851, in Tennessee. He came to Texas as a boy settling near McGregor in Comanche Springs prior to 1882, the year McGregor was founded. He was the last one remaining of a family of 7 brothers. Survivors include one son, Ed Baker of McGregor; four daughters, Mrs. Lena Leeth of Hico, Mrs. C. C. Basham and Mrs. Alene Dixon of McGregor and Mrs. A. J. Hill of Harlingen. Mr. Baker died at his home in McGregor Sunday, February 6, 1944. Burial was in Comanche Springs Cemetery by Amsler Funeral Home. Honorary pallbearers were Cpl. Floyd Dixon, Lt. (j. g.) Wayne A. Dixon, Charles Ray Basham, Hern Hudson, Nolen Draper, Charlie Leeth, Clinton Leeth, J. B. Leeth, Raymond Leeth, Roy Leeth and Joe Maxwell, all grandsons of the deceased. McGregor Mirror: Feb 11 (4-3), 1944.

LA GAYROLD BOND, age 3, and his three month old sister, SHARON BOND, burned to death in a house fire on the William's farm near McGregor Tuesday. The Bond family was sitting around the stove when coal oil which had been placed on the fire a few minutes before exploded. Mr. Bond's clothing caught fire and he ran out of the house to try to keep his buring clothing from igniting the house. The explosion set the entire room afire. Mrs. Bond, her clothing in flames, was able to get her 5 year old daughter, Zonella Bond, to safety. The flames were so bad that the family was unable to return to the house to rescue the two younger children. Mr. Bond, age 31, is a carpenter in McGregor. Mrs. Bond is a 27 year old housewife. Amsler Funeral Home was in charge of funeral services. McGregor Mirror: Feb 18 (1-4), 1944.

SOLOMON PERALES died in McGregor on February 17, 1944, at age 20. He was born in Texas on May 22, 1923, the son of Jose L. Perales and Commcepcion Navarro of Mexico. Informant was Ronaldo Rodriguez. Solomon lived on the John Bennett farm near McGregor. Burial was in McGregor Cemetery by Amsler Funeral Home. Amsler Funeral Home Records, Book #3.

MARGARET SUE GUTHRIE, age 4, was accidently shot Friday, February 18, 1944. She was born on June 20, 1940. Her sister, Marie Guthrie, age 8, lost both her hands in the same incident. Their 5 year old brother, Lloyd Guthrie, accidently discharged a 12-gauge shotgun while both parents, Mr. and Mrs. W. A. Bond, were at work at the Bluebonnet Ordnance Plant. Burial was in McGregor Cemetery by Lee Undertakers. Survivors include her parents, three sisters, Virgie Lou, Wanda Faye and Marie Guthrie; four brothers, Billie Joe, P. W., Jr. and Lloyd Ray and Donald Wayne Guthrie. McGregor Mirror: Feb 25, (1-1), 1944.

DUDLEY O. HENRY was killed in action on January 24, 1944. He was the husband of Peggy Phelan Henry of Waco, formerly of McGregor. Her parents are Mr. and Mrs Carl Phelan. McGregor Mirror: Feb 25 (5-1), 1944.

PATRICIA BRENNAN, age 13, died in Austin. She was the only child of Mr. and Mrs. Mike Brennan, who formerly lived in McGregor. Those from McGregor who attended the funeral included Mr. and Mrs. Jack Garrett, Paul Garrett, Mrs. Maureen Garrett, Mr. and Mrs. Clyce Allen, Mr. and Mrs. Moran Meador, Mr. and Mrs. Ed Grady and Misses Cora Mae Meador and Johnnie Meador. Burial was Sunday in Austin. McGregor Mirror: Feb 25 (8-2), 1944.

ALBERT KARNOWSKI, age 81, died at his home near Whitehall Wednesday, March 1, 1944. He had been a resident of Bell County for the past 52 years. Mr. Karnowski was born in Germany but came to America at age 21, locating in Washington County, Texas. A year later he moved to Straw's Mill near Gatesville and finally settled in Whitehall. Survivors include his wife; one son, P. H. Karnowski; one daughter, Mrs. Ernest Wiese of Whitehall and Buckhorn. Burial was in Buckhorn Cemetery by Amsler Funeral Home. McGergor Mirror: Mar 3 (4-5), 1944.

WALTER STEWART of Willis died in a Houston hospital Tuesday. He was the brother of Mrs. W. L. Sharp and Mrs. W. A. Hamilton of McGregor. McGregor Mirror: Mar 3 (5-1), 1944.

ROBERT TUCKER, age 91, died at his home in McGregor Friday. Burial was in Oakwood Cemetery in Waco by Compton's Funeral Home. Survivors include his wife; five daughters, Mrs. N. R. Boyles of Coleman, Mrs. J. L. Smith of Dallas, Mrs. G. B. Coleman, Mrs. W. D. Warnick, Mrs. S. P. Bailey of Waco; three sons, C. A. Tucker of Dublin, Frank Tucker of Gadson, Arizona, Robert Tucker of Christiana, Tennessee. Mr. Tucker was born in Murfreesboro, Tennessee but had lived around McGregor for 40 years. McGregor Mirror: Mar 3 (7-4), 1944.

CARL P. SYDOW of Decatur, Texas, was buried in McGregor Cemetery this week. Carl was born in 1875. He was a brother and uncle to Mrs. Louis Kelm and family. McGregor Mirror: Mar 10 (4-3), 1944.

FRITZ FISHGRABE died at his home six miles west of Moody Sunday. He was born in Germany but came to Washington County, Texas, as a lad of 16 years. Fritz had lived in the Buckhorn community for the past 39 years. Burial was in Buckhorn Cemetery by Amsler Funeral Home. Survivors include his wife; four daughters, Mrs. August Houy and Mrs. W. H. Webber, Jr. of Moody, Mrs. Fred Kattner of The Grove and Mrs. Robert Comer of Pasadena, California; four sons, Charlie Fischgabe of Temple, Otto and Reuben of Moody and Pvt. Ernest Fishhgrabe of the U. S. Army serving in England; two sisters, Mrs. J. E. Wright of McGregor and Mrs. William Templemeyer of Indianopolis, Indiana. McGregor Mirror: Mar 10 (7-3), 1944.

CHARLES RAY RICHARDSON, age 14, died in a Waco hospital Monday. He died of injuries sustained when he was run over by a truck in Crawford. Burial was in Compton Cemetery near Crawford by Lee Undertakers. Survivors include his parents, Mr. and Mrs Charles Richardson of Crawford; one sister, Mrs. Addie Travis of Houston. McGregor Mirror: Mar 10 (8-2), 1944.

JUAQUANITA DIAZ died on March 19, 1944, in a Waco hospital at age 7 months. She was born in McGregor on August 16, 1943, the daughter of Ben Diaz and Margaret Gonzales. Burial was in McGregor Cemetery by Amsler Funeral Home. Amsler Funeral Home Records, Book #3.

WILLIAM H. GOLLIGHER. Card of Thanks. We wish to thank friends and neighbors for sympathy shown us during our recent sorrow at the death of our father-in-law and grand-father, William H. Golligher. J. N. Fletcher and grand-children. William was born on June 10, 1860 and died on March 21, 1944. Burial was in McGregor Cemetery beside J. T. Fletcher. McGregor Mirror: Mar 31 (8-6), 1944.

ROBERT "BOB" HARRIS, age 68, died at his home Monday. He had lived in McGregor for more than 40 years where he was employed by the McGregor

Miling ang Grain Company. Survivors include his wife; two daughters, Mrs. Alleyne Davies of Waco and Mrs. Gena Mae Smith of Austin; one son, Roscoe Harris of McGregor. Burial was in McGregor Cemetery by Lee Undertakers. McGregor Mirror: Apr 7 (8-5), 1944.

MARSHALL BENTON WICKER, age 86, died at the home of his daughter, Mrs. Guy Snelson on Saturday. He was a native of Angleton, Texas, but when his health began to fail he made his home here. Burial was in Angleton by Lee Undertakers. Survivors include three daughters, Mrs. Guy Snelson of McGregor, Mrs. Alice Buels of Corpus Christi, Mrs. Fred Moore of Velasco, Texas; two sons, W. L. Wicker of Freer, Texas and Dallas Wicker of Abilene; one brother, George of Waco; two sisters, Mrs. Etta Shears of Clayton, Indiana, Mrs. Phoebe Terrell of Stilesville, Indiana. McGregor Mirror: Apr 14 (5-2), 1944.

PRISCILLA KIRKLAND FOWLER died at the home of her daughter in Lacoy Monday, April 3, 1944. She was born on March 23, 1855. Mrs. Fowler, age 89, had lived in Oglesby until a few years ago when she went to live with her daughter. Survivors include four daughters, Mrs. Metta Harrison of Los Angeles, Mrs. E. M. Mimms of Lacy, Mrs. Maude Davis of Turnersville and Miss Clara Fowler of Austin; two sons, Oscar of Osage and Tom Fowler of Oglesby. Burial was in Osage Cemetery beside Daniel G. Kirkland. McGregor Mirror: Apr 14 (5-3), 1944.

TED O. HARRIS died Saturday in a Abilene hospital. He was born in 1907. Burial was in Post Oak Cemetery near Oglesby by Lee Undertakers. Survivors include his mother, Minnie Harris; three sisters, Mrs. Viola Franklin of California, Mrs. Neil McBride and Mrs. Walter Wehring of McGregor; three brothers, R. T. Harris of Moody, Sam Harris of California and J. L. Harris of West Columbia, Texas. McGregor Mirror: Apr 14 (8-2), 1944.

FLETA MORRIS died at the family home near McGregor on Friday, April 14, 1944. She was born in 1885. Burial was in McGregor Cemetery by Lee Undertakers beside two children who preceded her in death. Survivors include her husband, Clarence A. Morris (1884-1945); her mother, Mrs. George W. Connally, Sr. of McGregor; two sisters, Mrs. Ludora Nobles and Mrs. Mary Settles of McGregor; four brothers, Beverly and George of McGregor, Crit of Wharton and Wallace Connally of California. McGregor Mirror: Apr 21 (5-3), 1944.

MATT B. GILL, age 27, was instantly killed when he was struck by an airplane propeller while working at Waco Army Air Field Wednesday. Mr. Gill was a civilian employee of the sub-depot at WAAF at the time of the accident. Survivors include his wife; one son of Hillsboro; parents, Mr. and Mrs. Jeff Gill of Oglesby; two brothers, Delbert who is in England; and one sister. Burial was in Coryell Church Cemetery. McGregor Mirror: May 5 (1-2), 1944.

JOSEFA V. MENDOZA died May 4, 1944, in Crawford, Texas at age 58. She was born in Mexico on March 19, 1886, the daughter of R. Villalabos and Vincenta Guarez. Her husband was Daniel Mendoza of Crawford. Burial was in McGregor Cemetery by Amsler Funeral Home. Amsler Funeral Home Records, Book #3.

BURL A DAVIS, second son of the late Gordon Davis of Oglesby, was killed in action in Italy on April 21, 1944. His brother, Lt. Royce O. Davis, was killed last August in a plane crash in Idaho and another brother, Lt. Hubert Davis, is stationed in England. Sergeant Davis entered the service when the national guard was mobilized into the 36th Division in 1940. He had been awarded a purple heart for wounds which he received in October of 1943. He was the son on the late Gordon Davis of Oglesby and grandson of Mrs. A. P. Davis of Oglesby. Survivors include his wife, Mrs. Melba Davis; their one year old child. His wife and child reside in Jonesboro with her parents. McGregor Mirror: May 5 (5-2), 1944.

B. O. BRIDGES, age 82, died at his home in Temple Tuesday. Burial was in a Temple Cemetery by Hewitt Funeral Home. Mr. Bridges had make his home in McGregor at one time with his daughter, Mrs. E. E. Bouldin. Survivors include his daughters, Mrs. E. E. Bouldin of McGregor, Mrs. Alma Langston of San Antonio, Mrs. L. O. Stewart of California, Mrs. H. R. Wood of Big Spring and Mrs. Ollie Ammons of Houston; two sons, L. A. Bridges of Odessa and W. M. Bridges of McGregor. McGregor Mirror: Jun 9 (4-4), 1944.

JESS HARRIS died Friday of a heart attack while he worked in the switchwards at Cleburne, Texas. He had been an employee of the Santa Fe Railway for more than 30 years. Jess married Myrtle Evans of McGregor. Survivors include his wife; one son, Capt. Weldon Harris who is stationed in Florida; five brothers, Dan and Ben Harris of McGregor, Jim Harris of Greenwood, Virgil Harris of Indian Gap and Joe Harris of San Antonio. Burial was in Oakwood Cemetery by Hewitt Funeral Home of Waco. McGregor Mirror: Jun 9 (5-4), 1944.

BESSIE STEWART died at her home near Clifton, June 1, 1944. She was born on December 9, 1878. Burial was in Harris Creek Cemetery. Miss Stewart had been an invalid for several years. Survivors include her sister, Miss Mamie Stewart; two brothers, Carl and T. A. Stewart. The family had lived near McGregor until about 2 years ago when their farm was absorbed by the Bluebonnet Ordnance Plant. McGregor Mirror: Jun 9 (5-6), 1944.

NANCY ANN POLLARD, age 68, died Friday June 9, 1944, in her home in Oglesby where she had lived for the past 49 years. She was born on November 24, 1876. Burial was in Eagle Springs Cemetery by Lee Undertakers. Pallbearers were Lenord Marshall, Ted Pollard, Jake Clearman, Billy Pollard, Morris Lynch, Ernest Pollard. Survivors include her husband; eight children, S. L. Pollard of Brownwood, Travis and Albert Pollard of McGregor, Marshall of Houston, Mrs. F. H. Campbell of Oglesby, Mrs. F. E. Clark of Breckenridge, Mrs. Edwin Rhodes of Dallas, Mrs. C. W. Westerfield of Valley Mills. McGregor Mirror: Jun 16 (5-3), 1944.

ODIS J. GOBER died in McGregor on June 15, 1944, at age 10. He was born in Coryell County on June 17, 1934, the son of Ernest P. Gober and Clara A. Woodall. Burial was in McGregor Cemetery by Amsler Funeral Home. Amsler Funeral Home Records, Book #3.

ANNA B. DAVENPORT, age 85, died Thursday in her home in the Bethany community situted five miles east of Moody. She was the widow of the late T. J. Davenport. Anna was born in Effingham County, Illinois on July 6, 1858 but moved to Bethany, Texas in 1877. Survivors include her five children, Mrs. Minnie V. Thomas of Bethany, Mrs. Effie Cury of Waco, Carl Davenport of Bruceville, Hattie and W. E. Davenport of Austin. Burial was in Bethany Cemetery by Amsler Funeral Home. McGregor Mirror: Jun 30 (5-2), 1944.

HENRY A. FISHER died on June 22, 1944. Burial was in Ater Cemetery by Lee Undertakers. Mr. Fisher had lived in McGregor for about eighteen months, moving here from Oglesby where he had lived for 74 years. Survivors include his wife, Lou Fisher; children, Mrs. R. L. Lovelace of McGregor, Mrs. R. L. Weaver of Dublin, Barney Fisher of McAllen, Hollis Fisher of the U. S. Navy, Mrs. Charles Parsons of McGregor, Elin Fisher of Wharton, Eddie Fisher of Bay City and Mrs. M. R. Bates of Osage. McGregor Mirror: Jun 30 (5-3), 1944.

FRITZ LEHRMAN, age 77, died in a Waco hospital Monday, June 26, 1944. He was born in Germany but settled in Washington County, Texas, at age 19. In 1906 he moved to Coryell City. Survivors include five sons and five daughters, Mrs. Louise Muelhouse of Mosheim, Mrs. Bill Meyer of Coryell City, Mrs. Clara Robinson of Waco, Mrs. Minnie Hull of Washington state, Mrs. Elsie Alder of McGregor, Mr. Fred Lehrman of Roscoe, Theodore of Osage, Henry and Herbert of Coryell City, Alvin and Eric of McGregor. Burial was in Clifton Cemetery by Amsler Funeral Home. Pallbearers were J. H. Bubert, Elmer Bubert, Wilfred Meyer, D. D. Meyer, Carbon Lehrman and Jack Lehrman. McGregor Mirror: Jun 30 (8-4), 1944.

FELIX A. MORRIS, SR. died Sunday, July 1, 1944, at his home in Oglesby. He was born in Mansfield, Texas, on December 14, 1873, but had lived in Oglesby for the past 61 years. For 15 years he served as trustee of the Oglesby schools. Survivors include his wife, Emma L. Morris (1876-1964); one son, F. A. Morris, Jr.; one daughter, Mrs. Park Donaldson of McGregor; five grandchildren, Searcy Lee Hurst, Jack Morris, Felix Morris, Morris Donaldson and Marion Donaldson; brothers and sisters, Willard of Hamilton, A. E. Morris of Corsicana, E. B. Morris of Waxahachie, Mrs. Lavinia Allison of Temple, Mrs. Ethel Alexander of McGregor and Mrs. Julia Burleson of Inglewood, California.

Three children preceded him in death, Earl Morris, Mary Etta Morris and J. A. Morris. Burial was in Post Oak Cemetery by Lee Undertakers. Out-of-town relatives present at the funeral included Dr. C. C. Anderson of Bensus, Dr. W. D. Anderson and daughter of San Angelo, Mrs. David Sherrill and daughters of Levelland, Mrs. G. J. Morris and children of Lubbock, Mr. and Mrs. Louis Smith of Austin, Ennis Garren of Mosheim, Mr. amd Mrs. Cody Anderson, Mr. and Mrs. Billie Anderson and Mrs. Gordon Frady of Crawford, Will Anderson and W. E. Mize of Oklahoma, Mrs. Mary Shumate of Waco, Mr. and Mrs. Paul Morris and son of Corsicana, Billie Morris of Waxahachie, Mr. and Mrs. T. L. Allison of Temple, Mr. and Mrs. E. B. Morris of Waxahachie, Willard Morris of Hamilton, A. E. Morris of Corsicana and Mr. and Mrs. W. B. Alexander of McGregor. McGregor Mirror: Jul 7 (3-3), 1944.

LEITHA BURGESS GILLILAND, age 53, died this week. She was born in 1891. Leitha had lived in McGregor for the past 31 years. Burial was in McGregor Cemetery by Lee Undertakers. Survivors include her husband, Burt Gilliland; three daughters, Mrs. Pearl Jackson and Mrs. Georgia Jackson of Bakersfield, California, and Mrs. Hazel Windham of McGregor. McGregor Mirror: Jul 7 (8-4), 1944.

ELSIE ADLER, age 35, died in her home near McGregor on July 2, 1944. She was born on March 14, 1909, the daugher of H. F. Lehrman and Louise Mueller. Survivors include her husband, Gus Adler; one daughter, Carleen; four sisters, Mrs. Louise Muelhouse of Moshiem, Mrs. Bill Meyer of Coryell City, Mrs. Clara Robertson of Waco, Mrs. Minnie Hull of Washington state; six brothers, Fred Lehrman of Roscoe, Theodore of Osage, Henry and Herbert of Coryell City, Alvin and Eric Lehrman of McGregor. Burial was in McGregor Cemetery by Amsler Funeral Home. Pallbearers were Gilbert Williams, Billy Robertson, R. D. and Wilfred Meyer, Carbon and Milford Lehrman. McGregor Mirror: Jul 7 (8-6), 1944.

PASCAL LEE ARNOLD, age 67, died in a Houston hospital Wednesday. His wife, Ina May Arnold (1881-1931), preceded him in death in 1931. He came to Texas from Kentucky and had lived in McGregor for the past 37 years. Burial was in McGregor Cemetery by Lee Undertakers. Survivors include eight children, Mrs. Woodrow Lawson, Mrs. Raymond Campbell, Mrs. Mattie Lee Hatcher of Waco, O. L. Arnold of Waco, Bill and Weldon Arnold of the U. S. Army, Coy and Tom Arnold of McGregor. McGregor Mirror: Jul 21 (1-3), 1944.

EMIL RABBE, age 40, died in a Waco hospital Saturday, July 15, 1944. He was a well known farmer in the Coryell City Community. Survivors include his wife; one daughter, Johanna Katherine who is 9 weeks old; three sisters, Mrs. Ed Pietzsch of Waco, Mrs. Otto Giebler of Valley Mills, Mrs. Arnold Lander of Crawford; one brother, Bill Rabbe. Burial was in the Canaan Baptist Church Cemetery near Crawford by Amsler Funeral Home. Pallbearers were H. W. Dreyer, Ed Pietzsch, Otto Giebler, Herbert Massirer, Cleo Rabbe, Robert Pietzsch, Cooper and

Tilbert Willman. McGregor Mirror: Jul 21 (3-3), 1944.

FENTON WILLIAM MORGAN, age 53, died Sunday in a Waco hospital. Burial was in Oakwood Cemetery in Waco by Wilkerson-Hatch Funeral Home. Survivors include one son, J. F. Morgan of Walla Walla, Washington; two daughters, Mrs. Netie Morgan Rowe of Dallas and Miss Wilma Loree Morgan of Waco; one sister, Mrs. Fred Bredin of Houston. McGregor Mirror: Jul 28 (6-1), 1944.

MR. MACLIN, brother-in-law of Mr. and Mrs. Clay Chapman, died in Waco Saturday. Burial was in McGregor Cemetery. McGregor Mirror: Jul 28 (7-3), 1944.

HUGH HONNOLL, son of Mr. and Mrs. J. R. Honnoll of McGregor, was killed when a Grayhound bus he was driving collided with a truck near Sequin, Saturday. Burial was in Eddy Cemetery. Survivors include his parents; three brothers, Cleo Honnoll of Houston, Dean R. Honnell of the U. S. Marines in Wilmington, N. C. and Felix Honnoll of Dallas. McGregor Mirror: Jul 28 (8-5), 1944.

VIOLA DAY, former resident of McGergor, died in a Amarillo hospital Saturday. Burial was in the local cemetery in Borger. A resident of Borger for 17 years, Mrs. Day was born in Gabsden, Alabama, on November 26, 1886. She came to Borger with her husband, L. P. Day, in June of 1928. He has been in the garage business since coming to Borger. Survivors include her husband; six brothers, Ross Green of Texarkana, R. P. Green of Waco, Charlie Green of Lometa, Joe Green of Palestine, Jim Green of McGregor and Park Green of Lingleville; a sister, Mrs. Henry Farrar of Waco. Mrs. Day will be remembered here as Viola Green. McGregor Mirror: Aug 11 (4-3), 1944.

HIRAM T. GRANTHAM died at his home in Clifton Wednesday. Mr. Grantham moved to Clifton from McGregor 16 years ago where he was identified with the First State Bank of McGregor. Burial was in the Meridian Cemetery. Survivors include his wife; one son, Darrell Grantham of Waco; four brothers, Will of Corsicana, Luther of Arkansas, N. J. and John Grantham of McGregor; one sister, Mrs. E. C. Huckabee of Corsicana. McGregor Mirror: Aug 18 (1-3), 1944.

ROY COLLINS was shot by his wife Wednesday. He died of the wound. McGregor Mirror: Aug 18 (1-2), 1944.

CHARLES RAY BASHAM, son of Mr. and Mrs. C. C. Basham, was killed in a palne crash August 21, 1944, at Chatham Field in Georgia. His body was brought to McGregor for burial in Turnersville by Lee Undertakers. Survivors include his parents; his wife; one son; three sisters, one of whom is serving her country as a nurse stationed in Italy. McGregor Mirror: Sep 1 (1-5), 1944.

MRS. LUTHER HERING, age 51, died Monday in a Waco hospital. Burial was in Rosemound Cemetery in Waco. Survivors include her husband, L. L. Hering; one son, Ensign Charles F. Hering of Austin now of the U. S. Navy; father, Marion Townsend of Sugar Grove, Arkansas; two brothers, Merritt Townsend of Ada, Oklahoma and Richard Twonsend of Lorena. Pallbearers were Robert Hering, Albert Hering, Herbert Hering, Charles Hering, J. C. Hering and Neal McBride. McGregor Mirror: Sep 15 (4-1), 1944.

REV. DALE ROACH, age 30, died at his home southeast of McGregor Saturday, September 16, 1944. Burial was in Old Perry Cemetery by Lee Undertakers. Survivors include his wife; two sons, Dale Jr. and David Austin Roach; one step-son, Raymond Landious; parents, Mr. and Mrs. J. B. Roach; two brothers, Austin and Ferguson; sisters, Mrs. Freeman Morgan of McGregor and Mrs. Mona James of West Virginia. McGregor Mirror: Sep 22 (5-2), 1944.

MRS. D. M. JORDAN, wife of Dr. D. M. Jordan a pioneer physician of Oglesby, died at her home Wednesday. Burial was in Moody Cemetry by Lee Undertakers. Survivors include one son; Dr. D. W. Jordan of Brady; two daughters, Mrs. C. DeJernett of Dallas and Mrs. W. Guy Draper of Temple; two grandsons, Wendell W. Jordan, Jr. of U. S. Navy and D. V. Jordan, Jr. of Brady; one grand-daughter, Mrs. Ben Thomson of Fort Knox, Kentucky. McGregor Mirror: Sep 22 (5-5), 1944.

HANNA ALMEDA CAMPBELL, age 85, died at the home of her daughter, Mrs. Jack Harris Wednesday, September 13, 1944. Burial was in Oakwood Cemetery in Waco. Survivors include her daughter, Mrs. Jack Harris; two sons, J. M. Turner of Mart and Robert L. Campbell of Beaver, Pennsylvania; three brothers, R. A. Horne of McGregor, Tom Horne of Bay City and Cliff Horne of Plainview; five sisters, Mrs. J. D. Hay of Waco, Mrs. Elgiva Harris of Plainview, Mrs. Mack Harris of Los Angeles, Mrs. C. R. Smith of Hamilton and Mrs. R. E. Jones of Olton. Mrs. Campbell was born in Moody but had lived in Plainview for the past 16 years. McGregor Mirror: Sep 22 (7-1), 1944.

M. S. SEWELL died in McCaulley, Texas, Friday, September 22, 1944. Burial was in a McCalley Cemetery. Mr. Sewell had lived in McGregor until about 20 years ago. McGregor Mirror: Sep 29 (5-3), 1944.

GRACE TAYLOR, formerly of McGregor, died in Houston of September 25, 1944. Miss Taylor was the daughter of the late Col. Nathaniel Alston Taylor. A native of Houston, she spent her childhood in Abilene, attended Chapel Hill Female College then returned to Houston in 1912. Grace was a well known author of poetry. Survivors include her sister, two brothers, Paul G. Taylor of Houston and Alston D. Taylor of Los Angeles. McGregor Mirror: Oct 6 (3-1), 1944.

MINNIE B. MILLER, age 61, died at the home of her daughter in Crawford Saturday, September 30, 1944. Mrs. Miller was born in Hamilton on

January 6, 1883, but moved to Coryell Church with her father, Mr. C. H. Terry. She met and married John J. MIller of Osage. Survivors include her husband, John J. Miller (1882-1952); three daughters, Mrs. S. M. Roe of Waco, Mrs. Joe Chamblee and Mrs. Walter Mattlage of Crawford; two sons, Pvt. Elba Miller in New Guinea and Sgt. Joel Miller of Sardinia; three brothers, Sam and Jim Terry of McGregor, Eargle Terry of Colorado; one sister, Mary Terry of McGregor. Burial was in Crawford Cemetery by Amsler Funeral Home. Pallbearers were John Farmer, Walter Mattlage, John Chamblee, Ed Anderson, Edward Roe and Jeff Bland. McGregor Mirror: Oce 6 (4-3), 1944.

JOHN HENRY LONG, age 66, of Valley Mills, died at his home Tuesday. Burial was in Valley Mills Cemetery. Survivors include his wife; two daughters, Mrs. John Troutt of Osage and Mrs. Harrison Troutt of Waco; one son, Melvin Long of Valley Mills; two brothers, D. F. Long of Gatesville and J. W. Long of McGregor; two sisters, Mrs. Maggie Woods of McGregor and Mrs. Mary H. Brackney of Waco. McGregor Mirror: Oct 6 (5-4), 1944.

WALTER M. KNIGHT, age 43, died at a Dallas hospital Tuesday, October 10, 1944. He had lived in Crawford most of his life but had been employed recently at the North American Aviation Plant in Dallas. He was born December 2, 1900, the son of Mr. and Mrs. H. L. Knight of Crawford. Burial was in Crawford Cemetery by Amsler Funeral Home. Survivors include his wife; three step-children, Martha, Billie and Julius; two sisters, Mrs. Jim Hering of McGregor and Mrs. Chester Wells of Waco; one brother, Harry L. Knight of Dallas. McGregor Mirros: Oct 13 (8-1), 1944.

BEN STANLEY HARRIS, age 59, died at the home of his son, Joe E. Harris, in McGregor Sunday, October 8, 1944. He was born January 20, 1885, the son of W. D. Harris amd Mary Ellen Cline Harris. Survivors include his wife, Beulah L. Harris (1886-1962); six sons, Joe Harris of McGregor, Ben T. Harris of Alvin, Homer H. Harris of Brooks Field in San Antonio, W. D. Harris of Camp Barcley in Abilene, C. V. Harris of South Bosque, Elmer L. Harris of the U. S. Army overseas; two daughters, Mrs. A. J. Furman of Rockport and Mrs. J. B. Tindell of McGregor; four brothers, J. W. Harris of Decatur, W. V. of Indian Gap, S. Dan Harris of McGregor and Joe Harris of San Antonio. Burial was in McGregor Cemetery by Amsler Funeral Home. McGregor Mirror: Oct 13 (8-3), 1944.

MARY J. WRIGHT died in a Hillsboro hospital Saturday October 21, 1944. Burial was in Ridge Park Cemetery in Hillsboro. Miss Wright was well known in McGregor, having lived her for many years before moving to Waco some 20 years ago. Survivors include two sisters, Mrs. J. E. Boyd of Hillsboro and Miss Bettie Wright of Waco. McGregor Mirror: Oct 27 (2-6), 1944.

DEATHS IN CENTRAL TEXAS, VOL. II

JOHN FREDERICK BICKEL, age 85, died at his home near McGregor Monday, November 6, 1944. John was born in Germany on June 27, 1859, the son of F. Jacob Bickel and Marie Richlier. He came from Germany to Waco at age 27, but had lived in McGregor for 58 years. When he left Germany he had made arrangements to work for and live with Grandmother Pace. Survivors include four daughters, Mrs. O. G. Horne of Montevello, California, Mrs. Homer Ruff, Mrs. Wendell Bray and Miss Kate Bickel of McGregor; one son, F. E. Bickel of McGregor. Burial was in Harris Creek Cemetery by Amsler Funeral Home. McGergor Mirror: Nov 10 (5-2), 1944.

MRS. JOANER NETTLES TALLEY, age 68, died at the family home in Crawford Wednesday, November 1, 1944. She was born near Watertown, Tennessee, in 1876, but made her home in Coryell in 1899. She had just recently moved to Crawford. Survivors include her husband, S. D. Talley (1873-1952). Burial was in Osage Cemetery by Amsler Funeral Home. McGregor Mirror: Nov 10 (5-3), 1944.

MRS. MONTTIE WICKER, age 67, died at the home of his sister in Oglesby Monday. She was born in 1877. Burial was in Davidson Cemetery by Lee Undertakers. Survivors include two daughters, Mrs. Leola Graham of Oglesby and Mrs. Ruby Martin of Waco; one son, Gaines G. Wicker of the U. S. Army; five grandchildren; one brother, E. W. White of Beeville; three sisters, Mrs. A. Davidson, Mrs. J. W. Davidson of Pecan Grove and Mrs. B. E. Clowers of San Jose, California. Pallbearers were O. M. Davidson, J. T. Davidson, Wes Davidson, Gus Davidson, Bill Gibson, Ulmer White and Craig Davidson. McGregor Mirror: Nov 10 (5-6), 1944.

CHESTER MONEY, age 58, died in Waco Saturday. Burial was in Rosemound Cemetery in Waco. Survivors include his wife, Mrs. Effie Money; one son, Clay Money of Houston; one daughter, Mrs. R. L. Ewing of Corpus Christi; five brothers, E. L. Money of Houston, V. G. Money of Sparks, W. C. Money of Los Angeles, C. E. Money of Waco, T. P. Money of Port Arthur; one sister, Mrs. W. S. Baker of McGregor. McGregor Mirror: Nov 17 (7-6), 1944.

EDWIN C. WIECHERING died Thursday, November 16, 1944, at the home of his mother, Mrs. F. Wiechering. Edwin was born in 1904. He had lived in Houston until ill health forced him to move in with his mother. Burial was in McGregor Cemetery by Lee Undertakers. Mr. Wiechering, age 38, had make his home in McGregor until about 6 years ago when the family moved to Chapel Hill. In 1941 he moved to Houston where he was a carpenter. Survivors include his wife; three children Helen Marie, Raymond and Berniece; mother, Mrs. F. Wiechering; two brothers, Walter of McGregor and Harold now serving overseas; three sisters, Hattie and Mrs. Albert Niemeier of McGregor and Alma of Dallas. His father and a sister, Hallie, preceeded him in death several years ago. McGregor Mirror: Nov 24 (4-2), 1944.

DEATHS IN CENTRAL TEXAS, VOL. II

OTTO SANDHOFF, age 68, died near Prairie Chapel community November 20, 1944. Otto was born on April 10, 1876, and came from Germany with his parents, Mr. and Mrs. August Sandhoff, at the age of 9. Burial was in Coryell City Cemetery by Amsler Funeral Home. Survivors include his wife, Wilhilmine Sandhoff (1887-1973); eight children, August Sandhoff of Waco, Mrs. Annie Hoppe and Mrs. Mattie Griffith of Valley Mills, Edd Sandhoff of Osage, Mrs. Elsie Pieper, O. H. Sandhoff of Crawford, Lonnie Sandhoff of McGregor, Willie Sandhoff of the U. S. Army in the Phillipines. McGregor Mirror: Nov 24 (4-2), 1944.

"BOOTSY" DIXON, age 28, died on August 15, 1944. He was born in McGregor and graduated from McGregor High School in 1935. In 1939-1940 he attended Independent Junior College in Kansas and in 1941-1942 completed his second year at Ottawa University in Kansas. In May of 1942 he entered the armed services and on December 18, 1942, received his commission in the Navy at Corpus Chirsti Naval Station. He was killed while on a routine patrol flight. He had been listed as missing in action until August 15, 1944. Survivors include his mother, Mrs. Allene Baker Dixon of McGregor; father, Jim Dixon of Waco; two sisters, Mrs. Alta Mae Hudson and Mrs. Margaret Draper of McGregor; one brother, Lloyd Dixon in the armed services. McGregor Mirror: Nov 24 (4-3), 1944.

JOHN THOMAS "DICK" LAWSON, age 78, died at his home in McGregor, Friday, November 17, 1944. Dick was born in 1865 and came to Texas from his home in North Carolina in 1887. Survivors include his wife, Martha C. Lawson (1867-1952); one son, Herbert Lawson of McGregor; three daughters, Mrs. Martha Stewart of Alexandria, California, Mrs. Earl Zackefoose of Little Rock, Arkansas, and Mrs. Edna McEver of McGregor. Burial was in McGregor Cemetery by Lee Undertakers. McGregor Mirror: Nov 24 (5-1), 1944.

JOHNNIE R. HOLT. CARD OF THANKS. Thanks for the comforting words becuase of the loss of our son and brother, T-Sgt. Johnnie R. Holt, who gave his all to the cause for a better world. Mr. and Mrs. I. G. Holt of McGregor; Grady Holt and wife, D. Holt overseas, Mrs. Marvin Camp Hulen, Marvin D. Holt of McGregor, Mr. and Mrs. G. B. Clift of Waco. McGregor Mirror: Nov 24 (5-4), 1944.

MRS. W. T. WOODLOCK died on Tuesday in an Austin hospital. She was the former Elsie Holst, daughter of Mick Holst and niece of the late Mrs. Julius Johnson of McGregor. She taught school for the county until her marriage to W. T. Woodlock of Gatesville. Survivors include her husband; three sons, Lawrence Holst Woodlock of San Antonio, Joe and John Hugh Woodlock; a daughter, Laura Lee Woodlock of Gatesville; her father, Mr. Nick Holst of San Antonio; one brother, Louis Holst of San Antonio. McGregor Mirror: Nov 24 (5-5), 1944.

DEATHS IN CENTRAL TEXAS, VOL. II

ANNIE IRENE COLLARD of Oglesby died at the family home on November 25, 1944. Burial was in Coryell Church Cemetery by Lee Undertakers. Survivors include her brothers and sisters, Mrs. Maggie Wood of Oglesby, Mrs. Lem Alexander of Ft. Worth, Mrs. Rigney of Burkburnett, Mrs. Dave Bright of Waco, F. G. Collard of Oglesby, D. F. Collard of Gatesville, Charles Collard of Bell, Colorado, John Collard of Spearman and Otis Collard of Dallas. McGregor Mirror: Dec 8 (4-4), 1944.

MRS. A. L. BLANTON, age 57, died at her home in McGregor, Wednesday, December 6, 1944. She had been connected with the U. S. Postal Service in McGregor for the past 10 years, since the death of her husband, Chester Blanton. Mrs. Blanton was born on October 14, 1881 in Moody, Texas, the daughter of James. H. High and Mary Bishop High. Survivors include two children, Miss Ann Blanton, cadet nurse at Hillcrest Hospital in Waco and Bill Blanton with the U. S. Army in Europe; two sisters, Mrs. Tap Wells of McGregor and Mrs. C. S. Fostoria of Ohio; five brothers, B. F. High of McGregor, John of Moody, Bill of Carlsbad, New Mexico, Tom of Walters, Oklahoma and Rev. Frank High of Waco. Burial was in McGregor Cemetery by Amsler Funeral Home. McGregor Mirror: Dec 8 (5-4), 1944.

MARGARET MARIAN ISBILL, age 23, was born in McGregor on February 16, 1921. She was killed in an airplane crash at the municipal airport in Omaha, Nebraska Thursday, December 7, 1944. Margaret was employed as a Ferry Pilot, earning her wings at Avenger Field as a WASPS. She was not piloting the plane at the time of the accident. At the age of 11 years she had lost her mother, Carrie Lee Sanderford Isbill, by death and her second mother, Mrs. Katherine Perkins Isbill, came to love her as though they had been of one blood. Survivors include her parents, Mr. and Mrs. Grady Isbill; one sister, Mrs. Jane Carver; one brother, H. G. Isbill, Jr. Burial was in McGregor Cemetery by Amsler Funeral Home. McGregor Mirror: Dec 15 (8-4), 1944.

A

AARS, Mrs. Jesse 108
ABBE, George 65
ABBE, Milford 65
ABBE, Mrs. S. M. 40
ABBE, Roseann 64
ABBE, S. G. 65
ABLE, Irene 143
ABLE, Mrs. E. G. 89
ABBE, Mrs. S. M. 91
ABEL, Mrs. W. G. 32
ABBE, Will 65
ABSKER, Mrs. John 17
ACREE, Elizabeth 4
ACREE, Fred 4
ADAMS, Donald 112
ADAMS, Mrs. Don 121
ADAMS, Mrs. H. C. 111
ADAMS, Nellie 91
ADAMS, Sallie 112
ADAMS, Sandra 111
ADCOCK, Albert 83
ADCOCK, Annie 81
ADCOCK, Clyde 83
ADCOCK, Ethel 81
ADCOCK, George 83
ADCOCK, Hubert 83
ADCOCK, Jesse 83
ADCOCK, Jimmy 83
ADCOCK, Mary 83
ADCOCK, Mrs. G. F. 25
ADCOCK, Roy 83
ADKINS, Billie 4
ADKINS, Bonnie 4
ADKINS, Jerry 4
ADKINS, Mattie L. 4
ADKINS, Mrs. Rice 41
ADKINS, Mrs. V. A. 92
ADKINS, Owana 4
ADLER, Carleen 150
ADLER, Elsie 149, 150
ADLER, Gus 150
ALEXANDER, _____ 20
ALEXANDER, Clifford 99
ALEXANDER, C. W. 36, 65
ALEXANDER, Emma 65
ALEXANDER, Ethel 149
ALEXANDER, Henry 65
ALEXANDER, Jack 99
ALEXANDER, James 99
ALEXANDER, Jo Anne 65
ALEXNADER, John 65, 99
ALEXANDER, L. D. 36, 65
ALEXANDER, Mary 99
ALEXANDER, Morris 45, 65
ALEXANDER, Mrs. G. L. 20, 21
ALEXANDER, Mrs. John M. 136
ALEXANDER, Mrs. L. D. 77
ALEXANDER, Mrs. Lem 156
ALEXANDER, Mrs. Ramsey 73
ALEXANDER, Mrs. W. B. 14
ALEXANDER, Paul 99
ALEXANDER, R. H. 16, 96, 99
ALEXANDER, Tom 99
ALEXANDER, W. 36
ALEXANDER, W. B. 36, 65, 150
ALEXANDER, Weldon 99
ALEXANDER, White 65
ALLEN, Azoline 106
ALLEN, Clyce 145
ALLEN, Connally 71
ALLEN, Dike 10
ALLEN, Ernest 35
ALLEN, Gladys 55
ALLEN, Grace 30
ALLEN, Jim 34
ALLEN, Mrs. B. J. 102
ALLEN, Mrs. K. A. 117
ALLEN, Mrs. Sloan 108
ALLEN, Mrs. Z. G. 91
ALLEN, Ollie D. 56
ALLEN, Sam 118
ALLISON, Georgia 17
ALLISON, Jay 126
ALLISON, Lavinia 149
ALLISON, Maggie 105
ALLISON, Mary E. 126
ALLISON, Mrs. J. L. 14
ALLISON, Mrs. T. L. 17
ALLISON, Sarah 126
ALLISON, Thomas 126
ALLISON, T. L. 150
ALVARADO, C. 134
AMMONS, Ollie 148
AMSLER, Mrs. Sam 31
AMSLER, Mrs. Walter 104
AMSLER, Sam 31
AMTHOR, A. W. 31
AMTHOR, Bertha 31
AMTHOR, J. M. 31
AMTHOR, Mrs. Richard 42
AMTHOR, Mrs. Gus 115
AMTHOR, Will H. 31
AMTHOR, William 30
ANDERSON, Anna 76
ANDERSON, A. P. 76
ANDERSON, Arnett 76

ANDERSON, Billie 150
ANDERSON, C. C. 150
ANDERSON, Clark 34, 45
ANDERSON, Clem 25, 133
ANDERSON, Cloree 47
ANDERSON, Cody 150
ANDERSON, Donald R. 133
ANDERSON, E. 6
ANDERSON, Ed 76, 153
ANDERSON, Edwin 70
ANDERSON, Elsie 136
ANDERSON, Elvin 25
ANDERSON, Floyd 133
ANDERSON, Garland 6
ANDERSON, Jerry 133
ANDERSON, John 1, 34, 45
ANDERSON, Ione 45
ANDERSON, Jo Anne 133
ANDERSON, Kathryn 45
ANDERSON, Leonard 6, 22, 42
ANDERSON, Lewis 70
ANDERSON, L. H. 36, 138
ANDERSON, L. L. 138
ANDERSON, Low 45
ANDERSON, Lula 73
ANDERSON, M. 133
ANDERSON, Mary 25
ANDERSON, Minnie 71
ANDERSON, Mrs. A. P. 45, 65
ANDERSON, Mrs. Clark 34
ANDERSON, Mrs. Ed 99
ANDERSON, Mrs. H. W. 41
ANDERSON, Mrs. John 76
ANDERSON, Mrs. Leonard 43
ANDERSON, Mrs. S. J. 83
ANDERSON, Nick E. 6
ANDERSON, Travis 6
ANDERSON, Truman 6
ANDERSON, W. D. 150
ANDERSON, Will 150
ANDERSON, William 36
ANDERSON, Wynell 133
ANDREWS, Montie 138
ANTHON, Annie 70
ANTHON, Florence 87
ANTHON, Garland 87
ANTHON, John 87
ANTHON, Mamie 87
ANTHON, Mrs. S. C. 87
ANTHON, Rufus 87
ANDERSON, William 36
ARBUCKLE, Homan 57
ARBUCLKE, Otho 57
ARCHER, Ruby 118

ARMES, Mrs. Troy 68
ARMOND, Elizabeth 21
ARMSTRONG, Alex G. 89
ARMSTRONG, Alfred M. 89
ARMSTRONG, Anna B. 86
ARMSTRONG, Elizabeth 44
ARMSTRONG, Jack 89
ARMSTRONG, Mrs. Frank 5, 10
ARMSTRONG, Mrs. R. M. 23
ARMSTRONG, Willie 89
ARNOLD, Bill 150
ARNOLD, Coy 150
ARNOLD, Ina 150
ARNOLD, Mrs. C. C. 64
ARNOLD, O. L. 150
ARNOLD, Pascal 150
ARNOLD, Tom 150
ARNOLD, T. T. 139
ARNOLD, T. W. 139
ARNOLD, Watson 22
ARNOLD, Weldon 150
ARP, Emma 111
ARP, Wayne 111
ARROWOOD, Bartley 61
ARROWOOD, John 61
ARROWOOD, Kathryn 61
ARROWOOD, Lila B. 61
ARROWOOD, Mrs. J. 27, 75
ASH, Buster 104, 113
ASH, Effie 103, 113
ASH, Eula 131
ASH, George 103, 113
ASH, Jim 104
ASH, Joe 104, 113
ASH, John 103, 104
ASH, Mat 104
ASH, Mrs. John 46
ATKINS, Billie 75
ATKINS, Bonnie 75
ATKINS, Charlie 76
ATKINS, Della 81
ATKINS, George 75
ATKINS, Jack 76
ATKINS, Jerry 75
ATKINS, Junius 76
ATKINS, Owana 75
ATKINS, Peggy 4
ATKINS, W. T. 4, 75
AUSTIN, Martha 69
AUTREY, Mrs. Baybil 28
AUTRY, Mrs. S. P. 130

BADGER, R. T. 113
BAGGETT, Ella F. 121
BAGGETT, Mrs. J. W. 99
BAGGETT, Mrs. M. L. 121
BAKER, Addie 97
BAILEY, Mrs. S. P. 146
BAKER, Ed 144
BAKER, Ella 116
BAKER, Hamilton 144
BAKER, Helen 97, 98
BAKER, J. T. 116
BAKER, Mrs. Morgan 99
BAKER, Mrs. W. S. 154
BAKER, Paul 99
BAKER, W. S. 98
BAKER, Wellor 98
BAKKE, Mrs. Harold 32
BALDRIDGE, Mrs. F. E. 139
BALLEW, Lizzie 65
BANDO, Ada 12
BANDO, Ada L. 12
BANDO, Charles 12
BANDO, M. L. 12
BANKE, Mrs. A. F. 69
BANKHEAD, Effie 86
BANKHEAD, F. M. 15
BANKHEAD, Ida 15
BANKHEAD, Mrs. Ernest 56
BANKHEAD, O. D. 36
BANKHEAD, Will 15
BANKHURST, Mrs. Rivers 73
BANNISTER, C. D. 85
BANNISTER, J. M. 85
BANNISTER, Luther 85
BANNISTER, Martha 85
BANNISTER, M. L. 85
BANNISTER, Tiny 85
BANNISTER, T. R. 85
BANNISTER, W. T. 85
BARBER, Mrs. Raymond 24
BARGAS, Lillie 80
BARNARD, Doyle 123
BARNARD, Emmett 123
BARNARD, Mrs. R. F. 43
BARNARD, Mrs. R. T. 29
BARNES, Agnes 51, 125
BARNES, Laura 118
BARNET, Mary 37, 38
BARNHART, Mrs. O. L. 97
BARNUM, H. B. 70
BARRETT, Frank 71
BARRON, Millie 18
BARRON, Mrs. Willie 91
BARTEK, Mrs. M. V. 82

BARTLES, Frederick 94
BARTLES, Albert 94
BARTLES, Fritz 94
BARTLES, Hardy 94
BARTLES, Herman 94
BARTLES, Louise 94
BARTLES, Walter 94
BARTON, Mrs. Clyde 121
BASHAM, Charles 144, 151
BASHAM, Mrs. C. C. 144, 151
BASS, Cohen 122
BASS, Ella 122
BASS, Herman 122
BASS, Peggy S. 122
BASS, Richard 122
BASS, Ruby 122
BASS, Trav 122
BASS, W. J. 122
BATES, Amelia C. 87
BATES, Bernice
BATES, Burrews 87
BATES, Charles 131
BATES, Lee 72, 87, 132
BATES, Marion 87, 132
BATES, Mrs. Gid 58
BATES, Mrs. M. R. 149
BATES, Roy 131
BATES, T. B. 132
BATES, Will 87, 132
BAUGH, M. V. 22
BAYBORN, _____ 73
BEACHEM, Alex 50
BEACHEM, Minnie 50
BEACHEM, Will 50
BEAL, Mr. 72
BEASLEY, Mrs. Marion 89
BEATY, Carrie 32, 58
BEATY, Cora 31
BEATY, E. B. 41
BEATY, Eugene 41
BEATY, Felix 32
BEATY, Frances 32, 58
BEATY, Frank 58
BEATY, John 32, 58
BEATY, Joyce 41
BEATY, Kirk 32
BEATY, Luther 31, 58
BEATY, Nora 41
BEATY, Nugent 41
BEATY, Otha 41
BEATY, Sam 32, 58
BEATY, Walter 58
BEATY, Wayne 41
BECK, Mrs. J. H. 44

BECKER, Mrs. W. H. 126, 133
BECKWORTH, Mrs. Emma 55
BEEBE, D. H. 123
BEEBE, Margie 56, 123
BEERWINKLE, Fritz 76
BEERWINKLE, T. G. 76
BEKKELUND, Mrs. J. S. 93
BEKKEN, Mrs. J. G. 100
BELL, Miss 40
BELL, Mrs. Paul 102
BELL, Mrs. Roland 123
BENNETT, B. D. 25
BENNETT, Clifford 48
BENNETT, Curte 135
BENNETT, Duane 25
BENNETT, John 14, 134, 144
BENNETT, Mary 25
BENNETT, Mrs. H. W. 42
BENNETT, Mrs. R. W. 80
BENNETT, Nancy 25
BENNETT, Nathan 25
BENNETT, Ray 25
BENNETT, Verna 25
BERCHLER, Mr. 144
BERESFORD, Mrs. Paul 22, 88, 119
BERMINGHOUSE, Miss 96
BERRY, Mrs. Louis 54
BERRY, Sarah (Sallie) 9
BERTS, Mrs. W. R. 28
BICKEL, Ernest 114
BICKEL, F. E. 98, 154
BICKEL, F. J. 114, 154
BICKEL, J. F. 114
BICKEL, John F. 98, 154
BICLEL, Kate 98, 114, 154
BICKEL, Marie 154
BICKEL, Mary "Mollie" 98
BICKEL, Pat 114
BILLINGSLY, Mrs. A. W. 141
BINGHAM, Mrs. Ford 102
BINNS, Mrs. A. S. 104
BISCHOFF, Edwin 3, 107
BISCHOFF, Fred 3, 107
BISCHOFF, Frederick 107
BISCHOFF, F. W. 3
BISCHOFF, Herman 3, 107
BISCHOFF, Louis 3, 107
BISCHOFF, Mrs. Edwin 33, 109
BISCHOFF, Mrs. F. W. 3
BISCHOFF, Mrs. Lewis 42, 97
BISCHOFF, Mrs. William 3
BISHOP, Alice E. 127
BISHOP, Emma 109, 110
BIVINS, Mrs. J. C. 58

BLACK, Bob 5
BLACK, Tom 5
BLACK, Dr. W. T. 5
BLACK, L. E. 5
BLACK, Mrs. 89
BLACK, Vallie 111
BLACK, W. T. 111
BLACKBURN, Isla 131
BLAILOCK, Betsie 44
BLAILOCK, Harry 113
BLAILOCK, Mary 113
BLAILOCK, Russell 113
BLAIR, E. E. 11
BLAIR, Herbert 11
BLAIR, Robert 11
BLAIR, T. E. 11
BLAIR, W. O. 11
BLAKE, C. F. 58, 101
BLAKE, Jiggs 101
BLAKELEY, Mrs. Murry 41
BLANCHARD, Irene 143
BLANCHARD, Mrs. Paul 102
BLANCO, Anna 132
BLANCO, F. 132
BLANCO, Feodono 132
BLANCO, Jewel 132
BLAND, Carrie 31
BLAND, Jeff 31, 153
BLAND, Willie 31
BLANTON, Ann 156
BLANTON, Anna 12
BLANTON, Augustus 12
BLANTON, Bill 156
BLANTON, Billie 12
BLANTON, Chester 156
BLANTON, Ella 91
BLANTON, Earl 29
BLANTON, George 91
BLANTON, James 12, 91
BLANTON, Jim 29
BLANTON, Mildred 29
BLANTON, Mrs. A. L. 27, 156
BLANTON, Mrs. Bassel 117
BLANTON, Mrs. Chester 106
BLANTON, Ray 29
BLANTON, Royce 30
BLANTON, Ruby 29, 30
BLANTON, Sid 50
BLANTON, Verne 29
BLANTON, Wilma 29
BLASSINGAME, Mrs. Charles 141
BLEWETT, Mrs. J. W. 120
BLISSETT, Tom 40
BLOODWORTH, Mrs. John 52

BLOUNT, Andrew 115
BLOUNT, J. H. "Don" 115
BOARSDATTER, Bertha 92, 93
BOEMER, Walter 116
BOHNE, Bill 9
BOHNE, Elda 9
BOHNE, John 9
BOHNE, Henry 9
BOHNE, Mrs. John 14, 111
BOHNE, Rueben 9
BOHNE, Selma 9
BOLDING, Mrs. Billy 136
BOLGER, Mrs. Glen 91
BOLTE, Mrs. Herman 9
BOLTINHOUSE, Allie 123
BOND, LaGayrold 144
BOND, Mrs. T. K. 103, 113
BOND, Sharon 144
BOND, Zonella 145
BOND, W. A. 144
BOOTON, Elizabeth 133
BORBELL, Adolphus 51
BOREN, Eula 13
BOSTIK, B. J. 130
BOSTIK, Bonnie N. 123
BOSTIK, John G. 130
BOSTIK, Mrs. D. M. 130
BOSTIK, S. P. 130
BOTKINS, B. B. 97
BOTKINS, Charles 97
BOTKINS, Jessie B. 97
BOTKINS, P. J. 97
BOULDIN, E. E> 98
BOULDIN, Everett 98
BOULIN, Louise 94
BOULDIN, Mrs. E. E. 148
BOUNDS, Eleanor 53
BOWDOIN, Mrs. Bill 141
BOYD, Annie 105
BOYD, Bertie 83
BOYD, Claud 105
BOYD, Clyde 84
BOYD, Fred 84
BOYD, Laurine 83
BOYD, Henry 83
BOYD, Howard 83
BOYD, Minnie 83
BOYD, Mrs. J. E. 111, 153
BOYD, Pitson 84
BOYD, Summer 84
BOYD, Tom 84
BOYD, Wayne 105
BOYD, Wilma 83
BOWDEN, Mrs. Willie 27

BOWIE, Mrs. R. R. 16
BOWLIN, Mrs. W. L. 51
BOYLE, Margaret 50
BOYLES, Mrs. N. R. 146
BOYCE, Alice 59
BOYCE, Frank 59
BOYCE, J. B. 59
BOYCE, P. B. 59
BRACKNEY, Mailon 71
BRACKNEY, Mary 153
BRADFORD, Iva 111
BRADSHAW, Annie 87
BRADSHAW, Dick 70
BRADSHAW, Etta 89
BRADSHAW, Frances 70
BRADSHAW, Franklin 89, 143
BRADSHAW, Grady 89, 143
BRADSHAW, Howe 89, 143
BRADSHAW, Joe 70, 89, 143
BRADSHAW, Jonas 70
BRADSHAW, J. S. 89
BRADSHAW, Link 89, 134, 143
BRADSHAW, Luit 89, 143
BRADSHAW, Mrs. F. P. 54
BRADSHAW, Mrs. Joe 143
BRADSHAW, O. P. 70
BRADSHAW, Price 70
BRADSHAW, W. L. 134
BRADSHAW, W. P. 35, 70
BRAMLETT, Harriett 5
BRANDES, Mrs. Ernest 133
BRANDES, Catherine A. 115
BRANDES. Edward 115
BRANDES, Irene 115
BRANDES, Mrs. Ben 115
BRANDES, Mrs. Ernest 126
BRANDES, Mrs. Sam 115
BRANUM, C. G. 67
BRASWELL, J. A. 141
BRASWELL, W. H. 141
BRAUER, Mrs. Dick 125
BRAY, Mrs. Wendell 98, 114, 154
BRAY, Mrs. Will 92
BRAZELTON, Mandy 33
BRAZIEL, Herbert 88
BRAZIEL, Martha J. 88
BRAZZIL, Bob 46
BRAZZIL, Mrs. Aubrey 68
BREDIN, Mrs. Fred 151
BREEDING, Mrs. E. R. 73
BREEDING, Mrs. George 121
BREEDING, Mrs. J. R. 32
BRENNAN, Mike 145

BRENNAN, Mrs. Mike 117, 145
BRENNAN, Patricia 145
BREVILLOT, Jessie 46
BREWER, Mrs. Arthur 143
BRIDGES, B. O. 148
BRIDGES, L. A. 148
BRIDGES, W. M. 148
BRIGHT, Dave 77
BRIGHT, Mrs. Dave 156
BRIM, Sarah 95
BRINKLEY, Austin 73
BRINKLEY, Bill 73
BRINKLEY, Bob 28
BRINKLEY, Bryan 130
BRINKLEY, Clark 130
BRINKLEY, Cliff 73
BRINKLEY, Clyde 130
BRINKLEY, Edna 130
BRINKLEY, Fay 28
BRINKLEY, George 73
BRINKLEY, Henry 73
BRINKLEY, Jesse 73
BRINKLEY, Kelly 73
BRINKLEY, Lee 73
BRINKLEY, Missoura 92
BRINKLEY, R. L. 28
BRINKLEY, Robert 130
BRINKMEYER, Mrs. Charles 116
BRINKMEYER, William 116
BRITTAIN, Mrs. Ed 94
BRITTAIN, Mrs. Edgar 57
BROACH, B. 68
BROACH, Frank 68
BROACH, Kate 68
BROCK, Jace 63
BROCK, Jacob 63
BROCK, Olivia 93
BROCK, Ollie 112
BROCK, Tom B. 63
BROCKELMANN, Mrs. Fred 85
BROCKEMAN, Henry 42
BROCKERMEYER, Albert 101, 127
BROCKERMEYER, Carl 101, 127
BROCKERMEYER, Dorothy 127
BROCKERMEYER, Fred 101, 127
BROCKERMEYER, Henry 101, 127
BROCKERMEYER, Lillie 101, 127
BROCKERMEYER, Minnie 101, 127
BROCLERMEYER, Reinhardt 101, 127
BROCKERMEYER, Robert 101, 127
BROCKERMEYER, Ruth 127
BROCKERMEYER, William 101
BROCKSCHMIDT, Mrs. Frtiz 33
BROOKS, Mrs. Collin 142
BROOKS, Mrs. Paul 42
BROWN, A. Harley 35
BROWN, Albert 138
BROWN, Anita 35
BROWN, Atlas 139
BROWN, Bell 35
BROWN, Ben 22, 87
BROWN, Betty 119
BROWN, B. M. 139
BROWN, C. D. 48
BROWN, Dorothy 119
BROWN, Edna 22, 87, 119
BROWN, Edwin 88
BROWN, Ernest 48
BROWN, Eve 100
BROWN, Eva 48
BROWN, Florence 38, 43
BROWN, George 35
BROWN, Hayne 138
BROWN, Ira 138
BROWN, James E. 22, 87, 119
BROWN, Jason 43
BROWN, Jasper 29, 138
BROWN, J. Edward 22
BROWN, Jennings 35
BROWN, Jesse 139
BROWN, John 78, 139
BROWN, J. T. 29
BROWN, Ladene 29, 30
BROWN, Martha 84, 88, 134
BROWN, Minerva 78
BROWN, Mrs. Elmer 32
BROWN, Mrs. Jesse 22, 90
BROWN, Mrs. Jim 82
BROWN, Mrs. J. T. 29, 43
BROWN, Mrs. Raymond 40
BROWN, Mrs. Turk 39
BROWN, Oscar 34
BROWN, Porter 88, 119
BROWN, Ray R. 139
BROWN, Raymond 29, 30
BROWN, Roy 143
BROWN, Sammy 29, 30
BROWN, Stephen 34
BROWN, Tally 78
BROWN, Thoedore 48
BROWN, Thomas 143
BROWN, Virginia 119
BROWN, Wesley 78
BROWN, William 22
BROWNING, Ben 121
BROWNING, Calvin 121
BROWNING, Dick 121
BROWNING, Fred 121

BROWNING, Jack 121
BROWNING, Jess 121
BROWNING, Raymond 121
BROWNING, Tom 121
BRUCE, E. T. 42
BRYAN, W. T. 66
BRYANT, Mrs. Oscar 67
BRYANT, Oscar 32
BUBERT, Elmer 96, 149
BUBERT, Henry 96
BUBERT, Hubert 96
BUBERT, J. H. 149
BUBERT, Josephine 96
BUBERT, Leo 96
BUBERT, Mac 96
BUCK, Anne 65
BUCK, Minnie 65
BUCK, William 65
BUCKBEE, Bettie 70
BUCKBEE, Mrs. Tom 119
BUCKBEE, Tom 70
BUCKNER, Alice 31
BUCKNER, Dorea 109
BUCKNER, Mrs. Frank 94
BUCKNER, Mrs. Len 126
BUCKNER, Mrs. Lynn 71
BUELS, Alice 147
BUICE, H. W. 61
BUICE, Mrs. J. H. 43
BUICE, Ralph 132
BUICE, W. A. 61
BULLINGTON, Mrs. James 102
BUNCH, Mrs. A. B. 80
BUNYARD, Ola Mae 57
BURCH, Addie 55
BURKNEY, Mamie 74
BURKS, Alfred L. 86
BURKS, Mrs. Floyd 61
BURKS, Ollie O. 86
BURLESON, J. A. 120
BURLESON, J. M. 120
BURLESON, J. R. 120
BURLESON, Julia 14, 149
BURLESON, Lucy 120
BURLESON, Mrs. J. R. 75
BURNS, Minerva 91
BURT, Mrs. J. A. 66
BURTON, Frances 81
BURTON, Lee 81
BURTON, Luther 82
BURTON, L. V. 82
BURTON, M. W. 81
BURTON, Reva 73
BURWELL, Katherine 22

BURWELL, Mrs. James 22
BUSCHMEIER, Miss 125
BUSTER, A. G. 1
BUTH, Charlotte 140
BUTH, Frederick 140
BUTH, Mrs. Fritz 140
BUTLER, Bill 80
BUTLER, Clarence 15
BUTLER, Mandie 95
BUTLER, Miles 15
BUTLER, Mrs. 102
BUTLER, Mrs. Jim 82
BUTLER, Mrs. Winn 89
BUTTS, Mrs. Henry 130
BYFORD, A. B. 138
BYFORD, Annie M. 138
BYFORD, Betty 138
BYFORD, Burnard 138
BYFORD, Cody 100, 138
BYFORD, Gaston 138
BYFORD, J. P. 138
BYFORD, Mary 138
BYFORD, Mrs. J. P. 138
BYFORD, Shirley 138
BYFORD, Winnie 138
BYFORD, W. O. 138

C

CAGLE, Mrs. Bill 25
CAGLE, Mrs. J. V. 136
CAGLE, Mrs. N. J. 142
CALDWELL, Alma 88
CALDWELL, Bill 81
CALDWELL, Frank 81
CALDWELL, George 81
CALDWELL, Harry 81
CALDWELL, Lycurgus 81
CALDWELL, Ralph 81
CAMERON, William 89
CAMPBELL, Cullen 73
CAMPBELL, Dolly 73
CAMPBELL, E. K. 84
CAMPBELL, Eula 114
CAMPBELL, Floyd 24, 114
CAMPBELL, Hanna 152
CAMPBELL, J. R. 84
CAMPBELL, Leona 51
CAMPBELL, Mrs. F. E. 80
CAMPBELL, Mrs. F. H. 149
CAMPBELL, Mrs. Floyd 74
CAMPBELL, Mrs. H. A. 137
CAMPBELL, Riley 24
CAMPBELL, Robert 152
CAMPBELL, R. T. 73

CAMPBELL, Thomas 51
CAMPBELL, Tishey 24
CAMPBELL, W. M. 24
CAMPBELL, William 73, 114
CANADY, Emma 47
CANNON, Ethel 119
CANNON, James L. 119
CANNON, Jay 119
CANNON, J. L. 70
CANNON, Leita F. 119
CANNON, Lois 119
CANNON, Mildred 70
CANNON, Ovie 119
CANNON, Watt 119
CANNON, Will 119
CANOUGH, Mrs. Jake 123
CANTWELL, Mrs. Asa 89
CARNES, G. N. 107
CARR, Mrs. Frank 121
CARROLL, Mrs. Jim 26
CARRUTH, Mrs. Frank 112
CARTER, Charles 55
CARTER, Clarence 55
CARTER, Jack 55
CARTER, Johnnie 55
CARUTHERS, Eldon 13
CARVER, Jane 156
CARY, Una 47
CASEY, Frances E. 4
CASEY, J. C. 7
CASEY, J. T.
CASEY, John 4
CASEY, Laura 7
CASEY, Lillie 18
CASEY, Mrs. R. M. 4
CASEY, Mrs. Tom 7
CASEY, R. E. 7
CASH, Mrs. C. W. 119
CASS, Jim 4
CASS, Mrs. E. B. 52
CASS, Mrs. J. F. 77
CASTILLO, Desidero 118
CASTLEMAN, Charles 94
CASTLEMAN, R. H. 94
CATES, Jennie 102
CAUDLE, James 57
CAUDLE, Louis 57
CAUDLE, Mrs. J. L. 78
CAUDLE, Nellie 57
CAUFIELD, George 22
CAUFIELD, Henry 21
CAUFIELD, Katie 91
CAUFIELD, Mrs. George 117
CAUFIELD, Wiley W. 21

CAULEY, Mary 60
CAVABESS, Mrs. H. P. 75
CAVITT, Annie 94
CAVITT, J. F. 96
CAVITT, Laura 60
CAVITT, Mrs. Joe 22
CAVITT, Mrs. W. R. 15, 102
CAVITT, S. A. 94
CAWTHORN, Jack 35
CAWTHORN, Mack 35
CAWTHRON, Carloyn 41
CAWTHRON, Mrs. Jack 41
CEFUS, Nancy 46
CEFUS, Ned 46
CEMENT, Mrs. R. H. 36
CHABLEE, Molly 132
CHAMBERS, Mollie 87
CHAMBERS, Mrs. R. W. 126
CHAMBERS, Vella 31
CHAMBLEE, John 153
CHAMBLEE, Mrs. Frank 73
CHAMBLEE, Mrs. Joe 153
CHAMBLEE, Mrs. J. T. 23
CHAMBLEE, Ralph 23
CHAMBLEE, Roger 23
CHAMBLEE, Roland 23
CHAMINS, D. E. 126
CHANDLER, Mrs. Atha B. 66
CHANDLER, Mrs. Jim 61
CHANDLER, Mrs. Witt 138
CHANEY, Mrs. Clyde 131
CHANEY, Nute 13
CHANEY, Virgil 12
CHAPIN, Brady 4, 68
CHAPIN, Cecil 4, 68
CHAPIN, Charlie 4
CHAPIN, C. N. 68
CHAPIN, E. A. 68
CHAPIN, Elbert 68
CHAPIN, Ernest 4
CHAPIN, Hugh 4, 68
CHAPIN, Joe 4
CHAPIN, Liby F. 3
CHAPIN, Mrs. C. N. 3
CHAPIN, Ross 4, 68
CHAPMAN, C. H. 7
CHAPMAN, Clay 16, 64, 151
CHAPMAN, Mrs. Neal 104
CHERRY, Mrs. E. L. 55, 126
CHESSER, Charlie 50
CHESSER, Earl 50
CHESSER, Nellie 50
CHILCOAT, Carrie 87
CHILCOAT, Jessie 61

CHILCOAT, J. R. 98
CHILCOAT, Mrs. J. B. 86
CHILDRES, Mrs. Clyde 21
CHRISTIAN, Samantha 55
CHRISTIE, John 41
CHRISTIE, Lillie 69
CHRISTIE, Nellie 70
CHRISTIE, Opal 29
CHRISTIE, S. V. 7
CHRISTIE, W. F. 72
CHRISTIANSEN, Mr. 72
CHRISTOPHER, Mrs. A. 36
CHUNN, Mrs. Richard 65
CLABAUGH, Mrs. Sam 133
CLAIRBORNE, Bettie 66
CLAIRBORNE, Chas 12
CLAIRBORNE, Delmar 12
CLAIRBORNE, G. W. 66
CLAIRBORNE, I. P. 6, 11
CLAIRBORNE, Mrs. 6
CLAIRBORNE, Pattie 66
CLAIRBORNE, Rae 12
CLARK, Agnes 75
CLARK, J. S. 75
CLARK, Mrs. E. C. 58
CLARK, Mrs. Ernest 28
CLARK, Mrs. F. E. 149
CLARK, Mrs. J. W. 105
CLARK, Mrs. L. C. 38
CLARK, Mrs. R. D. 23
CLARK, R. D. 75
CLAWSON, Edwin 102
CLAWSON, Ernest 102
CLAWSON, Ivy 102
CLAWSON, Leonard 102
CLAWSON, W. N. 102
CLAYBROOK, J. E. 97
CLAYTON, Mrs. Earl 28, 130
CLEARMAN, A. Jake 136
CLEARMAN, Billie 136
CLEARMAN, Bob 138
CLEARMAN, Henry 138
CLEARMAN, Jack 136
CLEARMAN, Jake 138, 148
CLEARMAN, Jennie 16
CLEARMAN, Joe B. 136
CLEARMAN, Lucinda 138
CLEARMAN, Mary L. 136
CLEARMAN, Phillip 136
CLEARMAN, Ray 136
CLEARMAN, Robert V. 138
CLEARMAN, Sam 138
CLEMENTS, C. C. 131
CLEMENTS, E. R. 131

CLEMENTS, G. C. 117
CLEMENTS, Glen 117
CLEMENTS, J. H. 131
CLEMENTS, J. W. 131
CLEMENTS, Lonnie 131
CLEMENTS, Manning 117
CLEMENTS, Mrs. J. W. 117
CLEMENTS, Olen 117
CLEMENTS, Roy 117
CLEMONS, Dolores 65
CLEMONS, Donald 57
CLEMONS, George 59
CLEMONS, Harrie 59
CLEMONS, James Obie 59
CLEMONS, Ruth 65
CLEMONS, Sallie 59
CLEMONS, Tom 59
CLEMONS, Wenford 57, 59
CLEMONS, W. H. 57
CLEMONS, Willie 57
CLENDENEN, Mrs. Paul 100
CLENDENEN, Paul 100
CLIBOURNE, Pattie 36
CLIFT, G. B. 155
CLIMER, Ruby 46
CLINE, Mrs. Harvey 128
CLONCH, Ella 141
CLONCH, J. E. 141
CLONCH, Mae 141
CLONCH, Morgan 141
CLOPP, Henry 56
CLOPP, Lonnie 56
CLOPP, Mrs. J. D. 56
CLOPP, Walter 56
CLOUD, Mrs. A. B. 91
CLOWERS, Lottie 24
CLUCK, Arthur 113
CLUCK, Charlie 113
CLUCK, Frankie 113
CLUCK, Johnnie 113
CLUCK, Mildred 113
CLUCK, Sam 113
CLUCK, W. L. 113
COAHOGON, Vera 99
COATS, Mrs. T. C. 105
COFFELT, George 103
COFFELT, L. 103
COFFELT, Robert 103
COFFMAN, Mrs. T. A. 135
COKER, Pearl 32
COLE, Addie 118
COLE, Alexander 118
COLE, Ben 82
COLE, Clyde 118

COLE, Edna L. 118
COLE, Gracie 118
COLE, Harry 118
COLE, Ida 33
COLE, Joe 33, 118
COLE, M. F. 82
COLE, Mrs. Everett 89
COLE, Mrs. W. R. 100
COLEMAN, Mrs. Charlie 6, 111
COLEMAN, Mrs. G. B. 146
COLLARD, Annie 156
COLLARD, Charles 156
COLLARD, D. F. 156
COLLARD, F. G. 156
COLLARD, Georgia 65
COLLARD, Harrell 65
COLLARD, John 156
COLLARD, Mrs. Felix 43
COLLARD, Mrs. Leslie 53
COLLARD, Otis 156
COLLINS, Mr. 122
COLLINS, Roy 151
COLLINS, Vera 122
COLVIN, Mrs. W. C. 102
COMER, Jim 31
COMER, Josie 31
COMER, Mike 31
COMER, Mrs. Robert 146
COMER, Mrs. S. A. 31
COMPTON, Bertha 142
COMPTON, Mattie 72
COMPTON, Mrs. Frank 142
COMPTON, Mrs. Lovie 80
COMPTON, Mrs. J. T. 29, 43
COMPTON, Mrs. Vic 138
COMPTON, P. O. 138
CONLEY, C. G. 120
CONLEY, Gail 120
CONLEY, James 120
CONLEY, N. C. 38, 120
CONLEY, Walter 38
CONNALLY, Ben 15, 135
CONNALLY, Beverly 147
CONNALLY, Chris 55, 126
CONNALLY, Clarence 55
CONNALLY, Crit 147
CONNALLY, Ernest 55, 126
CONNALLY, Fred 44
CONNALLY, George 34, 147
CONNALLY, Gertrude 135
CONNALLY, Grover 83
CONNALLY, Henry 44
CONNALLY, H. F. 55
CONNALLY, Irene 93, 112
CONNALLY, Julia A. 55, 126
CONNALLY, Lanham 135
CONNALLY, Lee 126
CONNALLY, Leo 44
CONNALLY, L. N. 44
CONNALLY, Maggie 6
CONNALLY, Miss 95
CONNALLY, Mrs. Albert 74
CONNALLY, Mrs. F. O. 39
CONNALLY, Mrs. Frank 113
CONNALLY, Mrs. George 147
CONNALLY, Mrs. Lee 71, 109
CONNALLY, Mrs. Tom 15
CONNALLY, Naler 83
CONNALLY, Nep 135
CONNALLY, Ollie 44
CONNALLY, Pled 44
CONNALLY, Roy 55, 126
CONNALLY, Price 135
CONNALLY, Tom 55, 83
CONNALLY, Wallace 147
CONNALLY, William 55, 126, 135
COOK, A. F. 7, 108
COOK, Anna 119
COOK, Ben 108
COOK, Cecil 7
COOK, Charlie 108
COOK, Chester 119
COOK, Gus 119
COOK, Henry 82
COOK, J. B. 82
COOK, Jennings 83
COOK, John 108
COOK, L. D. 82
COOK, Marion 83
COOK, Mrs. E. C. 86
COOK, Mrs. G. H. 95
COOK, Mrs. J. H. 82
COOK, Mrs. Price 97, 115
COOK, Mrs. W. M. 97
COOK, Mrs. W. T. 53
COOK, Mrs. Stanley 102
COOK, N. J. 108
COOK, Tom 7, 108
COOK, Will 108
COOPER, A. D. 73
COOPER, Arthur 109
COOPER, Mary A. 138
COOPER, Mrs. A. R. 110
COOPER, Mrs. Jesse 45
COOPER, Mrs. John 14
COOPER, Mrs. L. P. 73
COOPER, Mrs. Noah 110
COOPER, Mrs. W. W. 19

COOPER, Nora 118
COOPER, Preston 73
COOPER, Walter 73, 139
COPELAND, Olene 97
CORBELL, Adolphus 51
CORBELL, Agusta 50
CORBELL, Horace 51
CORBELL, William 50
CORBETT, Mrs. W. C. 38
CORY, Richard 63
COSGROVE, Francis 50
COSGROVE, Frank 50
COSGROVE, Jack 50
COSGROVE, Patrick 50
COSGROVE, Sarah 50
COUCH, Bess 133
COULTER, Mary I. 123
COUSINS, C. L. 36
COUSINS, Dick 36
COUSINS, J. H. 12
COUSINS, John 36
COUSINS, Marion 36
COUSINS, M. H. 36, 66
COUSINS, Mrs. 23
COUSINS, Mrs. Richard 66
COUSINS, Pattie 36
COUSINS, R. O. 66
COUSINS, Richard 36
COUSINS, Will 36
COUSINS, Willis 36
COVEY, Mrs. D. S. 68
COWSERT, Mrs. H. L. 141
COX, Alpha 40
COX, Alsie 113
COX, Bob 7
COX, Caleb 7
COX, Doris 113
COX, Dowd 46
COX, Elizabeth 7
COX, Harvey 46
COX, Isaac N. 71, 126
COX, Jennie 86
COX, Joe 46, 71, 109
COX, John 71, 109, 126
COX, Keith 113
COX, Ola 102
COX, Malinda 70
COX, Mrs. Billie 102
COX, Mrs. L. C. 131
COX, Mrs. Joe 102
COX, Mrs. Roy 40, 74
COX, Mrs. W. C. 117
COX, Mrs. W. W. 51, 125
COX, Newt 7

COX, O. N. 71
COX, Otis 109, 126
COX, Richard 46
COX, Sallie 83
COX, Sarah 19, 89
COX, W. C. 71, 109, 126
COX, Wess 113
COX, Willie 113
CRAIN, Charles Z. 46
CRAIN, Delia 132
CRAIN, Earl 117
CRAIN, George 132
CRAIN, Glenn 31, 46, 84
CRAIN, Joe 132
CRAIN, Joel N. 46, 84
CRAIN, Lawton 132
CRAIN, Lena 46
CRAIN, Mae 89
CRAIN, Martin 132
CRAIN, Mavis 46
CRAIN, Mae 143
CRAIN, Mrs. Earl 49
CRAIN, Mrs. E. N. 81
CRAIN, Mrs. Glen 92
CRAIN, Mrs. J. N. 117
CRAIN, Newt 84
CRAIN, Riley 46
CRAIN, S. Ross 46
CRAIN, Watt 46, 84, 117
CRAVEY, Gennie 30
CRAWFORD, D. C. 66
CRAWFORD, E. D. 65
CRAWFORD, J. M. 65
CRAWFORD, M. H. 66
CREEKMORE, Sarah 100
CRELIA, Clyde 131
CRELIA, Eula 131
CRELIA, Hoyt 131
CRELIA, James A. 131
CRELIA, Leslie 131
CRELIA, Lester 131
CRELIA, Rosa 131
CRENSHAW, Boss 131
CRENSHAW, Mary 131
CRENSHAW, Mrs. D. M. 131
CROCKETT, R. R. 26
CROSS, James 102
CROSS, Lloyd 102
CROSS, Mrs. Tom 102
CROSS, Tommie 102
CROUCH, A. B. 48
CROUCH, Burl A. 48
CROUCH, Carolyn 142
CROUCH, Earl 108

CROUCH, E. W. 48, 142
CROUCH, Halbert 142
CROUCH, Hurl 108
CROUCH, Irma 111
CROUCH, James M. 142
CROUCH, J. C. 48
CROUCH, John 19
CROUCH, J. M. 48
CROUCH, Letha 50
CROUCH, Marshall 142
CROUCH, Mrs. Charlie 6
CROUCH, Mrs. E. W. 69
CROUCH, Mrs. William 50
CROUCH, Pearl 142
CROUCH, Rachel 142
CROUCH, Willie A. 89
CROW, Bunion 137
CROW, George 137
CROW, Houston 62
CROW, Jess 137
CROW, J. F. 137
CROW, Mrs. W. E. 102
CROWDEN, Mrs. A. J. 29, 43
CRUMLEY, Sue 65
CRUMP, Mrs. G. C. 45
CRUMP, Sallie 65
CRYER, Mrs. Cecil 27
CUENOD, Ellen 133
CUENOD, E. M. 133
CUENOD, Eugene 133
CUENOD, Henry 133
CUENOD, Leonce L. 132
CUENOD, Louanne 133
CUENOD, Lucien 133
CUENOD, Megda 133
CUENOD, Maud 133
CUENOD, Mrs. Paul 132
CUENOD, Mrs. Rene 133
CUENOD, Paul 132, 133
CULBRETH, E. E. 90
CULBRETH, Frank 90
CULBRETH, Homer 90
CULBRETH, J. K. 90
CULBRETH, Mrs. E. W. 90
CULBRETH, W. G. 90
CULP, Mrs. Roy 23, 114
CULP, Ola 114
CULPEPPER, A. L. 117
CULPEPPER, Ben 76
CULPEPPER, Donnell 117
CULPEPPER, E. A. 76
CULPEPPER, Freddie 76
CULPEPPER, J. B. 117
CULPEPPER, Margie 76

CULPEPPER, Mrs. Bryon 32
CULPEPPER, Mrs. Joe 117
CUMMINGS, Billy 35
CUMMINGS, Bob 35
CUMMINGS, E. B. 35
CUMMINGS, Jess 35
CUMMINGS, Matilda 51
CUMMINGS, Morgan 35
CUMMINGS, Rebecca 35
CUNNINGHAM, J. P. 42
CURB, Byron 80
CURB, Nora 80
CURRY, C. C. 39, 59
CURRY, E. L. 39
CURRY, Eva 39
CURRY, Izora 39
CURRY, Jep 39
CURRY, J. L. 39
CURRY, J. M. 39
CURRY, J. O. 39
CURRY, Mrs. C. C. 11
CURY, Effie 149
CUTBIRTH, Mrs. L. L. 100

D

DAFFON, Miss 52
DALTON, A. L. 26
DALTON, Alton 9
DALTON, Burnice 71
DALTON, El 117
DALTON, Martin 19
DALTON, Mrs. B. E. 117
DALTON, Mrs. Len 95
DALTON, Mrs. Wash 71
DALTON, M. V. 9, 68, 69
DALY, Edna 107
DALY, Joseph 107
DALY, Mrs. J. C. 107
DALY, Russell 107
DAMON, Mrs. Jim 76
DANIELS, Claude 40
DANIELS, J. V. 40
DANIELS, Wesley 12
DARDEN, Raymond 132
DARSEY, Mrs. Thomas 13, 14
DARSEY, Tom 29
DARSEY, Willie 14, 29
DAUGHERTY, Mary 60
DAVENPORT, Anna 149
DAVENPORT, Carl 149
DAVENPORT, Hattie 149
DAVENPORT, Mrs. D. P. 104
DAVENPORT, T. J. 149
DAVENPORT, W. E. 149

DAVIDSON, Craig 154
DAVIDSON, Estelle 46
DAVIDSON, Gus 154
DAVIDSON, J. T. 154
DAVIDSON, Mattie 113
DAVIDSON, Mrs. A. 154
DAVIDSON, Mrs. Aubrey 21
DAVIDSON, Mrs. B. E. 154
DAVIDSON, Mrs. J. W. 154
DAVIDSON, O. M. 154
DAVIDSON, Mrs. Quincy 21
DAVIDSON, Wes 154
DAVIES, Alleyne 146
DAVIS, Addie 113
DAVIS, B. A. 130
DAVIS, Bert 24
DAVIS, Berturm 123
DAVIS, Burl 24, 148
DAVIS, Charlie 105
DAVIS, Claude 105
DAVIS, Elizabeth 130
DAVIS, Elvin 114
DAVIS, Ethel 63
DAVIS, Gordon 24, 136, 148
DAVIS, H. D. 24, 130
DAVIS, H. L. 130
DAVIS, Hubert 24, 148
DAVIS, Hupert 130
DAVIS, James M. 130
DAVIS, Jennie 3
DAVIS, Jessie 130
DAVIS, J. M. 24
DAVIS, John 105, 112
DAVIS, Lee 50
DAVIS, Marvin 130
DAVIS, Maude 147
DAVIS, M. E. 24
DAVIS, Melba 148
DAVIS, Mrs. Albert 24
DAVIS, Mrs. A. P. 130, 148
DAVIS, Mrs. Bert 123
DAVIS, Mrs. C. J. 124
DAVIS, Mrs. High 54
DAVIS, Mrs. Sam 114
DAVIS, Mrs. W. C. 82
DAVIS, Mrs. Wes 87
DAVIS, Oscar 105
DAVIS, Royce 24, 130, 136, 148
DAVIS, Ruth 24, 136
DAVIS, Virgie 45
DAVIS, W. H. 63
DAWSON, Bobbie L. 131
DAWSON, Frank 130
DAWSON, James D. 130

DAWSON, Lucy 100
DAWSON, Mrs. P. D. 83
DAWSON, Roy 8
DAY, L. P. 151
DAY, Mrs. John 53
DAY, Viola 151
DEAN, Amanda 51
DEBECK, J. L. 45
DEBECK, Mrs. M. L. 45
DEBECK, William 45
DEBECK, W. L. 45
DEBORDE, Hazel 123
DEFORD, J. C. 72
DEJERNETT, Mrs. C. 79, 152
DEJERNETT, Reubin 79
DEJORNETT, Mrs. Segale 1
DEJOURNETT, Mrs. C. R. 1
DENNIS, Mrs. R. S. 110
DENSMAN, D. M. 63
DENSMAN, John 63
DERTING, Amanda 13
DESHAUNGH, Elizabeth 71
DeSHAZO, Eluira 126
DEW, Kenneth 22
DEW, William 22
DEWITT, Mrs. Charles 130
DIAZ, Audre 98
DIAZ, Ben 98, 125, 146
DIAZ, George 98
DIAZ, Juan 125
DIAZ, Juaquanita 146
DIAZ, Margaret 125, 146
DIAZ, Ramona 125
DIBBLE, Addelia 100
DIBBLE, Carlton 100
DIBBLE, Sam 100
DICKERSON, Mrs. M. M. 132
DICKERSON, Mrs. Otto 52
DILLARD, George 71
DILLARD, Tom 71
DILLARD, Wilma 71
DILTZ, Cary 48
DILTZ, Mrs. C. B. 47
DILTZ, Theo 48
DISHOUGH, Mrs. I. L. 86
DITTO, Bessie 79
DIXON, Alene 144, 155
DIXON, Bootsy 155
DIXON, Floyd 144
DIXON, Jim 155
DIXON, Lloyd 155
DIXON, Wayne 144
DODSON, B. F. 97, 114
DODSON, Ramona 97, 115

DODSON, Lee 115
DODSON, Wiley 115
DOMSTEAD, Mrs. Leo 121
DONAHOO, Bill 31
DONAHOO, Lynn 31
DONALDSON, Gertrude 129
DONALDSON, Marion 149
DONALDSON, Morris 149
DONALDSON, Mrs. Park 149
DONALDSON, Park 14
DONOHO, Lena 143
DORMAN, J. Layton 58
DORMAN, Myrtle 58
DOSHER, Sam 27
DOSSETT, Walter 117
DOTSON, Mrs. D. G. 144
DOTY, Gladys 109, 135
DOTY, Harlon
DOTY, Mrs. Luther 2
DOTY, Sarah 92
DOTY, Tinsley 92
DOVE, Betty 23
DOVE, Mrs. J. H. 22
DOWIS, J. M. 53
WOWIS, Mrs. T. M. 80
DOWIS, Nannie 52
DOWIS, W. J. 52
DOWLER, Mrs. A. E. 54
DRAKE, Earl 30
DRAKE, Oma 40
DRAPER, Claxton 21
DRAPER, George 21
DRAPER, Joe 91, 111
DRAPER, Margaret 155
DRAPER, Mona 21
DRAPER, Monette 1
DRAPER, Mrs. 5
DRAPER, Mrs. George 41
DRAPER, Mrs. Guy 1, 79
DRAPER, Mrs. W. Guy 152
DRAPER, Nolen 144
DRAPER, W. Guy 21
DRAUGHON, Mrs. J. B. 66
DREYER, Herbert 62
DREYER, H. W. 150
DREYER, Marvin 62
DREYER, Mrs. Henry 62
DREYER, Wilma 58
DRISCAL, Eula 93
DUNBAR, Vida 133
DUNCAN, Annie 28
DUNCAN, Bonnie 28
DUNCAN, Byran 28
DUNCAN, Clark 28

DUNCAN, Clyde 28
DUNCAN, C. E. 64
DUNCAN, Elbert 64
DUNCAN, Gladys 28
DUNCAN, Laura 28
DUNCAN, Mrs. Carl 70
DUNCAN, R. E. 64
DUNCAN, Riley 28
DUNCAN, Robert 64
DUNCAN, Ruby 91
DUNCAN, Spurgeon 28
DUNCAN, Sturgeon 73
DUNCAN, Therman 28
DUNCAN, Volney 28
DUNCAN, Walter 28
DUNN, Lena 47
DUNN, Lillie 113
DUNN, Mrs. D. D. 64
DUNSON, Cecil 65
DUNSON, Jack 65
DUNSON, Kelton 65
DUNSON, Mrs. G. W. 65
DUNSON, Wingred 65
DUTTON, Mrs. Isla 55
DYESS, Mrs. M. R. 23
DYESS, Mrs. Richard 90
    E

EARLY, Odessa 36
EARLY, Mrs. Willie 36
EARP, Mrs. Jessie 7
EASTER, J. E. 101
ECHART, Grace 134
ECHOLS, Alma 77
ECHOLS, Annie 40
EDMOND, Mrs. Charlie 54
EDMONDS, Clara 109, 135
EDMONDS, Mrs. Newt 2
EDMONDSON, Annie 105
EDMONDSON, Mrs. Paul 112
EDNEY, Helen 12
EDSALL, Jimmy 35
EDWARDS, Bill 136
EDWARDS, Calvin 16
EDWARDS, Jessie 8
EDWARDS, John 45
EDWARDS, Mrs. W. B. 78
EDWARDS, Mrs. B. L. 24
EDWARDS, R. D. 91
EDWARDS, Sarah L. 45
EDWARDS, T. N. 31
EILERS, Helene 17
ELKINS, Mrs. Roger 3
ELLIOTT, Alice 105

ELLIOTT, Carl 92
ELLIOTT, Frances 92
ELLIOTT, L. E. 74
ELLIS, Arthur 52
ELLIS, Bettie Jo 58
ELLIS, Elmer 58
ELLIS, Jim 52
ELLIS, J. F. 16
ELLIS, John 52
ELLIS, Lee 52, 132
ELLIS, Maggie 52
ELLIS, Mrs. Lee 82
ELLIS, Ora 52
ELLIS, Wallace 58
ELMS, Grady 119
ELMS, H. L. 119
ELMS, Morris 119
ELMS, Richard 119
ELMS, Samuel 119
ELMS, Ursie 119
EMBRY, J. M. 118
EMBRY, Joe M. 138
EMBRY, W. H. 118
EMBRY, William 118
ENGLAND, Ada 101
ENGLAND, Billie 75
ENGLAND, C. W. 129
ENGLAND, George 32
ENGLAND, Isla 75
ENGLAND, Ivin 4, 32
ENGLAND, Jerry 4, 32
ENGLAND, Lena 47
ENGLAND, Lou 4, 32
ENGLAND. Mrs. Stanford 83
ENGLAND, Paul 75
ENGLAND, Rachel 5
ENGLAND, Rolin 32
ENGLAND, Stanford 32, 75
ENGLEBRECHT, Malinda 14
ENGLEBRECHT, Mrs. H. T. 2
ENGLISH, Ruby 30
ERNST, Mrs. Elliott 133
ESTUS, Missy 67
ETHRIDGE, Jennie 60
ETHRIDGE, Mrs. Dick 87
ETZELL, Mrs. Leon 28
EUPHAM, Billie Helen 103
EUPHAM, Mrs. Dwain 103
EVANS, Bill 123
EVANS, Dora I. 118
EVANS, Jim 29
EVANS, Henry 28
EVANS, Mrs. E. J. 63
EVANS, Mrs. Henry 130

EVANS, Mrs. Walter 125
EVANS, Mrs. W. P. 51
EVANS, Myrtle 148
EVANS, Reece 72
EVERETT, Addie 100
EVERS, Christine 103
EVERS, Courtney 103
EVERS, Doi 58
EVERS, F. J. 103
EVERS, H. P. 103
EVERS, John L. 103
EVERS, M. H. 103
EVERS, Parke D. 58
EVERS, W. J. 103
EVETTS, Elmer 118
EVETTS, Elvena "Venie" 118
EVETTS, Frank 118
EVETTS, Hazel 118
EVETTS, Mrs. Travis 113
EVETTS, Mrs. W. O. 54
EVETTS, Samuel 118
EVETTS, W. M. 118
EWING, Mrs. O. C. 80
EWING, Mrs. R. L. 154

F

FAIRCHILD, Ellis 31
FALKENBERG, Mrs. Adloph 2
FALL, Howard 41
FALL, Mary 41, 42
FAMBROUGH, Eva M. 1
FARMER, Earl 141
FARMER, Henry 100
FARMER, John 153
FARMER, Mrs. I. T. 25
FARMER, Paul 100
FARMER, Stephen 100
FARRAR, Mrs. Henry 151
FARRELL, Charles 15
FARRIS, C. L. 127
FARRIS, Edna P. 127
FARRIS, Frank 127
FARRIS, Fred 127
FARRIS, J. F. 127
FARRIS, Leon 127
FARRIS, Mrs. A. L. 110
FARRIS, Ora 117
FARRIS, R. A. 127
FARRIS, W. E. 127
FARROW, Billy 95
FARROW, E. D. 95
FARROW, John 95
FEGETTE, Mrs. John 73
FEGETTE, Mrs. Morgan 99

FEHLER, Ben 3, 33
FEHLER, Charles 3
FEHLER, C. W. 3
FEHLER, Fritz 3
FEHLER, H. 3
FEHLER, H. C. 85
FEHLER, Henry 33
FEHLER, Herbert 3, 33
FEHLER, J. F. 3, 33, 85
FEHLER, Mrs. F. H. 84, 88, 134
FEHLER, Mrs. Fritz 32
FEHLER, Mrs. Henry 85
FEHLER, Sophia F. 3
FEHLER, William 34
FERGUSON, Vernice 79
FEWELL, Herman 100
FICKLE, Annie 107
FIELDS, Lena 87, 132
FIELDS, Mrs. J. F. 14
FIELDS, Mattie 29
FISCHER, Minnie 110
FISHCGRABE, Charlie 146
FISCHGRABE, Ernest 110, 146
FISCHGRABE, Fritz 146
FISCHGRABE, Minnie 30
FISCHGRABE, Mrs. Fritz 110
FISHGRABE, Otto 146
FISHGRABE, Reuben 146
FISHER, Barney 149
FISHER, Eddie 149
FISHER, Elin 149
FISHER, Henry 149
FISHER, Hollis 149
FISHER, Lou 149
FISHER, Mattie 139
FISHER, Onavea 139
FISHER, Willie 70
FISK, Alvin 50, 109
FISK, B. D. 50, 109
FISK, Edna 50, 109
FISK, G. G. 50
FISK, Gilbert 109
FISK, Oliver 50, 109
FISK, Oscar 50, 109
FISK, Ross 50, 109
FLACK, Mrs. Henry 72
FLEET, Cecil 105
FLEMING, Billie 133
FLEMING, Mrs. Bus 133
FLETCHER, Bay 52
FLETCHER, Carroll 52
FLETCHER, C. R. 23
FLETCHER, J. N. 23, 146
FLETCHER, J. T. 23, 146
FLETCHER, L. P. 23, 52, 64
FLETCHER, Mrs. Bay 112
FLETCHER, Mrs. L. P. 52
FLETCHER, Mrs. W. A. 141
FLETCHER, Virgil 52
FLEWELLEN, Rebecca 82
FLOWERS, Mrs. George 92
FOOTE, Frederick 96
FORD, Bert 120
FORD, Claud 68
FORD, Henry 68
FORD, Owen 68
FORD, Ray 120
FORD, R. D. 68
FORD, R. S. 68
FORD, Sallie 68
FORD, Wesley 120
FORE, Hazel 69
FOSS, Hilda 93
FOSS, Mrs. T. G. 93
FOSS, T. G. 92
FOSS, Tom 93
FOSTER, Jessie 130
FOSTER, Margaret 81
FOSTER, Mrs. A. A. 135
FOSTORIA, Mrs. C. S. 156
FOUTS, Sarah 72
FOWLER, Clara 147
FOWLER, Mrs. Tom 87
FOWLER, Mrs. W. M. 82
FOWLER, Oscar 147
FOWLER, Priscilla 147
FOWLER, Tom 147
FOWLER, Virginia 55
FOWLER, Wiley 83
FOX, D. A. 56
FOX, Florine 62
FOX, L. C. 56, 131
FOX, J. C. 91
FOX, R. L. 62
FRADY, Esther 113
FRADY, Gordon 113
FRADY, Howard 113
FRADY, Joe 113
FRADY, Mrs. Gordon 150
FRADY, Mrs. J. J. 104
FRADY, Price 113
FRANCES, Vivian 79
FRANKE, Mrs. R. L. 97
FRANKLIN, Viola 147
FRANKS, Doc 51
FRANKS, George 51
FRANKS, John 43, 51
FRANKS, Milton 51

FREEMAN, Dan C. 57
FREEMAN, D. G. 28
FREEMAN, J. D. 57
FREEMAN, John 28, 57
FREEMAN, Mrs. J. D. 28
FREEMAN, Mrs. John 39, 90
FREEMAN, Mrs. Tom 104
FREEMAN, Roy 28, 57
FREEMAN, Tom 28, 57
FREYER, Jake 110
FREYER, Martin 110
FREYER, Mrs. Martin 2
FREYER, Mrs. Martin 2
FRY, Ruben 34
FRY, Sarah 74
FRYE, Mrs. Jimmie 76
FULP, Mrs. Julius 81
FULP, Mrs. L. B. 40, 91
FURMAN, Mrs. A. J. 153

G

GADDY, Mrs. T. W. 55
GAGE, A. B. 104
GAGE, F. B. 14
GAGE, Mrs. G. W. S. 104
GAGE, Robert 109
GAIN, J. H. 93
GAIN, O. O. 93
GALLMAN, Allen 36, 65
GALLMANN, Clara 65, 66
GALLMAN, Clifford 36
GALLMAN, Rob 65
GAMBLE, Mrs. Fred 117
GANN, Elbert 40
GANT, Frank 54
GARDNER, Althia 56
GARDNER, Charlie 56
GARDNER, Mary 105
GARDNER, Mrs. O. B. 56, 93, 105, 123
GARNETT, Mrs. W. S. 21
GARREN, Ennis 150
GARRETT, Bob 117
GARRETT, C. M. 98
GARRETT, D. M. 98
GARRETT, G. W. 98
GARRETT, Jack 117, 145
GARRETT, Manning 98
GARRETT, Maureen 145
GARRETT, M. C. 98
GARRETT, Mrs. M. M. 98
GARRETT, Mrs. Paul 117
GARRETT, Naomi 98

GARRETT, Paul 117, 145
GARRETT, Tom 117
GARTMAN, Lewis 143
GATLIN, A. C. 55
GATLIN, A. H. 55
GATLIN, A. S. 56
GATLIN, Dorothy 55
GATLIN, E. W. 55
GATLIN, J. A. 55
GATLIN, Virginia 55
GATLIN, W. H. 55
GAUER, Mrs. Addelia 112
GAUER, Mrs. Henry 2
GEE, Mrs. J. W. 61
GEE, Orvil 102
GEIBLER, Mrs. Otto 62
GELTEMEYER, Emma 51
GENTRY, Frances 82
GEORGE, Mrs. Lee 10
GIBBS, H. B. 133
GIBBS, Peggy 133
GIBSON, Bill 154
GIBSON, Mrs. E. B. 22
GIBSON, Mrs. E. L. 16
GIBSON, Mrs. Howard 111
GIEBLER, Mrs. Otto 150
GIEBLER, Otto 150
GILCREST, Mrs. L. 75
GILL, Delbert 147
GILL, Eula 133
GILL, Jeff 53, 147
GILL, Jim 53
GILL, Mary 53
GILL, Matt 147
GILLILAND, Andrew 48
GILLILAND, Belle 116
GILLILAND, Billie 48
GILLILAND, Burges 116
GILLILAND, Burt 150
GILLILAND, Columbus 116
GILLILAND, Grace 48
GILLILAND, Jeff 50
GILLILAND, Kathryn 48
GILLILAND, Leitha 150
GILLILAND, Lenore "Nora" 116
GILLILAND, Less 116
GILLILAND, Leroy 48
GILLILAND, L. R. 48
GILLILAND, Mattie 48
GILLILAND, Mrs. C. C. 48
GILLILAND, Mrs. Roy 115
GILLILAND, Roy 116
GILLILAND, William 116
GILMORE, Dora 69

GIPE, Ruth 99
GLASGOW, J. L. 91
GLASGOW, Levi 40, 91
GLASGOW, W. T. 91
GLASS, Mrs. J. M. 73
GLASS, Mrs. J. R. 73
GLAZE, C. 93
GLAZIER, J. A. 105
GLAZIER, Mary 105
GOBER, Clara 149
GOBER, Ernest 149
GOBER, Odis 149
GOBER, Sarah 80
GOBER, Miss 9
GOFF, Cecil 95
GOFF, Hershel 95
GOFF, L. P. 95
GOFF, Mamie 127
GOFF, Olivia 95
GOFF, Will 95
GOGETT, Mrs. Owen 35
GOGLIN, Mrs. P. 42
GOHLKE, Mrs. Bill 96, 116
GOHLKE, Mrs. Henry 96, 116
GOHLKE, Mrs. Herbert 14, 111
GOHLKE, Raymond 96
GOHLKE, Walter 96
GOLLIGHER, William 146
GONZALES, Agapito A. 134
GONZALES, Andores A. 134
GONZALES, Jewel 132
GONZALES, John 78
GONZALES, Margaret 125, 146
GOODE, Betty 101
GOODE, Joseph 98
GOODE, Mrs. George 26
GOODE, Robert 98
GOODE, Vernon 9
GOODWIN, Kenneth 110
GOODWIN, Mrs. Clara 121
GOODWIN, Mrs. Raymond 110
GOSSETT, Mrs. John 24
GRADY, Edward 46
GRADY, Colleen A. 46
GRADY, D. A. 64
GRADY, Ed 145
GRADY, Mrs. Tump 16
GRADY, Vernon 64
GRAHAM, Arch 90
GRAHAM, Cecil 82
GRAHAM, Charles 82
GRAHAM, C. W. 82
GRAHAM, Emmett 90
GRAHAM, Frances 82

GRAHAM, Frank 89
GRAHAM, H. B. 82
GRAHAM, Lane 90
GRAHAM, Leola 154
GRAHAM, Mack 90
GRAHAM, Mrs. Cecil 77
GRAHAM, Mrs. Earl 76
GRAHAM, Noah 79
GRAHAM, Ora 75, 82
GRAHAM, Tom 90
GRAHAM, Will 90
GRAHAM, W. N. 82
GRAMUNDER, Amelia 126
GRANTHAM, Darrell 151
GRANTHAM, Harry 121
GRANTHAM, Hiram 121, 151
GRANTHAM, H. T. 3, 108
GRANTHAM, James 121
GRANTHAM, J. D. 3
GRANTHAM, Jim 64
GRANTHAM, John 104, 108, 121, 151
GRANTHAM, J. R. 3
GRANTHAM, Lloyd 121
GRANTHAM, Luther 3, 121, 151
GRANTHAM, Mary 121
GRANTHAM, Mrs. Jim 46
GRANTHAM, Mrs. John 124
GRANTHAM, Nathan 121
GRANTHAM, N. J. 3, 151
GRANTHAM, Richard 3
GRANTHAM, W. B. 3
GRANTHAM, Will 121, 151
GRAVES, Minnie 79
GRAVES, Rannel 91
GRAVES, Stella 91
GRAY, Mrs. Emmett 64
GREEN, Alvin 17
GREEN, C. E. 18
GREEN, Charlie 151
GREEN, Clifton 91
GREEN, Curtis 18
GREEN, Ellen R. 18
GREEN, F. C. 18
GREEN, Frederick 18
GREEN, George I. 18
GREEN, Grundy 18
GREEN, Janelle 91
GREEN, Jim 17, 151
GREEN, Joe 151
GREEN. Kate 72
GREEN, Mrs. I. N. 27
GREEN, Mrs. Robert 87
GREEN, Mrs. Will 72

GREEN, Mrs. Victor 92
GREEN, Newton 18
GREEN, Park 17, 151
GREEN, Price 18
GREEN, Ross 151
GREEN, R. P. 151
GREEN, Viola 151
GREEN, W. A. 72
GREEN, Will 72
GREENHAW, Fern V. 45
GREENHAW, Lawrence 45
GREENHAW, Robert L. 45
GREGERY, Mrs. M. E. 93
GREGERY, Virginia 93
GRENHOWER, John 37
GRENHOWER, Mary 37
GRICE, W. R. 13
GRIFFIN, C. D. 8
GRIFFIN, Mary 8
GRIFFIN, Mrs. Anthony 111
GRIFFIN, Mrs. George 87
GRIFFIN, Mrs. J. D. 28
GRIFFIN, Mrs. Jim 130
GRIFFITH, Mattie 155
GRIFFITH, Mrs. Corrie 138
GRIMES, Elmira S. 4
GRIMES, Frederic M. 4
GRIMES, Mary E. 89
GRISSOM, Opal 93
GROFF, Mrs. Henry 2
GUAREZ, Vincenta 148
GUNDERLOY, Mrs. 52
GUNTER, Mrs. Herman 131
GUTHRIE, Billie 145
GUTHRIE, Donald 145
GUTHRIE, Lloyd 145
GUTHRIE, Marie 145
GUTHRIE, Margaret 145
GUTHRIE, P. W. 145
GUTHRIE, Virgie L. 145
GUTHRIE, Wanda F. 145

H

HAACK, Mrs. W. 39
HACKFELD, Ada 135
HACKFELD, Bertha 88, 134
HACKFELD, Clara 134
HACKFELD, Emil 88, 134
HACKFELD, F. W. 88
HACKFELD, Henry 88, 134
HACKFELD, J. H. 88, 134
HACKFELD, Otto 88, 134
HACKFELD, Pauline 133
HACKFELD, W. H. 134

HACKFIELD, Bertha 84
HACKFIELD, Emil 84
HACKFIELD, F. W. 84
HACKFIELD, Henry 84
HACKFIELD, J. H. 84
HACKFIELD, Otto 84
HACKNEY, Callie 108
HACKNEY, Doc 81
HACKNEY, H. E. 74
HACKNEY, Hoyle 81
HACKNEY, Hugh 81
HACKNEY, Louisa 81
HACKNEY, Mary 81
HACKNEY, Mrs. Hoyle 97
HACKNEY, W. L. 81
HACKNEY, W. W. 81
HADLEY, Mrs. H. M. 100
HAFERKAMP, Edgar 96
HAFERKAMP, Emma 80
HAFERKAMP, Mrs. Fred 96, 116
HAGLER, Mrs. J. O. 98
HALE, Elizabeth 63
HALEY, Laura 56, 123
HALEY, Sally 84, 117
HALL, Anna 128
HALL, C. B. 3, 15
HALL, Grady 130
HALL, Gustine 49
HALL, Harry 130
HALL, J. Baker 3
HALL, Louise 21
HALL, Mrs. H. T. 13, 14
HALL, Mrs. Ovater 32
HALL, Willie Mae 15
HALLE, Louise 42
HALLMARK, Fannie 138
HAMBLEN, A. L. 74
HAMBLEN, Arthur 93
HAMBLEN, Emily 93
HAMBLEN, Mrs. T. T. 73
HAMBLEN, Theodore 93
HAMBLEN, Thomas T. 93
HAMBLEN, T. T. 74
HAMBLEN, William 93
HAMBLIN, A. L. 112
HAMBLIN, Theodore 112
HAMBRICK, Emma 81
HAMBRICK, Park 103
HAMBRICK, Ray 103
HAMILTON, Anna 13, 19
HAMILTON, Charles 24
HAMILTON, Jean 104
HAMILTON, John F. 13, 19
HAMILTON, J. T. 13

HAMILTON, Marvin 40
HAMILTON, Mrs. Everett 141
HAMILTON, Mrs. John 19
HAMILTON, Mrs. W. A. 146
HAMILTON, Oliver 13, 19, 24, 104
HAMILTON, Opal 104
HAMILTON, Roy 13, 19
HAMILTON, Sam 40
HAMILTON, Stella 104
HAMILTON, W. A. 13, 16, 118
HAMILTON, W. J. 104
HAMON, D. C. 24
HANCOCK, Bettie 36
HANDLEY, Mrs. A. M. 7
HANDLIN, Rosa 123
HANEY, Mrs. E. R. 144
HANNA, Sallie 67
HANNA, Sam 67
HANNAH, Clytus 64
HANNAH, Connie 64
HANNAH, J. F. 64
HANNAH, L. P. 64
HANOVER, Anne 96
HANOVER, W. S. 96
HANOVER, W. V. 96
HARBOROUGH, Mrs. D. M. 35
HARDING, J. M. 85
HARDING, W. F. 18
HARDY, Jeff 60
HARDY, Mrs. Lon 60
HARE, Mrs. L. H. 73
HARE, Mrs. R. C. 73
HARGETT, Mrs. John 142
HARPER, Mrs. L. 104
HARPER, Noble 49
HARPER, Victor 49
HARRELL, Maude 76
HARRIS, Ardine 47
HARRIS, Ben 148, 153
HARRIS, Bettie 58
HARRIS, Buelah 153
HARRIS, Christine 17
HARRIS, C. V. 153
HARRIS, Dan 6, 131, 148
HARRIS, Elgiva 152
HARRIS, Elmore 26, 27, 153
HARRIS, Gertie 136
HARRIS, Herriet 76
HARRIS, Homer 153
HARRIS, Horace 83
HARRIS, Jess 148
HARRIS, Jim 148
HARRIS, J. L. 147

HARRIS, Joe 148, 153, 153
HARRIS, J. W. 153
HARRIS, Lee 47
HARRIS, Mary E. 88, 153
HARRIS, Melvin 47
HARRIS, Melvin 23
HARRIS, Minnie 147
HARRIS, Mrs. C. E. 137
HARRIS, Mrs. Dan 38, 80
HARRIS, Mrs. Jack 152
HARRIS, Mrs. Joe 24, 58
HARRIS, Mrs. Mack 137, 152
HARRIS, Myrtle 148
HARRIS, Neoma 13
HARRIS, Obe 13
HARRIS, R. M. 114
HARRIS, Robert 146
HARRIS, Roscoe 147
HARRIS, Roy 13
HARRIS, R. T. 147
HARRIS, Sam 147
HARRIS, S. D. 153
HARRIS, Ted 147
HARRIS, Tom 47
HARRIS, Virgil 148
HARRIS, Weldon 148
HARRIS, W. D. 88, 153
HARRIS, W. V. 153
HARRISON, Clara 85
HARRISON, Clarence 105
HARRISON, Darthulia 105
HARRISON, Harlan 105
HARRISON, Homer 105
HARRISON, Horace 76, 105
HARRISON, Laura 44
HARRISON, Metta 147
HARRISON, Mrs. O. S. 69
HARRISON, Mrs. W. R. 76
HARRISON, Will 105
HARRISON, William 105
HARTMAN, Lizzie 67
HARTMAN, Mrs. A. L. 67
HARTT, Mrs. C. G. 1
HARTT, Rosemary 1
HATTER, Carl 26
HATTER, Lou 45
HATTER, Mrs. L. W. 45
HATTER, Ray 45
HATTON, Robert 9
HAWKINS, Annie 34
HAWKINS, Ernest 95
HAWKINS, Lum C. 95
HAWKINS, Mrs. Harvey 14
HAWKINS, Mrs. J. L. 95

HAY, Benjamin 36
HAY, Mrs. J. D. 152
HAY, Mrs. Jim 137
HAYES, Mary 125
HAYES, W. H. 51
HAYNES, B. L. 24
HAYNES, Bonnie L. 129
HAYNES, Don 129
HAYNES, Faye 129
HAYNES, Grady 129
HAYNES, Holley 118, 129
HAYNES, Ira 129
HAYNES, Mary 24
HAYNES, Mrs. Albert 9
HAYNES, Mrs. B. L. 24
HAYNES, Mrs. Louie 9
HAYNES, Royu 129
HAYNES, Wheeler 129
HAYNES, W. L. 129
HAYS, P. 141
HAZELWOOD, Mrs. W. A. 131
HEADT, Louise 106
HEALER, Ada 139
HEARNE, Mary 9
HECKMAN, Minnie 65
HEFFT, Mrs. Alsteen 86
HEID, Anna 133
HEINSOHN, Ella S. 125
HEMPHILL, Ruby 53
HENAGER, Arnold 100
HENAGER, Dorothy 100
HENAGER, Guy 100
HENAGER, Lawanda 100
HENAGER, Mattie 87
HENAGER, Ruth 100
HENAGER, Wayne 100
HENEGAR, Mattie 132
HENDERSON, Corrie 126
HENDRICK, Mrs. J. W. 129
HENDRIX, Mrs. John 123
HENNEKE, Conrad 96
HENNEKE, Frank 96
HENRY, Dudley 145
HENRY, Lon 93
HENRY, Mrs. Lon 54
HENRY, Mrs. R. E. 129
HENRY, Peggy 145
HENRY, R. L. 38
HENSON, Columbus 63
HENSON, Francis 63
HENSON, H. W. 92
HENSON, Luther 92
HENSON, Mrs. G. B. 131
HENSON, Otis 63

HENSON, Willie 63
HERING, A. E. 62
HERING, Albert 85, 152
HERING, Ben 97
HERING, Bob 85
HERING, C. G. 85
HERING, Charles 152
HERING, Charlie 85
HERING, Edd 97
HERING, Henry 97
HERING, Herbert 152
HERING, J. C. 152
HERING, Jim 85
HERING, Leo 97
HERING, L. L. 152
HERING, Louise 84
HERING, Luther 85
HERING, Mrs. Albert 87
HERING, Mrs. A. W. 49
HERING, Mrs. Jim 153
HERING, Mrs. Luther 116, 152
HERING, Mrs. O. F. 97
HERING, Otto 97
HERING, Pearl 97
HERING, Robert 152
HERMAN, Mrs. M. C. 120
HERRING, C. F. 92
HERRING, Charlie 92
HERRING, Jim 92
HERRING, Lonnie 92
HERRING, Luther 92
HERRING, Mildred 92
HERRING, Mrs. J. F. 66
HERRING, P. H. 57
HERSTER, Mildred 92
HESSE, Elsie 96
HESSE, Emma 96
HESSE, E. W. 96
HESSE, Ernestine 96
HESSE, Gertrude 96
HESSE, Max 96
HESSE, Myrtle 96
HESSE, Oscar 96
HESSE, Richard 96
HEWITT, Bertha 96
HEYMAN, Mrs. Jessie 44
HICKERSON, A. J. 110
HICKERSON, Buck 14, 110
HICKERSON, Cicero 110
HICKERSON, Emma 14, 110
HICKERSON, Gussie 139
HICKERSON, H. C. 110
HICKERSON, Jack 110
HICKERSON, Lee 110

HICKERSON, L. R. 110
HICKERSON, Marcus 14
HICKERSON, Mary 110
HICKERSON, Mattie 14, 110
HICKERSON, Mrs. B. 14
HICKERSON, Tom 110
HICKERSON, Wash 110
HICKS, Matilda 137
HICKS, Mrs. W. R. 14
HIGGINBOTHAM, Elizabeth 47
HIGH, B. F. 25, 27, 106, 156
HIGH, Bill 156
HIGH, C. C. 27
HIGH, Darrel 104, 106
HIGH, Euna 133
HIGH, Felix 59
HIGH, Frank 156
HIGH, James 156
HIGH, Jerry 133
HIGH, J. D. 79
HIGH, J. F. 106
HIGH, J. L. 106
HIGH, John 44, 156
HIGH, J. R. 79
HIGH, L. D. 44
HIGH, Mary 156
HIGH, Mrs. B. F. 119
HIGH, Mrs. L. D. 79
HIGH, R. C. 79
HIGH, Susie 44
HIGH, T. J. 106
HIGH, Tom 156
HIGH, W. J. 106
HIGH, W. L. 106
HIGHSMITH, Mrs. Eugene 73
HIGHSMITH, Vernon 73
HILL, Armstrong 39
HILL, Mollie 110
HILL, Mrs. Andy 49, 81
HILL, Mrs. A. J. 144
HILL, Mrs. Ernest 81
HIMES, Maxine 117
HINES, Mrs. J. C. 108
HINMAN, Emma 4
HINMAN, D. B. 4
HINTON, Mrs. Roy 130
HINTON, Myrtle 28
HITT, Aubrey 36
HODDE, Charlotte 125
HODEL, Frank 85
HODGES, Amanda 51, 87
HODGES, Andrew 87
HODGES, Caroline G. 87
HODGES, Creed Clay 87

HODGES, E. G. 87
HODGES, Mrs. Andrew 51
HODGES, Mrs. Ernest 114
HODGES, Mrs. R. C. 7, 62
HODGES, Nora 87
HODGES, Ona 87
HODGES, Willie M. 87
HODNET, Mrs. Marshall 138
HOEHN, Mrs. Edward 18
HOFFMAN, Charlie 136
HOFFMAN, Sarah 136
HOLBROOK, Carlton 9
HOLBROOK, George 9
HOLBROOK, Jessie 9
HOLBROOK, J. W. 9
HOLBROOK, Lillie 9
HOLBROOK, Marburt 9
HOLBROOK, Mary 9
HOLBROOK, Mrs. Bill 76
HOLBROOK, Mrs. Ed 78
HOLBROOK, Mrs. Ernest 73, 139
HOLBROOK, Shirley 9
HOLBROOK, Walter 9
HOLLAND, Abbie 40
HOLLBROOK, John 4
HOLLINGSWORTH, Ernest F. 139
HOLLOWAY, Mrs. H. A. 54, 70
HOLMES, Mrs. D. H. 48
HOLST, Elsie 155
HOLST, Louis 155
HOLST, Mick 155
HOLST, Nick 155
HOLT, D. 155
HOLT, Frances 57, 133
HOLT, Grady 155
HOLT, I. G. 78, 155
HOLT, Johnnie 155
HOLT, Marvin 155
HOLT, Mrs. Ira Holt 78
HOLT, Mrs. Marvin 94
HOMAN, Alice 68, 86
HOMAN, C. D. 68
HOMAN, David 67
HOMAN, Dewey 68
HOMAN, Fred 68
HOMAN, James 68
HOMAN, Maude 68
HOMAN, Walter 68
HOMAN, Willie 68
HONEYCUTT, Katie 67
HONNOLL, Cleo 151
HONNOLL, Dean 151
NONNOLL, Felix 151
HONNOLL, Hugh 151

HONNOLL, J. R. 151
HOOD, Isom 47
HOOD, Lucy 1, 47
HOOD, Oliver 47
HOOVER, Mrs. John 29
HOPPE, Alvin E. 135
HOPPE, Annie 155
HOPPE, Carl 2, 109, 135
HOPPE, Christina 2
HOPPE, Doty 134, 135
HOPPE, Elizabeth 135
HOPPE, Emma 109
HOPPE, Erma 135
HOPPE, Irma L. 2
HOPPE, Mark 2, 109, 135
HOPPE, Olge 100
HOPPE, Oscar 2, 109, 135
HOPPE, Robert L. 135
HOPPE, Walter 2, 109, 134, 135
HORD, Sara 36
HORN, B. W. 18
HORN, Curtis 18
HORN, Frances 18
HORN, Leon 18
HORN, Mrs. Willie 106
HORNBEAK, Mozzell 70
HORNBUCKLE, Howard 58
HORNE, Annie 137
HORNE, Bob 42
HORNE, Cliff 137, 152
HORNE, Earl 42
HORNE, Flora 137
HORNE, H. E. 137
HORNE, Jack 137
HORNE, Mary 83
HORNE, Mrs. O. G. 98, 114, 154
HORNE, R. A. 83, 137, 152
HORNE, R. N. 83
HORNE, Roy 83
HORNE, Sam 46, 136
HORNE, Tom 137, 152
HORNE, William 42
HORNER, Mrs. P. W. 70
HORSTMANN, Carl 125
HORSTMANN, Caroline 125
HORSTMANN, Charlotte 125
HORSTMANN, Eliza 125
HORSTMANN, Fritz 125
HORSTMANN, William 125
HOUSTON, Mrs. H. F. 135
HOUY, Mrs. August 146
HOWARD, C. B. "Lin" 26
HOWARD, C. E. 67
HOWARD, C. G. 6

HOWARD, Charlie 52
HOWARD, Harvey 26
HOWARD, Julia 52
HOWARD, Lillie 67
HOWARD, Mrs. A. M. 129
HOWARD, Mrs. Ernest 75
HOWARD, Mrs. E. E. 53
HOWARD, Phil 26
HOWARD, Robert 67
HOWARD, Sam 26
HOWARD, W. S. 26
HOWE, A. R. 73
HOWE, A. W. 73
HOWE, Charles 73
HOWE, L. B. 73
HOWE, Riley 73
HOWE, Thomas 73
HOWELL, Mrs. Robert 77
HOWLAND, Hazel 104
HOWSER, Mrs. 79
HOY, Fanny 94
HOY, Jim 94
HUCKABEE, Mrs. E. C. 3, 121, 151
HUCKABEE, Mrs. W. C. 3
HUDDLESTON, Earl 91, 136
HUDDLESTON, Jack 102
HUDDLESTON, Mrs. J. E. 92
HUDLEY, Mrs. Howell 16
HUDSON, Alta M. 155
HUDSON, Frank 40
HUDSON, Hern 144
HUDSON, J. H. 40
HUDSON, John 114
HUDSON, Joe 40
HUDSON, Martha 40
HUDSON, Mrs. H. H. 114
HUDSON, Robert 40
HUERMANN, Mrs. Mark 40
HUESKE, Adolf 126
HUESKE, Amelia 126
HUESKE, August 126
HUESKE, Ben 126, 133
HUESKE, Caroline 85
HUESKE, Clayton 133
HUESKE, Ed 126, 133
HUESKE, Emma 126, 133
HUESKE, Erna 97
HUESKE, Frieda 97
HUESKE, Hulda 28
HUESKE, Leona 133
HUESKE, Mrs. Adolph 97
HUESKE, Mrs. W. G. 84, 88, 134
HUESKE, Neta 97

HUESKE, Pauline 133
HUESKE, Otto 126, 133
HUESKE, Tuscher 126
HUESKE, Will G. 126, 133
HULEN, Mrs. Marvin 155
HULL, Minnie 149, 150
HUMPHRIES, Curtis 11
HUMPHRIES, Freda 11
HUMPHRIES, Ida M. 11
HUMPHRIES, Juanita 11
HUMPHRIES, Leola 121
HUMPHRIES, Marie 46
HUMPHRIES, Mrs. T. O. 11
HUMPHRIES, Thelma 11
HUMPHRIES, Thomas 11
HUMPHRIES, T. O. 91
HUMPHRIES, Wanda 91
HUNNICUTT, Mrs. John 127
HUNT, Grace 86
HUNT, Ira 58
HUNT, Mrs. Burl 35
HUNTER, Mrs. Hal 64
HUNTER, Juanita 90
HUNTER, Mrs. E. H. 120
HUNTER, R. T. 90
HURLOCK, Manie 119
HURST, Searcy L. 149
HUTCHEON, Chester 29
HUTCHINS, _____ 48

I

INGRAM, H. C. 27
INGRAM, Lena K. 19
INGRAM, Martha 27
INGRAM, Mrs. Harris 56
INGRAM, Mrs. T. P. 82
INGRAM, Ollie 97
INGRAM, Polk 27
ISBELL, Jack 136
ISBILL, Carrie 156
ISBILL, Dawn 136
ISBILL, Grady 156
ISBILL, H. G. 156
ISBILL, Katherine 156
ISBILL, Margaret 156
ISBILL, Mrs. Edgar 135
ISBILL, Mrs. Paul 129
ISBILL, Paula 129
ISENHOUR, Lula 79
IVY, Mrs. Leonard 107

J

JACKMAN, Loy 114
JACKMAN, Speight 114
JACKSON, C. S. 3
JACKSON, E. A. 3
JACKSON, Ella 19
JACKSON, F. M. 3
JACKSON, Frances 20, 21
JACKSON, Frank J. 18
JACKSON, Georgia 150
JACKSON, J. A. 20
JACKSON, Jacob 21
JACKSON, J. F. 3
JACKSON, J. R. 3
JACKSON, Mary L. 3
JACKSON, Mae 83
JACKSON, May 20, 21
JACKSON, Mittie 20, 21
JACKSON, Myrtle 18
JACKSON, Pearl 150
JACKSON, Richard 3
JACKSON, S. D. 3
JACKSON, Uda V. 83
JACKSON, William 19
JACKSON, W. W. 3
JACKSON, Wyet 19
JACOBS, Anna 39
JACOBS, August 39
JACOBS, Claudine 39
JACOBS, Fritz 39
JACOBS, Henry 39

JACOBS, Hettie 39
JACOBS, J. S. 22
JACOBS, J. W. 22
JACOBS, Lonnie 39
JACOBS, Mary 22
JACOBS, Mrs. Roy 117
JACOBS, W. F. 22
JALONICK, Carl 11
JAMES, Mona 152
JAMESON, Mrs. A. L. 66
JAMISON, Mary L. 11
JAMISON, Mrs. Maurice 50
JANES, D. H. 52
JANES, Mrs. Haggard 139
JANES, Thomas 52
JARRETT, Mrs. Joe 84, 88, 134
JAYROE, Alton H. 136
JAYROE, Carl 136
JAYROE, Carol 51
JAYROE, Carroll 136
JAYROE, Clara 136
JAYROE, Coxswain L. 136
JAYROE, Creassie 138
JAYROE, Harold 136
JAYROE, John R. 136
JAYROE, Luke 51
JAYROE, Mary 51
JAYROE, Millie 31
JAYROE, Nathan 136
JAYROE, Robert 51
JAYROE, Sherrill 136
JAYROE, Wesley 136
JAYROE, W. T. 136
JECHKE, Laura 96
JECHKE, Walter 96
JECHKE, Willie 96
JEFFERIES, Mrs. Robert 76
JENKINS, Doris 79
JENKINS, Duane 83
JENKINS, Gloria 83
JENKINS, Harold 79
JENKINS, Henry 83
JENKINS, John 25, 83
JENKINS, Mrs. Frank 20, 21
JENKINS, Mrs. T. H. 79, 102
JENKINS, Nannie 81
JENKINS, Paul 83
JENKINS, Uda V. 83
JETER, Lizzie 100
JETT, Faye 34
JETT, I. N. 34
JETT, James 34
JETT, Paul 34
JOHNSON, Agnes 72

JOHNSON, Alf 11
JOHNSON, Allen 122
JOHNSON, Anne 133
JOHNSON, Buddy 122
JOHNSON, B. S. 133
JOHNSON, Cicero J. 86
JOHNSON, C. Julius 72
JOHNSON, Clifford 70
JOHNSON, C. W. 70
JOHNSON, Dolphius 34
JOHNSON, Emma 134
JOHNSON, Ernest 11
JOHNSON, Etta 34
JOHNSON, Eunice 21
JOHNSON, Eva 21
JOHNSON, Florine 5
JOHNSON, Floy 5
JOHNSON, Harry 5, 72
JOHNSON, Helen 5
JOHNSON, Howard 11
JOHNSON, Isham 86
JOHNSON, J. S. 11
JOHNSON, James D. 5
JOHNSON, James E. 5
JOHNSON, James E., Jr. 5
JOHNSON, John 5, 34
JOHNSON, Kate 72
JOHNSON, Kee 11
JOHNSON, Loy 5
JOHNSON, Mary 70
JOHNSON, Mrs. Arthur 89
JOHNSON, Mrs. Bud 50
JOHNSON, Mrs. Curtis 67
JOHNSON, Mrs. E. H. 27
JOHNSON, Mrs. Jim 103
JOHNSON, Mrs. Johnnie 112
JOHNSON, Mrs. Julius 22
JOHNSON, Mrs. Park 122
JOHNSON, Mrs. Paul 64
JOHNSON, Mrs. W. A. 50, 109
JOHNSON, Mrs. Will 122
JOHNSON, Nancy 34
JOHNSON, Neal 34
JOHNSON, N. J. 114
JOHNSON, Parker 122
JOHNSON, Paul 118, 122
JOHNSON, Pearl 22
JOHNSON, Priscilla (Drucilla) 10
JOHNSON, Rob 34
JOHNSON, Robert 114
JOHNSON, Roy 70
JOHNSON, Samuel 5
JOHNSON, Tull 118, 122
JOHNSON, Venice 114

JOHNSON, Virgil 34
JOHNSON, W. C. 86, 122
JOHNSON, William 5
JONES, Albert 134
JONES, A. T. 10
JONES, C. L. 65
JONES, Clydus 134
JONES, C. O. 16
JONES, Dan 18, 19
JONES, D. W. 101, 103
JONES, Edna 127
JONES, Emma 32
JONES, Eulalia 101
JONES, Frank 16, 134
JONES, F. T. 121
JONES, Harry 121
JONES, Henry 134
JONES, Herschell 121
JONES, H. H. 16
JONES, Homer 65
JONES, Ione 65
JONES, Jackson 65
JONES, James 5, 121
JONES, J. E. 121
JONES, Johnnie 143
JONES, Jonas 32
JONES, Leola 121
JONES, Lynn 121
JONES, Martha 10, 21, 101
JONES, Marylyn K. 121
JONES, Mrs. A. T. 112
JONES, Mrs. Ben 24, 58, 118
JONES, Mrs. Charlie 2
JONES, Mrs. C. O. 102
JONES, Mrs. D. W. 90
JONES, Mrs. I. T. 19, 69
JONES, Mrs. Jesse 13
JONES, Mrs. J. F. 11
JONES, Mrs. J. J. 101
JONES, Mrs. M. A. 65
JONES, Mrs. R. E. 137, 152
JONES, Mrs. Sam 82
JONES, Nancy 77
JONES, Nannie Dell 134
JONES, O. F. 101
JONES, Paul 143
JONES, P. E. 101
JONES, Ray 121
JONES, R. B. 65
JONES, Reva 121
JONES, Robert 134
JONES, Tom 134
JONES, Weldon 19
JONES, William H. 5

JONES, Willis 24
JORDAN, A. A. 80
JORDAN, Albert 9
JORDAN, C. T. 80
JORDAN, Doug 79
JORDAN, Dr. Dowell 1
JORDAN, D. M. 152
JORDAN, D. V. 152
JORDAN, Dr. D. W. 1, 152
JORDAN, Emma 80
JORDAN, Florie 10
JORDAN, James 80
JORDAN, Jim 9
JORDAN, J. J. 36
JORDAN, Louise 79
JORDAN, Mayme 79
JORDAN, Melinda Nickerson 1
JORDAN, M. L. 5
JORDAN, Mrs. D. M. 152
JORDAN, Mrs. M. L. 67, 79
JORDAN, O. K. 10
JORDAN, Roger 36
JORDAN, Sarah 80
JORDAN, Wiley 1
JORDAN, Wendell 79, 152
JORDAN, Windell 1

K

KAELIN, Amil 144
KAELIN, Jacob 144
KAELIN, Jake 144
KAELIN, Mary 144
KAELIN, Mrs. B. 144
KALSCHEUER, Fred 99
KALSCHEUER, Hans 99
KANADY, Red 34
KANE, Mrs. Bird 55
KARNOWSKI, Albert 145
KARNOWSKI, P. H. 145
KASTING, Mrs. Fred 102
KATTNER, Mrs. Fred 146
KEARNEY, Mrs. Bruce 102
KEEN, Mrs. Elmer 94
KELLEN, Mrs. Ocoee 80
KELLEY, Mrs. Dennis 131
KELLING, Mr. 63
KELLUM, Mrs. 28
KELLY, Eliza 8
KELLY, J. W. 47
KELLY, Mrs. Knox 97
KELLY, Mrs. Michael 21
KELLY, Wesley 47
KELM, Albert 97
KELM, Alfred 97

KELM, Emma 97
KELM, Emie 97
KELM, Martine 97
KELM, Mrs. Louis 146
KELM, Otto 97
KELM, Richard 97
KELM, Walter 97
KELSO, Frank 80
KELSO, Jim 80
KELSO, Lela 80
KELSO, P. G. 80
KELSO, Walter 80
KELTNER, Mrs. 18
KELTNER, Mrs. J. C. 25, 83, 93
KELTNER, Raymond 25, 83
KELTON, Mrs. E. S. 78
KEMP, Jim 1
KEMP, Lucy Hood 1, 52
KEMP, Mildred 1
KEMP, Washington 1, 52
KERLEY, Minnie 17
KESTLER, Mrs. C. W. 78, 112
KIDD, Frank 53
KIDD, J. L. 53
KIDD, M. C. 53
KILGORE, Glenn 81
KILGORE, Granville 81
KILGORE, H. C. 19
KILGORE, J. S. 80
KILGORE, Lottie 81
KILGORE, Oran 62
KILGORE, Ralph 81
KILLOUGH, Mrs. Ted 9
KILPATRICK, Billy 120
KILPATRICK, Eben 120
KILPATRICK, E. R. 86
KILPATRICK, Frances 120
KILPATRICK, Hubert 86
KILPATRICK, James 120
KILPATRICK, Lorraine 120
KILPATRICK, Mary 120
KILPATRICK, Mildred 120
KILPATRICK, Robert 120
KIMBLE, Mrs. W. G. 137
KING, Henry 91, 92
KING, John 64, 108
KING, LaJuanah 64
KING, L. E. 21
KING, Leon 91
KING, Luther 92
KING, Mary K. 92
KING, Mrs. J. W. 117
KING, Quince 92
KING, Tilman 92

KING, Tom 108
KINNAMON, Una 118
KINSEY, Luther 130
KINTZEL, Wilhelm 69
KINZ, Mrs. E. C. 89
KIRBY, Amanda 15
KIRBY, Carlos 118
KIRBY, C. L. 135
KIRBY, Jess 15, 135
KIRK, Edwin 133
KIRK, Lizzie 87
KIRK, Mollie 138
KIRK, Mrs. Edwin 72
KIRK, Mrs. E. M. 132
KIRK, Mrs. W. H. 19
KIRKLAND, Daniel 147
KIRKPATRICK, I. J. 124
KIRKPATRICK, Mary 124
KIRKSEY, Willie 10
KNESCHK, Adloph 3
KNESCHK, Agnes 3
KNESCHK, Emma 3
KNESCHK, Mr. 2
KNIGHT, Billie 153
KNIGHT, Claud 59, 123
KNIGHT, Harry 153
KNIGHT, H. L. 153
KNIGHT, Julius 153
KNIGHT, Martha 153
KNIGHT, Mattie 13
KNIGHT, Norma 123
KNIGHT, Walter 153
KNIPPEL, Louise 122
KNOWD, W. M. 60
KNOWLES, Claud 59
KNOWLES, Tom 59
KOEHLER, Adolf 61
KOEHLER, Ben 61
KOEHLER, Henrietta 61
KOEHLER, Hermina 24
KOEHLER, Mrs. Will 84
KOEHLER, Severin 61
KOEHLER, Walter 24
KOEHLER, Will 24, 85
KOEHLER, Willie 61
KOESTER, Carolyn 106
KOKEMOR, Mrs. W. M. 106
KOLB, Mrs. W. C. 139
KOPP, Clara 17
KOWIERSCHKE, Mrs. C. 103
KRAFT, Mrs. Mack 65
KRAUSE, Ella 125
KRAUSE, Hans 125
KRAUSE, Lydia 125

KRAUSE, Lothur 125
KREMPIN, Mrs. Will 85
KREYER, Alf 52
KROFT, Sam 1
KROLLAGE, Henry 25
KROLLAGE, Minnie 25
KROLLAGE, Mrs. Rudolph 18
KRUSE, W. H. 58
KUNZ, A. W. 51
KUNZ, E. C. 45
KUNZ, Elmer 51
KUNZ, Howard 51
KUTACEK, Mary 17

L

LACINA, Bessie 50
LACINA, Frank 50
LACINA, Mary 50
LACINA, John 50
LA FITTE, Mrs. Nettie 85
LAM, Easter 41
LAM, Elie
LAM, F. B. 41, 91
LAM, H. M. 41
LAM, John 41
LAM, Lafayette 41
LAM, Maggie 41
LAMB, Mrs. Murl 114
LAMB, Mrs. N. J. 114
LAMMERT, Anita 23
LAMMERT, Annie 23
LAMMERT, Arnold 23
LAMMERT, Edwin 23
LAMMERT, Ester 23
LAMMERT, Lonnie 23
LAMMERT, Ruby 23
LAMMERT, William 23
LAMMERT, Willie 23
LANCES, Mrs. J. 120
LANCH, Mrs. W. W. 88
LAND, Shelburn 35
LANDER, Arnold 112
LANDER, Mrs. Frank 110
LANDER, Mrs. Hennie 61
LANDER, Frank 112
LANDER, Frieda 112
LANDER, Joe 112
LANDER, Minnie 112
LANDER, Mrs. Arnold 150
LANDER, Sohpie 112
LANDIOUS, Raymond 152
LANE, Eddie 57, 133
LANE, Fred 57, 133

LANE, Jessie 57, 133
LANE, Jewel 113
LANE, J. W. 57, 133
LANE, Paul 57, 133
LANE, Robert 57, 133
LANE, Roy 57, 133
LANE, Samuel 57
LANE, Tommie 57, 133
LANFIRED, Elizabeth 2
LANFRIED, John 2
LANFRIED, Martha 2
LANFRIED, Will 2
LANGSTON, Alma 148
LANGSTON, Mrs. D. L. 80
LARKINS, Mrs. C. L. 106
LAWHUER, Rachel 93
LAWRENCE, Carl 115
LAWRENCE, Eddie 24
LAWRENCE, Irene 115
LAWRENCE, Joyce 115
LAWRENCE, Lavon 115
LAWRENCE, Lucy 115
LAWRENCE, Mittie 91
LAWRENCE, Mrs. 35
LAWRENCE, Mrs. W. D. 115
LAWRENCE, Savoy 91
LAWRENCE, Shirley 115
LAWRENCE, W. D. 115
LAWSON, Alexa 36
LAWSON, Dick 27, 155
LAWSON, J. T. 7, 155
LAWSON, Harry 36
LAWSON, Herbert 155
LAWSON, L. A. 36
LAWSON, Martha 155
LAWSON, Oliver 36
LAYNE, W. C. 67
LEACHE, Corrie 63, 126
LEACHE, C. Lytton 126
LEACHE, Edd 126
LEACHE, F. S. 126
LEACHE, J. D. 126
LEACHE, J. W. 126
LEAMONS, Donnie I. 104
LEAMONS, Nancy 104
LEAMONS, Shearman 104
LECHLER, Mrs. Joe 123
LEE, A. L. 21
LEE, C. R. 74
LEE, Flora 100
LEE, Frankie 131
LEE, George 74
LEE, G. W. 10, 21, 39, 74
LEE, Homer 74

LEE, Irene 21
LEE, Josephine 74
LEE, L. A. 74
LEE, Lena R. 21
LEE, Meda 73
LEE, Mrs. A. L. 31, 76, 77
LEE, Mrs. G. W. 112
LEE, Mrs. Robert 115
LEE, Myrtle 58
LEE, W. D. 8
LEE, William 21
LEE, Willie M. 7
LEE, W. J. 74
LEETH, Charlie 144
LEETH, Clinton 144
LEETH, J. B. 144
LEETH, Lena 144
LEETH, Raymond 144
LEETH, Roy 144
LEFEVRE, Eugene 132
LEFEVRE, Leonce 133
LEGG, N. R. 64
LEGGEN, Frances 27
LEHDE, Mrs. H. C. 78, 113
LEHRMAN, Alvin 149, 150
LEHRMAN, Carbon 149, 150
LEHRMAN, Christ 61
LEHRMAN, Eric 149, 150
LEHRMAN, Fred 149, 150
LEHRMAN, Fritz 61, 149
LEHRMAN, Henry 149, 150
LEHRMAN, Herbert 149, 150
LEHRMAN, Jack 149
LEHRMAN, Milford 150
LEHRMAN, Minnie 84
LEHRMAN, Theodore 149, 150
LEHRMAN, William 57
LEIZERT, Charles 62
LELONG, Clara 132
LEMLY, C. C. 46
LEONARD, Claude 30
LEONARD, Curtis 30
LEONARD, Earl 30
LEONARD, Edith 30
LEONARD, Erby 30
LEONARD, Ernest 30
LEONARD, J. E. 30
LEONARD, Lillian 30
LEONARD, Lula 30
LEONARD, W. J. 30
LEUBNER, Anna 97
LEUBNER, F. W. 97
LEWELLEN, Mrs. G. D. 55, 126
LEWELLEN, Mrs. N. D. 7

LEWIS, Freddie 77
LEWIS, Frankie 77
LEWIS, M. J. 77
LEWIS, Mrs. G. A. 35
LEWIS, P. P. 77
LEWIS, R. S. 77
LEWIS, Sarah 77
LIGHT, Susan 12
LINDER, Eliza 49
LINDER, John 49
LINDSEY, Earl 39
LINDSEY, J. H. 39
LINDSEY, J. S. 75
LINDSEY, Martin 39
LINDSEY, S. K. 75
LINDSEY, Turner 39
LINDSEY, Wilma 75
LIPPE, Albert 116
LIPPE, Edwin 116
LIPPE, Fred 11, 51
LIPPE, Henry 51
LIPPE, H. W. 4
LIPPE, Lena Steinkamp 4
LIPPE, Miss 11
LIPPE, Mrs. Henry 116
LIPPE, William 4
LIPPE, W. R. 4
LOCKE, Mrs. A. O. 133
LOCKHART, Odam 54
LOCKHART, Sylvia 54
LOCKSBY, Myrtle 49
LOCKWOOD, Mrs. Jesse 144
LOESCH, Agnes 140
LOESCH, Anna 18
LOESCH, Eldor 116, 140
LOESCH, Ella 96
LOESCH, Ernest 140
LOESCH, Erwin 140
LOESCH, Henrietta 106
LOESCH, O. C. 140
LOESCH, Otto 140
LOFLAND, Pierce 76
LOFLAND, Trena 76
LONG, D. F. 153
LONG, James 69
LONG, John H. 153
LONG, J. W. 153
LONG, Melvin 153
LONG, Mrs. Earl 56
LONG, Mrs. M. J. 134
LONG, Rufus 46
LONG, Sarah 46
LOPER, Arthur 63
LORENZ, Agnes 11

LORENZ, Emile 96
LORENZ, Fred 11
LORETZ, Mary 81
LOUTERBACK, Mrs. J. W. 105
LOVELACE, Mrs. R. L. 149
LOW, Daniel 60
LOWE, Adolph G. 6
LOWE, Minnie 6
LOWE, Mrs. John 110
LOWRIMORE, Mary A. 6
LOWRIMORE, Olin 6
LUCKIE, Emily 93
LUEDEKER, Annie 121
LUEDEKER, Edgar 121
LUEDEKER, Harold 121
LUEDEKER, Herbert 121
LUEDEKER, Lillian 121
LUEDEKER, Mrs. E. 85, 121
LUEDEKER, Mrs. Herbert 33
LUEDEKER, Willie 121
LUEDKE, Augusta 80
LUEDKE, Dan 80
LUEDKE, Henry 80
LUEDKE, Herman 80
LUEDKE, Otto 80
LUEDKE, Paul 80
LUEDKE, Walter 80
LUEDKE, William 80
LUEDTKE, Bertha 115
LUEDTKE, C. F. 58, 115, 125
LUEDTKE, Charlie 115
LUEDTKE, Ed 115
LUEDTKE, Elsie 115
LUEDTKE, Emma 125
LUEDTKE, E. R. 97, 98
LUEDTKE, Ernest 85, 115
LUEDTKE, Mrs. Ernest 42
LUNA, Alka F. 2
LUNA, Altha M. 1
LUNA, Cody 1
LUNA, Dorothy B. 1
LUNA, Edison 2
LUNA, Joe D. 2
LUNA, Thomas O. 1
LUNA, T. O., Jr. 1
LUSK, Mrs. J. A. 80
LYNCH, Allard 143
LYNCH, Francis 6, 42
LYNCH, Frank 143
LYNCH, Gene 43
LYNCH, Herbert 143
LYNCH, Jack 42
LYNCH, Jeanette 42
LYNCH, Jessie 143

LYNCH, John R. 143
LYNCH, Margaret 43
LYNCH, Mary 42
LYNCH, Mick 43
LYNCH, Morris 6, 43, 148
LYNCH, Mrs. Cliff 27
LYNCH, Mrs. T. N. 42
LYNCH, Nick 6
LYNCH, T. N. 6
LYNCH, William 143
LYON, Fannie 22
LYON, F. M. 16, 96
LYON, Louie 75
LYON, Mrs. D. H. 75
LYON, Mrs. F. M. 75
LYONS, Mrs. Ernest 46
M

MACK, Mrs. Adolph 2
MACLIN, Mrs. J. L. 7
MACLIN, Mr. 151
MAGEE, Evelyn 31, 88
MAGEE, Jack 31, 89
MAGEE, Marcelle 31, 89
MAGEE, Rosalyn 31, 88
MAGEE, Silas 31
MAGEE, Stella 88
MAGEE, William 88
MAGEE, Willie M. 31, 89
MAKOWSKI, Henrietta 30, 110
MAKOWSKI, Milton 110
MAKOWSKI, William 30
MALOTT, Mrs. Jack 95
MANGUM, T. A. 67
MANLEY, Claud 59
MANN, A. J. 16, 26, 38, 79
MANN, Mrs. Hunter 55, 126
MANN, Mrs. John D. 136
MANN, Mrs. Ollie 76, 117
MANN, Wayne 80
MANNING, Bettie 95
MANNING, Tom 41
MANSKE, Anna 10
MANSKE, Dr. Gayart 10
MANSKE, Herbert 10
MANSKE, Mrs. Walter 42
MANSKE, Otto
MANSKE, Paul K. 10
MANSKE, Walter 10
MANSKER, Daisy 74
MANSKER, Don 74
MANSKER, Joe 74
MANSKER, Mary 74
MANSKER, Mrs. Don 48

MANSKER, Mrs. Joe 127
MANSKER, Mrs. Tom 88
MANSKER, Tom 74
MARASKO, Mrs. August 3
MARR, Mrs. Ray 53
MARRS, Florence 17
MARSHALL, Beatrice 123
MARSHALL, Charles 123
MARSHALL, C. W. 123
MARSHALL, Dorothy 123
MARSHALL, Ethel 35, 40
MARSHALL, Glenn 123
MARSHALL, Lenord 149
MARSHALL, Lester 78, 123
MARSHALL, Louise 123
MARSHALL, Loy 123
MARSHALL, Loyce 123
MARSHALL, Marvin 123
MARSHALL, Mollie 78
MARSHALL, Roy 123
MARSHALL, Tom 78
MARTIN, _____ 66
MARTIN, Bryon 112
MARTIN, Bruns 112
MARTIN, Clara 112
MARTIN, F. L. 112
MARTIN, F. M. 112
MARTIN, Harry 66
MARTIN, H. L. 66
MARTIN, Jay 131
MARTIN, Joe 112
MARTIN, J. R. 112
MARTIN, Marcia 66
MARTIN, M. B. 10, 64, 112
MARTIN, Mrs. Bruns 120
MARTIN, Mrs. Joe 38
MARTIN, Mrs. J. R. 38
MARTIN, Mrs. Weldon 42
MARTIN, Nora 72
MARTIN, Othar 112
MARTIN, Peter 112
MARTIN, P. C. 112
MARTIN, R. J. 66
MARTIM, Ruby 154
MARTIN, S. W. 112
MARTIN, Weldon 38
MARYSIP, Mrs. Michael 102
MASSIRER, Adam 137
MASSIRER, Ella 110
MASSIRER, George 137
MASSIRER, Hattie 66, 137
MASSIRER, Herbert 110, 150
MASSIRER, Jacob 137
MASSIRER, John 110, 137

MASSIRER, Lillian 137
MASSIRER, Lorene 66
MASSIRER, Louis 110
MASSIRER, Mrs. John 110
MASSIRER, Phillip 137
MASSIRER, Walter 66, 110
MATHESON, Mrs. Lonnie 60
MATTHER, W. E. 23
MATTHEWS, Arthur 76
MATTHEWS, Laura 94
MATTHEWS, Maude 94
MATTHEWS, Mrs. Sam 130
MATTHEWS, Nancy E. 56
MATTHEWS, Victor 94
MATTHEWS, W. A. 94
MATTHEWS, W. C. 56
MATTHEWS, William 94
MATTHEWS, Woodrow 94
MATTLAGE, Mrs. Charles 85
MATTLAGE, Mrs. Henry 17
MATTLAGE, Mrs. Walter 153
MATTLAGE, Walter 153
MATTIZA, Henry
MATTIZA, Joanna 137
MATTIZA, John 17
MATTIZA, Mrs. Herbert 102
MAUHLER, _____ 98
MAUNGER, Ernestine 96
MAXWELL, Eleanor 141
MAXWELL, Joe 144
MAXWELL, Joseph 141
MAXWELL, Mrs. J. C. 98
MAXWELL, Paul 141
MAXWELL, Rita 141
MAXWELL, Rita M. 141
MAYER, Mrs. Jack 6
MEADOR, Cora Mae 46, 145
MEADOR, Duff 45
MEADOR, Ernest 46
MEADOR, John 25, 46
MEADOR, Johnnie 145
MEADOR, Leitha 130, 131
MEADOR, Mary 25, 46
MEADOR, Moran 46, 145
MEADOR, Mrs. Earnest 68
MEADOR, Myrtle 46
MEADOR, W. S. 46
MEADOWS, Alma 92
MEADOWS, Annie 93
MEADOWS, Ben 93
MEADOWS, Harvey 93
MEADOWS, John 92
MEADOWS, Sam 93
MEADOWS, W. R. 16

MEEKS, Mrs. 10
MEEKS, Mrs. Mecca 139
MEISKE, Henrietta 85
MEISKE, Emma 33
MEISKE, William 85
MENDOZA, Daniel 148
MENDOZA, Josefa 148
MERCHANT, Mrs. Cleo 45
MERIDETH, Mary 91
MERITT, Earl 118
MARITT, Quince 118
MERKS, Margaret 88
MERRITT, Earl 136
MERRITT, Mrs. Bob 72
MERRITT, Mrs. Frank 105
MERRITT, Velma 100
MERTEN, Mrs. Herman 53
MERTINS, Gus 11
MERTINS, Mrs. Ed 70, 119
MEYER, Charlotte 57
MEYER, D. D. 149
MEYER, Mrs. Bill 149, 150
MEYER, Mrs. H. A. 111
MEYER, Mrs. H. F. 85
MEYER, Mrs. Jack 111
MEYER, R. D. 150
MEYER, Wilfred 149, 150
MEYER, Wilhelmine 95
MILES, Mrs. J. L. 142
MILES, Sam 110
MILES, Vesta 109
MILLENDER, Jimmie 128, 129
MILLER, Bertha 135
MILLER, Bettie 33
MILLER, Bunyan 91
MILLER, Charles 40
MILLER, Elba 153
MILLER, Emma 86
MILLER, E. O. 86
MILLER, Francis 111
MILLER, George 111
MILLER, James 85, 86, 131
MILLER, Jim 111
MILLER, Joe 85
MILLER, Joel 153
MILLER, John 33, 153
MILLER, Martha 91
MILLER, Mattie 40
MILLER, Minnie 152
MILLER, Mr. 7
MILLER, Roy 33
MILLER, T. A. 86
MILLER, T. C. 86
MILLER, Thomas 40

MILLER, William 33
MILLS, Euso 51
MILSTEAD, Maude 30
MIMMS, Mrs. E. M. 147
MINNIS, Mrs. O. H. 46
MINNIX, Albert 82
MISELY, Mary E. 121
MITCHELL, Bryan 82
MITCHELL, Elibe C. 82
MITCHELL, Elmer 118
MITCHELL, Garland 82
MITCHELL, Lula Mae 8
MITCHELL, Mrs. John 81
MITCHELL, Mrs. L. E. 50, 109
MITCHELL, Mrs. Willie 32, 108
MITCHELL, Nancy 82
MITCHELL, Sarah 82
MITCHELL, Vergie 82
MITCHELL, Waldene 8
MITCHELL, Walter 8
MIZE, Mrs. J. C. 7
MIZE, Mrs. J. M. 73
MIZE, Mrs. M. E. 73
MIZE, Mrs. Melvin 139
MIZE, Mrs. R. L. 53
MIZE, Mrs. Walter 108
MIZE, W. E. 150
MOATS, Odessa 8
MOBLEY, Mrs. Newt 103
MOFFETT, H. L. 69
MOFFETT, Mrs. Dwight 124
MOGLE, Carl 17, 39
MOGLE, C. W. 31
MOGLE, Pauline 17
MOILLETT, Mrs. O. S. 69
MONCRIEF, C. E. 23
MONCRIEF, Mrs. W. R. 77
MONCRIEF, Robert 22
MONCRIEF, Sallie 23
MONEY, Chester 154
MONEY, C. E. 154
MONEY, Clay 154
MONEY, Effie 154
MONEY, E. L. 154
MONEY, T. P. 154
MONEY, V. G. 154
MONEY, W. C. 154
MONTGOMERY, Elmo 64
MONTGOMERY, John 96
MONTGOMERY, Mrs. John 49
MONTGOMERY, Mrs. W. T. 21, 127
MOON, Grandpa 25
MOONEY, Arthur 86
MOONEY, Carl

MOONEY, C. D. 86
MOONEY, Edward M. 17
MOONEY, H. G. 67
MOONEY, Jess 86
MOONEY, Jim 17, 18
MOONEY, Merle 64
MOONEY, Mrs. Arthur 82
MOONEY, Mrs. J. L. 41, 58
MOONEY, Mrs. L. A. 127
MOONEY, Mrs. N. B. 17, 64
MOONEY, O. L. 17
MOONEY, Oll 64
MOONEY, Sallie 86
MOONEY, Thomas E. 17
MOONEY, Will 17, 86
MOONEY, William 58
MOORE, C. M. 53
MOORE, C. O. 7
MOORE, Dan L. 7
MOORE, Frank 53
MOORE, Gladys 36
MOORE, Hugh 53
MOORE, Ida 53
MOORE, Joe 53
MOORE, Mae 53
MOORE, Mrs. B. J. 139
MOORE, Mrs. Fred 147
MOORE, Mrs. M. L. 36
MOORE, Mrs. R. Q. 45
MOORE, R. P. 53
MOORE, Virge 60
MOOREHEAD, Henry 55
MOOREHEAD, Joseph 55
MOOREHEAD, Millie L. 55
MOORES, E. S. 133
MOORES, Euna 133
MOORES, Mrs. W. A. 106
MORGAN, Ethel 35
MORGAN, Fenton 151
MORGAN, G. G. 135
MORGAN, J. F. 151
MORGAN, Lee 35
MORGAN, Mrs. Freeman 35, 152
MORGAN, Mrs. Tom 35
MORGAN, Wilma 151
MORRIS, _____ 129
MORRIS, A. E. 14, 71, 149, 150
MORRIS, Annie 129
MORRIS, Betty 109
MORRIS, Billie 150
MORRIS, Bonnie 31
MORRIS, Buster 31, 62, 129
MORRIS, C. A. 115
MORRIS, Charlie B. 14

MORRIS, Clarence 147
MORRIS, Earl 150
MORRIS, E. B. 149
MORRIS, Emma 17, 149
MORRIS, Ernest 14
MORRIS, F. A. 14, 129, 149
MORRIS, Felix 92, 129, 149
MORRIS, Fleta 147
MORRIS, Gilford 14
MORRIS, G. J. 150
MORRIS, J. A. 150
MORRIS, Jack 106, 129, 149
MORRIS, James A. 129
MORRIS, J. C. 106
MORRIS, J. E. 115
MORRIS, Jerry 106
MORRIS, J. H. 14
MORRIS, John 86, 106
MORRIS, Lilla M. 14
MORRIS, L. P. 115
MORRIS, Miller 106, 131
MORRIS, Mary E. 150
MORRIS, Mary Lou 14
MORRIS, Mrs. A. E. 54
MORRIS, Mrs. Jim 74
MORRIS, Mrs. Wilder 128
MORRIS, Mrs. Will 71, 126
MORRIS, Nancy 115
MORRIS, Olivia 16
MORRIS, Paul 14, 150
MORRIS, R. C. 115
MORRIS, R. E. 17
MORRIS, Searcy L. 129
MORRIS, Willard 14, 149, 150
MORRIS, William 115
MORRISON, Dave 82
MORRISON, Henry 82
MORRISON, John 82
MORRISON, Johnnie 17, 82
MORRISON, Lucian 17
MORRISON, Mrs. P. 11
MORRISON, Oscar 17
MORRISON, P. P. 17
MORRISON, Thomas 82
MOSLEY, Les 105
MOTE, Bob 45
MOTE, J. A. 45
MOTE, Jessie 100
MOTE, Joe 45
MOTE, John 45
MOTE, Morgan 45
MOTE, Tommie 45
MOTE, Whit 45
MUEGGE, Albert 116

MUEGGE, Alton 116
MUEGGE, Alvin 116
MUEGGE, August 116
MUEGGE, Doris 94
MUEGGE, Fred 116
MUEGGE, Gayheart 116
MUEGGE, Henrietta 116
MUEGGE, Lonnie 115
MUEGGE, Mrs. Alvin 106
MUELHOUSE, Louise 149, 150
MUIR, Bill 4
MUIR, Thomas H. 4
MUNIZ, Miguel 141
MUNIZ, Rebecca 141
MURPHY, Lenora 98
MURPHY, Mary A. 99
MURPHY, Waldean 98
MURRAY, Florence 85
MURRAY, Jeff 85
MURRY, Ann 128
MURPHY, C. H. 30
MURPHY, Charles 26
MURPHY, Cyph 26
MURPHY, E. C. 26, 40
MURPHY, Eph 30
MURPHY, Ernest 26
MURPHY, Mrs. E. C. 35
MURPHY, Mrs. Eph 30
MURPHY, Mrs. Jess A. 122, 127
MUTSCHER, Sophie 101
MYERS, Luch 53

MC

McADA, Mrs. W. L. 54
McANNALLY, Bud 48
McBRIDE, Mrs. Frankie 7, 42, 93
McBRIDE, Neal 152
McBRIDE, Mrs. Neil 147
McBRIDE, N. H. 93
McCAIN, Mrs. Julian 30
McCARTER, Mrs. Webb 86
McCAULEY, E. R. 33, 49
McCAULEY, Mrs. W. A. 33
McCAULEY, Nora 33, 49
McCAULEY, W. A. 33, 49
McCLENNAN, Kate 21
McCLENTOCK, John 25
McCLINTON, C. A. 83
McCLINTON, E. E. 83
McCLINTON, George 83
McCLINTON, Johnnie 83
McCLINTON, Lillie 73
McCORKLE, Iva Nell 47

McCORKLE, J. C. 34
McCORKLE, John 34
McCORKLE, Mrs. Oscar 47
McCORKLE, Nancy 34
McCORKLE, Oscar 34
McCORKLE, Otha 34
McCOLLUM, A. L. 44
McCOLLUM, C. H. 139
McCOLLUM, Charles 44
McCOLLUM, C. M. 44
McCOLLUM, Ida 44, 98
McCOLLUM, James 44
McCOLLUM, M. A. 139
McCOLLUM, Mrs. Odie 14
McCOLLUM, O. H. 44
McCULLOUGH, Mrs. Charlie 155
McCULLUM, Oscar 139
McCULLUM, Samuel 44
McCOLLUM, Tom 44
McDANIEL, Mrs. J. C. 8, 105
McDANIEL, Mrs. R. S. 69
McDONALD, Barbara 41
McDONALD, Clarence 41
McDONALD, Claud 41
McDONALD, Cliff 41
McDONALD, Dewey 41
McDONALD, Doc 41
McDONALD, Emmett 41
McDONALD, F. R. 41
McDONALD, Homer 41
McDONALD, I. N. 120
McDONALD, Jerry 41
McDONALD, John 40
McDONALD, J. V. 41
McDONALD, Martha 41
McDONALD, O. P. 40, 41
McDONALD, Phoebe 41
McDONALD, Rose 41
McDONALD, Sam 41
McDONALD, Will 41
McDORMETT, Mrs. 59
McELROY, Mrs. Ruby 110
McENTIRE, Ernest 80
McENTIRE, G. A. 80
McENTIRE, George 80
McENTIRE, H. B. 80
McENTIRE, Joseph 38, 79
McENTIRE, Lula 36, 79
McENTIRE, Mrs. J. R. 6
McENTIRE, Mrs. Ralph 29
McENTIRE, Mrs. R. D. 118
McENTIRE, Ralph 6, 38, 80
McEVER, Bobbie J. 7
McEVER, Brice

McEVER, Dick 7
McEVER, Earl L. 7
McEVER, Ed 6
McEVER, Edna 155
McEVER, Margaret 103
McEVER, Mrs. E. C. 102
McEVER, Thomas J. 6
McFADDEN, Mary 46
McFALL, Joe 132
McFATRICK, Mrs. Theo 118
McGAUGHEY, Mrs. Almon 50, 109
McGINTY, Mrs. A. E. 101
McGOWEN, Mrs. A. N. 41
McGREGOR, J. H. 66
McGREGOR, Mrs. J. W. 99
McGREGOR, Mrs. Roxie 83
McGREGOR, Mrs. Thornton 54
McGUIRE, Daisy 123
McILHANEY, Mrs. R. N. 131
McKAMIE, Mrs. J. A. 53
McKEE, Mrs. T. J. 114
McKELVAIN, B. A. 72
McKELVAIN, Isla 72
McKELVAIN, Jim 72
McKELVAIN, Mrs. N. A. 72
McKELVY, Mrs. J. W. 54
McKELVY, MRs. W. L. 103
McKINNEY, Bob 32
McKINNEY, James 74
McKINNEY, June 32, 127
McKINNEY, Mandy 81
McKNIGHT, Mrs. R. L. 22
McMAHAN, Bert 141
McMAHAN, Dave 141
McMAHAN, Doris 141
McMAHAN, H. 141
McMAHAN, William 141
McMAHON, Donna 95
McMILLAN, Mrs. James 74
McMINN, Mrs. Clyde 65
McMULLEN, Arthur 36
McMULLEN, Bill 36, 101
McMULLEN, Fannie 27
McMULLEN, Jim 36
McMULLEN, Joe 27
McMULLEN, Lloyd 36
McMULLEN, Mrs. Jim 27
McMULLEN, Paul 36
McMULLEN, Rozella 36
McMULLEN, R. T. 36
McMULLEN, W. A. 36
McMULLIN, Mrs. R. T. 136
McMURTRY, Mrs. Carl 113
McNEIL, Glynda 29, 30

McNEIL, G. R. 30
McNEIL, Raymond 30
McNIEL, A. A. 109
McPEAK, Sarah 126
McWILLIAMS, Emily 71
McWILLIAMS, Jess 71
McWILLIAMS, Joe 71
McWILLIAMS, Layton 71
McWILLIAMS, Lonnie 71
McWILLIAMS, Mrs. W. A. 71
McWILLIAMS, Tommie 71
McWILLIAMS, Tommy 71
McWILLIAMS, Walter 71

N

NAIL, Mrs. Ben 105
NALER, Calvin 36
NALER, George 36, 83
NALER, Mary 36
NALER, Mrs. Wilis 56
NALER, Sallie 83
NALER, Tom 83
NALER, Zola 36
NALER, Willis 83
NALER, Carrie 113
NANCE, Charlie 11
NANCE, C. T. 11
NANCE, Joel 11
NANCE, Lonnie 11
NANCE, Morris 11
NANCE, Mrs. Oscar 71
NANCE, Tom 11
NANCE, Wesley 11
NATION, Howard 35
NATION, Uncle Charlie 23
NAVARRO, Concepcion 141
NAYLOR, Cecil 141
NAYLOR, Dewey 141
NAYLOR, Ennis 141
NAYLOR, Mae 141
NAYLOR, Mrs. William 142
NAYLOR, Sam 141
NAYLOR, William 141
NEAGLE, D. M. Walter 144
NEAGLE, Emmett 144
NEAGLE, India 144
NEAGLE, John 144
NEAGLE, Joseph 144
NEELY, Annie 137
NEELY, Effie 107
NEELY, Robert 102
NEELY, Sarah 107
NEELY, Will 102
NEFF, Ione 22

NEFF, Mrs. Ben 22
NEFF, Pat M. 53
NELSON, Ernest 108
NELSON, F. D. 32, 121
NELSON, H. C. 121
NELSON, Johnnie 93
NELSON, Leroy 108
NELSON, Mildred 32
NELSON, Mrs. A. T. 33, 49
NELSON, Mrs. C. W. 62
NELSON, Mrs. Ivy 131
NELSON, Mrs. Johnny 87
NELSON, T. N. 108
NELSON, Willie 93
NELSON, W. W. 2
NEVILLE, Eva 133
NEWBERRY, Ella 138
NEWMAN, Billy 137
NEWMAN, Frances 7
NEWMAN, Jack 137
NEWMAN, Mrs. L. N. 137
NEWMAN, Mrs. R. L. 137
NEWMAN, Mrs. Robert 140
NEWMAN, Pearl 98, 101
NEWMAN, R. L. 137
NICHOLS, Ola 44
NICKERSON, Melinda 1
NIEMEIER, Albert 96
NIEMEIER, C. 115
NIEMEIER, Carl 96
NIEMEIER, Charlie 96, 116
NIEMEIER, Ernest 96, 116
NIEMEIER, H. 115
NIEMEIER, Hattie 154
NIEMEIER, Henrietta 96
NIEMEIER, Henry 96, 116
NIEMEIER, Herbert 96
NIEMEIER, Minnie 96, 116
NIEMEIER, Mrs. Albert 154
NIEMEIER, Mrs. Ernest 19
NIEMEIER, Nagel 96
NIEMEIER, Will 96, 116
NIEMEIER, Willie 140
NIEMEIER, Willis 96
NIETZSEHKE, Caroline 62
NITSCHE, Mrs. E. 3
NOBLES, Ludora 147
NOLAN, Don 111
NOLAN, E. B. 69
NOLAN, John 111
NOLAN, Mae 9
NOLAN, Mrs. 11
NOLAN, Mrs. Ray 55
NOLAND, Mrs. Dovey 105

NOLAND, Mrs. John 138
NORMAN, Marky 136
NORMAN, Mrs. E. R. 135
NORMAN, Mrs. Tom 35
NORMAN, Sarah 136
NORTHAM, Mabe 35
NORTON, Mrs. 72
NOWLIN, John B. 19
NOWLIN, John E. 19
NOWLIN, Sarah 92
NUNLEY, John 78
NUNLEY, Minerva 78
NUNLEY, Mrs. Tally 103
NUNLEY, Tally 78
NUNLEY, W. B. 78
NUNLEY, Wesley 78

O

O'CONNER, Mrs. Joe 110
ODELL, Mrs. W. C. 73
OGLESBY, Ford 101
OGLESBY, Frank 101
OGLESBY, Ida 101
OLIVER, Alice 127
OLIVER, Audie 127
OLIVER, Gertrude 117
OLIVER, Haley 127
OLIVER, James 127
OLIVER, John 127
OLIVER, Lee 127
OLIVER, Lewis 128
OLIVER, L. J. 127
OLIVER, Mrs. Audie 42
OLIVER, Will 128
OLSON, Mrs. Henry 42
OSBORN, Mrs. Joe 51
OSWALD, Mrs. Woodward 100
OSWALD, Woodrow 100
OTTO, Sophie 85
OWEN, Mrs. W. W. 16
OWEN, Willie Mae 16
OWENS, Charles 13
OWENS, Mollie 7
OWENS, Mr. 40
OWENS, Harry 13
OWENS, William 13
OWENS, W. J. 68
OWENS, Zona 34
OXFORD, Frances 79
OXFORD, Jeremiah 79
OXFORD, Sam 79
OXFORD, Sarah 79

P

PACE, Emma 111
PACE, E. R. 138
PACE, Gideon 98
PACE, Mary 138
PACE, Russell 139
PACE, W. D. 98, 138
PACK, Bernice 55
PACK, C. M. 55
PACK, Hassie 29
PACK, J. B. 13
PACE, Lilburn 120
PACK, Mrs. G. W. 120
PACK, W. H. 13
PACKINGHAM, Mrs. W. B. 141
PAGE, Jim 40
PAPE, Caroline 69
PARKEE, J. T. 15
PARKER, Cynthia A. 5
PARKER, Mrs. Otis 120
PARKER, Mrs. Owen 107
PARKER, Mrs. W. P. 108
PARKER, Sadie 32
PARKER, Quanah 5
PARKER, Winnie 107
PARKLOW, W. E. 63
PARKS, Billy 111
PARNUM, Mrs. J. E. 18
PARRISH, Mrs. Charlie 2
PARROTT, Marion 133
PARROTT, W. E. 133
PARSONS, Ethel 119
PARSONS, Mrs. Charles 149
PARSONS, Mrs. Vern 42
PATRICK, Mertie 130
PATTERSON, John M. 12
PATTERSON, Julia 95
PATTERSON, L. S. 12
PATTERSON, Madge 112
PATTERSON, Mary 99
PATTERSON, Mrs. Charles 4
PATTERSON, Ted 100
PATTERSON, Walter 12
PATTON, Arp 99
PATTON, Carrie 35
PATTON, E. 99
PATTON, E. R. 99
PATTON, Malinda 99
PATTON, Martha 9, 99
PATTON, W. E. 9, 99
PATTON, William S. 99
PAUK, Mary 113
PEACE, Emma 5

PEACE, Joe C. 10
PEACE, Joe P. 5
PEACE, Mrs. R. M. 5
PEACE, R. M. 5
PEACE, R. N. 10
PEACE, R. R. 10
PEARSON, Mrs. Ray 104
PECK, Jacob 72
PECK, O. T. 72
PECK, William 72
PEEL, Frank 84
PEEL, S. W. 84
PENITO, Leone 91
PENNINGTON, C. P. 77
PENNINGTON, Oma 10, 36
PENNINGTON, Otto 36
PENNINGTON, Vesta 36, 70
PENNY, Mrs. Otis 99
PERALES, Consepcion 141, 145
PERALES, Joe 141, 145
PERALES, Ronaldo 145
PERALES, Solomon 145
PERALES, Maria 118
PERKINS, Grady 26, 61
PERKINS, Jasper 26
PERKINS, J. W. 61
PERKINS, Kate 72
PERKINS, Katherine 156
PERMENTER, Armond 131
PERMENTER, B. J. 131
PERMENTER, H. A. 131
PERMENTER, Luella 131
PERMENTER, Mrs. Bill 99
PERMENTER, Rena 131
PERMENTER, W. H. 131
PERMENTER, Winnon 131
PERMENTER, Woodrow 131
PERRY, Lillie 66
PERRY, Mrs. E. A. 112
PETERS, Mrs. Will 61
PETERSON, Anne 65
PETERSON, C. J. 72
PETERSON, Mrs. O. F. 77
PETERSON, Sallie 72
PETREE, Mrs. Eddie L. 136
PETREE, Mrs. J. S. 52
PETTIGREW, Mrs. J. A. 82
PETTUS, Mamie 30
PETTWAY, L. 15
PETTWAY, Mildred N. 15
PETTWAY, Mrs. L. 8
PETTY, Mrs. A. A. 53
PEZAN, Alice 30
PFIEFFER, Evelyn 138

PHELAN, Carl 36, 145
PHILLIPS, A. L. 78
PHILLIPS, Hessie 78
PHILLIPS, L. L. 78
PIEPER, Elsie 155
PIERCE, Claude 137
PIETZSCH, August 62
PIETZSCH, Ed 150
PIETZSCH, Mrs. Ed 62, 150
PIETZSCH, Robert 62, 150
PILGRAM, Emma 47
PIMENTO, Coke 36
PINKNEY, Mrs. C. A. 127
PIRES, Noreto 144
PLACE, Brittain 56
PLACE, Frank B. 56
PLACE, Jessie 56
PLACE, Thomas H. 56
PLEDGER, Mrs. W. P. 135
PLEDGER, W. P. 135
PLEMONS, C. T. 120
PLEMONS, Evett 120
PLEMONS, G. W. 120
PLEMONS, Harrell 120
PLEMONS, J. T. 120
PLEMONS, L. H. 120
PLEMONS, Mary 62
PLEMONS, Mrs. Mack 102, 103
PLEMONS, Mrs. O. B. 103
PLEMONS, O. B 120
PLEMONS, Pearl 71
PLEMONS, R. H. 120
PLEMONS, Vernon 120
PLEMONS, Walter 120
PLEMONS, William B. 120
POE, Mrs. J. A. 34
POE, Sterling 58
POETZCH, Mrs. Emil 19
POLLARD, Albert 149
POLLARD, Billy 148
POLLARD, Cora 82
POLLARD, Ernest 148
POLLARD, Florence 59
POLLARD, Marshall 149
POLLARD, Mrs. Ernest 4
POLLARD, Mrs. Ted 112
POLLARD, Nancy 148
POLLARD, S. L. 148
POLLARD, Ted 148
POLLARD, Travis 148
POLLY, Bertie 143
POLLY, Millie 143
POLSTON, A. M. 48, 115
POLSTON, Berniece 41

POLSTON, Bill 115
POLSTON, Elijah 115
POLSTON, Gladys 41
POLSTON, Iva 41
POLSTON, Jack 41, 115
POLSTON, Jesse 115
POLSTON, Jim 115
POLSTON, Joe H. 115
POLSTON, Lizzie 116
POLSTON, Lucy 116
POLSTON, Mrs. Jack 41
POLSTON, Scott 115
POLSTON, Virgil 115
POLSTON, Willard 115
POMERANKE, Wilma 47
POOL, C. 43
POOL, Jasper 43
POOL, Miss 29
POOL, W. N. 43
PORTER, Edna 119
PORTER, Fred 22
PORTER, J. M. 22
PORTER, Mrs. Fred 108
PORTERFIELD, Florence 69
PORTERFIELD, Frank 69
PORTERFIELD, George 24
PORTERFIELD, Henry 69
POERTEFIELD, Howard 46
PORTERFIELD, John 46
PORTERFIELD, Kate 35
PORTERFIELD, Mrs. Arthur 88
PORTERFIELD, O. R. 69
POTTER, Gerald 16
POTTER, Jerry 89
POTTER, Mrs. O. S. 16
POTTER, Orville 89
POTTER, Virginia 104
POSS, Mrs. J. D. 20, 21
POWELL, Jim 59
POWELL, Mrs. Blonde 75, 82
POWELL, Mrs. J. N. 24
POWELL, Sam 59
POWERS, Mrs. W. H. 44
PRENTICE, Allie 111
PREWITT, Edith 32
PRICE, Mrs. Mildred 99
PRIMM, Nathan 27
PRINCE, Belle 92
PRINCE, Henrietta 128
PRINCE, Mrs. A. P. 131
PRITLE, Bert
PRITLE, Irl 35
PRITLE, Marie 35
PRITLE, M. S. 35

PRITLE, Otis 35
PRITLE, Peggy
PRITLE, Sallie 36
PROVENT, Marie L. 19
PRUITT, Mrs. Jesse 6, 111
PUNDT, Mary 80
PUTMAN, Frank 67
PUTMAN, W. A. 67

Q

QUEBE, Bertha 78
QUEBE, B. O. 28
QUEBE, Fred 28
QUEBE, Gus 28
QUEBE, Hazel 78
QUEBE, Helen 78
QUEBE, Henry 27, 28, 78
QUEBE, Mildred 78
QUEBE, Mrs. Heinz 28
QUEBE, W. F. 28

R

RABBE, Bill 62, 150
RABBE, Clara 58
RABBE, Cleo 150
RABBE, Ella 62
RABBE, Emil 62, 150
RABBE, Ernest 58, 62
RABBE, Henry 14
RABBE, Johanna K. 150
RABBE, Mrs. H. 111
RABBE, Mrs. William 14
RABBE, Ottilia 26, 62
RABBE, Wallace 14, 111
RABBE, William 26, 58, 62
RABBE, W. L. 14, 111
RABBE, W. W. 111
RACHUY, Hattie 99
RAGGLESWORTH, Mr. 62
RAGSDALE, John 100
RAGSDALE, Martha 100
RAGSDALE, W. T. 100
RAINBOLT, Mary 82
RAMSEY, C. L. 138
RAMSEY, J. M. 98
RAMSEY, Mrs. Boomer 87, 98
RAMSEY, Mrs. B. P. 80
RANKIN, Lois 47
RANKIN, Mrs. V. B. 3
RAPP, Carl 17
RAPP, George 17
RAPP, Henry 17

RAPP, Pauline 17
RAPP, Pius 17
RASCHKE, Estelle 109
RASCHKE, George 109
RASCHKE, Louise 109
RASCHKE, Mrs. George 2
RATHJEN, Herbert 18
RATHJEN, Willie 18
RATHMAN, Mrs. William 31
RAY, Davis 91
RAY, Mrs. Jeff D. 86
RAY, W. D. 57
REDMAN, Ella 32
REECE, Bob 45
REECE, Robert 45
REDMAN, Ella 108
REED, Aruld 65
REED, Frank 66
REED, George 66
REED, Glen 64
REED, Horace 64
REED, Jack 47
REED, Jessie 47
REED, Leonard 64
REED, Mack 26, 64
REED, M. F. 64
REED, Mrs. Badger 113
REED, Mrs. Frank 65
REED, Mrs. George 81
REED, Mrs. K. A. 53
REED, Wallace 66
REED, Warren 64
REED, William 66
REED, W. J. 47
REEDER, Charles 34
REEDER, E. C. 34
REEDER, Ruth 34
REEVES, A. C. 127
REEVES, Cledyth 127
REEVES, Ella 7
REEVES, Ed 127
REEVES, E. W. 117, 127
REEVES, Farris D. 127
REEVES, John E. 127
REEVES, Louisa 81
REEVES, Ora 127
REEVES, Pat 127
REEVES, Roland 127
REEVES, Ruth Ann 117
RENEAU, Mrs. Ralph 71
RENFRO, Cal 49
RENFRO, Cliff 49
RENFRO, Lloyd 50
RENFRO, Lula 55

RENFRO, Mrs. M. F. 62
RENFRO, Sallie 49
RENFRO, T. J. 49, 50
RETHMEIER, Sophie 34
REY, James 48
REYNOLDS, Airel 86
REYNOLDS, Bill 85
REYNOLDS, Edith 22
REYNOLDS, Frank 86
REYNOLDS, Hazel N. 86
REYNOLDS, John 101
REYNOLDS, Louie H. 86
REYNOLDS, Mrs. A. E. 13, 19
REYNOLDS, Ora 86
RHEA, Mrs. D. B. 83
RHODES, H. B. 59
RHODES, Mrs. Edwin 149
RICHARD, Mrs. Ray 28
RICHARDS, Dean 51
RICHARDS, Dick 129
RICHARDS, Mrs. G. C. 100
RICHARDSON, Charles 142, 146
RICHARDSON, Claud 142
RICHARDSON, Doris 134
RICHARDSON, Ethel 86
RICHARDSON, J. W. 103
RICHARDSON, Mary J. 142
RICHARDSON, Mrs. Charlie 138
RICHARDSON, Pearl 134
RICHARDSON, W. O. 142
RICHLIER, Marie 154
RICHTER, Albert 140
RICHTER, Carl 140
RICHTER, Fritz 140
RICHTER, Minnie 139
RICHTER, Otto 140
RICKLIN, Anna 114
RIDDLE, B. C. 36
RIDDLE, Bryan 36, 65
RIDDLE, Howard 37, 65
RIDDLE, J. I. 36
RIDDLE, J. J. 69
RIGNEY, Mrs. 156
RILEY, Bud 5
RILEY, J. T. 5
RILEY, Ola 47
RILEY, Marvin 47
RILEY, Melvin 47
RILEY, R. J. 48
RILEY, Ruby 122
RILEY, W. M. 52
RILEY, Zack 5
RINEHART, Mrs. Paul 69
RITCHIE, Mrs. Curtis 33, 49

RITCHIE, Rev. 62
RITTAN, Emma 83, 84
ROACH, Austin 152
ROACH, Clarence 127
ROACH, Dale 152
ROACH, David 152
ROACH, Eleanor 129
ROACH, Eliza 127
ROACH, Elmore 129
ROACH, Ernest 67
ROACH, Ferguson 152
ROACH, F. M. 129
ROACH, Frank 127
ROACH, George 45
ROACH, J. B. 67, 152
ROACH, Jim 45
ROACH, John 127
ROACH, Lear 67
ROACH, Lucian 45
ROACH, Martin 127
ROACH, Meredity 67
ROACH, Mrs. B. G. 45
ROACH, Mrs. Lucian 137
ROACH, Olis 67
ROACH, Roy 129
ROACH, W. K. 67
ROBERTS, Bill 2
ROBERTS, Bob 88
ROBERTS, Bonita M. 142
ROBERTS, Dorothea 142
ROBERTS, Jack G. 142
ROBERTS, Henry 88
ROBERTS, Mary 88
ROBERTS, Mrs. W. W. 120
ROBERTSON, Billy 150
ROBERTSON, Clara 150
ROBERTSON, Jim 137
ROBERTSON, Mrs. Train 137
ROBERTSON, Sam 53
ROBINETT, Lillie 138
ROBINSON, _____ 20
ROBINSON, Bettie 33
ROBINSON, Billie 144
ROBINSON, Charlie 40
ROBINSON, Clara 149
ROBINSON, Darrell 144
ROBINSON, Donald 144
ROBINSON, Ernest 40
ROBINSON, Ethel 40
ROBINSON, James 40
ROBINSON, Jimmie 143, 144
ROBINSON, Margaret 51
ROBINSON, Mrs. H. P. 103, 104, 113

ROBINSON, Mrs. Jim 35
ROBINSON, Mrs. Miller 29, 118
ROBINSON, Phillip 144
ROBINSON, Raymond 144
ROBINSON, Walter 144
ROBINSON, Will 40
ROBINSON, Winnie 138
ROBUCK, Mrs. 113
ROE, A. L. 105
ROE, Della 105
ROE, Edward 105, 153
ROE, H. C. 105
ROE, J. W. 105
ROE, Mrs. Henry 62
ROE, Mrs. S. M. 153
ROE, Ralph 105
ROE, R. Q. 105
ROE, Rufus 105
ROE, S. M. 105
ROGERS, Arthur 68
ROGERS, Joe M. 68
ROGERS, John 68
ROGERS, Mrs. Ross 5, 10
ROGERS, Mrs. W. F. 111
ROGERS, Nannie 60
ROGERS, W. G. 68
ROGERS, Zella 66
ROHLOFF, A. 58
ROHLOFF, Ludwig 62
ROHLONN, Miss 26
ROLAND, Mrs. R. L. 130
ROLLINS, Mrs. Lother 28
ROLOFF, Annie 17
ROSE, Nettie 118
ROSS, Henry 81
ROSS, J. C. 81
ROSS, Kate 48, 81
ROSS, Mrs. F. H. 144
ROSS, Mrs. Jess 3
ROSS, W. W. 48, 81
ROUTH, Elmo 131
ROUTH, Ethel 77
ROWE, Netie 151
ROWE, Thlitha 50
ROZELLE, Mrs. Olan 9
RUCKER, Marvin 111
RUCKER, Mrs. Marvin 57
RUCKER, Mrs. Tom 6
RUCKER, Nancy 111
RUCKER, Thomas 6, 111
RUFF, Mrs. Homer 98, 114, 154
RUSH, Epp 53
RUSH, J. A. 53
RUSH, John 53
RUSH, Walter 53
RUSSELL, Fannie 102
RUSSELL, Joe Bob 15
RUSSELL, Glen 15
RUSSELL, Mrs. George 89
RUSSELL, Mrs. R. B. 126
RUSSELL, Robert 102
RUSSELL, Sallie 27
RUSSELL, W. G. 103
RYAN, Joyce 84
RYAN, Mary 84

S

SADLER, Lillian 136
SAFFLE, Mr. 62
SAFLEY, Mrs. Bob 127
SAKUTH, Mrs. David 104
SALES, Gordon 8, 105
SALES, Josie 8
SALES, Mary 56, 123
SALES, Mrs. R. W. 91
SALES, R. W. 8, 105
SALES, T. S. 8, 105
SAMMONS, T. G. 126
SAMPSON, Mrs. Yeager 52
SANDEL, Myrtle 66
SANDERFORD, Carrie 156
SANDERS, Bertha 142
SANDERS, Bill 142
SANDERS, Fred 142
SANDERS, Henrietta 59
SANDERS, H. H. 47
SANDERS, John 142
SANDERS, J. R. 48
SANDERS, Kate 81
SANDERS, Lawrence 59
SANDERS, Martha 142
SANDERS, Minnie 142
SANDERS, Mrs. Harry 115
SANDERS, Otto 142
SANDERS, Robert 3
SANDERS, William 59, 142
SANDHOFF, August 155
SANDHOFF, Edd 155
SANDHOFF, Lonnie 155
SANDHOFF, Mrs. Lonnie 84
SANDHOFF, O. H. 155
SANDHOFF, Otto 155
SANDHOFF, Wilhilmine 155
SANDHOFF, Willie 155
SANDLIN, Emma 68
SANFORD, Betty 91
SAVELY, Mrs. R. L. 40
SAWYER, Joe 11

SCARBOROUCH, J. S. 38
SCHAEFER, Mrs. Theo 140
SCHEELE, Mrs. R. 85
SCHEELE, Rufdolph 97
SCHEPERS, Ella 42
SCHEPERS, Esther 53
SCHEPERS, Joan 42
SCHEPERS, Joe 42
SCHEPERS, Joseph 53
SCHEPERS, J. W. 42, 53
SCHMALRIEDE, Ben 106
SCHMALRIEDE, Eldon 106
SCHMALRIEDE, Fred 106
SCHMALRIEDE, Ted 106
SCHMALRIEDE, Walter 106
SCHMALRIEDE, William 106
SCHNEIDER, Christine 59
SCHNEIDER, Mrs. Henry 140
SCHOMELL, Ruth 136
SCHRADER, Mrs. Edwin 102
SCHRADER, Mrs. Otto 140
SCHROEDER, Charlie 97
SCHROEDER, Bertha 84, 109, 134, 135
SCHROEDER, D. H. 88
SCHROEDER, Mrs. Arthur 2
SCHROEDER, Mrs. Will 97
SCHUESSLER, Mrs. Geroge 103
SCHULTE, H. C. 32
SCHULTE, Mrs. H. 32
SCHULTE, Mrs. Henry 33
SCHUTTE, Mrs. Melvin 33
SCHULTZ, Frieda 39
SCHULTZ, Wilhima 97
SCHUTT, Eliza 125
SCHWARZ, Guenther 119
SCHWARZ, Helmuth 119
SCHWARZ. M. J. 119
SCHWARZ, Peggy 119
SCHWARZ, Teddy 119
SCHWETTMANN, H. C. 96
SCHWETTMANN, Mrs. Ernest 62
SCOTT, Alice 77
SCOTT, Crawford 77
SCOTT, D. B. 16, 51
SCOTT, Emma 51
SCOTT, Ethel 51
SCOTT, F. M. 51
SCOTT, Frank 51
SCOTT, Ola 51
SCOTT, Mable 51
SCOTT, Mrs. E. A. 106
SCOTT, Susan 51
SCOTT, Walter 51

SCOTT, W. H. 51
SCRUGGS, Ada 115
SCRUGGS, Charlie 88
SCRUGGS, John 88
SCRUGGS, Mrs. John 85, 97
SCRUGGS, Tom 88
SCULLY, Hattie 111
SEAGRAVES, Mrs. B. M. 141
SEARCEY, Arthur 74
SEARCEY, C. B. 74
SEARCEY, Charles 74
SEARCEY, Dot 74
SEARCEY, Henry 74
SEARCEY, James 74
SEARCEY, Jim 74
SEARCEY, Lawton 74
SEARCEY, Sarah 74
SEARCEY, Wade 74
SEARCY, Annie 129
SEARCY, Graham 111
SEARCY, Maggie 82
SEARCY, Mrs. G. W. 136
SEARCY, Mrs. Jim 111
SELEMAN, Mrs. John 106
SENTERFIT, Mrs. R. F. 16
SERGER, Mrs. August 17
SETTLES, Mary 147
SEWELL, M. S. 152
SEYBOLD, Louise 110
SHAFFER, Wayne 27
SHALLER, Louise 59
SHAMBLEE, Roger 71
SHANNON, R. L. 21
SHARP, Lorraine 46
SHARP, Mrs. Charlie 4
SHARP, Mrs. N. T. 55
SHARP, Mrs. W. L. 146
SHEARS, Etta 147
SHEFFIELD, Mrs. Ollie 118
SHELBY, E. 68
SHELTON, Billy G. 16
SHELTON, Pete 16
SHEPARD, Maggie 10
SHEPARD, Will 10
SHEPPARD, Bob 77
SHEPPARD, Craig 77
SHEPPARD, John 77
SHEPPARD, Ross 77
SHEPPARD, Sim 76
SHERRILL, Mrs. David 150
SHIRLEY, Alice 41
SHIRLEY, Ben 41
SHIRLEY, F. A. 41
SHIRLEY, Frank 18

SHIRLEY, Joel 41, 91
SHIRLEY, Leta 41
SHIRLEY, Mary 18
SHIRLEY, Moxie 41
SHOFFER, Mrs. R. C. 131
SHOFNER, John 61
SHOFNER, Tom 61
SHOPE, Baxter 29
SHOPE, Festus 29
SHOPE, Helen 29
SHOPE, Mrs. Baxter 29
SHOPE, S. F. 29
SHOPE, Theron 29
SHOPE, Z. F. 29
SHORT, H. D. 27
SHORT, Lula 5
SHORT, Mahaley 16
SHORT, Mark 24
SHORT, Mrs. Ellison 24
SHORT, Mrs. F. M. 83
SHOUMAN, Charles 8
SHOUMAN, J. K. 8
SHOUMAN, W. J. 8
SHUMATE, Mary 150
SIEWART, Annie 69
SIEWERT, Emma 69
SIKES, Clinton 132
SIKES, Roy 132
SIKES, Mrs. W. E. 132
SILER, Mrs. W. J. 2
SILHIEMER, Dora 80
SIMMA, Mrs. H. 4
SIMONS, Mrs. Jeff 50
SIMMONS, Frank 91, 104
SIMMONS, John 91
SIMMONS, Mrs. Charity 83
SIMMONS, Mrs. Jeff 109
SIMMONS, Mrs. Jim 82
SIMMONS, Mrs. W. A. 85
SIMMONS, Robert 91
SIMMONS, W. S. 91
SIMPSON, Maggie 52
SIMS, Clyne 10
SIMS, Edgan 10
SIMS, Harry 104
SIMS, Helen 104
SIMS, Henry 10
SIMS, Joe E. 104
SIMS, Louisa 39
SIMS, Mrs. J. C. 104
SIMS, Myrtle 68
SIMS, Nancy 70
SKELTON, Jim 101
SKELTON, Mrs. L. D. 101

SKELTON, Paul 101
SKINNER, Mrs. John 133
SLAUGHTER, Mrs. L. L. 136
SLESS, Ervin 102
SLESS, George 102
SLIGHT, J. E. 131
SLIGHT, Mrs. J. E. 131
SLOAN, Noll 101
SLOANE, Mrs. E. O. 34
SMILEY, Kathleen 134
SMITH, Addie 80
SMITH, Alonzo 70
SMITH, Alvin 65
SMITH, Annie 65, 113
SMITH, Calvin 80
SMITH, Charlie 70
SMITH, Cynthia 29
SMITH, Doris 70
SMITH, Edith 12
SMITH, Ellis 80
SMITH, Emma 48, 69
SMITH, Fannie 49
SMITH, Floyd 80
SMITH, Foster 39
SMITH, Gena Mae 147
SMITH, Gid 83
SMITH, Gustine 49
SMITH. Haley 127
SMITH, Harold 80
SMITH, Henry 49
SMITH, Ira 70
SMITH, Iva 70
SMITH, Jacob 49
SMITH, Jake H. 16
SMITH, J. H. 132
SMITH, John 116
SMITH, Lee 128
SMITH, Lora 103
SMITH, Louis 150
SMITH, Lovie 53
SMITH, Mae 80
SMITH, Mary 70, 80
SMITH, Minnie 72
SMITH, Mrs. A. D. 65
SMITH, Mrs. Andrew 67
SMITH, Mrs. Artie 103
SMITH, Mrs. C. A. 62
SMITH, Mrs. C. R. 152
SMITH, Mrs. D. C. 137
SMITH, Mrs. Frank 117
SMITH, Mrs. Henry 96
SMITH, Mrs. J. L. 146
SMITH, Mrs. J. T. 50
SMITH, Mrs. M. F. 16

SMITH, Mrs. Perry 94
SMITH, Opal 66
SMITH, R. A. 108
SMITH, Robert 132
SMITH, Roberta 70
SMITH, Robbecke 117
SMITH, Rubye 97
SMITH, Tom 83
SMITH, Velma 59
SMITH, Volney 96
SNELSON, Mrs. Guy 147
SNIDER, Billy 139
SNIDER, Catherine 139
SNIDER, Cecil 139
SNIDER, Eugene 139
SNIDER, Florence 139
SNIDER, Jewel 139
SNIDER, Jim 139
SNIDER, Mildred 139
SNIDER, Robert 139
SOWDERS, Mrs. Elmer 94
SPARKS, Amos 103
SPARKS, Clarence 103
SPARKS, Della 129
SPARKS, H. A. 107
SPARKS, Jerry 103
SPARKS, Laura 107
SPARKS, Maggie 107
SPEARS, Mrs. Hub 108
SPEIGHT, Don 114
SPENCER, Albert G. 58
SPENCER, Cecil 30
SPENCER, Frank 58
SPENCER, Louise 30
SPENCER, Terry 58
SPICER, Mrs. J. L. 45
SPIKER, Ida 17
SPIKER, Tina 17
SPRADLEY, Otha 10
SPRINGFIELD, Sybil 100
SPRINGMAN, Lillie 137
SRADER, Ed 63
SRADER, H. E. 27, 75
SRAHER, Mary 27
SRADER, Mrs. Ed 23
SRADER, S. L. 27, 75
SRADER, Symantha 63
SRADER, William 27
SRADER, W. L. 75
STANDEFER, Mrs. C. S. 23
STANDIFER, Sallie 44, 139
STANFORD, Mrs. A. F. 141, 142
STANWORTH, Rosalie 38
STAPP, Anna 104

STAPP, Ed 104
STAPP, F. M. 104
STAPP, G. 104
STAPP, Jim 104
STAPP, John 104
STEBBINS, Rosa 112
STEBBINS, Rose 93
STELEA, Eleanora 96
STEM, Bessie 23
STEPHENS, Leola 98, 101
STEVENS, Amanda 73
STEVENS, Bessie 148
STEVENS, Carl 148
STEVENS, Mamie 148
STEVENS, Mrs. Cal 127
STEVENS, Mrs. Gove 127
STEVENS. T. A. 148
STEWART, Jim 79
STEWART, Katherine 97
STEWART, Martha 155
STEWART, Mary 79
STEWART, Mrs. L. O. 148
STEWART, Mrs. Otto 94
STEWART, Mrs. Paul 97, 112
STEWART, Mrs. P. P. 95
STEWART, Mrs. W. P. 114
STEWART, Walter 144, 146
STILES, Mrs. Robert 101
STILSON, Mrs. Ben 82
STINE, Mrs. 12
STINKE, Mada 80
STOCKBURGER, Charlie 107
STOCKBURGER, Davis 107
STOCKBURGER, Edith 107
STOCKBURGER, Garner 107
STOCKBURGER, Ida 107
STOCKBURGER, John 107
STOCKBURGER, Leonard 107
STOCKBURGER, Lobert 107
STOCKBURGER, Mrs. Clarence 107
STOCKBURGER, Mrs. L. W. 38
STOCKBURGER, Mrs. Robert 28
STOCKBURGER, R. A. 107
STOERMER, Mrs. Fred 136
STOKES, Gene 35
STOLZ, Albert 99
STONE, C. C. 64
STONE, Earl 6, 111
STONE, Emma 119
STONE, Eva 6, 111
STONE, Fannie 43
STONE, G. C. 28
STONE, George 28
STONE, G. L. 48

STONE, J. L. 6, 111
STONE, Mart 48
STONE, Mrs. Oscar 27
STONE, Mrs. W. J. 28
STONE, R. R. 48
STONE, Sarah 48
STONE, Vacie 9
STONE, William J. 9
STONE, W. J. 48
STONE, W. W. 6, 28
STORY, Mr. 2
STORY, Rev. T. G. 2
STOUT, Mary 116
STOVER, Mrs. Marvin 10
STRICKER, Mrs. Albert 143
STRICKER, Mrs. Otto 143
STRICKLAND, Alvis 132
STRICKLAND, Mrs. Doshey 105
STRICKLAND, Mrs. Doyle 48
STRICKLAND, Mrs. E. W. 77
STRONG, Mrs. Ewell 33
STUBBLEFIELD, Albert 120
STUBBLEFIELD, Bryan 120
STUBBLEFIELD, Cecil 120
STUBBLEFIELD, Ray 120
STUBBLEFIELD, T. W. 120
STULL, Bina 116
STURGES, E. A. 56
STURGES, Julia 56
STURGES, Mrs. E. A. 56
STURGES, Oliver 56
SULLINS, L. 18
SULLINS, Mrs. Luther 18
SULLINS, Mrs. R. V. 68
SUMMERS, Amos 67
SUMMERS, Dock 67
SUMMERS, Guy 67
SUMMERS, Jack 67
SUMMERS, J. S. 86
SUMMERS, Mrs. Cleo 80
SUMMERS, Mrs. Guy 123
SUMMERS, Pete 67
SUMMERS, R. C. 86
SUMMERS, Roy 67
SUMMERS, Rufus 67
SUMMERS, T. F. 86
SURRETT, J. E. 69
SURRETT, J. P. 69
SURRETT, Mollie 69
SURRETT, Pearl 142
SUTTON, _____ 79
SUTTON, Dora 34
SUTTON, Mrs. R. G. 11
SUTTON, Otto 34

SWAFFORD, Lena 81
SWAN, Mrs. Will 11
SWANSON, Mrs. Ray 3
SWIFT, J. B. 16
SWIFT, Joe 16
SWIFT, Mrs. J. B. 138
SYDOW, Carl P. 146
SYLER, Gertrude 109, 135
SYMANK, Mrs. Ernest 140
SYMANK, Mrs. John 140
SYMANK, Mrs. Willie 140
T

TALLEY, Fred 31
TALLEY, Joaner n. 154
TALLEY, S. D. 154
TANNER, George 66
TANNER, J. W. 66
TANNER, J. W. N. 66
TANNER, Mary 66
TARPLEY, Sarah 79
TATE, Mrs. A. L. 50, 109
TATE, S. L. 44
TAYLOR, Alston 152
TAYLOR, Emma 62
TAYLOR, Grace 152
TAYLOR, Ida Lee 55
TAYLOR, J. E. 75
TAYLOR, Mrs. J. B. 45
TAYLOR, Mrs. S. W. 12
TAYLOR, Nathaniel A. 152
TAYLOR, Paul 152
TAYLOR, Walton 15
TAYLOR, W. C. 75
TEMPLEMEYER, Mrs. William 146
TEMPLETON, Mrs. Ben 56
TERRELL, Phoebe 147
TERRY, Albert 44
TERRY, Anna 44
TERRY, C. H. 153
TERRY, Charles 44
TERRY, E. 153
TERRY, Jim 153
TERRT, Leroy 100
TERRY, Mary 153
TERRY, Mrs. A. F. 58
TERRY, Mrs. Albert 13, 19
TERRY, Mrs. J. 36
TERRY, Sam 153
TERRY, Thelma 36
THAMES, Mrs. Travis 55
THETFORD, Bettie 31
THETFORD, Ella 31
THETFORD, Foy 31

THETFORD, George 31
THETFORD, Lee 31
THETFORD, Mrs. C. L. 31
THETFORD, Onietra 31
THOMAS, Arthur 60
THOMAS, Ben 60
THOMAS, Clarence 60
THOMAS, H. C. 25
THOMAS, Hershel 60
THOMAS, Ivy 60
THOMAS, John 25
THOMAS, Lahan 56
THOMAS, Lucian 60
THOMAS, Minnie 149
THOMAS, Morris 45
THOMAS, Mrs. Gene 87
THOMAS, Mrs. O. E. 75
THOMAS, Rachael 56
THOMPSON, Bessie 97
THOMASON, E. J. 5, 15, 118
THOMPSON, Dick 24, 91
THOMPSON, Gus 90
THOMPSON, J. R. 91
THOMPSON, LaVerne 46
THOMPSON, Martha 21
THOMPSON, Melton 91
THOMASON, Mrs. E. J. 31
THOMPSON, Mrs. Horace 55
THOMPSON, Mrs. W. M. 65
THOMSON, Mrs. Ben 152
THREAT, Mrs. R. H. 132
THURMOND, Mrs. 23
THWING, Mrs. Frank 108
TIDSDALE, Mrs. Tom 143
TINDELL, Mrs. J. B. 153
TINSLEY, Mrs. L. E. 7
TIPTON, Arthur 132
TISCHLER, Emma 133
TOLBERT, Della 4
TOLBETT, Mrs. W. C. 52
TOLER, Mrs. R. M. 102
TOLLIVER, Mrs. E. S. 82
TOMLINSON, Arward 129
TORRENCE, Mrs. H. T. 111
TOUCHON, Mrs. Max 133
TOUTT, Mrs. H. R. 45
TOWNSEND, Ella 116
TOWNSEND, Marion 152
TOWNSEND, Meritt 116, 152
TOWNSEND, M. F. 116
TOWNSEND, Richard 116, 152
TRAPP, Alice 76
TRAVIS, Addie 146
TROUTT, Mrs. Harrison 153
TROUTT, Mrs. John 153
TUBB, Mrs. W. W. 138
TUBBS, Nannie 128, 129
TUBBS, W. T. 128, 129
TUCKER, C. A. 146
TUCKER, Frank 146
TUCKER, John 107
TUCKER, Mrs. C. S. 77
TUCKER, Robert 146
TURNAGE, Alcus 86
TURNER, J. M. 152
TURNER, Mrs. W. A. 7
TYSON, Agnes 86

U

UNDERWOOD, Mrs. Lattie 56

V

VAHRENKAMP, Bernice 112
VAHRENKAMP, Carolina 85
VAHRENKAMP, E. C. 113
VAHRENKAMP, Ed 78
VAHRENKAMP, Ervin 62
VAHRENKAMP, F. 78, 113
VAHRENKAMP, Fred 78, 97
VAHRENKAMP, Frederick 112
VAHRENKAMP, F. Will 78
VAHRENKAMP, H. A. 78, 113
VAHRENKAMP, Herbert 62
VAHRENKAMP, Lillie 112
VAHRENKAMP, Marvin 62
VAHRENKAMP, Minnie 59, 142
VAHRENKAMP, Otto 78, 113
VAHRENKAMP, Sophie 113
VAHRENKAMP, Will 112
VAHRENKAMP, William 85
VANDIVER, Allen 82
VANDIVER, Bill 54
VANDIVER, Charles 54, 82
VANDIVER, George 54, 82, 105, 114
VANDIVER, High 82
VANDIVER, Homer 82
VANDIVER, Jim 114
VANDIVER, Lonnie 82
VANDIVER, Mrs. C. A. 105
VANDIVER, Tad 82
VANDIVER, Walter 82
VASSELL, J. R. 8
VASSELL, Minnie 8
VILLALOBOS, R. 148
VOWELL, L. C. 89
VAUGHN, Mrs. M. M. 22
VOWELL, Mrs. Roy 32

VOWELL, W. A. 89

W

WADE, Emby M. 4
WADE, Houston 79
WAFFORD, Edna 28
WAGGONER, F. 47
WAGGONER, James T. 47
WAGGONER, Jay 48
WAGGONER, Mary 47
WAGGONER, Seymour 47
WAGGONER, Willard 47
WALDROP, Mrs. Elmo 108
WALKER, A. J. 134
WALKER, Ann 128
WALKER, Dan 79
WALKER, Edna 134
WALKER, Elizabeth 131
WALKER, Elma 79
WALKER, Evelyn 38
WALKER, F. C. 134
WALKER, Foy 58
WALKER, Frank 128, 129
WALKER, G. B. 79
WALKER, George 79, 128, 129, 134
WALKER, Jack 128, 129
WALKER, Janelle 79
WALKER, Jimmie 111
WALKER, Joe T. 60
WALKER, J. W. 31
WALKER, Margaret 31
WALKER, Marie 111
WALKER, Mary 60, 87
WALKER, Mrs. Bob 54
WALKER, Mrs. Ed 108
WALKER, Mrs. James 111
WALKER, Mrs. Hugh 28, 130
WALKER, Nadine 79
WALKER, R. J. 134
WALKER, Robert 38
WALKER, Ruby 86
WALKER, Samuel 38
WALKER, S. E. 134
WALKER, Sidney 38
WALKER, T. E. 38
WALKER, W. F. 87
WALKER, William 134
WALL, Mrs. G. B. 29, 43
WALLACE, Bill 70
WALLACE, Elisha 31
WALLACE, Homer 54
WALLACE, Ike 54
WALLACE, I. W. 70

WALLACE, Jesse 31
WALLACE, Jim 54
WALLACE, Joe 80
WALLACE, Jo Ella 54
WALLACE, John 54
WALLACE, Kathleen 80
WALLACE, Lula Beth 80
WALLACE, Mary 31
WALLACE, Mrs. Elva 38, 80
WALLACE, Mrs. Elver 80
WALLACE, Mrs. F. Birch 103
WALLACE, Mrs. John 18
WALLACE, Mrs. Smiley 54
WALLACE, Prudie 31
WALLACE, Virgil 54
WALLACE, William 54
WALTER, Benton 18
WALTER, Charlie 62
WALTER, Curtis 18
WALKER, Foy 87
WALTER, Fred 62
WALTER, George 62
WALTER, Helen 62
WALKER, Hugh 87
WALTER, Jesse 62
WALTER, Jim 62, 87
WALTER, John 62
WALKER, L. S. 11
WALTER, Otis 18
WALTER, Lizzie 18
WALTER, Mary 62
WALTER, Mattie 62
WALTER, Milton 62
WALTER, Mrs. J. F. 82
WALTER, William 62
WALTERS, Charlie, Jr. 57
WALTERS, Forest 46
WALTERS, Garland 71
WALTERS, Jack 71
WALTERS, John 71
WALTERS, Johnnie 120
WALTERS, Juanita Jo 71
WALTERS, Mrs. Charles 101
WALTERS, Mrs. Charlie 133
WALTERS. Mrs. C. W. 120
WALTERS, Mrs. Will 71
WALTERS, Sonny 101
WALTERS, Thomas 16
WALTON, Dora 29, 118
WALTON, G. R. 118
WALTON, Mrs. F. B. 29
WALTON, Mrs. T. B. 118
WARD, Mrs. Sam 27
WARDLAW, Mrs. Jack 55, 126

WARLICK, Katie 70
WARNICK, Mrs. E. S. 6
WARNICK, Mrs. W. D. 146
WARNICK, Willie 8
WARNICK, W. L. 1, 8, 25
WARREN, Isham 52
WARREN, J. G. 27
WARREN, Josephine 52
WARREN, Mrs. C. L. 83
WARREN, Mrs. Frank 53
WASHINGTON, Mrs. D. 66
WASHBURN, Mrs. Dale 1
WASHBURN, Mrs. Elmo 112
WATSON, Mrs. J. R. 27
WAYLAND, Mrs. Ray 64
WEAVER, Allie Wood 5
WEAVER, Mrs. Allen 104
WEAVER, Mrs. R. L. 149
WEAVER, Sam 5
WEBB, Earl 137
WEBB, Eliza 134
WEBB, John M. 137
WEBB, Lois 137
WEBB, Mrs. C. W. 55, 126
WEBB, Mrs. J. M. 62
WEBB, Mrs. Lonnie 102
WEBB, Mrs. W. W. 17
WEBB, Phil 137
WEBB, Sarah 137
WEBB, S. T. 135
WEBBER, Mrs. W. H. 146
WEBER, Arnold 18
WEBER, Mary F. 18
WEBER, Mrs. Fritz 18
WEBSTER, Mrs. Jim 24
WEDEKING, Sophie 78
WEEK, Mrs. Drury 66
WEEKLEY, Chloma 111
WEEKLEY, John 111
WEEKLEY, Pat 111
WEEKLEY, Vallie 111
WEEKLY, Mrs. C. M. 5
WEHMEYER, Louise 95
WEHRING, Albin 33
WEHRING, Alvin 109
WEHRING, Ben 33, 109
WEHRING, Elsie 33, 109
WEHRING, Henry 33
WEHRING, Herbert 109
WEHRING, Johanna 33, 109
WEHRING, Mary 33, 109
WEHRING, Mrs. Walter 147
WEHRING, Walter 109
WEHRING, William 33

WEHRMANN, Fred C. 122
WEHRMANN, Henry 110, 122
WEHRMANN, Sophie 30, 110
WEISE, Minnie 127
WEISS, Adolf 18
WEISS, Albert 18
WEISS, Ben 18
WEISS, Charlotte 18
WEISS, Ed 18
WEISS, Emanuel 18
WEISS, Emma 116
WEISS, Ernest 18, 100
WEISS, Fritz 18, 19
WEISS, Joyce 100
WEISS, Lonnie 19
WEISS, Mrs. Albert 111
WEISS, Mrs. Ed 95
WEISS, Roy 99, 100
WEISS, Walter 18
WELCH, Bryan 54
WELCH, Joe 54
WELCH, John 54
WELCH, Mrs. D. W. 55
WELCH, Sarah 54
WELCH, William 54
WELLMAN, Charlie 110
WELLMAN, Fritz 30, 110
WELLMAN, Henry 110
WELLMAN, Mrs. Charles 30
WELLMANN, Frederich 110
WELLMANN, Roy 110
WELLMANN, Sophie 110
WELLS, Clydus 94
WELLS, Letitia 60
WELLS, Lydia 109, 135
WELLS, Mrs. Chester 153
WELLS, Mrs. T. A. 94, 95
WELLS, Mrs. Tap 27, 133, 156
WELLS, Mrs. Terry 2
WELLS, Mrs. Tom 71
WELLS, R. A. 94
WELLS, T. Adolphus 60
WELLS, T. E. 60, 95, 106
WELLS, Tom 95
WELLS, W. W. 60
WENDT, Frieda 32
WENDT, Friedarike 32
WENDT, F. W. 32
WENDT, John 32
WENDT, Louie 32
WENDT, Mrs. F. W. 85
WENDT, William 32, 85
WENER, Mrs. 113
WESCHKE, Minnie 61

WEST, Inez 104
WEST, Mrs. G. S. 12
WEST, Mrs. R. E. 104
WEST, Susie 93
WESTERFELD, Charles 62
WESTERFIELD, Mrs. Alfred 9
WESTERFIELD, Mrs. Butler 123
WESTERFIELD, Mrs. Charles 14, 111
WESTERFIELD, Mrs. C. W. 149
WESTERFIELD, Mrs. Ernest 14, 111
WESTERFIELD, Mrs. John 71
WESTERFIELD, Nettie 62
WHATLEY, Sallie 11
WHEAT, Billy 130
WHEAT, Edwin 130
WHEAT, J. V. 35
WHEAT, Lee 35
WHEAT, Mrs. J. V. 130
WHEAT, Mrs. Lee 25
WHEAT, Mrs. Lucile 51
WHEAT, Paul 130
WHEELER, Dr. 19
WHEELER, L. E. 47
WHEELER, Lula 47
WHEELER, R. L. 47
WHEELER, William 47
WHIGHAM, Daisy 86
WHIGHAM, Dick 24
WHIGHAM, Paul 24
WHIGHAM, Mrs. Jim 24
WHILDEN, Homa 87
WHILDEN, Mary L. 87
WHILDEN, Ruth 87
WHILDEN, W. H. 87
WHITE, Ada 91
WHITE, Carl 2, 15
WHITE, Charles 15
WHITE, E. W. 154
WHITE, Ida 118
WHITE, Jack 102
WHITE, Joe 68
WHITE, Lewis 40
WHITE, Lottie 111
WHITE, Mrs. E. L. 39
WHITE, Mrs. George 2
WHITE, Mrs. W. R. 103
WHITE, R. Dean 95
WHITE, Smith 15
WHITE, Thersa J. 5
WHITE, Ulmer 154
WHITEMAN, Florence 32
WHITLOCK, Agnes 86
WHITLOCK, Alpha 8
WHITLOCK, Cleo 117
WHITLOCK, John 78
WHITLOCK, Minnie 72
WHITLOCK, Mrs. T. S. 136
WHITLOCK, Robbie Lora 8
WHITLOCK, Talmage 136
WHITLOCK, William 8
WHITTENBURG, C. C. 30
WHITTENBURG, Clarence 98
WHITTENBURG, Earl 99
WHITTENBURG, Louis 99
WHITTENBRUG, Mrs. Frank 99
WHITTENBURG, Mrs. S. A. 63
WHITTENBURG, Willie 99
WIBLE, Claud 77
WIBLE, Doug 77
WIBLE, India 77
WIBLE, William 77
WICKER, Dallas 147
WICKER, Gaines G. 154
WICKER, George 147
WICKER, Marshall 147
WICKER, Mrs. Monttie 154
WICKER, W. L. 147
WICKLIFFE, Ervin 70
WIECHART, Mrs. W. C. 33
WIECHERING, Alma 154
WIECHERING, Berniece 154
WIECHERING, Edwin 154
WIECHERING, Hallie 154
WIECHERING, Harold 154
WIECHERING, Helen M. 154
WIECHERING, Mrs. F. 154
WIECHERING, Raymond 154
WIECHERING, Walter 154
WIESE, Anna 95
WIESE, Ben 95
WIESE, Carl 95, 101
WIESE, Fred 95, 101
WIESE, Gilbert 110
WIESE, Henry 101
WIESE, Hulda 101
WIESE, Irene 76
WIESE, Lena 30
WIESE, Louise 95
WIESE, Mrs. Ben 3, 107
WIESE, Mrs. Charlie 110
WIESE, Mrs. Ernest 107, 145
WIESE, Mrs. Fred 85
WIESE, Mrs. William 85
WIESE, Nellie 46
WIESE, Otto 101
WIESE, Robert 101
WIESE, Walter 101, 110
WIESE, Will 101

WIESE, William 95
WIETHORN, Emma 122
WIETHORN, Gus 23, 61, 62, 122
WIETHORN, Henry 23, 62, 122(2)
WIETHORN, Louis 23, 122
WIETHORN, Louise 23, 122
WIETHORN, Minnie 137
WIETHORN, Mrs. Henry 106
WIETHORN, Mrs. Louis 33
WIETHORN, William 122
WILDERER, John 17
WILEY, Mrs. R. D. 14
WILHITE, Alice J. 1
WILHITE, Chester 1
WILKERSON, R. A. 35
WILLIAMS, A. Kirk 108
WILLIAMS, Alanzo 52
WILLIAMS, Ava 95
WILLIAMS, Bessie 57
WILLIAMS, Cooper 51, 125
WILLIAMS, Delia 52
WILLIAMS, Doris 55, 125
WILLIAMS, Ellie 16
WILLIAMS, Frilba 52
WILLIAMS, Gilbert 150
WILLIAMS, Gip 16
WILLIAMS, Harry 33
WILLIAMS, Holvey 33
WILLIAMS, James 52
WILLIAMS, J. C. 51
WILLIAMS, Jesse 52
WILLIAMS, Jim 16, 42
WILLIAMS, John 16, 108, 125
WILLIAMS, Johnnie 55
WILLIAMS, Kirk 57
WILLIAMS, Lee V. 125
WILLIAMS, Martha 104
WILLIAMS, Mary 51, 125
WILLIAMS, Mollie 46
WILLIAMS, Moses 52
WILLIAMS, Mr. 54
WILLIAMS, Mrs. 92
WILLIAMS, Mrs. Lee 102
WILLIAMS, Mrs. Robert 104
WILLIAMS, Mrs. Sam 16
WILLIAMS, Nora 52
WILLIAMS, Ollie 16
WILLIAMS, Peeler 33
WILLIAMS, Robert 33
WILLIAMS, Samuel 57
WILLIAMS, Sarah 91
WILLIAMS, Tom 16
WILLIAMS, Valura 52
WILLIAMS, V. W. 51, 125

WILLIAMS, Walter 52
WILLIAMSON, Lillian 91
WILLIAMSON, Mrs. Marvin 80
WILLINGHAM, Ruth 127
WILLIS, Infant 4
WILLIS, Jimmie L. 4
WILLIS, John 4
WILLIS, Lucy 1, 52
WILLIS, Martha J. 4
WILLMAN, Cooper 150, 151
WILLMAN, Lena 112
WILLMAN, Martha 24
WILLMAN, Tilbert 150
WILLMANN, Albert 84
WILLMANN, Catherine 57
WILLMANN, Ernest 57, 84
WILLMANN, Fritz 84
WILLMANN, Henry 84
WILLMANN, Lena 84
WILLMANN, Minnie 84
WILLMANN, Tilbert 84
WILLMANN, W. 84
WILLMANN, William 57
WILLMANN, Willie 84
WILLS, Howell 89
WILMAN, Mrs. Ernest 140
WILSON, Mrs. Ben 27
WILSON, Mrs. F. R. 118
WILSON, Mrs. G. R. 29
WILSON, Mrs. Monroe 131
WINCHELL, Margaret 89
WINCHELL, Mrs. Oliver 16, 89
WINDHAM, Hazel 150
WINGROVE, F. R. 15
WINSTON, Mrs. T. N. 97
WINTERS, Jane 54
WISE, Martha 85
WISE, Willford 116
WITT, A. F. 121
WITT, Albert 12, 61
WITT, Annie 121
WITT, Bill 137
WITT, Charlie 137
WITT, Eddie 137
WITT, Emma 122, 137
WITT, Fred 122
WITT, Frieda 62
WITT, Henry 19
WITT, Holly 19
WITT, Mrs. Fred 23, 85, 122
WITT, Mrs. Marion 22
WITT, Mrs. Rene 103
WITT, Otto 137
WITT, Sarah 12

WITT, Paul 62, 137
WITT, Pearl 12
WITT, Raymond 12
WITT, Rudolph 137
WITT, W. P. 12
WITTE, Albert 42
WITTE, Fred 42, 97
WITTE, Mrs. Albert 97
WITTE, Mrs. Walter 57
WITTE, Sophie 42
WITTE, Willie 42, 97
WOLSCHK, Mrs. R. C. 23
WOLSCHK, Gus 3
WOLSCHK, Miss 2
WOMACK, Corda 13
WOMACK, Adeline 13
WOMACK, Jack 13
WOMACK, J. B. 13
WOMACK, J. H. 13
WOMACK, Lawson 13
WOMACK, Mamie 80
WOMACK, Nina L. 13
WOMACK, Presley 13
WOMACK, Ramsey 13
WOMACK, Ted 13
WOMACK, Waymon 13
WONLARD, W. A. 35
WOOD, Allie D. 5
WOOD, John A. 15
WOOD, Maggie 156
WOOD, Mrs. H. R. 148
WOOD, Mrs. T. J. 91
WOOD, Mrs. Tom 27
WOOD, Olive 94
WOODALL, Clara 149
WOODLOCK, Joe 155
WOODLOCK, John 155
WOODLOCK, Laura 155
WOODLOCK, Lawrence 155
WOODLOCK, Mrs. W. T. 155
WOODLOCK, W. T. 155
WOODS, Jennie 65
WOODS, L. A. 65
WOODS, L. C. 36, 65
WOODS, Maggie 153
WOODS, Mrs. Carrol 88
WOODS, Nora 65
WOODSON, Mrs. Burbank 22, 88
WOODSON, Mrs. W. B. 119
WORTHY, Sallie 83
WRIGHT, Anna 128
WRIGHT, Bettie 31, 111, 153
WRIGHT, Charlie 55
WRIGHT, Elam 95

WRIGHT, Ella 128
WRIGHT, Ernest 111
WRIGHT, Fred 111
WRIGHT, George 95
WRIGHT, G. W. 95
WRIGHT, Hattie 111
WRIGHT, Helen 70
WRIGHT, Henry 128
WRIGHT, J. F. 55
WRIGHT, Jobe 128
WRIGHT, John D. 18
WRIGHT, Johnnie L. 128
WRIGHT, John W. 55, 128
WRIGHT, Kathleen 70
WRIGHT, Lee 128
WRIGHT, Marvin 128
WRIGHT, Mary 111, 128, 153
WRIGHT, Mrs. J. E. 146
WRIGHT, Mrs. Jobe 54, 70
WRIGHT, Mrs. T. R. 115
WRIGHT, Mrs. Wallace 70
WRIGHT, R. D. 11
WRIGHT, Roy 128
WRIGHT, Sam 128
WRIGHT, Will 128
WRYE, Garland 123
WRYE, Myrtle 123
WRYE, Robert 122
WYNN, Lena 19

Y

YARBOROUGH, Mrms. B. G. 36, 65
YATES, Joe 39
YATES, Mrs. R. P. 53
YOUNG, Etta 69
YOUNG, J. B. 5
YOUNG, Mary 96
YOUNG, Mrs. Vennie 137
YOUNG, W. J. 93
YOUNGBLOOD, J. H. 131
YOUNGBLOOD, Mrs. J. H. 45
YOUNGBLOOD, Orvid 45

Z

ZACHARIAS, Artelia 97
ZACHARIAS, Julius 97
ZACKEFOOSE, Mrs. Carl 155
ZETZMANN, Clara A. 134
ZIMMERMAN, C. E. 135
ZIMMERMAN, D. L. 135
ZIMMERMAN, Donald R. 135
ZIMMERMAN, H. Olin 135
ZIMMERMAN, Katie 135

ZIMMERMAN, W. R. 135
ZIPPER, Charles 98

www.ingramcontent.com/pod-product-compliance
Lightning Source LLC
Chambersburg PA
CBHW080431230426
43662CB00015B/2247